CW01160497

Women's Writing and Mission in the Nineteenth Century

Until now, the missionary plot in Charlotte Brontë's *Jane Eyre* has been seen as marginal and anomalous. Despite women missionaries being ubiquitous in the nineteenth century, they appeared to be absent from nineteenth-century literature. As this book demonstrates, though, the female missionary character and narrative was, in fact, present in a range of writings from missionary newsletters and life writing, to canonical Victorian literature, New Woman fiction and women's college writing. Nineteenth-century women writers wove the tropes of the female missionary figure and plot into their domestic fiction, and the female missionary themes of religious self-sacrifice and heroism formed the subjectivity of these writers and their characters. Offering an alternative narrative for the development of women writers and early feminism, as well as a new reading of *Jane Eyre*, this book adds to the debate about whether religious women in the nineteenth century could actually be radical and feminist.

Angharad Eyre currently teaches in the English Department at Queen Mary University of London and lives in the city with her husband and two small children.

The Nineteenth Century Series
Series editors: Joanne Shattock and Julian North

The series focuses primarily upon major authors and subjects within Romantic and Victorian literature. It also includes studies of other nineteenth-century British writers and issues, where these are matters of current debate: for example, biography and autobiography; journalism; periodical literature; travel writing; book production; gender; non-canonical writing.

Recent in this series:

Women's Letters as Life Writing 1840–1885
Catherine Delafield

Reading Transatlantic Girlhood in the Long Nineteenth Century
Edited by Robin L. Cadwallader and LuElla D'Amico

Dickens and the Bible
'What Providence Meant'
Jennifer Gribble

Gender, Writing, Spectatorships
Evenings at the Theatre, Opera, and Silent Screen in Late Nineteenth-Century Italy and Beyond
Katharine Mitchell

Women's Writing and Mission in the Nineteenth Century
Jane Eyre's Missionary Sisters
Angharad Eyre

Writing for Social Change in Temperance Periodicals
Conviction and Career
Annemarie McAllister

For more information about this series, please visit: www.routledge.com/The-Nineteenth-Century-Series/book-series/ASHSER2017

Women's Writing and Mission in the Nineteenth Century
Jane Eyre's Missionary Sisters

Angharad Eyre

Routledge
Taylor & Francis Group
NEW YORK AND LONDON

First published 2023
by Routledge
605 Third Avenue, New York, NY 10158

and by Routledge
4 Park Square, Milton Park, Abingdon, Oxon, OX14 4RN

Routledge is an imprint of the Taylor & Francis Group, an informa business

© 2023 Angharad Eyre

The right of Angharad Eyre to be identified as author of this work has been asserted in accordance with sections 77 and 78 of the Copyright, Designs and Patents Act 1988.

All rights reserved. No part of this book may be reprinted or reproduced or utilised in any form or by any electronic, mechanical, or other means, now known or hereafter invented, including photocopying and recording, or in any information storage or retrieval system, without permission in writing from the publishers.

Trademark notice: Product or corporate names may be trademarks or registered trademarks, and are used only for identification and explanation without intent to infringe.

Library of Congress Cataloging-in-Publication Data
Names: Eyre, Angharad, author.
Title: Women's writing and mission in the nineteenth century :
Jane Eyre's missionary sisters / Angharad Eyre.
Description: New York, NY : Routledge, 2023. |
Series: The nineteenth century series ; 1 |
Includes bibliographical references and index. |
Identifiers: LCCN 2022021165 (print) | LCCN 2022021166 (ebook) |
ISBN 9781032366227 (hardback) | ISBN 9781032366234 (paperback) |
ISBN 9781003332961 (ebook)
Subjects: LCSH: Women missionaries in literature. | Femininity in literature. |
English literature–19th century–History and criticism. |
English literature–Women authors–History and criticism. |
LCGFT: Literary criticism.
Classification: LCC PR468.M58 E97 2023 (print) |
LCC PR468.M58 (ebook) | DDC 820.9/9287–dc23/eng/20220915
LC record available at https://lccn.loc.gov/2022021165
LC ebook record available at https://lccn.loc.gov/2022021166

ISBN: 9781032366227 (hbk)
ISBN: 9781032366234 (pbk)
ISBN: 9781003332961 (ebk)

DOI: 10.4324/9781003332961

Typeset in Sabon
by Newgen Publishing UK

For my family

Contents

List of Figures ix
Acknowledgements x
List of Abbreviations xiii

Introduction 1

Prologue—Ann Judson and Harriet Newell:
Immortalising the Female Missionary 21

PART I
1830–1870 45

1 Tales of Female Missionary Sacrifice: Tracts,
   Collective Biographies and Newsletters 47

2 Missionary Self-Sacrifice in the Domestic Sphere:
   The Tracts and Novels of Martha Sherwood,
   Hesba Stretton and Dinah Craik 82

3 Novel Approaches to Missionary Sacrifice:
   Charlotte Brontë and Elizabeth Gaskell 108

PART II
1880–1900 143

4 Missionaries of the New: Sarah Grand,
   Olive Schreiner and Margaret Harkness 145

5 Women, Religion and Power: University Women's
  Missionary Writing   186
  Conclusion   227

  Bibliography   230
  Index   246

Figures

P.1	Portrait of Ann Judson, *Memoir of Mrs Ann H. Judson*	29
1.1	'Burning of the Wives and Slaves of Runjeet Sing, June 1839', *Memoirs of British Female Missionaries*	74
2.1	'His eye, as he passed the door, caught little Henry sitting on the mat…', *The History of Little Henry and his Bearer Boosy*	87
2.2	'"Our Father," she said, in a faint whisper', *Jessica's First Prayer*	91
3.1	Portrait of Ellen Nussey, Brontë Society *Transactions* (1898)	123
4.1	'He, watching over Israel, slumbers not, nor sleeps'. Stave of music from Mendelssohn's *Elijah*, as used by Sarah Grand in *The Heavenly Twins*	155
5.1	Photograph of Constance Maynard and her staff at Westfield College, 1888	189

Acknowledgements

This book comes out of my PhD research and so, in many ways, has been in gestation for more than ten years. As a result, there are a great many people to thank, who have been involved in some way in supporting me and my work over these years. This book also, though, came about thanks to a chance meeting at a conference, so I would first like to thank the British Association for Victorian Studies, who had sponsored my attendance at their conference by way of an ECR travel grant, and Professor Joanne Shattock, who – as well as having been an inspiration to my work – encouraged me to submit a book proposal to her series.

In practical terms, this book would simply not exist without the assistance of research institutions, librarians and archivists. The PhD programme at Queen Mary University of London (QMUL) provided me with excellent supervision, development opportunities and funding for research trips. Following this, fellowships granted by the Harry Ransom Center (University of Texas at Austin) and the John Rylands Centre (University of Manchester) provided invaluable access to archival material and, equally importantly, time and space to conceptualise my research. In addition, my archival research into missionary women's publications and women's colleges was an incredibly positive experience, and I would like to thank archivists at SOAS, University of Birmingham, Lady Margaret Hall and Royal Holloway for opening their collections to me, answering my many questions and generally helping me access some truly wonderful material. Particular thanks go to QMUL Archives, for permission to reproduce the image of Constance Maynard and her staff, as well as working with me and colleagues on a Maynard-related symposium in one of the most enjoyable collaborations I've experienced to date. Thanks also, of course, to the British Library, which provided permission for the use of most of the other images in this book, and without which I would not have been able to complete this research.

I would also like to thank my editors at Routledge for their help in making this book a reality. Mitchell Manners, Anita Bhatt and Jennifer Abbott kept me on track while being considerate of the many challenges Covid lockdowns and outbreaks represented to this project. And thanks also go the readers who reviewed my book proposal: their suggestions were helpful and their enthusiasm for the project was motivational.

I am tremendously grateful to all the colleagues who have helped me develop as a scholar. First and foremost, my PhD supervisor Professor Nadia Valman has been a never-failing source of support and encouragement, and I am privileged to have worked with such an exceptional teacher and scholar – who was also great fun to work with. Also invaluable were the numerous opportunities for paid research work she offered, notably for her script 'I am Human – a Walking Tour of the Royal London Hospital', which I felt honoured to be working on. While on QMUL's PhD programme, I was also lucky enough to work with Professor Annie Janowitz, who provided rigorous challenge, kindness and sparkling wine (essential for working through Heidegger); and Professor Thomas Dixon, who provided a fresh perspective on my work, as well as incredibly rewarding opportunities for development and collaboration. Professor Cora Kaplan also provided much-appreciated constructive challenge as respondent at one of my first PhD conferences. My PhD examiners, Professors Elisabeth Jay and Ruth Livesey, have been inspirations; their thorough reading and engagement with my work made for an intellectually satisfying viva, and they have been very patient with the many requests for references that have come their way. Another inspiration has been Professor Sue Morgan who, despite not having any formal connection with my academic career, has always been so supportive and has been instrumental in providing publication opportunities (as well as being another very patient writer of references!). For me, these people all represent the best of academia, in that they have been such unselfish teachers and mentors, and I count myself very lucky to have met them.

I have been fortunate enough to collaborate with colleagues from around the world who share my research interests. Special thanks go to Drs Elsa Richardson and Jane Mackelworth, with whom I really enjoyed co-producing the Maynard symposium at QMUL all those years ago, and co-writing the introduction for the *Women's History Review* special issue that came out of it. Thanks also to Drs Naomi Hetherington, Rebecca Styler, Claire Stainthorp and Richa Dwor for the rewarding collaboration that resulted in *Nineteenth-Century Religion, Literature and Society*, and the enjoyable get-togethers in London that involved. Thanks to Drs Flore Janssen and Lisa C. Robertson for their invitations to work with them on their projects concerning Margaret Harkness, which have always been most valuable and rewarding; to Dr Pauline Phipps for the fascinating conversations about Constance Maynard; and to everyone at the London and South East Branch of the Gaskell Society for talking with me about Gaskell and her relationship with Charlotte Brontë. Thanks to Drs Molly Livingston, Angela Runciman and all those involved in the British Women Writers Conference for helping me find my feet while I was temporarily an independent scholar in the US; and to Dr Janine Hatter and everyone else involved in the Victorian Popular Fiction Conference for always making me feel at home in British Victorian studies.

Thanks also to my colleagues and friends at QMUL. Members of my PhD cohort have been a source of great moral support over the years, and I am especially thankful for the friendship of Drs Elizabeth Robertson, Kirsty Rolfe, Peter Jones and Lara Atkin. Dr Suzanne Hobson and Professor Andrew van der Vlies had responsibility for the training and development of my PhD cohort – thanks to them for their support and friendship. Thanks also to Professor Clair Wills for taking me on as a research assistant on her project *Lovers and Strangers: An Immigrant History of Post-War Britain*, which, in addition to providing some financial support, was a fascinating learning opportunity. The Victorian teaching team are always a pleasure to work with, especially Professor Catherine Maxwell, and Drs Matt Ingleby and Angela Dunstan, whose passion, support and friendship I really value.

And of course, the writing of a book is not confined to the professional world, but necessarily, and perhaps increasingly, happens in the home. I am therefore grateful to my husband Richard and my children, Holly and Robert, for their patience with this situation. More than this though, I will forever be thankful to my husband for his boundless confidence in me and his enthusiastic interest in my work, for keeping me motivated at difficult times and for always being keen to talk through the tangles of my arguments and help me out of thickets – usually on a good long walk through our favourite bits of Washington, D.C. or London. Thanks also to my Dad, who showed me from a very young age what it meant to love your subject, and to love teaching it, and who has always been an invaluable reader of my work. And thanks to my Mum and my sister who have always been there for me when I needed them. I am also very grateful to my mother-in-law Deborah, who has provided consistent encouragement and support; my friend Laura, who let me work downstairs in her home while she watched my very young baby; and my wonderful childminder Avril Cole.

Finally, many of the friends and colleagues I am grateful to are from the precarious community of early career academia (a description that seems increasingly flexible in terms of time). These are people who, despite the lack of steady employment and despite the psychological impact of precarity, are collaborating to produce events and publications that are the lifeblood of the profession. Working alongside them has taught me so much. Some of those I have worked with may by now have left academia for alternative careers and occupations, where I hope they receive more appreciation for their talents. The official dedication of this book is to my family. But this book is also dedicated to all those who would have written books just as good as this one – and better – if they had had the same support and financial backing.

Abbreviations

CMS	Church Missionary Society
LMH	Lady Margaret Hall, University of Oxford
LMS	London Missionary Society
RTS	Religious Tract Society
SPCK	Society for the Promotion of Christian Knowledge
SPFEE	Society for the Promotion of Female Education in China, the East (also known as the Female Education Society, or FES)
SPG	Society for the Propagation of the Gospel in Foreign Parts
WMMS	Wesleyan Methodist Missionary Society

Introduction

I stood motionless under my hierophant's touch. My refusals were forgotten – my fears overcome – my wrestlings paralyzed. The Impossible – i.e. my marriage with St John – was fast becoming the Possible. All was changing utterly, with a sudden sweep. Religion called – Angels beckoned – God commanded – life rolled together like a scroll – death's gates opening, shewed eternity beyond: it seemed, that for safety and bliss there, all here might be sacrificed in a second.[1]

Like many readers, I have been fascinated and puzzled by the St John Rivers episode of *Jane Eyre*. Why did Charlotte Brontë offer her heroine the option of a missionary life? Why did Jane refuse? And what would her life have been like had she chosen the mission field over Mr Rochester? Researching this final question led me to a rich vein of early nineteenth-century female missionary biography, which made Brontë's inclusion of the missionary plot far more understandable. It also prompted me to wonder why there were not more female missionary characters in nineteenth-century novels as, I was assured, there were not. But when I adapted this question, and asked instead, how elements of the female missionary character might be present in nineteenth-century novels and life writing, I suddenly seemed to see them everywhere. The governess who stands up to save her charge from seduction, the nurse who sacrifices her life to read psalms to the victims of an epidemic, the college principal who encourages her graduates in their social work – these are all versions of the nineteenth-century female missionary character. She seemed to provide a strong, proto-feminist identity for women, and her presence and influence needed to be further explored.

While scholars have noted the influence of missionary history on the St John episode of Charlotte Brontë's *Jane Eyre*, few have appreciated the novel's extended engagement with the female missionary narrative as it was being told through the first half of the nineteenth century, in women's life writing and fiction.[2] As the above extract shows, Brontë was aware that the moment of religious calling in the narrative was a moment of high drama. It was a moment when the woman missionary struggled

DOI: 10.4324/9781003332961-1

between her duty to God and the dictates of the Victorian cult of domesticity; when she 'counted the cost' of her decision, which might cause her to sacrifice her health, and even her life, in the mission; and when she understood herself as an instrument in God's plan for the salvation of the world. Both heroic and self-sacrificial, authoritatively independent and self-effacingly passive, the female missionary character as she emerged from the narrative was full of contradictions. But, as Brontë understood, she and her narrative had the power to disrupt familiar constructions of Victorian femininity.

The prevalence of the female missionary narrative in the first half of the nineteenth century has largely been overlooked by literary scholars.[3] Indeed, until recently scholarship about nineteenth-century women's literature has generally had a blind spot when it comes to religion. We have therefore been presented with a paradox: though it is clear from mission history that the mission movement was often at the heart of nineteenth-century women's lives, we are asked to believe that it was not present in women's fiction of the time – and that the missionary plot in *Jane Eyre* is marginal and anomalous. Meanwhile, though historians have considered how aspects of mission experience affected Victorian women's subjectivities, the significance of the female missionary narrative specifically for the ideology of femininity has not been fully understood.[4] In this book, in addition to tracing, for the first time, the presence of the female missionary narrative and character in women's writing through the nineteenth century, I argue that is only by analysing the narrative and its adaptations that we can see the complex, uneven developments in the ideology of Victorian femininity as they were negotiated by women writers.[5]

Nineteenth-Century Missionary Women and Mission History

The number of professional women missionaries officially appointed to work in the foreign mission field by mission societies was relatively small until the latter part of the nineteenth century. However, throughout the century, women were heavily involved in the foreign and home mission movements: many women went out to the foreign mission field as missionary wives; a number went to work in urban missions and city settlements; most women from religious backgrounds would have been involved in supporting the mission through fundraising or other means; and the majority of women, especially those from religious backgrounds, would have been aware of and have read female missionary biographies.

Around the 1820s, in a fundamental shift of policy, the mission movement began to discourage intermarriage between western male missionaries and converted native women. Though initially the marriages had been seen as both expedient for mission objectives and as consistent with the Christian belief in universal kinship, they became seen as damaging, as missionary husbands were culturally influenced by their native wives as much as – or more than – their wives were influenced by them. To maintain the respectability of their agents in the field, mission societies determined that it would be necessary to send out missionary couples rather than single men where at all possible.[6] At this time, mission leaders were also calling for unmarried female missionaries to carry out educational work among women, especially in India.[7] In response, in 1834, the Society for the Promotion of Female Education in the East (SPFEE) was formed. Managed by a committee of women, this organisation was non-denominational and not associated with any particular mission; its recruits joined the Basel mission, the Wesleyan Methodist Missionary Society (WMMS) and the London Missionary Society (LMS), among others.[8] Some mission societies saw this pool of unmarried women workers as potential wives for single, or widowed, male missionaries; however, others were concerned that marriage took women away from valuable work and represented a poor return on the investment of recruiting, training and supporting the woman missionary.[9] In any case, mission societies soon felt a need to take on themselves the recruitment process for the large number of female missionaries they required. In 1858, the WMMS started its Ladies Committee, which was formed entirely of women – mostly wives and other family members of the Society's general committee – and operated independently of its parent Society.[10] And, in a move that reflected the wider-scale recruitment and training of unmarried female missionaries, the LMS began its systematic recruitment of women missionaries in 1875, with the Church Missionary Society (CMS) following in 1887.[11] These societies represented the cross-denominational evangelical Christianity that dominated the mission movement for most of the nineteenth century. Meanwhile, from the late 1860s, High Church Anglicans, subscribing to the Anglo-Catholic doctrine of service, established 'Anglican Sisterhoods' – settlements of charitable single women at home and abroad – through the Society for the Propagation of the Gospel in Foreign Parts (SPG) and the Society for the Promotion of Christian Knowledge (SPCK).[12]

Until recently, scholars have tended to overlook the extent of early nineteenth-century women's diverse involvement in mission, being often more interested in examining the professional female missionary in the late nineteenth and early twentieth centuries.[13] Indeed, there has been a tendency to create a teleological narrative of women missionaries' progress towards professionalisation and to devalue earlier women's experiences in mission.[14] However, as Alison Twells and Catherine Hall have shown, women in the very first decades of the nineteenth century were active in mission societies as supporters and fundraisers; furthermore, Twells has acknowledged missionary wives in the field as 'active missionaries', despite not being professionals.[15] Meanwhile, Emily Manktelow and Claire McClisky have emphasised the importance of missionary couples and families to the mission movement's deployment of middle-class evangelical domesticity in the field.[16]

There has also been a suggestion that the increased professionalism of missionaries in the second half of the century, in concert with increasing secularisation and the decline of evangelicalism, led to a decrease in evangelical fervour in missionary women.[17] However, from the 1850s on, Hudson Taylor's China Inland Mission recruited a large number of highly educated candidates, despite being less overtly professional and more religiously enthusiastic.[18] Similarly, in the 1880s and 1890s, the strongly evangelical Westfield College in London was successful in inspiring a number of highly educated women for the CMS. The continuing presence of the evangelical missionary movement, and the increasing number and status of women within it, was a significant fact of the second half of the nineteenth century, which has been largely ignored by scholars. Helpfully, Alison Twells has drawn attention to the large portion of society she calls the 'missionary public', who, at this time of supposed secularisation, were still enthusiastically following the mission movement and lionising its heroes.[19]

Maintaining this powerful missionary public and disseminating the mission's influence was the task of missionary writing. Missionaries were prodigious writers; letters, reports, newsletters, biographies and memoirs abound in the archives of the mission societies.[20] The SPFEE publicised its work through its newsletter, the *Female Missionary Intelligencer* and the WMMS Ladies' Committee produced a quarterly, *Occasional Papers*. Moreover, biographies of missionaries, including female missionaries, became bestsellers in the Victorian literary marketplace, as religious publishers continued to enjoy the strong position they had established in the early decades of the nineteenth century as part of the evangelical revival.[21] Such biographies and newsletters would have formed the staple diet of evangelical readers in families where fiction was frowned upon.

Female missionary biographies and newsletters have been somewhat overlooked in mission history. Traditionally, this history focused more on statistics, theology and male missionary leaders.[22] The recent flowering of studies on women's missionary experience, missionary families, the emotional side of missions, encounters between women missionaries and indigenous peoples, and the experiences of indigenous peoples and converts themselves is a positive development.[23] However, these studies have often, perhaps necessarily, been concerned with specific missionary environments and have largely been based on unpublished, archival materials, which has led to a somewhat atomised women's mission history, from which it is difficult to see what direct impact these experiences had on wider nineteenth-century culture. Concentrating instead on published missionary writing reveals that the textual representations of women missionaries communicated to the missionary public back home tended to encourage a generic view of the female missionary, whether she was in the South Sea Islands or Newfoundland, an Anglican or a Methodist.[24] The WMMS's *Occasional Papers* received intelligence from correspondents stationed in a variety of countries, who were presumably engaged in a multiplicity of strategies, but culled from these letters only the topics they wanted to present as part of the general experience of women missionaries. British missionary women were readers of these texts as well as writers and were subject to a range of British cultural forces before they were recruited by mission societies; these home-grown influences shaped their subsequent experiences in the field.

Crucially, of course, female missionaries operated in the Empire, and mission history has increasingly explored the complex ways in which missions interacted with the imperial project. Mission was not analogous with empire; as scholars have pointed out, British missions operated in regions that never became part of the empire, and non-British missions operated within the empire.[25] While Christianising and civilising have been seen as processes working hand in hand, mission leaders were often suspicious of the effects of the civilisation brought by empire, and disapproving of settler communities' morality.[26] Missionary philosophy also countered many of the theories on which imperial hierarchies were based, such as essentialist ideas of racial difference.[27] However, for a variety of reasons, missionaries often found themselves in collusion with imperial power, and certainly assumed the position of authoritative power granted them as white westerners by the conditions of empire.[28] Missionary women could, and did, wield colonial power in the way that Gayatri Spivak has described: they 'spoke for' the subaltern woman, erasing her subject status in order to construct themselves in opposition as imperial subjects.[29] They could also utilise Victorian ideas of the subaltern woman and the superiority of Christian womanhood to enable their own authoritative self-representation, as Antoinette Burton and Clare Midgley have argued was the case for women philanthropists.[30] However, I argue that, for women in the mission field, the presence of the indigenous woman, at times confounding the colonial image of the subaltern – especially in the case of the woman convert – made it more difficult to create authoritative self-images. The woman missionary's position was a complex one; speaking for the subaltern in newsletters, she was also 'spoken for' in obituary and biography. My study explores the appropriative strategies of power used by women missionaries over their native converts, but also seeks to understand how female missionaries' own objectification in a narrative of ideal femininity based on self-sacrifice caused them to subjugate native others.

The presence of the mission movement throughout nineteenth-century Britain was a powerful influence, which, with its doctrines of universal kinship and millenarian world view, was able to challenge the secular ideology of racial difference and the imperial project. At the same time, women's engagement in this radical mission movement, and the presence of the female missionary in nineteenth-century writing, complicated Victorian gender ideologies.

Religion, the Female Missionary and Gender Ideology in Women's Studies

As is well known, nineteenth-century society was highly religious, and its culture was at times dominated by evangelical, missionary Christianity.[31] However, the groundbreaking works of women's studies, which began the task of uncovering and recovering nineteenth-century women's literature and experiences, were reticent when it came to religion's place in nineteenth-century women's lives. Interpreting the nineteenth century from the location of second-wave feminism, scholars tended to focus, perhaps overly, on the themes of sexual relations and a struggle for 'selfhood'. Often seeing religion as simply another aspect of the patriarchy, they looked instead for how women writers rebelled against this force, and how they internalised their oppression.[32] Indeed, early feminist scholars can be accused of creating a narrative in which Victorian women gradually, and inevitably, freed themselves from the ideology of Victorian femininity to become secular, liberated, first-wave feminists.[33] As Valerie Sanders has acknowledged, there has been an assumption that religious women of this period were conservative and 'anti-feminist'.[34] This narrative refuses to accept the validity of nineteenth-century women's affective experience that departs from that of modern-day feminists; in consequence, the experiences of women negotiating the ideal models of femininity in terms of religious duty are invisible. Similarly, women writers who found religious constructions powerful for their feminist philosophies are misinterpreted as self-contradictory; for example, scholars have been dismayed by the 'paradox' inherent in many feminist writers' work culminating in self-sacrifice.[35]

Scholars have also adopted an instrumentalist approach to interpreting women's expression of religious belief: women are seen as adopting their faith for the opportunities which it provided.[36] There is an assumption on the part of some mission historians, for example, that women professed Christian piety in order to take part in professional activities, such as nursing or management, available in the mission field.[37] Similarly, Martha Vicinus (among others) has suggested that women were unconsciously sublimating their sexual drives into religious fervour and philanthropy.[38] Such instrumental interpretations fail to recognise the authenticity of women's religious experience and neglects to examine the complex ways in which emotion was intertwined with evangelical faith for women in the nineteenth century.

Recent historical and literary scholarship has pointed to the necessity of reviewing the role religion played in women's lives, and how, rather than being a simple patriarchal force, subjugating women, religion could be an empowering aspect of a woman's life. Historians such as Linda Wilson and Alison Twells have shown that religion was integral to nineteenth-century women's developing subjectivities and could justify a wealth of activity outside the home.[39] Similarly, scholars such as

Sue Morgan, Jacqueline deVries and Julie Melnyk have pointed to how women played active roles in shaping evangelical ideologies and theology.[40] Fascinatingly, scholars such as Sharon Marcus and Naomi Lloyd have also begun to explore how women experienced same-sex desire as part of their religious practice.[41] However, though Elisabeth Jay's *Religion of the Heart* opened the way for more studies of how evangelical religion was experienced, expressed and even shaped, through women's literature, progress in this field has been slow.[42] Anne Hogan and Andrew Bradstock's collection demonstrated how understanding the centrality of Christianity in the lives and work of women writers can lead to new explanations and interpretations of nineteenth-century literature, showing that women writers were using Christianity to critique society and develop Christian theology.[43] Nevertheless, Jude Nixon had to remind readers in 2004 that in order to fully understand nineteenth-century women's novels, we have to understand women's experiences of religion.[44]

Probably the most important Christian ideology that women were engaging with was that of femininity and the separate spheres. This ideology has mainly been understood as a secular force, and the cause of women's subjugation, coming about as a middle-class response to nineteenth-century socio-economic developments that led to men's work being sited increasingly outside the home, and women's respectability being tied to her confinement in the home. Certainly, by the Victorian period, writers such as Dickens, Ruskin and Coventry Patmore were establishing domesticity as a secular religion. However, doubts have been cast on whether the socio-economic reality of the period really did cause a separation of work along gender lines, with some scholars suggesting that the ideology emerged more as a result of the evangelical reform of society. The conduct books, sermons and other religious literature of the first half of the nineteenth century displayed an increased rhetoric of passive domesticity; home and family became associated with religion, and (in a somewhat circular fashion) woman came to be seen as more spiritual than man by virtue of remaining in the home and becoming the heart of its sanctifying influence on her husband and children.[45] Scholars have disagreed about the extent of domestic ideology's cultural dominance; Philippa Levine has argued that it was psychologically all-pervasive, while Vickery has suggested that domestic advice literature was largely ignored by women and should be interpreted as a conservative reaction to women's greater activity.[46]

While the religious ideology of domestic femininity was certainly experienced in some form by most women, it is most important to bear in mind that it was not always experienced as a subjugating ideology. Scholars have understood the ideology's rhetoric around 'woman's mission' to be a powerful justification for women's activity in the public sphere, for example, in the form of philanthropy.[47] And Alison Twells has convincingly argued that early nineteenth-century women could experience a religious 'missionary domesticity' which authorised their power in an expansive sphere of activity.[48] As the century progressed, domestic ideology's emphasis on the moral superiority of women feminised evangelical religion as well as giving women symbolic power. Evangelicalism's emphasis on simplicity and feeling in religion, combined with its privileging of the individual relationship with God, rather than adherence to tradition or authority, allowed women to write and act within the evangelical culture on an almost equal footing with men.[49] Moreover, the evangelical mission to convert society relied heavily on the activities of women, and I would suggest that it was women's success that led to a feminisation of evangelical practices.[50] Christine Krüger has also suggested that Victorian women writers benefited from a cultural inheritance of a dissenting tradition of women preachers, which provided empowering narratives and models of womanhood for their novels and for their understanding of their own identities.[51]

The potential of female missionary narratives to provide empowering identities for women was even greater, I argue, than those of women preachers, as the mission movement's scale, cross-denominational nature and sheer number of publications made it ubiquitous in nineteenth-century society. The figure of the missionary, moreover, was able to blur the boundaries between preaching and teaching, as Clare Midgley has noted; while female preaching was forbidden, the female missionary was encouraged to take the word to women in the zenana and could depict her missionary work with native men as acceptable female 'influence'.[52] Early biographies would compare the female missionary to earlier Christian women of the Bible but would also align her with the original missionaries: the Apostles.[53] The female missionary character could therefore be figured as a prophet, without incurring the disapproval incurred by female preachers – Peterson has even seen the female missionary as allowing militant and political identities for women, which is born out in my studies of missionary writings.[54]

At the same time, though, the radical influence of religion and the female missionary should not be overstated; the role of religion and the female missionary in the development of domestic ideology is complex. Almost as soon as she entered discourse, writers were emphasising the domestic and feminine aspects of the female missionary, and, as the century went on and the cult of domesticity became entrenched in Victorian society, women writers began to revise earlier portraits of women missionaries to minimise any of their less-than-ideal or unfeminine traits. As part of a two-way process, the female missionary also influenced the ideology of domestic femininity, adding the trait of missionary self-sacrifice to the ideal that all Victorian women were expected to emulate.[55]

In addition to engaging with the ideology of domestic femininity to present the female missionary, women writers and missionaries could also draw on elements of missionary masculinity and religious androgyny. Recent cultural and literary studies of masculinity, while generally valuable and illuminating, have not added much to our understanding of how the male missionary embodied or challenged ideas of masculinity through the century. In focusing solely on fiction, Claudia Nelson's *Boys Will be Girls* omits any mention of missionary biography, which would have been as influential a tool in educating young men. Meanwhile, John Tosh conflates the missionary with the soldier, tying their supposedly shared brand of masculinity to the national, heroic epic of imperialism, and does not attempt to trace how missionary masculinity might have changed through the century.[56] Mission history is producing fascinating studies of missionary experiences of masculinity, especially in the encounter with indigenous cultures, but there is still work to be done to see how these experiences influenced the ideology of masculinity in the metropole. Norman Vance's 1880s study of religious masculinity posited that chivalric, militant presentations of male religious heroes – missionaries as well as soldiers – were developed in the mid-century as a response to a public perception of religious men as effeminate.[57] It is these militant aspects that many women missionaries and writers can be seen to be drawing on in their depictions of the female missionary through the century. In some ways this is not that surprising; in the early nineteenth century, religion was not necessarily gendered. Nelson's study shows how, in fiction up to the 1870s, boys and girls were alike taught the Christian virtues of the 'Angel' of domestic ideology.[58] Moreover, Julie Melnyk has noted how Christ could feature in women's theological writing a model of feminised man and a preview of an androgynous life to come after the Apocalypse.[59] By the end of the century, although Victorian gender ideologies had become starkly polarised, religious New Woman writers were able to construct their visions for an ideally androgynous future on this tradition in theological writing and, particularly, on the figure of the female missionary.

Examining the Female Missionary Narrative in Life Writing, Archives and Fiction

This book examines the textual female missionary figure and the female missionary narrative as they were written, experienced and rewritten by women through the nineteenth century. Rather than simply a literary construct, this figure appears in life writing as well as fiction because, I argue, the female missionary character was important for real missionary women's construction of their subjectivities.[60] In turn, these women's development of the figure in their life writing provided women writers with a rich, complex character through which to explore the possibilities for women within religious ideas of womanhood.[61]

My methodology of examining life writing alongside literary fiction to understand the idea and influence of the female missionary presupposes that written texts have a complex relation to historical reality and ideology. Some scholars have argued that the 'real' experience of women of the past (as it emerges from diaries and letters) contradicts and ignores the official ideology of femininity (as it was transmitted in conduct books, for example); however, this neglects the equally 'real' experience of nineteenth-century women writing more publicly directed texts, such as letters for publication or introductions to biographies, which provide ample evidence of complex interaction with gender ideology.[62] Moreover, as Vickery acknowledges, when it comes to the rhetoric-laden documents of the New Woman writers, texts often have their own agendas and do not transparently communicate the 'truth'.[63] Equally, while Rhonda Semple uses a variety of materials in her quest to understand the woman missionary, she neglects to think about how the purposes of texts such as obituaries and missionary applications might render them more or less reliable as evidence of the 'real' woman missionary's character.[64] As I argue, missionary biographies aimed didactically to create the female missionary as a role model for women more generally; thus, depiction of the figure changed as the century wore on and cultural ideas about women and femininity changed. Other scholars, arguing that women writers self-consciously constructed public selves in diaries, letters and newsletters, have concluded that we must give up on the belief that texts can illuminate history, and treat all forms of writing as fictions.[65] However, I am unconvinced by this, as I am by arguments suggesting that women writers 'professed' one thing, while thinking and doing directly the opposite.[66]

Usefully, recent work by historians such as Sharon Marcus, Sue Morgan and Jacqueline deVries has posited a more complicated, productive relationship between 'real-life' texts such as diaries and more ideological works such as conduct books or even novels: Marcus sees each as 'reflecting' and 'reinforcing' the other.[67] As religious historians have noted, evangelical culture encouraged Christians to read the personal religious experiences of others in order to better understand their own; women learned to understand their affective experiences within the frameworks of other women's life writing and expressed their subjectivity using the accepted conventions and tropes of this evangelical literature.[68] More than this though, women's writing not only reflects the dominant cultural ideologies – their appropriation of the conventions of previous texts adapts them.[69] I argue that for female missionaries, especially, such adaptation was necessary, as they not only understood themselves through texts, but their construction of themselves in this way took place within, or was tested by, their experience in the complex space of the mission field. I read female missionaries' own letters and diary entries with a sensitivity to the process of negotiation taking place in their attempts to express their affective experience using existing forms, and identify where tropes are creatively adapted to encompass elements of these women's subjectivity not expressed before.

Recent histories of emotions have suggested that there was a reduction in the philosophical vocabulary of feeling in the nineteenth century, as earlier typologies were subsumed in the overarching category of 'emotions'.[70] Emotions historians have also argued that historical subjects understood their feelings according to the available cultural vocabulary of emotion.[71] It follows that religious women in the nineteenth century, faced with a limited and contested vocabulary of emotions in contemporary philosophy, would reach for the rich vocabulary of feeling represented in evangelical literature from the eighteenth and early nineteenth centuries. Missionary life writing demonstrates how women expressed and constructed their emotional experiences of religion with reference to an almost timeless religious conviction, which clashed, often painfully, with nineteenth-century societal expectations. Despite editors' desires to construct their subjects as particular kinds of religious heroines, the challenging emotions of these memorialised women's inner lives often emerged from the biographies to influence subsequent women readers and writers.

A variety of forms of life writing appear in this book, including: the single-subject missionary biography; the collective missionary biography; published missionary correspondence in missionary newsletters; circulated missionary correspondence; college newsletters; unpublished autobiography or religious accounts of life events; and diaries. It is difficult to find material written by missionary women in the first half of the century, especially when looking at the archives of mission societies that did not recruit single women missionaries until the late nineteenth century.[72] The archives of the LMS and WMMS, however, contain personal letters from missionary couples, dating from as early as 1818, and the newsletters of the WMMS and the SPFEE contain letters and editorials written by missionary women from the 1850s. While the LMS and the SPFEE's newsletter, *The Female Missionary Intelligencer*, have been widely studied, the WMMS Ladies Society and its *Occasional Papers* has been under-researched.[73] The correspondence from women missionaries published by this paper has an interesting relationship to female missionary biography; both are engaged in presenting an ideal female missionary figure, but often the correspondence reveals fissures between this ideal and the actual woman missionary on the ground. To explore how the woman missionary in the later part of the nineteenth century had changed from the ideal presented in the early nineteenth century, I accessed the archives of the CMS and SPG, alongside the archives of the women's colleges that supplied these mission societies with graduates. Here also the forms of circulated correspondence and the newsletter were still highly significant for women missionaries' construction of subjectivity.

Although scholars have suggested that missionary biography was significant for nineteenth-century women's developing subjectivities, and noted its influence on the development of the Victorian realist novel, this form is still under-researched in literary studies.[74] My study examines a variety of forms of missionary biography from the 1820s to the 1870s to explore how the female missionary figure and narrative was constructed and contested over these decades.

However, it is in fiction that perhaps the most interesting contestations of the female missionary character and narrative took place. Women writers in the nineteenth century, who conceived of writing as a religious duty, can be seen as missionary writers. Most obviously falling into this category are the evangelical writers of children's tracts, and I explore those writing between 1810 and 1870 for how they were using themes and characters from female missionary life writing. However, women novelists throughout the nineteenth century can also be examined through the female missionary lens to reveal how the female missionary character influenced their understanding of themselves and their art. Moreover, creative adaptations of the missionary character and narrative are even more highly visible in the novel, especially when they fail. Scholars have pointed to the fragmented, even 'hysterical', nature of the prose of women writers such as Charlotte Brontë; I argue that it was the attempts of such authors to contain the female missionary character and narrative within a psychologically realist yet convention-bound genre that caused such splintering of their texts. Rachel DuPlessis has argued that the Victorian novel's plot of love and marriage was insufficient for the narratives that women wanted to tell;[75] religious women such as Brontë wanted to express their authoritative religious subjectivity and the ways in which the female character was becoming constrained. Later, at the turn of the century, New Woman writers created new literary forms to incorporate the female missionary narrative as a powerful metaphor for feminism.

For all texts, biographical and fictional, I take the religious beliefs of the women writers seriously; rather than psychoanalysing them to determine what they might really have been feeling, I try to read their words with an understanding of the evangelical faith and missionary awareness many of them had grown up with. I argue that this common inheritance of pious, didactic literature, enjoining women to be spiritual, to renounce selfishness and to sacrifice themselves if necessary, provided these women with an emotional and heroic framework through which to interpret and describe their own experiences. Rather than dismissing contradictions, I attempt, within the context of evangelical religion and the female missionary narrative, to reconcile and explain these moments of apparent inconsistency or emotional incoherence.

Themes and Structure

The overriding subject of this book is how the female missionary figure and her narrative came to feature in nineteenth-century literature and culture in ways that influenced the developing ideology of femininity, early feminism and the development of women's literary forms. In the Prologue, I provide illustrations of some of the first female missionary characters and forms of the narrative and also introduce some of the narrative's themes. In addition to engaging in the presentation and construction of religious (or pious) femininity, the female missionary narrative has at its heart a requirement for missionary self-sacrifice. How this sacrifice was conceived – as a display of angelic passivity or as a heroic act – and to what extent it was embraced or avoided by missionary women writers had implications for the development of feminine ideologies and for the resulting form of their writing.

Marriage is also a central theme in the female missionary narrative. As scholars have noted, the (usually temporary) prohibition placed on marriage for professional women missionaries by some mission societies challenged ideas of natural, domestic femininity.[76] Equally, the marriages arranged by mission societies ran the risk of making marriage too transactional; marrying a missionary solely for the opportunity this provided of becoming a missionary wife in the field could be regarded as too mercenary a reason for marriage.[77] Though Talia Schaffer has suggested that there were many non-romantic understandings of marriage in the nineteenth century, she acknowledges that, in novelistic treatments of marriage, when reasons for marriage become too mercenary, they are usually disavowed by authors as beyond the pale.[78] Moreover, while Lawrence Stone's grand narrative of romantic marriage advancing hand-in-hand with the increase of individualism in the modern era has been largely discredited, I would argue that his interpretation of nineteenth-century marriage as sanctifying, and even requiring, romantic love – especially of a wife for her husband – is correct.[79] Claire McClisky has also noted the spiritual importance of married love in Christian circles and her findings concerning missionaries' attitudes to marriage mirror my own.[80] Missionary women's life writing consistently displays anxiety about whether the missionary woman is: approaching marriage in the correct spirit; attempting to disentangle romantic feelings for missionary suitors from their desires to enter the mission field; and trying to divine whether their missionary marriage is indeed God's plan for them. Furthermore, when the female missionary narrative enters the world of the nineteenth-century novel, where the marriage plot had traditionally dominated, the problems inherent in missionary women sacrificing romance and marriage are amplified, and become highly visible in ruptures of the textual form.

Another common theme of the female missionary narrative is the importance of friendships and other relationships between women, as part of religious practice and conversion. These intimate religious practices present women as authoritative and confident missionary agents working within nineteenth-century Christian communities, and their written descriptions of their experience of faith and doubt can be interpreted as an early form of women's theology.[81] Moreover, within the evangelical community's publishing practices, what began as a gifting of spiritual support between friends often became part of circulated religious publications, as women developed missionary networks and newsletters and were encouraged to edit biographies of other religious women. As the century went on, and women obtained positions of authority – for example, headships of girls' schools and colleges in missions, colonies and at home – or attempted to forge new, independent lives for themselves, the missionary narrative continues to be present in texts written, circulated and published by these women.

In this study, I do not aim to provide a comprehensive survey of the female missionary narrative and character in nineteenth-century women's writing. Rather, I provide case studies of women writers in particular decades of the century, writing in particular genres, in order to show the influence of missionary writing, characters, plots and tropes in a detailed manner while still tracing this influence across the century.

I start with a prologue introducing two of the first female missionary biographies, from the 1820s and 1830s: the American *Memoirs of Mrs Ann H. Judson*, edited by James Davis Knowles, and *Memoirs of Mrs Harriet Newell*, edited by Leonard Woods. These early examples of the first female missionary narratives already showed how the female missionary character held in tension feminine passivity and heroic authority, especially when it came to missionary sacrifice. Chapter 1 starts where the prologue leaves off, to trace the influence of Ann Judson's memoir. I outline how her biography was written and rewritten between 1839 and 1870, appearing in British and American collections of tracts and biographies, to demonstrate how the character of the female missionary changed through the decades. This chapter also examines other collected biographies of missionary women for their depiction of female missionary action and sacrifice and examines the writing of women missionaries themselves in the WMMS Ladies' Committee newsletter.

Chapter 2 turns to more fictional sources, tracking the movement of female missionary tropes from missionary life writing into the domestic genres of the children's tract and the governess story. I explore the missionary self-identities of Martha Sherwood, 'Hesba Stretton' and Dinah Craik and read their work for elements of the female missionary narrative and character. Seeing their 'holy child' and governess characters as domestic proxies for the female missionary has wide implications for the interpretation of a range of Victorian domestic fiction, as governess fiction has been understood as a substantial sub-genre of this fiction. As part of exploring these implications, Chapter 3 provides a close reading of the missionary plot of Charlotte Brontë's governess novel *Jane Eyre*. This chapter demonstrates how, in this novel, Brontë engages with the female missionary character in all her complexity. However, it also argues that, when the time came for Brontë to be memorialised, her biographers presented her – perhaps surprisingly – in the manner of an ideal female missionary. In telling this story, I demonstrate how Gaskell was influenced by Brontë's friend Ellen Nussey as well as by her own understanding of women's missionary duty, which can be seen emerging in her previous novel *Ruth*.

In Part II, we take up the search for the female missionary narrative in women's literature of the late nineteenth century. Chapter 4 shows that the female missionary figure still had power for women writers in the

1880s and 1890s, by providing readings of writings by the more religious of the New Woman writers. Sarah Grand explicitly presented herself and the New Woman mission as Christian. And while Olive Schreiner and Margaret Harkness struggled with agnosticism, both produced texts full of religious imagery, containing recognisable female missionary figures. Finally, Chapter 5 returns to missionary women's life writing, this time looking at the writings of religious college women, who often supported missions as part of their college life and sometimes went on to become missionaries themselves. The writings of these women at the turn of the century reveal which aspects of the female missionary character and narrative continued to be useful in sustaining women's authoritative activity in the world.

Understanding the influential nature of the female missionary narrative and character through the Victorian period sheds new light on women's history and literature. The fact that there was a continuing presence of female missionary writing at the turn of the twentieth century shows the figure's enduring usefulness for women, in that women in the progressive movements of higher education and socialism were able to adapt her and her narrative to sustain them in their own missions. If we acknowledge that modern-day feminism has its roots in the first-wave feminism of the 1880s and 1890s, we must also think about how religious aspects of that feminism, including aspects of the female missionary, have impacted modern-day activism and feminist subjectivities.

Notes

1 Charlotte Brontë, *Jane Eyre*, ed. by Margaret Smith (Oxford: Oxford University Press, 1993), p. 441.
2 Some scholars, such as Valentine Cunningham, have seen this episode of Brontë's as inspired by the existence of female missionaries, or by male missionary narratives, '"God and Nature Intended You for a Missionary's Wife"' in *Women and Missions, Past and Present, Anthropological and Historical Perceptions*, ed. by Fiona Bowie, Deborah Kirkwood and Shirley Ardner (Oxford: Berg, 1993), pp. 85–105 (pp. 96–8); see also Mary Ellis Gibson, 'Henry Martyn and England's Christian Empire: Rereading *Jane Eyre* through Missionary Biography', *Victorian Literature and Culture* (1999), 419–42. Recent scholars, though, have seen Brontë as engaging extensively with missionary ideas, for example, Winter Jade Werner, *Missionary Cosmopolitanism in Nineteenth-Century British Literature* (Columbus, OH: Ohio State University Press, 2020), pp. 109–42.
3 This is despite attention being drawn to female missionary biographies in the early 2000s by Clare Midgley and Linda Peterson. See Midgley, 'Can Women be Missionaries? Envisioning Female Agency in the Early Nineteenth-Century British Empire', *Journal of British Studies*, 45 (2006), 335–58; and Peterson, 'Women Writers and Self Writing', in *Women and Literature in Britain 1800–1900*, ed. by Joanne Shattock (Cambridge: Cambridge University Press, 2001), pp. 209–30.

16 Introduction

4 Catherine Hall was among the first to draw attention to women's involvement in supporting the mission movement in *White Male and Middle-Class: Explorations in Feminism and History* (Cambridge: Polity, 1992), 223–4; more recently, excellent work has been published on women's experience of mission, as supporters and as missionaries – for example, see Alison Twells, *The Civilising Mission and the English Middle Class, 1792–1850: The Heathen at Home and Overseas* (London: Palgrave Macmillan, 2009); and Emily Manktelow, *Missionary Families: Race, Gender and Generation on the Spiritual Frontier* (Manchester: Manchester University Press, 2013).

5 In this concept of ideologies developing unevenly, I am influenced by Mary Poovey's work, *Uneven Developments: The Ideological Work of Gender in Mid-Victorian England* (Chicago, IL: Chicago University Press, 1988).

6 See Werner, pp. 111–2; and Manktelow, pp. 23–38.

7 Peter Williams, ' "The Missing Link": The Recruitment of Women Missionaries in some English Evangelical Missionary Societies in the Nineteenth Century', in *Women and Missions*, ed. by Bowie et al., pp. 43–69 (p. 45).

8 Ulrike Sill, *Encounters in Quest of Christian Womanhood: The Basel Mission in Pre- and Early Colonial Ghana*, Studies in Christian Mission (Leiden: Brill, 2010), pp. 38–43; Cunningham, p. 91; George G. Findlay, *The History of the Wesleyan Methodist Missionary Society*, 5 vols. (London: J.A. Sharp, 1921–24), Vol. IV, p. 20.

9 Williams, ' "The Missing Link" ', in *Women and Missions*, ed. by Bowie et al., p. 65; Sill, p. 44.

10 Findlay, pp. 20–1.

11 Williams, ' "The Missing Link" ', in *Women and Missions*, ed. by Bowie et al., p. 65.

12 Elisabeth Jay, *Faith and Doubt in Victorian Britain* (London: Macmillan, 1986), p. 33; See also Cecilie Swaisland's history of the High Church Anglican mission in South Africa in 'Wanted – Earnest, Self-Sacrificing Women for Service in South Africa: Nineteenth-Century Recruitment of Single Women to Protestant Missions', in *Women and Missions*, ed. by Bowie et al., pp. 70–84 (pp. 76–81).

13 Midgley has discussed this lack of study, p. 336.

14 Elizabeth E. Prevost, in her study of women and African missions, for example, tellingly titles one of her chapters 'Towards the Professionalization of Female Evangelism' in *The Communion of Women: Missions and Gender in Colonial Africa and the British Metropole* (Oxford: Oxford University Press, 2010), p. 75; also see Rhonda Semple, *Missionary Women: Gender, Professionalism, and the Victorian Idea of Christian Mission* (Woodbridge: Boydell, 2003), pp. 6–18.

15 Hall, *White Male and Middle-Class*, pp. 223–4; Twells, pp. 84–123; Norman Etherington has also noted the active nature of missionary wives in this period, *Missions and Empire* (Oxford: Oxford University Press, 2005), pp. 182–3.

16 Manktelow, pp. 12–4; Claire McClisky, '(En)gendering Faith?: Love, Marriage and the Evangelical Mission on the Settler Colonial Frontier', in *Studies in Settler Colonialism: Politics, Identity and Culture*, ed. by Fiona Bateman and Lionel Pilkington (Basingstoke: Palgrave Macmillan, 2011), pp. 106–21; Twells has also noted the importance of engagement with the mission movement as important for the development of the British middle-class, pp. 43–53.

17 Hilton, p. 5.
18 Williams, '"The Missing Link"', in *Women and Missions*, ed. by Bowie et al., pp. 45–6.
19 Twells, pp. 178–205.
20 Anna Johnston, *Missionary Writing and Empire 1800–1860* (Cambridge: Cambridge University Press, 2003), p. 3. Ian Bradley also notes the importance of missionary writing in his *Call to Seriousness: The Evangelical Impact on the Victorians* (London: Cape, 1976).
21 See Nancy Cutt, *Ministering Angels: A Study of Nineteenth-Century Writing for Children* (Wormley: Five Owls Press, 1980), pp. xi, 27; and Dennis Butts, 'Introduction', in *From the Dairyman's Daughter to Worrals of the WAAF: The Religious Tract Society, Lutterworth Press and Children's Literature*, ed. by Dennis Butts and Pat Garrett (Cambridge: Lutterworth Press, 2006), p. 7.
22 Williams, 'The Missing Link', in *Women and Missions*, ed. by Bowie et al.; C. Peter Williams, *The Ideal of a Self-Governing Church: A Study in Victorian Missionary Strategy* (Leiden: Brill, 1990); Bebbington, p. 12.
23 See, for example, Claire McClisky, Daniel Midena and Karen Valgårda (eds), *Emotions and Christian Missions: Historical Perspectives* (Basingstoke: Palgrave Macmillan, 2015); Dorothy L. Hodgson, *The Church of Women: Gendered Encounters Between Massai and Missionaries* (Bloomington, IN: Indiana University Press, 2005); Modupe Labode, 'From Heathen Kraal to Christian Home: Anglican Mission Education and African Christian Girls, 1850–1900', in *Women and Missions*, ed. by Bowie et al., pp. 126–144.
24 Anna Johnston valuably outlined how missionary writing could affect Victorians' imperial self-perception. However, her study is limited by her focus on one mission organisation (the LMS) and her inclusion of mainly male missionary writers.
25 Etherington, pp. 1–5.
26 Brian Stanley, 'Christianity and Civilization in Evangelical Mission Thought, 1792–1857', in *Christian Missions and the Enlightenment*, ed. by Brian Stanley (Richmond, VA: Curzon, 2001), pp. 169–97 (pp. 193–5).
27 Jane Samson, 'Ethnology and Theology: Nineteenth-Century Mission Dilemmas in the South Pacific', in *Christian Missions and the Enlightenment*, ed. by Stanley, pp. 99–122 (pp. 102–9); See also Twells, pp. 12–5.
28 Patricia Grimshaw and Andrew May, 'Reappraisals of Mission History: An Introduction', in *Missionaries, Indigenous Peoples and Cultural Exchange*, ed. by Patricia Grimshaw and Andrew May (Eastbourne: Sussex Academic Press, 2010), p. 2.
29 Gayatri Chakravorty Spivak, 'Can the Subaltern Speak', in *Marxism and the Interpretation of Culture*, ed. by Cary Nelson and Lawrence Grossberg (Urbana, IL: University of Illinois Press, 1988), pp. 295–306.
30 Burton, *Burdens of History: British Feminists, Indian Women, and Imperial Culture, 1865–1915* (Chapel Hill, NC: University of North Carolina, 1994), pp. 30–1; Midgley, 'From Supporting Missions to Petitioning Parliament: British Women and the Evangelical Campaign against *Sati* in India, 1813–30', in *Women in British Politics, 1760–1860: The Power of the Petticoat*, ed. by Kathryn Gleadle and Sarah Richardson (Basingstoke: Macmillan, 2000), pp. 74–92.

18 *Introduction*

31 Twells, pp. 178–83; Elisabeth Jay, *The Evangelical and Oxford Movements* (Cambridge: Cambridge University Press, 1983), pp. 1–5.
32 See Susan Gilbert and Sandra Gubar, *Madwoman in the Attic: The Woman Writer and the Nineteenth Century Literary Imagination* (London: Yale University Press, 1979); and Elaine Showalter, *A Literature of Their Own: British women writers from Charlotte Brontë to Doris Lessing* [1982], 2nd edn (London: Virago, 2009).
33 See, for example, Martha Vicinus, 'Introduction', in *Suffer and be Still: Women in the Victorian Age*, ed. by Martha Vicinus (London: Indiana University Press, 1972), pp. vii–xv (pp. ix–x).
34 Valerie Sanders, *Eve's Renegades: Victorian Anti-Feminist Women Novelists* (Basingstoke: Macmillan, 1996), pp. 6–9.
35 Showalter, *A Literature of Their Own*, pp. 195–201; see also Anne Heilmann, *New Woman Strategies: Sarah Grand, Olive Schreiner, Mona Caird* (Manchester: Manchester University Press, 2004), p. 126.
36 On this tendency, see Naomi Lloyd, 'Evangelicalism and the Making of Same-Sex Desire: The Life and Writings of Constance Maynard' (unpublished doctoral thesis, University of British Columbia, 2011), p. 8.
37 Semple, p. 36.
38 Vicinus, 'Introduction', in *Suffer and Be Still*, ed. by Vicinus, p. xi.
39 Twells, pp. 84–112; Linda Wilson, *Constrained by Zeal: Female Spirituality Amongst Nonconformists, 1825–75* (Carlisle: Paternoster, 2000), p. 11.
40 Sue Morgan and Jacqueline deVries (eds), *Women, Gender and Religious Cultures in Britain, 1800–1940* (Abingdon: Routledge, 2010); Julie Melnyk (ed.), *Women's Theology in Nineteenth-Century Britain: Transfiguring the Faith of their Fathers* (London: Garland, 1998).
41 Sharon Marcus, *Between Women: Friendship, Desire, and Marriage in Victorian England* (Oxford: Princeton University Press, 2007), pp. 63–5; Lloyd, p. 8–9.
42 Elisabeth Jay, *The Religion of the Heart: Anglican Evangelicalism and the Nineteenth-Century Novel* (Oxford: Clarendon, 1979).
43 Anne Hogan and Andrew Bradstock (eds), *Women of Faith in Victorian Culture: Reassessing the Angel in the House* (Basingstoke, Macmillan, 1998).
44 Nixon, 'Introduction', in *Victorian Religious Discourse: New Directions in Criticism*, ed. by Jude Nixon (Basingstoke: Palgrave Macmillan, 2004), pp. 1–26 (pp. 3–4).
45 Amanda Vickery describes this ideology in 'Golden Age to Separate Spheres? A Review of the Categories and Chronology of English Women's History', *The Historical Journal*, 36 (1993), 383–414 (pp. 383–7); see also Hall, *White Male and Middle Class*, pp. 84–9; Catherine Hall and Leonore Davidoff, *Family Fortunes: Men and Women of the English Middle Class 1780–1850* (London: Routledge, 2002), pp. 179–92; and Philippa Levine, *Feminist Lives in Victorian England: Private Roles and Public Commitment* (Oxford: Blackwell, 1990), p. 31.
46 Philippa Levine, *Victorian Feminism 1850–1900* (London: Hutchinson, 1987), pp. 12–3; Vickery, pp. 391–408.
47 Barbara Caine, *Victorian Feminists* (Oxford: Oxford University Press, 1992), pp. 42–5, 107; Judith Walkowitz, *City of Dreadful Delight: Narratives of Sexual Danger in Late-Victorian London* (Chicago: University of Chicago Press, 1992), pp. 57–63.

48 Twells, p. 268.
49 Jay, *Religion of the Heart*, pp. 40, 104; Hilton, p. 19.
50 Bradley notes this feminisation, pp. 40–1; Walkowitz also argues that the male urban settlements in the late nineteenth century emulated female practices of philanthropy, *City of Dreadful Delight: Narratives of Sexual Danger in Late-Victorian London* (Chicago, IL: University of Chicago Press, 1992), p. 70.
51 Christine, Krueger, *The Reader's Repentance: Women Preachers, Women Writers and Nineteenth-Century Social Discourse* (London: University of Chicago Press, 1992), p. 5.
52 Midgley, 'Can Women be Missionaries?', pp. 352–3.
53 James Davis Knowles, *Memoirs of Mrs. Ann H. Judson*, 3rd edn (London: Wightman and Co., 1830), p. 9; Daniel C. Eddy, *Heroines of the Missionary Enterprise; or Sketches of Prominent Female Missionaries* (London: n.p., 1850), p. v.
54 Peterson, 'Women Writers', in *Women and Literature*, ed. by Shattock, pp. 209–230.
55 I demonstrate this two-way process of cultural influence in Chapter 1.
56 John Tosh, *Manliness and Masculinities in Nineteenth Century Britain* (Harlow: Pearson, 2005), p. 187.
57 Vance, *The Sinews of the Spirit: The Ideal of Christian Manliness in Victorian Literature and Religious Thought* (Cambridge: Cambridge University Press, 1985), pp. 5–7.
58 Claudia Nelson, *Boys Will be Girls: The Feminine Ethic and British Children's Fiction 1857–1917* (New Brunswick, NJ: Rutgers University Press, 1991), pp. 2–23.
59 Julie Melnyk, 'Introduction', in *Women's Theology in Nineteenth-Century Britain*, ed. by Melnyk, pp. xii–xviii (pp. xvi–xvii).
60 Alison Booth argues that women's life writing in general was important for the development of women's subjectivities, *How to Make It as a Woman: Collective Biographical History from Victoria to the Present* (Chicago, IL: University of Chicago Press, 2004), pp. 2–3.
61 Throughout this book, I tend to use the descriptor 'female missionary' when referring to the textual figure and 'missionary woman' when referring to real missionary women.
62 Vickery, pp. 389–91.
63 Ibid., p. 401.
64 Semple, p. 48.
65 Virginia Brereton, quoted in Wilson, p. 27.
66 Vickery, p. 391.
67 Marcus, pp. 36–40.
68 Wilson, p. 11; Candy Gunther Brown, *The Word in the World: Evangelical Writing, Publishing and Reading in America 1789–1880* (Chapel Hill, NC: University of North Carolina Press, 2004), p. 11.
69 Morgan and deVries, 'Introduction', in *Women, Gender and Religious Communities*, ed. by Morgan and deVries, pp. 2–3.
70 Thomas Dixon, *From Passions to Emotions: The Creation of a Secular Psychological Category* (Cambridge: Cambridge University Press, 2003), pp. 2–3.
71 Nicole Eustace, Eugenia Lean, Julie Livingston, Jan Plamper, William M. Reddy and Barbara H. Rosenwein, 'AHR Conversation: The Historical Study of Emotions', *American Historical Review*, 117 (2012), 1487–531 (pp. 1495–504).

20 *Introduction*

72 Johnston encounters this problem in her study based on the writings of the LMS, which did not recruit single women missionaries until 1875, p. 7.
73 For example, Anna Johnston's study of missionary writing relies on the LMS archives, p. 7; Cunningham bases his missionary article mainly on LMS sources; and Midgley uses LMS and SPFEE sources alongside missionary memoir in 'Can Women be Missionaries?'.
74 Midgley, 'Can Women be Missionaries?'; Peterson, 'Women Writers', in *Women and Literature*, ed. by Shattock; Jay, *Religion of the Heart*, pp. 2–3; more recently, female missionary biography formed a tantalisingly small part of Alison Booth's study of women's collective biographies.
75 Rachel Blau DuPlessis, *Writing Beyond the Ending: Narrative Strategies of Twentieth-Century Women Writers* (Bloomington, IN: Indiana University Press, 1985), p. 27.
76 Sill, p. 54; see also Susan Thorne, 'Missionary-Imperial Feminism', in *Gendered Missions: Women and Men in Missionary Discourse and Practice*, ed. by Mary Taylor Huber and Nancy C. Lutkehaus (Ann Arbor, MI: University of Michigan Press, 1999), pp. 46–7.
77 Though, as is discussed in Chapter 1, there is evidence that a number of missionary wives approached marriage in this way.
78 Schaffer, *Romance's Rival: Familiar Marriage in Victorian Fiction* (Oxford: Oxford University Press, 2016), pp. 7–10.
79 Lawrence Stone, *The Family, Sex and Marriage in England 1500–1800* (London: Weidenfeld and Nicolson, 1977), pp. 136–8, 202–6; for critique, see Schaffer, pp. 19–20.
80 McClisky, '(En)gendering Faith?', in *Studies in Settler Colonialism*, ed. by Bateman and Pilkington, pp. 110–113.
81 Melnyk, 'Introduction', in *Women's Theology in Nineteenth-Century Britain*, ed. by Melnyk, pp. xi–xii.

Prologue
Ann Judson and Harriet Newell: Immortalising the Female Missionary

Introduction

This is not the story of the American missionaries Ann Judson and Harriet Newell. Rather, it is the story of their afterlives, as the female missionary characters who, through their posthumous biographies, played a significant role in the construction of nineteenth-century British femininity. Most of the women writers we will meet in this book would have read their stories as children in religious households or schools. Even if they did not, the female missionary figure haunted the dominant evangelical culture of the Victorian era, beginning with the biographies of Ann Judson and Harriet Newell.

The *Memoir of Mrs Ann H. Judson* was published in London in 1829. It followed the memoir of her fellow missionary Harriet Newell, published in 1816, and Ann Judson's own *Account of the American Baptist Mission to the Burman Empire – in a Series of Letters, Addressed to a Gentleman in London* (1823), a new edition of which had appeared in 1827. The London gentleman referred to in her title was the prominent Wesleyan Joseph Butterworth. As well as publishing her *Account*, Butterworth hosted Judson while she was in Britain between 1821 and 1822, introduced her to William Wilberforce and promoted the mission through his networks. One would therefore expect the British public who had been following the American Baptists' mission to be interested in her posthumous biography. What happened over the next few years, though, can only have been unexpected – the memoir was a publishing sensation.

In 1829, Judson's *Account* was out of print in Britain, and there had not been a new British edition of Newell's memoir for over ten years. Despite this, Judson's biography sold out its first two, 'considerable', British editions in just six months, was re-issued twice in 1830, and was in its ninth London edition by 1838. Moreover, the Religious Tract Society (RTS) responded to the popularity of the memoir by publishing its own versions of Judson's story a number of times between 1832 and 1856, and she became a staple of collective biographies of religious women.[1] In this way, Judson's story was told and retold throughout the nineteenth century, and her popularity continued into the twentieth century.[2]

I will examine the retellings of Judson's life in the next chapter. Before this, though, it is important to introduce the original biography: its character, the traditions it drew on, and what made it so significant. It is also important to explore the somewhat less successful memoir of Harriet Newell, and how her life story was also influential for women's missionary life writing. Exploring these early female missionary memoirs demonstrates how the biographers attempted to control the influence of their characters and inscribe them with a specifically feminine missionary identity. However, radical aspects of the female missionary do emerge, especially in the biography of Ann Judson, and this allowed religious women readers to interpret them in their own ways.

Traditions in Religious Life Writing

While the biographies of Ann Judson and Harriet Newell were among the first of female missionaries, they were not the first memoirs of religious women. They were also not the first missionary memoirs. Spiritual biographies of men and women proliferated in America and Britain following the evangelical revivals of the eighteenth century and, by the early nineteenth century, memoirs of male missionaries such as John Wesley and David Brainerd were an established genre.[3] Women's spiritual life writing usually took the form of conversion accounts or extended obituary letters published in religious magazines. Though women were not expected to present themselves publicly, there was an emphasis in evangelical religion on private reflection and self-examination that was often realised through journal writing and referenced in letters to friends and family, as part of that other evangelical duty of proselytising. As scholars have noted, from the time of Wesley's production of his *Journal* and *Arminian Magazine*, the lines between private and public writing began to be blurred, as he blithely published personal letters from ministers and female correspondents.[4] Within Methodist society, some published life writing dealt with 'exceptional' women – such as Mary Tooth's 1816 memoir of the female preacher Mary Bosanquet Fletcher (1739–1816) – but by the nineteenth century, these were limited in their influence, as Methodists attempted to erase women preachers from their history.[5] Spiritual biographies of more typical, domestic women were published across denominations, in Britain and America, by friends or family members. This life writing did not aim so much to depict an authentic, individual self (in the way that we have come to expect of modern autobiographies) as to produce exemplars of Christian practice to serve the religious community.[6]

The most emphasised aspect of female subjects in this spiritual life writing was their piety. For Calvinist evangelicals, pious behaviour, or living according to the pattern of Christ, was a sign that a person was predestined to salvation; for more moderate evangelicals, piety in everyday life could lead to salvation and could be attained by emulating the lives of other pious individuals. An important aspect of piety was resignation to the will of God and his Providence. This was especially important during the conversion process, which formed a familiar narrative within a person's life story and could be written up and circulated, or even published, as a standalone account during someone's lifetime. Conversion accounts tended to follow specific conventions and were often emotional as the subject recalled their painfully sudden awareness of their sinful nature; their despair as they feared they would never attain true piety and salvation; and their final resignation to the will of God, leading to happiness and conviction of salvation through Christ.[7] Though conversion accounts suggested a narrative closure at this point, evangelical conversion was usually a process; spiritual biographies therefore depicted their women subjects continually striving to live pious lives and celebrated their efforts and eventual success.

How an individual reacted to the onset of death was especially important in establishing their piety and determining whether or not they were saved, and the death scene was therefore crucial in spiritual memoirs. Evangelicals were encouraged to 'witness' the deaths of their friends and family members and to write accounts of deathbed behaviour that would suggest that the deceased had achieved salvation. Suffering pain and death with resignation was proof that an individual had piously resigned themselves to God's will, while happiness evidenced a person's evangelical 'conviction' of salvation. Similarly, taking pleasure in hearing prayers and hymns suggested the pious frame of an individual's mind, and hearing heavenly voices or experiencing visions of angels or departed loved ones was particularly convincing. Using one's last words – elevated in significance by the imminence of death – to convert mourners was a particularly good sign that someone was possessed of vital religion and its concomitant impulse to spread the word.[8] Evangelical societies published witnesses of good Christian deaths, alongside more extended obituaries and memoirs that included deathbed scenes, as evidence of the reality of salvation.

There was a potentially radical aspect to women's spiritual biographies, in that their own private writings, such as letters and diaries, were often quoted. As Krueger has noted, much of the material in religious women's letters would have been construed as preaching if they had spoken it in public.[9] Whether they were writing to convert friends, or believed their journals would someday be published, religious women's letters and journals have a self-conscious quality. However, these women's voices were heavily mediated and controlled by the family members, editors and publishers involved in presenting their subject's life story in a manner in which it could be emulated by other Christian women.[10]

Theoretically, in addition to female spiritual biography, the editors of Judson's and Newell's memoirs could draw on male missionary biographies. These were more monumental and more likely to be published in epic volumes, such as Wesley's biography of David Brainerd – or indeed the numerous biographies of Wesley himself. These were works about exceptional individuals, written in the manner of lives of the saints, rather than everyday exemplars of domestic piety, recorded in the ephemeral pages of religious magazines, and were popular perhaps as much for the exotic scenes and exciting situations they depicted as for their didactic presentation of a pious individual. The extent to which the biographers of Judson and Newell mixed the genres of domestic female spiritual memoir and heroic male missionary biography – how they both controlled and glorified their heroines – would have far-reaching implications for how women readers through the century would understand religious womanhood and femininity.

Controlling the Female Missionary Subject

In writing their biographies, Knowles and Woods knew they were doing something absolutely necessary to support the fledgling American missionary movement; Woods published his memoir of Newell as part of his work for the American Board of Commissioners for Foreign Missions and Knowles was commissioned to produce his memoir of Judson by the American Baptist Board of Missions. They also knew that what they were doing was controversial. The foreign mission movement was a venture of what was, in the early decades of the nineteenth century, the evangelical fringe of the American church and was viewed with some suspicion by mainstream Christians. Especially contentious was the idea of women leaving their homes for the mission field. Knowles knew that Judson's behaviour had been censured by some American women as unfeminine and 'inconsistent with prudence and delicacy', and he reported an example of this reaction:

> The remark of one lady respecting Mrs J. would express the feelings of many others. 'I hear,' said she, 'That Miss H. is going to India. Why does she go?' 'Why, she thinks it her duty; would not you go, if you thought it was your duty?' 'But,' replied the good lady with emphasis, '*I would not think it my duty.*'[11]

Until now, a woman's duty had been seen to lie at home. However, the mission movement required missionary wives, both to support male missionaries and to provide the example of Christian domesticity to the 'heathen'.[12] Woods and Knowles therefore had to establish their missionary heroines as appropriately pious and feminine, in order to demonstrate that a missionary destiny could be a respectable one for women. In addition, they needed their biographies to help mould female readers into pious, feminine helpmeets for future missionary men.[13] Hence, the memoirs exercised control on two levels: they managed the presentation of their female subjects, in order to influence the development of an appropriately feminine missionary subjectivity in their women readers.

They did this through the form of their biographies, editorial intervention and characterisation.

Harriet Newell

Leonard Woods constructed his memoir of Harriet Newell according to the model of women's spiritual life writing as it had appeared in American evangelical periodicals.[14] A very short introduction precedes Newell's own accounts of the religious events of her life, as they appeared in her journal and letters from 1806 (when she was thirteen years old). There is very little editorial intervention or explanation. Newell does not mention the missionary cause until late in 1810, when she records hearing about it from a female friend (presumably Ann Judson) who is going to join the mission to India. The first third of the memoir is therefore devoted to Newell's pre-missionary life and reads like the spiritual biography of a typical middle-class, New England woman.

The style of Newell's writings, selected by her editor, is also familiar, displaying her consciousness of writing within an established tradition, as part of a cause, for a potential audience of family, friends or wider congregation. In an explicit account of her conversion (a reflective document she produced as part of her religious practice), she compares her religious emotions to those she understands others had felt.[15] Her somewhat muted religious emotions made her account eminently suitable for a middle-class audience, who could find more extreme enthusiasm indecorous: 'My convictions of sin were not so pungent and distressing, as many have had [...] The ecstacies [sic], which many new-born souls possess, were not mine. But [...] I was filled with a sweet peace, a heavenly calmness'.[16] Her conversion narrative follows an established arc: following the usual trials of the world, she describes how her zeal diminished until, following contact with a revived Christian community, and certain religious ministers, her soul experienced a re-awakening, at which point she undertook Christian confirmation.

In the same way that spiritual life writing was dominated by its didactic aims, Woods's biography of Harriet Newell was mainly concerned with using the exemplary female subject and her martyrdom to validate the mission movement. In a preface, Woods justifies the publication of Newell's private papers by assuring the public that, while Newell would not have wished for publicity – she was an 'unambitious, delicate female' – he suggests that the importance of the cause makes both her and her work 'a kind of property' of 'the Christian community'.[17] In this way, as he asserts her exemplary femininity, he subjugates her life to the cause.

A number of documents by other authors are included in Woods's memoir alongside Newell's papers. Two of these documents were quite usual forms of spiritual life writing: a letter from Newell's husband to her mother providing his witness of her death, which concludes the main memoir; and Woods's sermon on the occasion of her death, which is included as an appendix and can be read as an obituary. However, Woods also appends a copy of a sermon he gave on the embarkation of the missionaries and, in later editions, he also adds an account of the American Mission Society and its progress following Newell's death. These additional documents have the effect of adapting the female spiritual biography form, so that it becomes even more associated with the religious cause rather than the individual it memorialises. The title page begins this process, as, in addition to describing the book as the *Memoirs of Mrs Harriet Newell*, it also lists the supplementary documents. Also prominent on the title page are the names of two men: Harriet Newell is most importantly the 'wife of the Rev. S. Newell, American Missionary to India'; and the memoir is compiled and includes sermons, by 'Leonard Woods D.D.'. Harriet Newell and her story are overshadowed by male actors in the mission, and the mission organisation, for which her life was sacrificed. On one of the first pages of the memoir, a quotation from Woods's obituary sermon further displaces Newell from the text – and from readers' memories: 'henceforth, everyone who remembers Harriet Newell, will remember the foreign Mission for America' (p. i). Rather than an active individual, she now simply stands for, and can be replaced by, the cause. Though Woods suggests that this process goes two ways – anyone remembering the mission will also remember Harriet Newell – the version of Newell that they remember will be that of the mission's first martyr. Indeed, Woods goes so far to suggest that this was Newell's sole purpose in life: she was destined by God to provide the society with its first 'martyr', and her virtues were to 'quicken and edify' other men and women to support missions (p. i).

When it comes to characterising the female missionary, as she was embodied by Newell, Woods uses a number of strategies to establish her as appropriately feminine. First, her missionary acts are depicted as fundamentally similar to a woman's domestic trials. Her decision to become a missionary – her struggle to determine God's plan for her talents – is presented in the same way as would be a domestic woman's struggle with faith or reaction to the prognosis of death. These struggles all required passive self-resignation to Providence, which was seen as evidence of piety, and was often portrayed as angelic and largely effortless in the case of women and children.[18] Newell's struggle, and her final decision to resign herself to God's Providential calling, are presented as simply evidence of her female piety. Moreover, Woods consistently analogises Newell's following of her missionary calling and her deathbed behaviour as examples of the same piety. In the biography, he uses similar language in his summaries of these events: she 'manifested remarkable tranquillity and resolution' (p. 119) on leaving America, and she 'calmly [...] expired' (p. 179). And in his sermon, he rhetorically conjoins the two events: 'her resolved and peaceful mind in the parting hour; and the fortitude and resignation which she afterwards exercised under her various afflictions'

(p. 210). Here, the embarkation scene strikingly prefigures her perfect, passive Christian death – that other 'parting hour'.

Woods's emphasis on Newell's death is important for a number of reasons. Fundamentally, the posthumous nature of the biography allows Woods complete control over his female missionary:[19] she is always a martyred saint of a cause, rather than a woman. In this way, Woods uses Newell's death to present the exemplary female missionary, conceptually inseparable from her essential and inevitable destiny. Through his selection of her personal papers, Woods suggests that she herself often anticipated her death: she talks of making this 'sacrifice' and accepting a missionary life or death with equanimity, as the will of Providence.[20] Her death is described both by the narrator and in letters from her husband, over the space of six pages, in a way that stresses her passive acceptance and saintliness in the face of suffering; while her husband refers to her as having some doubts immediately following the death of her child, he also insists that they 'were soon removed' and that 'she meekly yielded to the will of her heavenly father [...] she continually looked to God and passively rested on him'.[21] In his introduction to her death, Woods glosses this momentary struggle, saying that 'she calmly, and with apparent ease, expired' (p. 179). Further, the premature nature of her death – she was only nineteen – recalls child obituary literature, associating her all the more with passivity in death. Overall, the depiction of Newell's death is striking in its passivity and resignation, and proves that the female missionary's death can be just as exemplary as that of a domestic Christian woman. Indeed, in using the familiar form of the female spiritual biography, Woods in effect domesticates the missionary context, making the mission respectable for women.

More than this, though, Newell's exemplary femininity does not just survive the mission field – it is enhanced. The missionary context comes to represent the ideal opportunity for women such as Newell to live a life of true, feminine piety, devoted to God's cause, and feminine self-denial is epitomised in their martyrdom. In his funeral sermon, Woods credits Newell, and the female missionary more generally, with a natural, feminine domesticity, which makes her dutiful decision to leave her home and family – sorrowfully exchanging them for 'a land of strangers'[22] – even more selfless:

> The *wife of a missionary* [...] gives still more remarkable evidence of self-denial and devotion; - evidence I say *more remarkable,* because for *her* to forsake friends and country, is an instance of *greater self-denial.* The tie, which binds her to her relatives and her home, is stronger. Her mind is more delicate in its construction; more sensible to the tenderness of natural relations, and to the delights of domestic life. When, therefore, she forsakes *all,* for the name of Christ, she makes a higher effort; she offers a more costly sacrifice;

and thus furnishes a more conspicuous proof, that her love of Christ transcends all earthly affection.

(pp. 197–8)

In wanting to validate the mission movement over and above women's involvement, Woods paints the mission field not only as a place that is suitable for women, but as one that throws a woman missionary's femininity, especially her passive self-sacrifice, into sharp relief. Newell's brief life and typical religious life writing enabled her biographer to create the exemplary feminine, self-sacrificing missionary martyr for her nineteenth-century society.

Ann Judson

When Knowles came to write Ann Judson's biography, he was less able to adapt her life story to fit within the genre of domestic spiritual life writing. Indeed, Knowles displays anxiety concerning the form of biography he is writing, which is understandable given Ann Judson's life more resembled that of a male missionary than an exemplary religious woman. Presenting a woman in the manner of male saints such as Wesley and Brainerd was a radical idea, though; by this time, the recent women preachers of eighteenth-century Methodism had been largely erased from history, and despite Newell's memoir, female missionary heroines were not yet familiar.[23] Knowles responds to this context by justifying the female missionary actor, as well as his new genre of female missionary biography. He also uses editorial intervention far more than Woods had in his memoir of Newell, interrupting Ann Judson's accounts to explain or excuse her words and actions, in order to protect his female missionary from criticism. Finally, he attempts to portray her death in a manner that will prove her exemplary Christianity.

To justify women's participation in missionary work, in his first chapter, Knowles turns to Bible for precedent, arguing that it is 'full of testimony to the moral and intellectual worth of woman' and that it includes examples of early Christian heroines who, with their 'zeal', 'firmness' and 'intrepidity' pave the way for modern female missionaries.[24] Indeed, in telling the stories of the early female evangelists working alongside St Paul, it is implied that the Bible itself is an example of female missionary biography. Moreover, in what would become a common recourse of later nineteenth-century women writers and activists, Knowles praises the Christian world for recognising the 'true rank of women' (p. 10) in celebrating their active, respected role in their families and congregations – in contrast with non-Christian societies.[25]

Knowles also finds a precedent for the female missionary's controversial leaving of her home in American history. He notes that one of the first settlers of Salem (MA) was a woman – Lady Arabella Johnson – who

Figure P.1 Portrait of Ann Judson, *Memoir of Mrs Ann H. Judson*. © British Library Board. All Rights Reserved/Bridgeman Images.

accompanied her husband in their religious emigration from England in the 1620s and had recently been eulogised in a way that established her as an appropriately feminine Christian heroine. Knowles argues that Judson should be included in this 'tribute to female excellence':

> In the path of duty no sacrifice is with them too high or too dear [...] Timid though she may be, and so delicate [...] on such occasions she loses all sense of danger, and assumes a preternatural courage [...] Then she displays that undaunted spirit, which neither courts difficulties, nor evades them; that resignation, which utters neither murmur nor regret; and that patience in suffering, which seems victorious over death itself.
>
> (pp. 45–6)

In aligning Judson with such a specifically female form of piety and sacrifice, Knowles renders her far less controversial. This female heroine is self-sacrificing, timid, delicate, resigned and patient in suffering. She is reluctant, in that she does not 'court' difficulties, and her courage comes from some source other than herself – it is 'preternatural'.

However, when it comes to including Judson's own words, Knowles acknowledges that the autobiographical form of such life writing might not work to create the perfect example of a female missionary; a biography that features a woman's own personal writings might uncover emotions and thoughts difficult to reconcile with the public's expectations:

> The compiler has felt the difficulty of treating properly some topics which have a necessary connection with the narrative, and which have occasioned various feelings, in different bosoms. Some may think that he has touched them too lightly; while others may have wished that they should not be mentioned at all.
>
> (p. vi)

It is impossible to identify these topics with certainty, due to Knowles's assiduous lack of specificity in this passage – 'some topics' causing 'various feelings' in 'different bosoms'. Knowles's discomfort could suggest that he is referring to aspects of Ann Judson's life which occasioned emotional reactions, such as crises of faith. Knowles's anxiety around the nature of Judson's own words leads to (and is revealed by) his exerting a noticeable amount of editorial control over the memoir. He makes clear in his preface that he only included Judson's private writings 'so far as they [...] were suitable for publication' (p. v), and throughout the text, he displays a concern to direct the reader's interpretation of the narrative and reduce the possibility of 'incorrect' readings. In particular, he explicitly cuts short entries that deal with Judson's early struggles with faith – a subject Harriet Newell's biography seems to rehearse *ad infinitum*. He explains:

> The complaints and self-reproaches of uninspired saints, may possibly be injurious to some professors of religion [...] And the enemies of religion are liable to regard them as inexplicable inconsistencies and proofs that religion is the parent of melancholy, and is devoid of permanent and tranquil happiness.
>
> (p. 26)

To counter these 'enemies', Knowles continues his intervention to explain what Judson might have really meant and finds other quotations to enable him to insist upon her 'deep and habitual piety' (p. 109). His self-conscious move here of both opening and closing discussion about how much of a female subject's crises of faith to make public implies a fear that Judson's life might not be suitable to fulfil the purpose of a spiritual biography, which he defined in his introduction as being, like the Bible, 'to teach mankind, in the most emphatic manner, the happiness which springs from piety' (p. 9).

Ultimately, in the same manner as Woods, Knowles has most control over his subject – is able to define her and her meaning for the reader – in death. This is hard-won though, as Judson's was difficult to present as an exemplary Christian death. To a large extent, this problem was a result of the mission context: Knowles describes her as dying 'in a strange place [...] surrounded by strangers' (p. 266), as her husband was away on missionary business; consequently, an extended, reliable Christian 'witness' of her death was difficult to find. Knowles acknowledges that this is a problem: 'It would be consoling to know more of the state of her mind, during her sickness, and of her feelings in prospect of death' (p. 266). His publishing in full of Mr Judson's letters to his wife's mother about her death – following the conventions of spiritual biography and the example of Woods – cannot fully reassure the reader of her perfect Christian death, as they rather detail Mr Judson's anxious searching for details and provide mixed, unsatisfactory evidence. In one of his letters, Mr Judson writes almost desperately: 'I have no account whatever of the state of her mind, in view of death and eternity'.[26] In a later letter, though he has obtained the doctor's report that 'her mind was uniformly tranquil and happy in the prospect of death', he has also learned that her last words were unremarkable: 'I feel quite well; only very weak'.[27] Moreover, though the deathbed witnesses of the Burmese Christians were encouraging, there was a language barrier, and there were suggestions that Ann Judson was not fully compos mentis on her deathbed.

However, in publishing all the evidence available, Knowles was able to furnish his readers with the material for a satisfying conclusion. The words attributed to Judson on her deathbed by the Burmese Christians were highly affecting in their simplicity, and these became her accepted 'last words', being repeated as such in retellings of her biography through the century: 'The teacher is long in coming, and the new Missionaries are long in coming: I must die alone and leave my little one; but as it is the will of God, I acquiesce in his will'.[28]

Interestingly, Knowles goes on to add depictions of other, more conventional good Christian deaths, with which Judson can be linked and which can provide a more satisfying sense of closure for readers. Notably, these deaths are those of children, which suggests that Knowles, like Woods, is attempting to associate the female missionary martyr with the angelic passivity familiar from child obituary literature. After Mr Judson's letters, he immediately adds a poem by Sarah Boardman (one of the new missionaries who arrived after Ann Judson's death, and who became the second Mrs Judson) about the death of the Judsons' daughter 'little Maria', who lived for six months after her mother's death and is portrayed as 'innocent', 'serene', 'mild' and 'fragile'.[29] And in a final chapter that narrates the continuation of the mission, Knowles includes a letter from the missionary wife Mrs Wade, which describes the death of a child convert:

> Your last kind letter found me [...] watching the corpse of one of our dear scholars, who had, after a very painful illness, just passed into her eternal state. But her placid, smiling countenance, reproved my sadness and chided my tears, and I seemed to realise that angels were indeed hovering round her little bed [...] she *truly* sleeps in Jesus.[30]

The holiness of this death can be added, or superimposed by the reader, onto the previous experience of reading about Ann Judson's death, in the same way as the infant Maria is figured as being incorporated with her mother's body in the grave: 'softly pillowed on her breast'.[31]

As a 'departed servant of the Redeemer', presented, mediated and controlled by her biographer, Ann Judson, like Harriet Newell, could serve the goals of the mission, fostering 'pious feelings' and 'stronger desires for the universal triumph of the Gospel' in the hearts of readers (p. vi). But as we shall see, Knowles's biography also allowed Ann Judson to emerge in her own words, which served the mission – and women missionaries – in other ways.

Radical Autobiography and the Missionary Heroine

In many ways, a potentially radical female subject emerged from both the Newell and Judson memoirs simply as a result of the autobiographical form: as in other spiritual biographies, the women subjects spoke for themselves through the publication of their private writings. How they reconciled their missionary roles with religious ideas of femininity, though, led to some interesting adaptations of Christian discourse and of female spiritual biography. The aspects of the missionary role that required most reconciling with existing ideas of Christian womanhood seemed to be missionary marriage, the public role of women missionaries and women's missionary action.

Missionary Marriage

The circumstances of their marriages, arranged to facilitate the mission, preoccupied both Newell and Judson and, indeed, were potentially difficult to reconcile with society's understanding of femininity. Marriage was the cornerstone of domesticity – its necessary precondition – however, as Woods noted in his funeral sermon, missionary marriage required women to sacrifice the domestic sphere. Moreover, the connection of a woman's marriage first and foremost with a missionary *career* could strangely sever it from growing societal expectations of romantic love within marriage.[32] Even evangelicals believed that sentiments of love and attachment should be central to marriage, and Hannah More's popular novel *Coelebs in Search of a Wife* made such an evangelical marriage appear easy and natural. However, in the same way they wished to avoid expressions of excessive enthusiasm, evangelicals also advocated against marriages based on purely romantic impulse.[33] The private writings of Harriet Newell and Ann Judson make plain the dilemma: marrying without love could be seen as immoral or unfeminine, but romantic love could sway her from her duty to love God above all others and follow his path for her.

Although he does not acknowledge or explain these dilemmas, Woods includes a large amount of Newell's writing about her experience of receiving the dual proposal from Samuel Newell to become his wife and fellow missionary. Harriet took a number of months to make her decision, and her letters and journal entries on this subject in the memoir cover almost forty pages. She is emotionally disturbed by his proposal, which she refers to as 'long dreaded' and causing 'doubt, anxiety and distress'.[34] Her most elevated emotions are for the missionary career: she desires to 'follow God' to 'where millions of my fellow sinners are perishing for lack of vision'.[35] Though she does admit to feelings for her suitor, she does so with great ambivalence, writing to a friend that she is 'in great danger of being activated by a strong attachment'.[36] Instead of being a cause for celebration, this attachment is identified as a 'danger', as human affection should not be trusted to motivate her choice of a missionary life. Moreover, love for her suitor threatens to displace God in her affections, as she expresses with frustration in the next line of the letter: 'Oh, could I but give the ever-blessed God the first place in my affections, I should not be in danger of being misled by earthly objects'. Although these struggles were eventually replaced with a relatively consistent faith in her missionary destiny, and her letters suggest that she found happiness in marriage, the strength of emotion with which these worries are expressed over such a length of time shows how difficult the idea of marriage could be for religiously inspired women.

Unlike Woods, Knowles openly acknowledges and explains the female missionary dilemma in his biography. Judson's writings were likely as disordered as Harriet Newell's, but, as he did with her religious doubts, Knowles summarises for the reader:

> She was thus placed in a situation of peculiar difficulty and delicacy [...] in this case her embarrassment was increased, by the conflict which might arise between affection and duty [...] she might have some painful suspicions lest her affections might bias her decision to become a missionary; while female delicacy and honour would forbid her to bestow her hand, merely as a preliminary and necessary arrangement.[37]

While Knowles is hypothesising about Judson's experience, the considerations he posits for a young woman marrying a missionary certainly echo Newell's account. He rationally and honestly describes the dilemma as an unavoidable clash of society's and religion's expectations of women in marriage, leading to a risk that society will misread missionary women and see them as unfeminine. Knowles admits that the dilemma arises because missionary marriage is primarily connected with the cause, rather than affection; Adoniram Judson's offer of marriage includes 'of course, a proposition for her to accompany him in his missionary enterprise' (p. 35). Even more than this, Knowles delicately acknowledges the importance of love in marriage for women when he describes the marriage proposal as a point 'of the utmost consequence to her individual happiness' (p. 36) and breaks into this rational discussion with the exclamation that 'it was impossible to divest herself of her personal feelings!' (p. 36). Such feelings in Judson are interpreted as part of what Knowles terms her female 'honour' – a term that elevates her femininity to the point of nobility.

Significantly, Knowles acknowledges of the importance of love within evangelical marriages, along with an admission that missionaries might wrongly sacrifice love in favour of utility: men for a necessary 'helpmeet', and women for opportunity in the mission field. Both Woods and Knowles depict their female missionaries as emotionally disturbed by the idea of sacrificing love in marriage, possibly because the alternative – that women might see missionary marriage as merely the opportunity for a career – radically threatened the female missionary's femininity. However, the fact that the dilemma was even expressed and discussed in these biographies was in itself radical.

The Public Role of the Female Missionary

As readers of spiritual biography themselves, Newell and Judson understood the potentially public nature of their writings and used their personal writings to communicate their faith to friends and family. Both produced self-conscious accounts of their conversions which presented their spiritual journeys along the same lines as those that were published in religious periodicals to help others struggling with spiritual crisis. Indeed, in her account, Judson refers to receiving religious magazines containing conversion narratives from her chapel leader in response to her troubled state – she writes that she 'read the conviction and conversion of some, who, I perceived, had once felt as I now felt'.[38] The accounts of Judson and Newell were therefore written in such a way that they were perfect for publication and, in addition to being included in her biography, Ann Judson's account was published by both the Baptist Society in America and the RTS in Britain. Just as their religious subjectivities had been formed by previous women's religious writings, Newell and Judson went on to construct subsequent women's experiences of religion. As such, and in expressing their particularly female experience of faith, their writings can be seen as an early form of female theology[39] – one to which missionary activity is integral.

Throughout their biographies, Judson's and Newell's words reveal women's agency in transmitting religion through friendship and writing to be a radically significant force alongside the male authority of the church. In her account, as Judson instructs her readers about the importance of emotion in the conversion experience, she tells of how she was aided in her spiritual development by her aunt. When her considerations of her sin caused her anxiety and distress, and to repeatedly weep uncontrollably, her aunt instructed her to 'cherish' these feelings, which lead to conversion.[40] Judson also demonstrates her own role in transmitting religious theories, as she quotes a letter she wrote to a friend, in which she suggests that the increasing of extreme emotions is a sign of the growth in an individual of grace. Grace leads Christians to very definite standpoints, it causes them to 'hunger, thirst and strive' for holiness and to 'loathe, abhor and mourn' sin; and the growth of feelings leads to their dedication to their duty to convert others because 'they *feel* more for the worth of souls. As they are convinced daily of the dreadful nature of sin, so they will feel more anxious to save sinners from the consequences of it'.[41] Judson and Newell wrote many similar letters to friends. Knowles reports that those of Judson to unconverted friends 'breathe an earnest desire for their welfare, and a faithfulness in beseeching them to repent of their sins, and believe in the Redeemer' (p. 19). They understood that they had a religious duty to actively convert friends and family members, and the form in which they could achieve this, prior to taking on a formal missionary role, was the written form of the letter and narrative.

When they became the first missionary wives of the American missionary movement, both women would have been aware of the increased significance of their letters and private writings. Many missionary women, often on the voyage out to their postings, carried on correspondence with family members in which they entreated them to look to their souls, using the mortal danger of their own situation as an example to excite them into piety before it was too late.[42] Newell and Judson did this too, but also understood the future public value of their writings for the promotion of the mission and women's place in it. As Harriet Newell lay dying in Mauritius, she dictated her final words for her loved ones to her husband:

> She could say only a few words; but feared she should not have another opportunity [...] Tell them [...] from the lips of their dying sister, that there is nothing but religion worth living for [...] Tell them not to delay repenting [...] Tell them [...] that I have never regretted leaving my native land for the cause of Christ.[43]

In addition to using the authority given her final words by her impending death to attempt the conversion of her family, she is aware also of the need to communicate her belief in the importance of the mission.

Judson went further than simply writing to family, once she had become a missionary wife, she took on the role of promoting the mission and became, to a large extent, its public face. Due to ill health, she was the first of the missionaries to take furlough and, while she recovered in Britain and America, she addressed the wider public at meetings and wrote her *Account of the Burma Mission* – which she made sure would be disseminated in Britain by the London-based missionary supporter, Joseph Butterworth. Knowles justifies this public activity by Judson as useful to the cause:

> Christians [...] may serve the cause of the Redeemer, by circulating authentic accounts of the deplorable situation of the heathen nations, and statements of the nature, designs, and progress of the benevolent efforts which Christians are now making for the conversion of the world.
>
> (p. v)

Significantly, through justifying Judson's writings, Knowles sets a precedent for other Christian women writers, holding out the possibility of employment in the field of literature as part of the wider missionary cause.

Furthermore, when Knowles tries to follow Woods's practice of giving the history of the mission alongside his missionary subject, rather than overtaking Judson, the mission history becomes intertwined with her life story, as her life's work: 'It was thought desirable, to embody with a memoir of Mrs Judson, a connected narrative of the rise and progress of the Burma Mission. Her life is indeed, a history of that mission' (p. iv). As his biography proceeds, Knowles becomes increasingly dependent on Judson's writings to tell the eventful story of the mission. Even the progress the mission has made after her death is associated with her and can only be told to such a wide audience as part of the story of this famous female missionary leader, which makes it a rather unusual and significant female missionary 'autobiography'.

Female Missionary Heroism

Indeed, while Woods depicted his female missionary as a martyred feminine saint, requiring little reconciliation with established notions of femininity, Knowles was far more willing to allow his exceptional female missionary to stake her claim to a place in the tradition of heroic (male) missionary life writing.

Theoretically, it should not have been necessary for religious biographies to have been particularly gendered. Though Woods in his biography of Harriet Newell had gone some way to inscribing passive self-sacrifice to God's will as a specifically feminine missionary piety, there was a tradition of ascribing this same passivity to male religious martyrs – at least once the possibility for activism had diminished.[44] For example, David Brainerd's resignation on his deathbed was stressed in Wesley's eighteenth-century memoir of the missionary – he 'seemed to continue unmoved, in the same calm frame that he had before manifested; as having resigned all to God'.[45] And Sargent's 1819 memoir of Henry Martyn expounds him as exemplary of those 'whose excellence consists in a renunciation of themselves'.[46] One of the most important evangelical texts, read both in America and England, was William Wilberforce's *A Practical View*, which identified 'passivity and obedience' as the most necessary Christian virtues for both men and women.[47] Certainly, Harriet Newell and Ann Judson referred to being inspired by male role models such as Brainerd, Henry Kirke White and William Law. And women as much as men were enjoined to display active piety in the form of works in the world, which could be interpreted as including missionary work.[48]

However, in the early nineteenth century, writers were beginning to incorporate the passive deaths of male missionaries into the culture of chivalric heroism. Because there was a danger that these deaths could be seen as unnecessary sacrifices by a public not yet fully convinced of the utility of overseas missions, biographers worked hard to establish their religious martyrs within developing ideas of chivalric masculinity.[49] As Mary Ellis Gibson notes, when Macaulay wrote his hagiographic epitaph of Henry Martyn, he engaged tropes of spiritual quest and violent conquest.[50] Similarly, Sargent's biography painted Martyn as a resolute martyr, compounding self-sacrifice with active heroism in his description of missionary work as 'demanding the most painful sacrifices and the most arduous exertions'.[51] As Catherine Hall notes, the male missionary experience in the nineteenth century was made up of contradictions, piously aware that their strength came only from God, yet also believing it was their own manly agency in the mission field that would save the world.[52]

In writing his history of Ann Judson, Knowles was also keen to rehabilitate missionary self-sacrifice, meaning that his female missionary became included in this heroic, masculine mythology. In his memoir, the missionary wives are often spoken of in the same breath as their husbands; he writes that it was the resolution of both Mr and Mrs Judson to go out to India: 'they yielded themselves as willing sacrifices'.[53] When he describes the embarkation of his band of missionaries, he explicitly includes the wives and then proceeds to use the term 'missionaries' and 'men' in an inclusive way, in terms of 'mankind'. His overriding concern is to make an argument that heroic, gentlemanly characteristics should be celebrated in missionaries as they are in other fields of life:

> Why should such disinterested benevolence and heroic firmness fail to obtain the applause of men who are ready to admire and praise these qualities, when exerted on other occasions and for other objects? Why should not the voice of eloquence and the lyre of the poet, which delight to commemorate the self-denial, the patriotism, and noble daring of the wise and good, be mute, when the missionary departs on his errand of mercy?
>
> (p. 45)

Here, self-denial is listed alongside masculine tropes of patriotism and daring – again, notwithstanding the gender of the missionary. Indeed, it is Ann Judson who is the missionary subject of this paragraph; the preceding sentence reads, 'she knew well what she must surrender, and the objects which called for the sacrifice' (p. 45). It is *her* 'heroic firmness' and 'intrepid courage' (p. 45) that Knowles demands be recognised. Rather than passively accepting death, Knowles's female missionary faces her certain death in the mission field with masculine heroism.

Ann Judson's heroic action is most clearly displayed by herself, in her own account of her wartime experiences.[54] This account was written as a letter to her brother in-law, which, far from controlling, Knowles included in his biography, in full, without editorial interruption. For Knowles, this narrative was important as it elevated the suffering of the missionaries to a prominent position in world affairs and ensured the book's popular success. For evangelicals who were discouraged from reading fiction, this narrative could effectually fill the gap; as Knowles notes, 'it will be read with strange and painful interest. Fiction itself has seldom invented a tale more replete with terror' (p. 227).

Ann Judson's awareness of the value of her own narrative to the mission is obvious from how imperative she felt it was to write it. She casts her writing of the account as almost as heroic as her wartime experiences. Not only is she writing for a public – her friends and the mission's supporters – but in writing she is traumatically reliving the horrors she survived:

> I have frequently been induced to throw it aside altogether, but feeling assured that you and my other friends are expecting something of this kind, I am induced to send it with all its imperfections. This letter, dreadful as are the scenes herein described, gives you but a faint idea of the awful reality. The anguish, the agony of mind [...] impossible to delineate on paper, can be known by those only who have been in similar situations. Pray for us, my dear brother and sister, that these heavy afflictions may not be in vain, but may be blessed to our spiritual good, and the advancement of Christ's church among the heathen.[55]

The psychological and physical suffering – so extreme as to be uncommunicable – were, of course, caused by British imperial violence. However, Judson reframes her suffering within a narrative of heathenism: the drama of an imperial war is harnessed to the cause of the spiritual war being waged by the missionaries to further excite readers' feelings about the mission.

Judson's account presents numerous examples of her agency on behalf of her husband and the mission – including, on occasion, when he did not authorise it. When Adoniram Judson and the other prisoners were taken to the distant death prison of Oung-pen-la Ann Judson followed, even when it meant a five-mile trek across hard terrain with her family and possessions in tow. When she finally arrived and found her husband, she recalls that he, dismayed, said 'Why have you come? I hoped you would not follow, for you cannot live here', suggesting that even this pioneering missionary who seemed to be convinced of the value of missionary wives (after Ann Judson's death he remarried twice) believed that this was not fit behaviour for a woman at this time.[56] Knowles does not excise this anecdote from the record, nor the descriptions of Ann Judson's continuing resourcefulness and resolve in providing shelter for herself and her children and even inoculating the nearby village against smallpox.

Significantly, Knowles does not end his biography with the death of Ann Judson. Instead, he prints her *Address to Females in America Relative the Situation of Females in the East*. This document, the written version of her rallying cry to her countrywomen, can be read as an example of female preaching, with dramatic language and formal rhetorical devices: 'But will our feelings of pity and compassion [...] allow us to turn away – to dismiss the subject altogether without making an effort to rescue, to save? No! I think I hear your united voices echo the reply'.[57] Hardly passive, this publication reads as a call to arms. It provides a striking example of piety clothed in active, almost militaristic language: women are 'united' like an army and called to action – to 'rescue'. The rephrasing of this action to 'save' re-situates her call to arms in the context of the religious war: evangelical religion battling with the 'heathen' world. In this context, piety is expressed powerfully, existing side by side with active authority in woman.

In using these rousing and lively words of Judson's to close his biography instead of an obituary, Knowles adds to the ways available to depict women in biography. Moving away from the passive subject of spiritual biography, consigned to eulogy by her death, his female missionary remains in the imagination as an active subject, doing her heroic duty for the mission: 'although she who here uttered her thoughts and her benevolent desires, is gone to the world of spirits, yet, being dead, she still speaks'.[58]

Conclusion

The publishing of Ann Judson's (auto)biography was succeeded immediately by the reprinting of the earlier memoir of Harriet Newell. In a way, this ensured that the heroic female missionary Ann Judson would always be in tension with Woods's depiction of Harriet Newell as a childlike martyr. On the other hand, the publication of Ann Judson's *Memoir* allowed the public to read of Harriet Newell's life through another lens, through which the radical potential of her missionary life and writings could emerge. Throughout the century, the lives of America's first female missionaries would be told and retold, presented apart and together, labelled interchangeably as martyrs, saints or heroines. The characterisation of the female missionary was unstable, full of contradictions, as biographers struggled to control their subjects, whose voices, actions and deaths challenged notions of Christian femininity.

Notes

1. Clare Midgley noted the popularity of Judson's biography in 'Can Women be Missionaries? Envisioning Female Agency in the early Nineteenth-Century British Empire', *Journal of British Studies*, 45 (2006), 335–58 (pp. 342–8); Linda Peterson also pointed to the importance of Judson's biography for Victorian women's life writing, 'Women Writers and Self-Writing', in *Women and Literature in Britain 1800–1900*, ed. by Joanne Shattock (Cambridge: Cambridge University Press, 2001), pp. 209–30 (pp. 222–4); and Alison Booth also considered the case of Ann Judson in her study, *How to Make it as a Woman: Collective Biographical History from Victoria to the Present* (Chicago, IL: University of Chicago Press, 2004).
2. After a brief hiatus during the 1870s and 1880s, Judson's story was revived by Emma Raymond Pitman in her 1889 collective biography *Lady Missionaries in Foreign Lands*. This version of the story was republished a number of times between 1932 and 1950.
3. Scholars have acknowledged the importance of earlier religious writings for the genre as it emerged during the evangelical revival but tend to agree that the developments of the seventeenth and eighteenth centuries created the conditions for a specific kind of nineteenth-century evangelical life writing. See D. Bruce Hindmarsh, *The Evangelical Conversion Narrative: Spiritual Autobiography in Early Modern England* (Oxford: Oxford University Press, 2005), pp. 12–32, 321–2; and Peterson, 'Women Writers', in *Women and Literature*, ed. by Shattock, p. 222.
4. Hindmarsh, pp. 322–3; Amy Culley, *British Women's Life Writing, 1760–1840: Friendship, Community and Collaboration* (Basingstoke: Palgrave Macmillan, 2014), pp. 28–9; Christine Krueger, *The Reader's Repentance: Women Preachers, Women Writers, and Nineteenth-Century Social Discourse* (Chicago, IL: University of Chicago Press, 1992), pp. 43–6.
5. Culley, pp. 8–9. As Culley notes, the more popular 1817 biography of Fletcher downplayed her preaching, pp. 28–9.
6. Peterson, 'Women Writers', in *Women and Literature*, ed. by Shattock, pp. 223–4; Candy Gunther Brown, *The Word in the World: Evangelical Writing, Publishing and Reading in America 1789–1880* (Chapel Hill, NC: University of North Carolina Press, 2004); Mary Kupiec Cayton, 'Harriet Newell's Story: Women, the Evangelical Press and the Foreign Mission Movement', in *An Extensive Republic: Print, Culture and Society in the New Nation 1790–1840*, ed. by Robert A Gross and Mary Kelley (Chapel Hill, NC: University of North Carolina Press, 2012), pp. 408–16.
7. Hindmarsh, pp. 321–2.
8. Elisabeth Jay, *Religion of the Heart: Anglican Evangelicalism and the Nineteenth-Century Novel* (Oxford: Clarendon, 1979), pp. 154–60; Michael Wheeler, *Death and the Future Life in Victorian Literature and Theology* (Cambridge: Cambridge University Press, 1990), pp. 27–32.
9. Krueger, p. 43.
10. Midgley, pp. 341–5; Brown, pp. 98–9.
11. James Davis Knowles, *Memoir of Mrs. Ann H. Judson*, 3rd edn (London: Wightman and Co., 1830), p. 36 [emphasis in original].
12. On the early calls for women to join missions as missionary wives, see Ulrike Sill, *Encounters in Quest of Christian Womanhood: The Basel Mission in Pre- and Early Colonial Ghana*, Studies in Christian Mission (Leiden: Brill, 2010).

13 Anna Johnston has noted how, as the century progressed, female missionaries' stories were edited to fit a particular image of the missionary wife and helpmeet, *Missionary Writing and Empire, 1800–1860* (Cambridge: Cambridge University Press, 2003), pp. 33–4.
14 Cayton suggests that the familiar nature of Newell's biography was the reason for its popularity, 'Harriet Newell's Story', in *An Extensive Republic*, ed. by Gross and Kelley, pp. 413–4.
15 Laura M. Stevens discusses how engaging with emotional accounts of missionaries encouraged emulation in *The Poor Indians: British Missionaries, Native Americans, and Colonial Sensibility* (Philadelphia, PA: University of Pennsylvania Press, 2004), pp. 140–2. Also see Introduction for further discussion of the workings of emotions in religious writing and experience.
16 Harriet Newell, Diary [27 August, 1809], in *Memoirs of Mrs Harriet Newell*, ed. by Leonard Woods, 2nd edition (London: Booth and Co, 1816), pp. 7–8; Jay notes that British evangelicals were especially keen to downplay the necessity of violently emotional conversion at this time, p. 60.
17 Leonard Woods, *Memoirs of Mrs Harriet Newell*, pp. xi–xii. Further references to this work are given following quotations in the text.
18 Claudia Nelson notes how in early nineteenth-century fiction child and female death were equated and treated as a natural end to the passive life of the 'Angel in the House', *Boys will be Girls: The Feminine Ethic and British Children's Fiction 1857–1917* (New Brunswick, NJ: Rutgers University Press, 1991), pp. 6–23.
19 Midgley draws attention to this aspect of control male compilers had over their subjects in posthumous female missionary biographies, p. 341.
20 Harriet Newell, Letter, May 1811, in Woods, pp. 76–7.
21 Samuel Newell, Letter 10 December 1812, pp. 175–86 (pp. 179–81).
22 Harriet Newell, Diary, 17 April 1811, in Woods, p. 73.
23 Culley, pp. 28–9.
24 Knowles, p. 9. Further references to this work are given following quotations in the text. As Krueger has noted, this was a method of justification used by the Methodist women preachers earlier in the century, pp. 7–9, 25–6.
25 Antoinette Burton argues that late nineteenth-century feminists used a similar tactic to justify their engagement in imperial politics, in *Burdens of History: British Feminists, Indian Women and Imperial Culture 1865–1915* (London: University of Carolina Press, 1994), p. 7; however, as Clare Midgley has revealed, this discourse began far earlier, when women first engaged with the mission movement, 'From Supporting Missions to Petitioning Parliament: British Women and the Evangelical Campaign against *Sati* in India, 1813–30', in *Women in British Politics, 1760–1860: The Power of the Petticoat*, ed. by Kathryn Gleadle and Sarah Richardson (Basingstoke: Macmillan, 2000), pp. 74–92 (pp. 76–7).
26 Adoniram Judson, Letter, 7 December 1826, in Knowles, pp. 266–70 (p. 269).
27 Adoniram Judson, Letter, 4 February 1827, in Knowles, pp. 270–2 (p. 271).
28 Ibid., p. 271. Evangelical religion's privileging of simple piety has been noted by scholars, see Jay, p. 40; and Krueger, pp. 60–3.
29 Sarah Hall Judson (nee Boardman), Poem, in Knowles, pp. 275–6.
30 Mrs Wade, Letter, 28 June 1828, in Knowles, p. 303. [emphasis in original]
31 Sarah Judson, Poem, in Knowles, p. 276.

42 *Prologue*

32 Lawrence Stone argues that the sanctification of marriage through the seventeenth and eighteenth centuries led to love being strongly expected within marriage, especially of a wife for her husband, *The Family, Sex and Marriage in England 1500–1800* (London: Weidenfeld and Nicolson, 1977), pp. 136–8, 202–36. (See Introduction for more discussion of critical understandings of marriage in the nineteenth century.)
33 Jay, p. 134.
34 Newell, Diary, 17 April 1811, in Woods, p. 72.
35 Newell, Letter, May 1811, in Woods, pp. 76–7.
36 Newell, Letter, 12 June 1811, in Woods, p. 79.
37 Knowles, pp. 35–6. Further references are given following quotations in the text.
38 Judson, Account, in Knowles, pp. 12–9 (p. 16).
39 As Julie Melnyk has argued, though the field of theology was a masculine one in the nineteenth century, there was an overlap between religious and theological writing, and often expressed their theological ideas in letters and the periodical press, 'Introduction', in *Women's Theology in Nineteenth-Century Britain: Transfiguring the Faith of their Fathers*, ed. by Julie Melnyk (London: Garland, 1998), pp. xii–xviii (pp. xi–xii).
40 Judson, Account, in Knowles, p. 16.
41 Judson, Letter, 20 September 1807, in Knowles, pp. 26–7 (p. 27). [my emphasis]
42 For example, Abigail Beighton wrote continuously in this way to her sister and brother-in-law from the point of her embarkation from Gravesend in 1818 until her death in Penang in 1821, 'Correspondence of Thomas and Abigail Beighton', London, SOAS, MS 380689.
43 Samuel Newell, Letter, 10 December 1812, in Woods, pp. 175–86 (p. 182).
44 Linda Wilson, *Constrained By Zeal: Female Spirituality Amongst Nonconformists, 1825–75* (Carlisle: Paternoster, 2000), p. 156.
45 John Wesley, *An Extract of the Life of the Late David Brainerd Missionary to the Indians* (Penryn: Cock, 1815), p. 275.
46 Wesley, p. 279; John Sargent, *Memoir of the Rev. Henry Martyn*, 4th edn (London: J. Hatchard and Son, 1820), p. 2.
47 Catherine Hall, *White, Male and Middle Class: Explorations in Feminism and History* (Cambridge: Polity, 1992), p. 77; Elisabeth Jay, *Faith and Doubt in Victorian Britain* (London: Macmillan, 1986), p. 4. Scholars of masculinity have also noted the androgynous implications of subsuming manliness or womanliness in the Christian virtues. See Nelson, *Boys Will be Girls*, pp. 2–10; and John Tosh, *Manliness and Masculinities in Nineteenth Century Britain* (Harlow: Pearson, 2005), pp. 32–4, 87–92.
48 W. D. Bebbington, *Evangelicalism in Modern Britain: A History from the 1730s to the 1980s* (London: Unwin Hyman, 1989), pp. 10–2; Wilson, pp. 55–8.
49 Rhonda Semple explores in detail the ways in which missionary men anxiously laid claim to Victorian masculinity, 'Missionary Manhood: Professionalism, Belief and Masculinity in the Nineteenth-Century British Imperial Field', *Journal of Imperial and Commonwealth History*, 36 (2008), 397–415 (p. 407); Norman Vance also points to how religious male authors such as Kingsley and Hughes were attempting the same recuperation of the Christian hero, *The Sinews of the Spirit: The Ideal of Christian Manliness in Victorian*

Literature and Religious Thought (Cambridge: Cambridge University Press, 1985), pp. 5–7.
50 Mary Ellis Gibson, 'Henry Martyn and England's Christian Empire: Rereading *Jane Eyre* through Missionary Biography', *Victorian Literature and Culture*, 27 (1999), 419–42 (p. 419).
51 Sargent, p. 31.
52 Hall, pp. 224–5.
53 Knowles, p. 41. Further references are given in the text.
54 Peterson drew attention to the novelty of this presentation of the female subject as active in political and even military contexts, 'Women Writers', in *Women and Literature*, ed. by Shattock, pp. 209–30.
55 Ann Judson, Narrative, Letter 26 May 1826, in Knowles, pp. 227–61 (p. 261).
56 Ibid., p. 246.
57 Ann Judson, 'Address to Females in America Relative to the Situation of Females in the East', in Knowles, pp. 321–4 (pp. 321–2).
58 Knowles, p. 321.

Part I
1830–1870

1 Tales of Female Missionary Sacrifice
Tracts, Collective Biographies and Newsletters

Introduction

When Knowles's biography of the American missionary Ann Hasseltine Judson was published in 1829, it was by no means certain that a missionary heroine would be embraced by the British public. For most people in Britain, a woman's duty lay at home with her family – not in the mission field. The ideological belief in the essentially domestic nature of women (linked to the rise of the middle classes and the economic separation of the commercial from the domestic sphere) grew gradually more pervasive and strongly held between the 1830s and 1860s.[1] When, in the 1830s, the missionaries Charles Gutzlaff and Robert Morrison pointed out the necessity for women missionaries, especially in India, for reaching female populations, there was resistance from both men and women in Britain, and the leaders of the main mission movements were especially conservative in their ideas about women's role.[2] That the missionary population would develop in such a way that by the end of the century men would be outnumbered by women would have been, for many at this time, unthinkable. Nonetheless, from the 1830s onwards, following Knowles's immensely successful biography of Ann Judson, the figure of the female missionary became increasingly significant to British culture and ideas about femininity.

This chapter will show how women's writing in particular worked to form the female missionary figure in such a way that she was compatible with domestic ideology while still allowing women the authority to engage in missionary activities. Alison Twells and Kathryn Gleadle have shown that, in the early nineteenth century, and especially among Dissenting families, missionary activity was not seen as incompatible with domesticity.[3] I argue that religious literature, such as that examined in this chapter, contributed to the acceptability of missionary domesticity for women at the same time as gradually limiting the concept's original expansiveness. The texts examined in this chapter demonstrate how women writers, with the sponsorship of male religious leaders, increasingly entered the literary marketplace with their missionary life writing.

DOI: 10.4324/9781003332961-4

As the domestic evangelical movement discouraged the reading of fiction, the market was hungry for non-fictional, religious texts with interesting narratives.[4] While religious young women continued to read the widely available early nineteenth-century spiritual biographies, including Knowles's and Woods's original biographies of Ann Judson and Harriet Newell, they would increasingly have encountered the stories of these and other female missionaries within religious tracts and the new form of the collective missionary biography. These genres transformed the female missionary subject so that she became essentialised, idealised and elided with the figure of the domestic angel – thus creating an influential form of missionary femininity for women to emulate.[5]

In many ways, the self-sacrificial, domestic aspects of the ideal female missionary figure were useful to women missionaries and writers in their self-representation and promotion of woman's role in the cause. Even as single, proto-professional women missionaries began to take on a central role in the Wesleyan Methodist Mission Society (WMMS) in the early 1860s, the writings of Wesleyan missionary wives, published by the WMMS Ladies' Committee in their *Occasional Papers*, demonstrate a rhetorical utilisation of the feminine traits of the ideal female missionary. However, breaks in the ideal female missionary discourse, and the displacement of sacrifice in women missionaries' letters suggest that the depiction of the ideal female missionary was not as unified and stable as some conservative evangelicals might have wished.

I start this chapter by tracing what happened to the story of Ann Judson after Knowles's biography was published. Immediately, the biography inspired women to both write about and become missionaries, and firmly established the genre of female missionary biography in Britain. At the same time, Christian societies and supporters of mission seized upon Judson's story in particular, retelling and repackaging it in religious tracts and collective biographies. The editors of these adaptations (who were most often women) gradually changed the depiction of Judson, and the female missionary more generally, through their adaptive strategies of selection, abridgement and collation, resulting, in the end, in a far more domesticated and feminine missionary than had appeared in Knowles's original biography.

The final part of this chapter explores the writing of living women missionaries by analysing the first issues of the Wesleyan Methodist Missionary Society's Women's Committee newsletter, *Occasional Papers*. Alongside this case study, I read the collective biography of British women missionaries published in 1841 by Jemima Thompson, an enthusiastic mission supporter. These writings by women who identified as active missionaries show the conflict that women experienced in establishing the ideal female missionary figure for the public while at the same time attempting to escape the implications of this figure for their own lives.

Knowles's Memoir of Ann Judson: Inspiring and Reanimating Missionary Zeal

As we saw in the prologue, Knowles had, in his biography, justified Ann Judson's missionary writing by suggesting that Christians 'serv[ed] the cause of the Redeemer, by circulating authentic accounts' of both the conditions in 'heathen nations' and of the 'progesss' of Christian missions;[6] and, in so doing, presented such writing as a religious duty for any and all Christians, including women. British writers were not slow to take advantage of Knowles's encouragement, producing many such accounts, in the form of female missionary life writing. Major British female missionary biographies appeared, including the *Memoirs of Mrs Mary Ellis* (1835), the *Memoir of Mrs Stallybrass* (1836), the *Memoirs of Hannah Kilham* (1837) and the *Memoir of Mrs Margaret Wilson* (1840). Jemima Thompson's *Memoirs of British Female Missionaries* mentions at least six full biographies that, at the time of writing, were in some form of print and uses these as source material for her retellings of the lives of sixteen women who lived and died as missionaries between 1817 and 1839. And this collection is only one example of what Clare Midgley and Alison Booth have found to be a popular form of biography edited by women writers throughout the century, in which female missionaries often featured.[7]

Male and female missionaries explicitly praised female missionary biography for its role in supporting the mission. Most obvious was its impact in inspiring women to become missionaries. The Revd Joseph Fletcher writes in his introduction to the 1836 *Memoir of Mrs Stallybrass*: 'What cheerful consecrations of youth and talent, in all the exuberances of health and vigour, have been made [...] in consequence of the perusal of the lives of Harriet Newell and Mrs Judson'.[8]

More generally, though, the missionary wife Margaret Wilson of the Bombay mission believed that female missionary biography was valuable because it unveiled the achievements of women missionaries to the public. She made this argument in a review of Knowles's memoir of Ann Judson, which she wrote and published in the *Oriental Christian Spectator* (a periodical produced by her husband and the other men of the Bombay mission):

> It introduces us to individuals, formed by nature for a subordinate sphere of action [...] it draws aside the veil which modest and retiring virtue delights to throw over deeds of charity or of heroism, which she has herself achieved.[9]

While Wilson is clear that female missionaries are subordinate by nature, she draws attention to what she and others are achieving, using the strong term 'heroism'. There is a criticism here that missionary women are wrong to 'delight' in hiding their activities, as published virtues would be more helpful than female modesty in advancing Christianity. And while Wilson herself wrote this review anonymously, as a concession to her family, after she died, her husband unveiled her achievements by including extracts of the review and the account of her authorship in his biography.

What is perhaps most striking in Wilson's review, though, is her description of how Ann Judson's biography in particular affected her and – she imagined – other religious women: 'We rise from it with invigorated confidence, with our zeal animated, and with high admiration of the intrepid fortitude, and patient endurance, which this follower of the Divine Master was enabled to manifest and to sustain'.[10] This enthusiastic testimony from an active missionary woman demonstrates that female missionary biography, especially that which allowed the woman herself to speak and express her struggles, could be a powerful instrument for sustaining agents of the cause.

From Knowles to Clara Balfour: Feminising Ann Judson and the Woman Missionary

Though Knowles's biography of Ann Judson had inspired missionary wives and writers, British supporters of mission between the 1830s and 1860s knew that in order to grow the movement, especially among women (who had proved to be valuable fundraisers and activists in other religious causes, such as the campaign against the slave trade or the practice of sati[11]), the roles of the female missionary and missionary writer would have to be domesticated. The aspects of Knowles's Ann Judson that encouraged British religious women to see themselves as autonomous agents – the ability to make their own determination of God's plan for them and see it through, to express their religious experiences, to lead other women in religious causes, and even to play an active role in diplomatic or military scenarios as a member of a mission station in a hostile, foreign field[12] – risked turning the respectable classes against the idea of female missionaries altogether. As the ideology of separate spheres developed, women were increasingly being presented as ideally passive, domestic creatures. Evangelical doctrine for women, preached in tracts and manuals by women such as Hannah More as well as from the pulpit, emphasised the necessity of the Christian wife and mother in the home as a defence against the corrupting influence of the commercial sphere.[13] This domesticity of the ideal Christian woman would have to be reflected in women's missionary writing.

The increasing domestication of female missionaries can be seen most clearly in the changes that were made to the story of Ann Judson by women writers as they produced their own versions of the tale over three decades. As we saw in the prologue, the evangelical community placed less value on biographies being an authentic representation of the memorialised subject, and more on the usefulness of the story to advancing the cause.[14]

Editors of later versions of Judson's life story, therefore, adapted the story freely, making their own interpretations of Judson's character, often departing drastically from Knowles's characterisation. Moreover, the practice of reproducing other texts tended to reduce the significance of the biographer, turning them into a passive vessel for the transmission of a religiously useful message, which had implications for women writers and activists more generally.[15]

While there are a great number of retellings of Ann Judson's story by British and American editors, I have chosen to focus on those that were most available in Britain between 1830 and 1860. First, in Edinburgh in 1831, Knowles's story of Judson's life appeared, abridged and presented alongside a biography of Mrs Martha Laurens Ramsay, in *American Biography*, edited by Margaret Grierson ('Miss Grierson'), a writer of Sunday school books. In 1832, the RTS included Judson in its *Christian Biography*, as a subject alongside William Cowper, Revd Matthew Henry and Miss Anna Jane Linnard. Also in the 1830s, the RTS extracted Judson's account of her conversion for one of their short tracts. In 1841, the Revd James Gardner included another abridgement of Knowles's biography in his *Memoirs of Christian Females: With an Essay on the Influences of Female Piety*. And in 1843, the anonymous E.M.I. wrote a version of Judson's story specifically for children, 'Mrs Judson and Little Maria', which was published in a collection titled *Missionary Stories: Lessons from Heathen Lands*. In 1850, the American author Daniel C. Eddy's *Heroines of the Missionary Enterprise*, which included the life stories of the second and third as well as the first Mrs Judson, was published in London, edited by the Scottish Revd John Cumming (a second London edition was published in 1859, titled *Ministering Women, or Heroines of Missionary Enterprise*). In 1854, Clara Balfour published her version of Judson's story, *A Sketch of Mrs Ann H Judson*, in a collected edition that also included *A Sketch of Hannah Kilham*. These biographical sketches were also included in Balfour's 1854 *Working Women of the Last Half Century: The Lesson of Their Lives*, which ran to three editions (the last published in 1868). And in 1856, the RTS reprinted its abridgement of Knowles's biography in *Female Biography*, including her alongside three other American women subjects: Harriet Newell, Anna Jane Linnard and Susan Huntington.[16]

An evolution of Ann Judson's story can be inferred simply from the titles of the retellings: from the 1840s, the emphasis is increasingly on Judson as a woman, seen alongside other Christian 'heroines'. The form of the retellings also changed, from long abridgements of Knowles's biography in the 1830s to shorter abridgements and original adaptations in the 1840s and 1850s that included fewer extracts of Judson's own writings – if indeed they included any. However, even from the first retelling in 1831, there is evidence of editors re-interpreting Judson in order to present her and her piety as more specifically feminine and to create the ideal female missionary figure for the nineteenth century.

Knowles's original biography of Ann Judson did not rely on domestic gender ideology to justify her actions. In fact, when it came to listing her qualities as a woman, he was ambivalent:

> The important and sorrowful scenes through which she passed, calling for decision, activity, energy, and fortitude, were less favourable than the sheltered and quiet retirement of domestic life, for the cultivation of the softer and the gentler qualities and their effect may have been perceptible in her character. But a woman placed in her situation and tasked with her duties is not to be judged by any ordinary standard.[17]

Knowles admits Judson's failure to cultivate feminine virtues, but at the same time removes female missionaries from the class of 'ordinary' women, suggesting that they should not be judged on their femininity.

In Margaret Grierson's *American Biography*, however, this description of Ann Judson's character is rewritten to read:

> *None but* the scenes through which she passed could probably have developed sympathies so kind – love so constant – faith so fervent – piety so meek, gentle and submissive – energy so wonderful, so sublime! [...] May her bright example of self-denial and self-devotion animate others to follow in her footsteps.[18]

This manipulation of the original text, effectively reversing Knowles's interpretation of the effect of the situation of the mission field on women, demonstrates how domestic gender ideologies were being imposed upon the character of Judson. The narrator stresses her possession of more attractive, feminine characteristics; the dashes and exclamation marks communicate an almost incoherent enthusiasm; and the listing of positive qualities ends with Judson buried by a piling up of multiple adjectives, which say far more about what missionary supporters wanted to see in female missionaries than about Judson herself.

Grierson also paints an attractive picture, based on very little evidence, of an intimate friendship between Ann Judson and Harriet Newell at Bradford Academy:

> There commenced probably that early friendship, now perfected in heaven, when, in the words of the poet, so beautifully descriptive of the school-days of girlhood, she and Harriet Newell, 'both on one cushion, both at one sampler', inhaled together the principles of heavenly life.[19]

Friendship was seen as an important aspect of women's lives within evangelical culture.[20] As well as prefiguring the intimate friendship that is envisaged as possible in heaven, the female friendship between Judson and Newell is associated with feminine, domestic behaviours such as sitting, embroidering, on a cushion. The alteration of the facts to achieve this image shows Grierson's desire to portray Judson as part of a specifically feminine religious culture.

Grierson also emphasises Judson's identity as a wife and mother, especially when describing her death. While Knowles had not editorialised the domestic feelings of the Judsons, the material within Adoniram Judson's letters that Knowles included allowed Grierson to conclude her biography by painting a portrait of 'affecting domestic incidents': the lonely death of Ann Judson, and the grieving husband at the graves of both his wife and child, 'under the hope tree – Hopia – which stands at the head of their graves'.[21] E.M.I.'s children's tract 'Mrs Judson and Little Maria', as implied by the title, also focuses on Judson as a mother. Although Judson's account in Knowles's biography makes it clear that once she arrived at the prison in Oung Pen La, she could not look after herself or feed her child, let alone nurse her husband – and that Adoniram Judson had to take the child to the village to beg for milk from other mothers – E.M.I. reverses the situation, insisting that it was Ann who, as ideal wife and mother, nursed her family and begged in the village for milk.[22] Her tale, like Grierson's, ends with the mother and baby sleeping 'sweetly together under the Hope-tree' and selects a picture of this scene to illustrate the entire tract.[23] For Knowles, it was important to end his biography by presenting how the mission went on to be successful, and he finally concluded by using Ann Judson's own speech about the importance of mission work. For those who came after, it was more important to leave readers with an emotionally affecting, domestic image of Ann Judson, whose feminine example in death might inspire other women to actions of religious martyrdom.

By 1851, in Clara Balfour's *Sketch*, Ann Judson's femininity has become part of what makes her so particularly suitable and likely to be successful in her missionary work. Balfour's Judson is

> lovely and winning in the extreme – the light that beamed in her intelligent eyes, the smiles that played around her benevolent mouth, were a universal language all could understand. Her progress with the language was more rapid than her husband, and she soon began to speak to the women with whom she came in contact on the subject of religion.[24]

These feminine charms and smiles, partaking of an almost holy 'light', are interpreted as instrumental in 'winning' souls, especially in the female society invoked here. Despite painting the female missionary as a primitive, language-less, feeling-rather-than-thinking creature, Balfour is at pains to prove that Ann Judson was an example of woman as communicator and influencer rather than active evangelist. There is little evidence for her claim that Ann Judson was more advanced than her husband in the Burmese language – in fact, Adoniram Judson went on to translate large portions of the gospel – but Balfour suggests that this does not really matter, as it is through everyday domestic activities and intercourse that Ann Judson is able to introduce, very simply, Christian ideas.[25] Despite the success granted to her, the specifically female method of proselytising described here limits the female missionary to a role of somewhat passive domestic influence.

Balfour's attempts to construct Ann Judson as an appropriately domestic female missionary follow Grierson's in their creative licence. Although Ann and Adoniram Judson were in exotic and at times dangerous surroundings, Balfour goes to great lengths to emphasise the domestic nature of the Burma mission. The missionary couple take on a ready-made mission house 'surrounded by a garden […][with] some pleasant glimpses of the surrounding scenery'.[26] Such detailing of the 'home', especially the inclusion of a garden and 'pleasant' scenery for the reader's imagination, has the effect of domesticating what might otherwise be seen as a threatening, alien environment. In a similar way, before the narrative is inevitably taken over by the realities of Ann Judson's wartime experience, Balfour ensures that she is seen engaging in domestic tasks, 'carrying on a household', and even 'receiving visitors' in the true style of the Victorian wife and matriarch (p. 17).

Correct missionary marriage, in Balfour's retelling of Ann Judson's story, is of crucial importance as the bedrock of Victorian domesticity. For her, women's domesticity is their authorising discourse in the missionary cause as, she says, 'Christianity is eminently domestic in its influences' (p. 4). Women are domestically involved in child-rearing, teaching, sympathising, nursing and otherwise relieving suffering, and Balfour sees these as activities to be carried out in the mission field. Perfectly exemplifying the view that female missionaries were in the empire to disseminate the virtues of imperial domesticity, she argues that the influence of women is achieved through modelling the perfect Victorian family and its values – which she equates with Christianity – for the 'heathen':

> The example of a Christian wife, mother, and mistress of a family, and with her, of a home, where truth and love dwelt, was a visible manifestation of the loveliness of the religion sought to be imparted, a preaching all hearts would respond to, all minds would be impressed by. To render Christianity loveable, it must be shewn [sic] to be lovely. This is the office of the female missionary.
>
> (p. 5)

Female missionaries are seen here to be largely symbolic. They do not engage in rational intercourse with potential converts about Christian belief and scripture; they manifest a diffuse loveliness that mutely impresses the minds and hearts of the local population. The use of 'love', 'loveliness', 'lovable' and 'lovely' in this short paragraph empties the word of all meaning beyond the sentimental, taking the idea of evangelicalism as 'the religion of the heart' to extremes.

Balfour's concern to depict missionary marriage as a means to promulgate domestic values in the field leads her to excise any suggestion of romantic love from the Judsons' relationship; Adoniram's proposal is described in the terms of a business transaction:

> Without any intention of altering his determination as to the future, he made her an offer of his hand. It was quite in accordance with his manly character that he should, in asking her father's consent, set fully before him, as he had often doubtless done before her, the sacrifices which the wife of a missionary must undergo [...] To this appeal Ann Hasseltine had answered, 'I will go', and parental consent was not withheld to what they considered a sacred demand.
> (pp. 10–11)

Balfour's concern is to reconcile the missionary couple with the norms of the Victorian family: Adoniram asks parental permission and is established as appropriately masculine, while parental consent and the sacred demand are portrayed as of equal importance, neither conflicting with the other. There are echoes of Hannah More's evangelical novel *Coelebs in Search of a Wife* in the emphasis on family and the detail of how Adoniram and Ann Judson met through being part of the same society.

Knowles's more complex treatment of the female missionary marriage dilemma – in which women could not morally be motivated to a missionary life solely by romantic love of a man, but also could not marry merely as a means to become a missionary – is rarely seen in the retellings of Judson's story. Even abridgements of his text summarise Ann Judson's considerations in far less detail, acknowledging the anxiety the proposal occasioned, but quickly moving to a satisfactory conclusion. The marriage is described in far cooler language: the couple 'formed an acquaintance', and there was a 'mutual attachment', leading to 'a more intimate and endearing relationship'.[27] When Daniel Eddy, in his collection of American female missionary biography, turns briefly to Ann Judson, he re-interprets her struggle to accept the marriage proposal as simply a conscientious and rational consideration of the proposition to become a missionary: 'She was at times fearful that her disposition for what was in itself romantic and strange, would bias her judgement and lead her to pursue a course which she should regret'.[28] Similarly, Revd James Gardner abridges Knowles's text to depict Judson's struggle as a serious consideration of whether the opportunity was really a call from God, or only her own desire to spend her life among the 'heathen'.[29] It is the idea of becoming a missionary that has become romantically desirable in itself, rather than any idea of marriage.

Equally significant for the development of the female missionary identity, the more revisionist versions of Ann Judson's biography present the concept of her missionary sacrifices less as active martyrdom and more as passive, resigned suffering.[30] Of course, in the early nineteenth century, treatments of male missionary martyrdom often used the language of passive resignation. However, as the century wore on, presentations of missionary martyrdom became more gendered, and, by the mid-century, biographies of Ann Judson and other female missionaries were focusing on the passive missionary death as a more particularly female experience. Grierson's *American Biography* (1831) features a few lines of verse which link Ann Judson's female nature with her suffering: 'In her steps a woman's fear/ On her cheeks a woman's tear'.[31] Rather than faithfully present a missionary woman's character, Grierson is more concerned with how the story of a female missionary's sufferings and sacrifice can create emotional sympathy, stating that 'hardly anyone can read unmoved her eventful story' (p. 13). Judson's intrepidity is interpreted as being God-given, 'the proper fruit of faith – a holy courage, and holy confidence' rather than her own (pp. 124–7). In her preface, Grierson avoids all mention of the missionary's actions, allowing her only a rather vague 'diffusion' of precepts, which, of course, originate in heaven (p. 10). Judson's 'exalted heroism' is based only on her admirable capacity to 'suffer' (p. 282), and her self-sacrifice is the only message this author leaves us with: 'May her bright example of self-denial and self-devotion animate others to follow in her footsteps' (p. 283). While Balfour in 1851 presents Ann Judson's life somewhat less sentimentally, again, it is her ability to suffer which is admired – which elevates her even above angels, who 'cannot suffer' – and the author concludes with a reference to her laudable 'self-sacrifice'.[32]

As the retellings of Ann Judson's life change her character by emphasising her more feminine traits of domesticity and passive self-sacrifice, the form in which they appear also has an impact on the characterisation of the female missionary. Tract and collective biography especially reduced Ann Judson to the generic type of the exemplary Christian woman. When, in the 1830s, the RTS produced a tract about her, they focused only on her early life before she became a missionary's wife, selecting only her conversion account from the biography for re-printing. This account is highly generic, conforming to the pattern of conversion letters that would have been popular in evangelical magazines and other RTS publications. Judson's actions in the mission field are reported at the end of the tract, almost as an afterthought, as if to further prove the authenticity of her conversion: 'Mrs Judson, after a devoted life spent in promoting the gospel, as a missionary's wife in Burmah, and after unusual trials, departed this life, on the 24th Oct, 1826'.[33] The grammar of this sentence reduces the importance of her more particular experiences, using commas to relegate her role as a missionary's wife and the trials she experienced during the Anglo-Burmese war to parenthetical clauses. What is important for the RTS is the generality of her conversion experience and her activity promoting the gospel – these were things all Christian women could emulate. When Judson's conversion account came to be collected in the RTS's first series of tracts, it appeared alongside tracts on domestic deathbed scenes, warnings about preparing for death and advice to Christian parents on how to passively accept the death of infants.

The form of collective biography is especially interesting in how it reduced Judson, and other female missionaries, to a generic type, to be defined by their feminine suffering, passivity and domesticity.[34] While Midgley optimistically sees a kind of female solidarity being formed in collective biographies, Booth admits that the pressure of including a large number of lives leads prosopography to reduce differences between women to a 'single message'.[35] In their titles, both the RTS's *Christian Biography* and Grierson's *American Biography* erode Judson's individuality, making her simply an example of a religion or a nationality. This reduction of Judson's individual life story to simply an example of many Christian memoirs becomes extreme in biographies that collected together numerous missionary women's stories. Daniel Eddy, whose original collection included the lives of thirteen American women missionaries, is explicit that he believes that reducing the particularity of his women's stories is justified for the educative and inspirational value the resulting work will have for the mission cause: 'We deem it no impropriety to take them down, unwind the peculiarity of sect, and weave those honoured names in one sacred wreath, that we may dedicate it to all that love the cause of missions'.[36]

In these biographies, the role of female missionaries has become, through their death as much as their life's actions, to provide emotional symbols to stimulate interest in the cause of missions. Their individual value in terms of educating and proselytising is subordinate to their collective value as martyrs; and the original idea that biography presents authentic women, including their struggles, as examples that women could realistically emulate, has been lost.[37] The brevity required to describe each single life in these collective biographies also means that the words of the subjects themselves are most often entirely omitted. Instead, editors paraphrase until the women's individual actions are reduced to generic, impressionistic hagiography. Take, for example, Eddy's description of Ann Judson's actions among the prisoners in Oung Pen La: 'Like a ministering angel she moved among them, giving drink to the thirsty, food to the hungry, and clothing to the destitute'.[38]

Passive suffering and sacrifice of life become the most obvious characteristics of female missionaries in collective biographies. This is emphasised in collections that include a large number of female missionary memoirs; the evangelical necessity of focusing on the deathbeds, and the fact that a number of missionaries did not live long enough to achieve very much, means that the enduring subject of these books becomes the sacrificial death of English women abroad. The anonymous 'Authoress' of *Memoirs of Female Labourers in the Missionary Cause* (1839) refers to female missionary deaths almost always in the same breath as she mentions their lives or work. When she says that 'their example, their useful lives, and peaceful, happy deaths' will inspire her readers to become missionaries, it is difficult to know whether the life or death is meant to be more appealing. The lines of poetry she includes before her first subject align these two aims even more closely: ''Tis sweet to labour – sweet to die'.[39] Rather than their lack of action in the mission field rendering them unsuitable exemplars, their deaths instead make them perfect symbolic martyrs for the cause. For example, Jemima Thompson, in her 1841 collection, writes of Mrs Coulthart, who died only five months after landing in Jamaica, that

> She lived not in vain:
> 'Long do they live, nor die too soon,
> Who live till life's great work is done.'
> If that be to prepare for death, to be meet for heaven, and to glorify God on earth, then it was answered in the life of Mrs Coulthart.[40]

Mrs Coulthart's death itself is here seen as a female missionary act to glorify God, as it creates the emotional narrative necessary for these biographical collections to further the missionary cause. However, the extreme passivity of these sacrifices – Mrs Burton, for example, is said to barely care for her own mortality, valuing life only 'for the sake of being useful to others' – lessens any heroism their martyrdom could imply.[41]

The form of collective biography, and the paratexts that usually accompany these collections, also worked to feminise women missionaries and erode any differences between these women and their domestic counterparts. All the collective biographies discussed in this chapter made use of at least one preface or introductory essay – often written by a male representative of the Church, acting as sponsor to a woman editor – which effectively reconfigures and interprets the text to come.[42] In the case of the RTS versions of Ann Judson's memoirs, this process works both ways: once Ann Judson's conversion account appeared in its collected tracts, the other tracts surrounding it had an effect on the story's interpretation, but were also inflected by the novel concept of female missionary action abroad. As a result, a definition of specifically feminine Christianity emerges; in the same way that evangelical discourse was beginning to identify women as more essentially pious and spiritual than men, missionary supporters were defining women as particularly fit for the work of missions due to their god-given femininity.[43]

One of the tracts that appeared alongside the 'Early Life of Mrs Judson' in the RTS's 1830s collection was entitled 'Female Influence and Obligations'. This tract demonstrates how domestic femininity could be used as a justification for women's action outside the home, but also to negate any idea of women's agency in these actions. Women are noted as having been given 'peculiar powers' of influence by God and are told of motherhood that 'this talent God himself has lodged with you'.[44] And they are seen as 'peculiarly adapted' for charitable visiting: 'You [...] are disposed to weep with them that weep [...] your habits of life fit you to enter the scene of domestic affliction with the best prospects of doing good' (p. 3). Women are also seen as 'peculiarly fitted' for Sunday school teaching (p. 3) and, the tract remarks, 'even the distant heathen [...] are beginning to stretch out their supplicating hands to you' (p. 8). The passive construction of women being 'peculiarly' adapted or fitted reflects the lesson of this tract, which is to stress that all these talents and actions of women stem from God rather than their own characters:

> All your rich and distinguishing privileges are his gift, ever talent intrusted to your care is the property of your Maker, God. He has opened up before you, in this world of effort and hope, a wide field of usefulness, and directed you to enter and labour for him. [...] God himself is bringing about his great purposes by the use of means; by the instrumentality of human influence and human action.
>
> (pp. 4–5)

In the same way that women editors of missionary biography were acting as passive vessels to disseminate instructional material, women missionaries were passive instruments of God. While this religious doctrine had always to an extent been a rhetoric used of evangelical male missionaries such as David Brainerd, this highly gendered version dominated writing about female missionaries and played a part in entrenching passivity and resignation as part of domestic ideology.[45]

Prefaces to collective biographies also acted to gender the religious concept of piety, making it part of essentialised femininity. The anonymous compiler of *Memoirs of Female Labourers in the Missionary Cause* (1839) refers to a particularly 'female zeal', which she implies is all that is required to be a female missionary.[46] And the Revd James Gardner prefaced his 1841 missionary collection *Memoirs of Christian Females* with an 'Essay on Female Piety'.[47] In this essay, Gardner struggles to reconcile doctrinal orthodoxy – that each sex is alike in possessing original sin, wickedness and resistance to God – with his conviction that woman is more naturally suited to piety:

> It is impossible to deny, that in the memoirs of pious females the influence of Christianity is exhibited in some of its most interesting and beautiful aspects. Possessed of strong sensibilities theirs is peculiarly the religion of the heart [...] There is something, indeed, peculiarly attractive in the religion of a Christian female. [...] We cannot shut our eyes to the fact that, in the regular attendance on Divine ordinances, as well as in the maintenance and encouragement of

those schemes of benevolence which are the natural fruit of a pious mind, the female sex are [...] entitled to the highest commendation.[48]

Gardner here stresses the powerful sentimental and aesthetic value women have for the Church. Their affecting femininity, combined with piety and passivity, made them perfect missionary martyrs for the cause.

As essential feminine traits become all that is necessary to suit women for the mission field, so any difference between domestic and missionary women is dissolved. For example, Revd Richard Knill, providing an introduction to *Memoirs of Female Labourers in the Missionary Cause*, collapses any distinction between female missionaries and domestic religious women, when he misremembers the book's title and refers to the collection as simply 'Memoirs of Holy Women'. He also groups together domestic and missionary work as aspects of what all 'pious women of the present day' are engaged in, from the 'prayerful instructions of the nursery' and 'the self-denying labours of the Sunday-school' to fundraising for missions.[49] It is likely that the anonymous 'Authoress' of this collection did not see much difference between the lives of the women she was memorialising in this text and the those of the young Christians she had also produced 'in neat and attractive binding': *Early Religion Seen in the Peaceful Happy End of Thirteen Young Children, who Lived and Died in the Lord* and *Select Memoirs of Young Christian Females who Lived and Died in the Lord*.[50] Children, domestic young women and female missionary martyrs were interchangeable for many examples of this genre of women's collective biography.

The alignment of missionary heroines with more domestic Christian women was especially effectively achieved through the physical presentation of their life stories alongside one another in collective biographies. Gardner's collection, though focusing mainly on missionary women, also contains stories of more domestic women and omits any mention of mission in the title he gives to his work, *Memoirs of Christian Females*.[51] Most of the retellings of Ann Judson's life discussed in this chapter also included the life of at least one other woman. In *Christian Biography* and *American Biography*, Judson becomes aligned with a particular passive, domestic femininity through being grouped with female subjects Anna Jane Linnard and Martha Laurens Ramsay, respectively. These wives, mothers and daughters are given the panegyric of heroism due to their everyday, female actions of doing their domestic duty, suffering and dying, all uncomplainingly and with resignation to God's will. The setting of Ramsay's story in particular alongside that of Ann Judson could be seen as a corrective to any threat of unfeminine behaviour in the latter, as Grierson explicitly says, in Mrs Ramsay's case 'No apology can be necessary. All the excellencies of Christian character as developed in the various duties of a daughter, wife, and mother, are exhibited in her conduct'. And attention is drawn to how fundamentally similar the two subjects are, despite appearances: 'the same principles and virtues, so conspicuous in these two individuals'.[52]

The overall message of these missionary biographies was that all women, whether called to duty in the mission field or simply destined to live or die at home, could embody the Christian virtues of piety, passivity and resignation in the face of suffering, self-denial and self-sacrifice – in fact, they were 'peculiarly' and naturally fitted to do so – and these virtues became part of the aesthetic of the ideal domestic angel. The provenance and religious commendation of these virtues had the power to elevate the lives of domestic religious women and justify their philanthropic activities in the community. However, extreme demands were now being made of all women – not just those with missionary vocations like Ann Judson – in terms of passivity and self-denial. Furthermore, the evolution of the missionary heroine into ideal domestic woman diluted any suggestion that missionary women had agency in their decisions or work and insisted that the main source of authority for women's missionary work lay in her ideal domesticity.

The preoccupation on the part of the authors of these texts with controlling the missionary woman's story, reducing it to a single message of passive piety, also led to a sort of arrested development in the literary form of the female missionary biography; the texts become more formulaic and didactic, and less concerned with presenting authentic portraits of women's religious and missionary experience. My next chapter will demonstrate how the developments in missionary biography set the terms for how mid-nineteenth-century religious women writers presented more domestic heroines in fiction. First though, it is important to explore how these literary developments affected women missionaries and mission supporters themselves – especially those that supported the movement for more professional roles for women in mission – both in how they understood their motivations and how they could depict themselves in their own missionary writings.

Female Missionary Writing 1841–1860: Jemima Thompson and the Wesleyan Ladies' Committee

Many of the editors of later collective missionary biographies were rather vague about the purpose of their texts. They suggested that readers' interest might be 'kindled' and that young women might model their behaviour on that of the female missionary – though their ability to emulate her example of passive sacrifice in the domestic sphere was stressed as much as the possibility of following her out to the mission field. For editors of texts who had more of a stake in supporting missions, this genre – and the discourse of the ideal female missionary it promoted – required some modification. For women editors of such texts, the stakes were even higher: not only did the discourse need to suit their pragmatic purpose of recruiting more women missionaries, but it also determined the scope of their self-representation as professional women in the mission movement. In this section, I therefore explore how the missionary supporter Jemima Thompson and the Wesleyan Methodist Missionary Society's (WMMS's) Ladies' Committee negotiated, appropriated and subverted the generic conventions of female missionary life writing and the presentation of the ideal female missionary.

Jemima Thompson was an enthusiastic mission supporter with family ties to both the London Missionary Society (LMS) and the Society for the Promotion of Female Education in China, India and the East (SPFEE). Her desire to become a missionary in the field was thwarted by her father, and her collective memoir can therefore be seen as another way for her to fulfil her felt missionary duty.[53] While her 1841 collection *Memoirs of British Female Missionaries* might appear, on first glance, to be just another collective biography praising female missionary sacrifice and suffering (such as that of Mrs Coulthart mentioned previously), it actually has a lot more in common with the original biography of Ann Judson. For example, Thompson privileges the voice of her subjects, providing extracts of their private writings, in the manner of Knowles and Woods. She makes the purpose and method of her text clear, using a preface and introductory essay to make the case for women's work in the mission field. And, as well as describing her missionaries' passive resignation in death, she also stresses their active piety in the work of the mission.

Thompson's commitment to including her missionary subjects' own voices is striking. Despite the brevity required in sketching the lives of sixteen missionary women, she includes journal and letter extracts in the majority of her sketches. Where these could not be sourced from official biographies, obituaries or published funeral sermons, she acquired more private papers and used these, confident in the approval of the evangelical community; for example, she quotes a conversion account her biographical subject Mrs Harvard had written 'for the private perusal of a friend'.[54] Like previous biographers, she insists that the words of these excellent women, more than editorial assurances, will prove how admirable they were and, therefore, should be made public for the advancement of Christianity. Furthermore, she uses extracts of female missionary letters to develop the evangelical tradition of deathbed witnessing. When there is a lack of information about the nature of a subject's death, she supplements the official deathbed witness or assurance of relatives by including letters written by the subjects themselves, shortly before their deaths. These presented by Thompson as equally valid forms of assurance. For example, in the case of Mrs Jowett, she writes:

> [Her] personal piety must be evident from this brief record of her works; and her state of mind in the prospect of dissolution cannot be so well exhibited by anything as by the following letter, which she only wrote two days before her decease.[55]

This privileging of textual evidence, from the pen of the deceased woman missionary, over eyewitness testimony, works to elevate the female missionary memoir from a literary form to an incarnation of Christian witness. It also allows the subject of the biography to speak, authentically, for herself, rather than having her last words reported or paraphrased.

In the same way as Knowles was didactic about the need for missionaries to follow in the footsteps of Ann Judson, Thompson includes introductory essays making this same point. As I have discussed, Knowles ended his biography with chapters on the current state of the Burma Mission and Ann Judson's own 'Address to Females in America Relative to the Situation of Females in the East', a combination that made plain the nature of the challenge, what was already being achieved, and the call to action. In her collective biography, Thompson included 'A Survey of the Condition of Women in Heathen Countries' and 'A Preliminary Essay on the Importance of Female Agency in Evangelizing Heathen Nations'.[56] As scholars have noted, these essays argue that the root of the problem in 'heathen countries' – what is holding them back from 'civilisation' – is their domestic arrangements: child marriage, infanticide and the lack of an 'Angel in the House' combine to show a need for domestic reform. Women missionaries, to access women in zenanas and as exemplars of domesticity, are therefore the answer.[57] In Thompson's view, though, it took more than domestic influence and angelic resignation to be a missionary woman: candidates should prepare thoroughly and intellectually for their work. Amongst her introductory material, Thompson includes a comprehensive and challenging reading list for aspiring women missionaries, covering history (ancient, modern and church); works of divinity, including Biblical criticism; philosophy; education; geography; and biographies of religious men and male missionaries.[58] Her exhortation is for women to make the most of the gifts that have been given them by God. Piety here lies not in simply accepting one's talents but in actively improving those talents, in order to be of use in the mission field.

Indeed, Thompson's collection is so focused on the practical aspects of preparation for missionary life, that there are few descriptions of beautiful piety and domesticity such as appear in other collective biographies of missionary women. Instead, she enthuses about her missionaries' agency, especially when they are at the point of making the decision to embark for the mission field. Far from passive, her subjects knew from an early age that they wanted to be missionaries and made efforts to marry missionaries or – unusually for this time period – to go out alone. Thompson tells the story of Mrs Norton, who managed to enter the mission field through taking a job as a governess with a family going out to India, and another who went out to nurse her sick missionary brother and successfully stayed on in the mission rather than being sent home after his recovery and marriage.

In fact, domesticity, in the form of marriage, is not portrayed by Thompson as an admirable attribute for a woman missionary. For Mrs

Norton, marriage is an end to her promising career; her tenure as the wife of a missionary was 'very short', as marriage was followed quickly by death (p. 54). Moreover, her marriage ensured that the official narrative of her life – a funeral sermon – focused solely on this brief period of her life as a missionary's wife. Thompson is left surmising that

> Probably [...] she accomplished more than is generally known, and it has been regretted that we have no particular detail of her labours and successes in the cause of the Redeemer in the island of Ceylon, or [...] in continental India.
>
> (p. 65)

For Thompson, marriage could lead to the sacrifice of missionary opportunity and the loss of a good story.

Thompson also problematises the concept of marriage as an embodiment of essential domestic feeling among women missionaries. Her missionary wives are not domestic angels and mothers – rather they are their husbands' partners, able to 'to share [...] the trials of his arduous labour'. In this form, marriage is portrayed as a positive opportunity for women looking for a useful occupation. It is also presented in terms of a business transaction, in the same way that Adoniram Judson's proposal to Ann Judson was described as business-like by Balfour; these women's approach to marriage reads as a necessary preliminary for realising their vocation in the mission field. Though this manner of viewing marriage had posed a dilemma for Ann Judson, in that it appeared to be indelicate behaviour for a woman, there is evidence that, by the 1830s, this was a common attitude among religious women: in an 1834 letter found in the WMMS archive, an anonymous female correspondent makes a marriage proposal to the Reverend Bunby:

> Allow me to say something about myself that you may be the better able to judge whether I am possessed of those qualifications which you [...] desire in a wife. For five years I have been in the society and have from the first felt desirous of being actively engaged in the work.[59]

Not only does a missionary vocation lead a woman to subvert the traditional courtship roles of men and women, but it also subverts the love letter genre into that of a job application. The qualities that this woman emphasises are more professional than domestic, and the desire is for the work, not the man.[60] In Thompson's collection, we see Mrs Coulthart embarking on missionary marriage in the service of her vocation. Before her marriage, she is described as having 'breathed most ardently a missionary spirit, and it became her unceasing desire that she might serve her Redeemer among the heathen'.[61] The use of 'ardent' and 'desire' in the context of mission, rather than in connection with her marriage, is typical, and the marriage only comes about because this desire becomes known to Christians who are looking for a wife for an eligible missionary about to embark for Jamaica. Thompson also uses the occupational language seen in the letter to Reverend Bunby, describing Mrs Coulthart as 'qualified for a missionary's wife', and quoting Mr Coulthart as saying that his wife was devoted to God, rather than to himself (pp. 18–9). Marriage is not romantic in these cases, and there is no suggestion that in treating marriage this way missionary women are making any kind of sacrifice.[62]

Of course, as we saw earlier, Thompson does include references to her subjects' self-sacrificial deaths. Compelled either by the prevailing discourse around female missionary martyrs, or by the generic convention of the collective memoir, she includes a number of long accounts of her subjects' peaceful, happy deaths from eyewitnesses. However, there are indications that Thompson is not entirely sincere in celebrating the deaths of missionary women. When she refers to Hannah Kilham as having 'fell a sacrifice', her archaic language points more to a self-conscious effort to write within the conventions of the genre than to a desire to inspire more sacrifices (p. 95). In her preface, she stresses the missionary women's 'honourable and useful lives', rather than their martyrdom, as most edifying (p. vii). Strikingly, in the cases where her missionary subjects did not achieve very much before their deaths, Thompson expresses obvious dissatisfaction with the accepted trope of redeeming sacrifice. Following the account of a Mrs Wilson's death in India (which takes the form of four paragraphs of her husband's deathbed witness), Thompson subversively changes the tone of the biography entirely and suggests that Mrs Wilson's death was perhaps her own fault:

> Mrs Wilson was evidently a sincere Christian. It may, however, be presumed, that even for the important privileges of devotion, she might be too inattentive to her health, neglecting exercise early in the morning, so essential to Europeans in India.
>
> (p. 26)

While admitting that she does not have enough information about this particular case, Thompson mobilises her general knowledge of missionary health and the Indian climate, to advise aspiring women missionaries that they should take the example of Mrs Wilson's death as a warning and avoid this kind of vain sacrifice, rather than emulate it.

Though one might expect female missionary newsletters to follow Thompson's subversive lead in suggesting that women missionaries should stay alive rather than martyr themselves, the editors of these papers had difficulty maintaining such a position. The female missionary newsletter – especially one edited entirely by women and written by a majority of female correspondents – was a new genre of the 1850s. The SPFEE launched its *Female Missionary Intelligencer* in 1854, and this publication included relatively conventional female missionary life writing in the form of obituaries and articles authored by male mission leaders as well as some letters from serving missionary women.[63] In contrast, in 1859, the Ladies' Committee of the WMMS started their newsletter, *Occasional Papers*, and featured longer editorials written by women members of the committee and more letters from serving missionary wives. The editors of both publications faced the challenge of representing themselves, as women missionaries, in a way that would inspire more women to support or join the mission movement; sustain their women missionaries in the field; and yet not contradict the ideal figure of the female missionary that had found so much acceptance in Victorian society. The challenge became quite explicit in the pages of the Wesleyan Ladies' *Occasional Papers* as they were starting the newsletter at the same time as they were beginning to recruit single women to work as unmarried teachers in mission schools. As the committee and missionary wives begin to define this new breed of female missionary in their writings, they reveal how far the conception of the ideal female missionary was useful for missionary wives in their self-understanding and presentation. Their descriptions of the different types of female missionary both circumscribed the authority of the new agent and guarded against any radical change to the conventional idea of the female missionary character – in fact, the wives' writing often re-inscribed the figure's characteristics of domesticity and passive self-sacrifice. However, in this moment of tension, these women's writings also reveal how, for the missionary wives, the requirement of these characteristics could be difficult and even psychologically untenable.

At first, it might seem paradoxical that an unmarried missionary could be defined in terms of domestic virtues, when the role often required women to sacrifice the possibility of marriage and family for a celibate life of duty – the SPFEE, for example, specifically prohibited its agents from marrying during their first five years of service.[64] Indeed, the role could have become highly controversial, given the importance of the cult of domesticity for Victorian women.[65] The Wesleyan missionary wives, though, portrayed the role and the temporary sacrifice of a domestic life positively, diminishing its emotional charge, stressing the rewards that unmarried missionaries would instead enjoy, and making clear the benefits to the cause that these agents would ensure. To a large extent, the belief among some evangelical women that missionary marriage was a means to an end, or a business transaction, reduced the idea that remaining unmarried was a sacrifice or that it necessarily made a woman less of a domestic creature. Now that there was this new opportunity for single women to follow their vocation into the mission field, they could be grateful that they no longer needed to marry and did not have to experience the same marriage dilemma as had Ann Judson or the Wesleyan missionary wives. The tone of the letters about this new agent is often almost jealous of the freedom these single women missionaries will have to carry out their work as they will be 'free from domestic ties' and 'unfettered by domestic cares'.[66]

The redeeming feature of the new single missionary was that her sacrifice of a personal domestic life was in the service of maintaining domestic values across the missions. The main reason she was necessary was that the domesticity recommended for female missionaries was actually proving challenging for the missionary wife. In the first issue of the *Occasional Papers*, published in March 1859, there is a letter from Mrs Walton, a missionary wife in Jaffna, who complains that her work in the mission school is keeping her away from her family:

> The entire responsibility [...] devolved on the Missionary's wife [...] and to render it really efficient required not only her general supervision, but her presence for several hours daily. When it is considered that a Missionary's family ought to be a living exemplification of the power and superiority of Christianity at home [...] it will be seen and felt that a Christian mother's place and sphere is almost exclusively with her own family.[67]

Mrs Walton here mobilises the philosophy of missionary marriage, that we have seen exemplified in Balfour's *Sketch of Mrs Judson*, to argue for the necessity of unmarried women missionaries. If the missionary wife is to preserve Victorian domestic authority, then it is harmful for her to take on more professional roles within the mission. While missionary wives might be able to generally supervise such schools, as wives and mothers in England supervised and assisted in Sunday schools, the main role of a missionary's wife is not in any way to carry out professional acts; she should simply be in the mission to provide, with her family, the symbolic function that is crucial in presenting Christianity to the local population.

Unmarried professional missionary teachers were therefore vital to carry out work in the mission's girls' schools and safeguard the domestic character of the missionary wife, in what could be seen as the beginnings of a division of labour.[68] However, almost immediately, the missionary wives start to write letters in which they make it clear that the committee must avoid recruiting women of excessive professionalism. One reason for this is that these sorts of women were seen as a possible threat to the authority of the missionary wife. From the beginning, the *Papers* make clear the position of this new female missionary in the hierarchy of the mission: they are to 'act under the direction of the Missionaries *and their wives*'.[69] Mrs Sanderson, despite expressing a need for unmarried women missionary teachers, expresses a fear in her letter that she will be sent 'ladies of middle age who would not be willing to submit to the directions and counsels of the Missionary's wife'.[70] The anxiety of the missionary wives is clear when they write positively of the prospect of single female missionaries, but are quick to qualify their enthusiasm by listing their requirements for such agents – often beginning and ending with 'piety', reinforcing the traditional view of the passive female missionary. For Mrs Jenkins, writing in February 1859, the single female missionary should be made in the image of the domestic missionary wife. The type of single woman she wants in the mission is: 'a pious, kind, active, well-informed, patient, cheerful, motherly body, who can cut out and teach needlework, keep house, manage servants and maintain neatness and order'. She does not envisage that these missionary teachers will proselytise or teach to any high standard, but rather that they will, like the Victorian mother, teach 'the *feeling of God*, of Sin, of Christ'.[71] This characterisation avoids any professionalisation of the female missionary role, portraying the single agent as a domestic 'mother', like the existing missionary women, despite her obvious sacrifice of marriage and biological motherhood for this role.

The rhetoric of domesticity and passive feminine influence was important to the Wesleyan missionary wives for their self-representation as well as for defining the new single female missionary. As I have mentioned, the requirements of domestic femininity were challenging for active women in the mission field, yet it was this idealised view of the female missionary that authorised these women to access useful work in the mission field. Describing the ideal candidates for the new single missionary role enabled the missionary wives to signal their allegiance to the virtues of the ideal female missionary. It was when they described their own work and progress that this rhetoric broke down and they reached instead for the more heroic, active language of earlier female missionary texts.

Because they wish to show evidence of the impact of their work, and their fundraisers' support, their letters are full of references to their activity, agency and even managerial prowess; Mrs Walton refers to her '*career* as the wife of a missionary' and revels in the 'large sphere for most important usefulness' it gives her.[72] Their active, almost professional, role in the missions is seen in their reports of their work, in which they appear superintending schools and instructing indigenous women in the gospel. This instruction was often of a high level, working alongside male missionaries' sermons, as Mrs Piercy describes in reference to her Female Class Meeting:

> They need leading on mentally as well as spiritually, to a more enlightened and sanctified state. [...] I try to enlighten their minds and consciences, and lead them on to more spiritual and stable religious experience. [...] The subject has been the same as the sermon. I go over the same ground, as nearly as I can, in a more simple and familiar way, interspersing questions, as with children.[73]

The emphasis on improving converts' 'mental' understanding of religion and 'stable' experience is at odds with the emotional, spiritual religious instruction usually expected from women teachers or mothers and more like that expected from a minister. To render a sermon in a 'simple and familiar way' also requires a great deal of understanding and skill, which Mrs Piercy deprecates with her parenthetical 'as nearly as I can'.

Many of the correspondents express that they share the goals of the Ladies' Committee and write with the long-term aims of the missions in mind. They opine on mission strategy, explicitly request funds, and craft their letters in order to maximise their potential for fundraising. Mrs Batchelor is notable in this regard. She wrote emotive descriptions of dying converts and promising orphans and followed these with direct appeals to readers, for example: 'Should any young friend who may read this feel desirous to assist the orphan Amurthee, they may do so by contributions of money for her support, and by remembering her in their prayers'.[74] Her suggestion of prayer as effective aid is almost an afterthought – necessary to display piety, but less useful than cold hard cash. Even more interestingly, Mrs Batchelor comes to the same conclusion as mission strategist Henry Venn was coming to at the same time on the importance of an indigenous church. In 1859, she writes:

> At present, agents from England are not so much needed as funds. [...] local agents may be employed. European ladies cannot be wholly domiciled amongst the girls, all they can do is superintend [...] The great desideratum is a training school; and if you could send out one or two ladies, fully qualified to train teachers, I think that for the present we should have our wants supplied.[75]

For Mrs Batchelor then, the new single female missionaries should be professionals – not passive paragons of domesticity.

In an even more complete break from the rhetoric of passive feminine influence, the missionary wives' language for describing their activity in the mission field contains militaristic metaphors, more suggestive of Knowles's emphasis on female missionary heroism than Balfour's Victorian femininity. For some women, this is surprisingly uncomplicated: Mrs Batchelor refers to beginning 'another year's campaign' and describes the local women as the mission's chief adversaries: 'they form the stronghold of idolatry, the keep of the castle of superstition' which, in the battle for souls, the missionary women must presumably storm.[76] And Mrs Jenkins writes of a site she surveyed for a new mission that 'it is a wonderful place for idolatry, one of its strongholds [...] it is a bold thought to attack such a place'.[77] This surveying for new mission sites was usually a task taken on solely by male missionaries, but the fact that Mrs Jenkins was involved suggests that, at this early stage, mission roles and aims were shared and the same militaristic language used by both male and female missionaries.

The enthusiasm women missionaries often displayed for their work has led scholars to question whether they were more inspired by the opportunities for agency provided by the mission field than by any religious conviction.[78] However, I argue that their enthusiasm should be interpreted as an expression of active piety, following the example of Ann Judson, and a rejection of the rhetoric of passive piety recommended for the ideal female missionary. The rejection of passive piety and patience is strikingly enunciated when Mrs Jenkins comments sarcastically that 'the Lord will provide is a comfortable promise'.[79] Though this sarcasm might appear to suggest that Mrs Jenkins is slipping in her performance of perfect piety, I argue this misses the point. Mrs Jenkins's undermining of the religious phrase 'the Lord will provide' is actually a searing criticism of the central mission authorities for their misinterpretation of piety. If mission societies simply sat back on their laurels and waited for God to provide for them, the missions would fail – true piety lay in taking action to fulfil God's will. The missionary wives saw their active work as being inspired by their religion; therefore, even if the language that they used to describe it was that of management and administration, it was overall a pious activity.

Active piety is so important to the Wesleyan missionary wives that it even breaks into their descriptions of the ideal single female missionary candidates. Like Thompson, they are clear that missionary candidates need to be rigorously prepared for their work. They suggest that books, especially religious biography, should be part of a missionary's training, as they can help prepare candidates to withstand difficulties. The suggestion is that reading about the religious trials of others – 'of distinguished missionary females' – will give candidates the powerful spiritual framework that will enable them to manage challenges rather than passively giving up and resigning the matter to God. More practically, candidates should have 'an aptitude for acquiring languages' and should even 'commence Tamil and Canarese in England'.[80]

Even when the missionary wives were describing the hardships of missionary life and the self-denial that was required of candidates, they do not use the language of passive suffering. Instead, they accentuate the heroism, nobility and potential rewards of the missionary life. The *Occasional Papers*' editors warn that women should not be misled by 'the glow of early zeal' to become missionaries, suggesting that this is a common experience in youth, but that they need to realise that the role and its hardships require instead 'true devotedness to Christ and his cause'.[81] Mrs Sanderson likewise reflects that 'it would be a pity to send to India young and thoughtless girls, who are perhaps led away by the romance of going to teach the daughters of the East' and stresses instead that the missionaries should be of a character 'not soon discouraged in arduous toil', who should 'count the cost before entering upon a life of self-denying duty'.[82] However, an anonymous article by 'A Missionary's Wife', printed in the same issue, paints a heroic picture of the female missionary which emphasises the role's potential for usefulness. She will be one of the 'noble examples of Christian courage, devotion and entire consecration to the Church's interest' who considers 'none of the treasures of this world as *precious* to them in comparison with perishing souls'. And she will find an 'appropriate sphere in the wide field' before her, in which to use her 'education' and 'mental or physical endurance'.[83] Becoming a missionary, even if one had to renounce marriage, is not about passive sacrifice but is instead an opportunity for heroic piety and action for the mission cause.

The missionary rhetoric that the Wesleyan Ladies' Committee and their correspondents are most conflicted about is that which surrounds the ultimate sacrifice that missionary women are often required to make. Like Thompson, the Wesleyan Ladies' Committee are concerned that female missionaries should live and work rather than die for the cause. Even as they warn candidates that they should be prepared to sacrifice, and be prepared for their health to fail, they stress that they will choose candidates based partly on their healthiness. In the very first editorial, the Ladies Committee make it clear that 'good health is essential' to be accepted as a WMMS female missionary, and Mrs Sanderson echoes this when she writes that teachers for her mission school should be 'possessed of good health and of common sense'.[84] They also emphasise the possibilities of rewards on earth as well as in heaven. An anonymous missionary's wife writes boldly: 'none ever took up this cross [...] who did not even in her work on earth reap rich compensation', suggesting the possibility of feelings of fulfilment from work.[85] One of the first single female missionaries, sacrificing a domestic life for the hardships of the mission field, described the sort of compensation she enjoyed through her work:

> You will be glad to know that those feelings which led me to offer myself to your Society [...] are daily on the increase [...] when I enter the school in the morning [...] my heart is filled with love and sympathy.[86]

While it is to be expected that missionary applicants highlighted their pious feelings when applying to missionary societies, Miss Wildish's letter suggests that an emotionally satisfying spirituality, as well as rewarding work, could sustain missionary women.[87]

However, one missionary wife demonstrates how important the idea of self-sacrifice could be in the missionary wife's self-representation. One of the main reasons Mrs Griffith celebrated the new unmarried female missionary was that 'we may now hope that missionaries' wives will live longer, and be able to prosecute their labours in the native female schools more cheerfully and confidently than heretofore'. However, it should be noted that all she asks is that they be allowed to live 'longer', rather than to avoid sacrifice altogether, and she takes the tone of martyrdom as she promises her support – 'I render you all the aid my poor shattered health will permit'[88] – as if her bad health is a badge of honour, self-consciously advertised.

As we have seen, martyrdom, especially that attended by passive resignation of the female missionary, was a dominant and emotional feature of female missionary writing by the middle of the century. It is not surprising that missionaries sometimes self-identified with this characterisation. In some ways, the *Occasional Papers* followed the trend of missionary life writing and mobilised emotional descriptions of their missionaries' self-sacrifice in order to inspire more women to support the cause. For example, they publish a memoir of Miss Beale, who died in the course of her work in Belize, which largely conforms to generic conventions of memoirs of martyrs. To stress her passive self-sacrifice, they quote the Revd George Sykes of the same mission: '[she] lived habitually in a state of preparation for death, many times expressing her entire resignation to the Divine will, willing to live, ready to die'.[89] However, the society still finds the news 'distressing', rather than edifying or triumphant, especially as she was 'in the strength of her days and in the midst of her usefulness'.[90]

The deaths and sacrifices that the women of the Wesleyan society do not find upsetting – in fact, they find them 'delightful' – are the deaths of native converts. At the point of the natives' deaths, the Wesleyan women are able to appropriate these converts as sentimental victims within a narrative of missionary salvation. Through the evangelical tradition of deathbed witnessing, and in the tradition of female missionary biography, British missionary women were authorised to narrate their converts' deaths, and the number of such accounts is evidence that they took on this duty with enthusiasm. Their writing of the deaths enabled them to take ultimate possession of the converts both in life and death, as they turned them into sentimental and edifying characters in the narrative of the mission more widely.[91]

In just the second edition of the *Occasional Papers*, two such deaths are described: that of Nalla Mooto, described by Mrs Batchelor, and that of a nameless native catechist, described by Mrs Polglase. There is an obvious power relation invoked through writing the deaths of this man and woman. The missionaries superintend this most private of human processes through their witnessing: though the native catechist's final words are for 'his friends who stood about him', they become the property of Mrs Polglase and the mission as she transcribes them into her narrative – the message of which is that his death 'showed the power of religion over death'.[92] The missionary women appear to have little personal feeling for the converts as individuals; the way they describe deaths focuses on proving the missionaries' actions have added 'more to the increasing number of redeemed and saved natives around the throne of God' (p. 26), and celebration of this always outweighs any feelings of sorrow at the loss of this person on earth, as does the additional pleasure the women gain from the spectacle of natives performing Christian deaths.

It becomes clear, however, when we look at the way in which the converts' deaths are described, that this is more than a simple appropriation of the native. Mrs Polglase gives a very detailed account of her native catechists' death:

> Rapid consumption weakened his body; but as his mortal frame grew weaker, his faith appeared to increase. A few hours before his death he said to his friends who stood about him, 'When I am gone, do not say I am *dead*, but only *removed*,' using a native word which signifies 'moving from one residence to another.' He then quoted 2 Corinthians v. 1; and soon after closed his eyes on this world.
> (p. 26)

Mrs Polglase makes sure to include details of any suffering, in the 'rapid consumption' and weakening of the man; the effect of this on the faith of the sufferer – it increased; his thoughts on his likely salvation, proven by his words of comfort to his friends; and the Biblical quotation that made up his last words. In fact, she presents the death of this native man using exactly the same narrative tropes that by the mid-century were being used by biographers almost exclusively for the presentation of female missionary sacrifice. While Mrs Polglase does not evince much sadness at the death, there is an implied emotional effect through the inclusion of friends around the deathbed requiring his comforting words, and of course in the detailed physical suffering of the man. Mrs Batchelor's account is very similar:

> while cholera was doing its work on the body of Nalla Mooto, her mind was greatly comforted by her daughter's reading to her the precious words of God. Few in England [...] can conceive of the sorrow and desolation which spread among families in this land when cholera makes its appearance [...] She expressed, in her last moments, a firm trust in Christ as her Saviour, and manifested great joy and peace of mind while her sorrowing child read to her.[93]

Cholera here, and the 'sorrowing child', heighten the emotional charge of the death – the desolation is such that it cannot be conceived. However, Nalla Mooto achieves a good evangelical death;[94] she not only passively, but joyfully accepts God's will, dying peacefully, in the manner of the missionary martyr Harriet Newell.

When the missionaries explain what these descriptions aim to achieve, they make clear that it is these deaths that will promote the cause of the mission – rather than their own. The editors of the *Occasional Papers* give explicit reasons for their inclusion of Mrs Batchelor's and Mrs Polglase's accounts of native deaths: it is in the service of 'increasing faith and effort in behalf of the long and deeply degraded daughters of India'.[95] The sacrifices are therefore imagined as achieving the same Christianising effect as the martyrdom of Ann Judson and Harriet Newell. Both Mrs Batchelor and Mrs Polglase refer to the deaths as providing 'encouragement' to mission supporters.

The power relations in these accounts, and the lack of any obvious emotion for the departed or orphaned, reveal the alienation at the heart of the female missionary's self-sacrificial narrative. Ultimately, missionary women might feel they had no place in the missionary narrative except through their deaths, which were narrated for the benefit of the cause. The Wesleyan wives' skilled creation of narratives of native sacrifice to replace those of female missionary sacrifice are necessary for their self-creation as active, professional missionary agents. Reluctant to sacrifice themselves in the cause, their transposition of the native convert to the centre of the missionary sacrifice narrative enabled the missionary women to take on professional identities that allowed for far longer, more fulfilling lives of action in the mission field.

The frontispiece to Jemima Thompson's *Memoirs of British Female Missionaries* graphically shows such a displacement of female missionary sacrifice. The picture depicts the 'Burning of the Wives and Slaves of Runjeet Sing' and features the wives in white robes, calmly ascending a burning pyre.[96] These are the 'degraded' daughters of India that the Wesleyan wives and female missionary biographers write about, who, due to their hopeless condition, provide the opportunity for Western female agency in the mission field. The effective portrayal of their extreme need is designed to inspire British women to act in support of the female missionary cause. However, the fact that Thompson is using their deaths for her own purposes is again another example of appropriation and a clear

Figure 1.1 'Burning of the Wives and Slaves of Runjeet Sing, June 1839', *Memoirs of British Female Missionaries*. © British Library Board. All Rights Reserved/Bridgeman Images.

transferral of the sacrificial imperative; while the picture's foregrounding of self-immolation – the most graphic form of self-sacrifice – could be seen as a metaphor for the female missionaries' sacrifices, it is the indigenous women and servants who are on the pyre.

Conclusion

While the missionary women of the Wesleyan society, and the supporter of female missionary professionalism Jemima Thompson never explicitly reject self-sacrifice and passive, domestic femininity as the ideal characteristics of the British female missionary, their presentation of active women missionaries – especially when this was self-presentation – problematised these traits and used strategies to displace those that were most troubling. While there was heroic value in some sacrifice and suffering, as established on a rhetorical level by Knowles, the tendency for later memoirs to valorise vain sacrifice and suffering, or passive femininity above useful activity, is implicitly challenged by Thompson's and the Wesleyan Ladies' Committee's more complicated and discriminating treatment of sacrifice. Psychologically, the sacrificial imperative placed upon the Wesleyan ladies as female missionaries led to their transferral of this onto the native converts in their power. However, the conformity of these narratives of sacrifice with those of earlier female missionary biographies shows that the writers were well aware of the power these stories held for the necessary support of the missionary cause, as they were equally aware of the necessity for continuing to present themselves, and any more professional female missionary agents, as respectably domestic.

Though a unified ideological depiction of the female missionary figure can be identified in missionary life writing by the 1860s, the continuing presence of Judson's own narrative, and the fissures and displacements in the discourse visible in missionary women's letters, and even collective biographies such as Thompson's, showed the instability of this figure and the continuing presence of disruptive ideas of female authority, proto-professionalism and heroism based in pious Christian action. These multiple facets of the female missionary figure emerging through letters, tracts and biography meant that religious women readers had access to an evangelical female subjectivity that was complex, varied and sometimes contradictory. In the next chapter, we will discover how women writers from evangelical backgrounds responded to the cultural prescription of femininity with an awareness of how much it owed to the female missionary figure – in all her complexity – and how they developed the rhetorical strategies of the missionary writers within fictional works. Their constructions of characters that blended the domestic angel and female missionary show the potential this elision had for models of female empowerment but also the serious drawback of basing such empowerment, paradoxically, on self-sacrifice.

Notes

1. For discussion of the pervasive influence of the separate spheres ideology, see Catherine Hall, *White Male and Middle Class: Explorations in Feminism and History* (Cambridge: Polity, 1992), pp. 84–9; and Catherine Hall and Leonore Davidoff, *Family Fortunes: Men and Women of the English Middle Class 1780–1850* (London: Routledge, 2002), pp. 179–92.
2. Though the Society for Promoting Female Education in the East (SPFEE) trained women missionaries from 1834, very few of these were officially employed by British missions before the 1860s. See Peter Williams, '"The Missing Link": The Recruitment of Women Missionaries in some English Evangelical Missionary Societies in the Nineteenth Century', in *Women and Missions: Past and Present, Anthropological and Historical Perceptions*, ed. by Fiona Bowie, Deborah Kirkwood, and Shirley Ardener (Oxford: Berg, 1993), pp. 43–69 (pp. 44–5); Clare Midgley has also shown how careful the leadership of the Society for the Promotion of Female Education in China, India and the East was in presenting the work of their female missionaries, especially in response to criticism in a discussion that unfolded in the pages of the *Christian Ladies Magazine* in the 1830s, 'Can Women be Missionaries? Envisioning Female Agency in the Early Nineteenth-Century British Empire', *Journal of British Studies*, 45 (2006), 335–58 (pp. 353–6).
3. Twells, *The Civilizing Mission and the English Middle Class, 1792–1850: The Heathen at Home and Overseas* (Palgrave Macmillan, 2009), pp. 5, 84; Gleadle, *The Early Feminists: Radical Unitarians and the Emergence of the Women's Rights Movement* (Basingstoke: Macmillan, 1995), pp. 6, 90–106.
4. Jay, *Religion of the Heart: Anglican Evangelicalism and the Nineteenth-Century Novel* (Oxford: Clarendon, 1979), pp. 196–8.
5. As we will see in this and the next two chapters, this elision was a two-way process: as early nineteenth-century middle-class culture demanded a domestication of the female missionary character, by the 1840s, a hardening, restrictive Victorian domestic ideology required all women to develop the traits of female missionary piety and self-sacrifice.
6. James Davis Knowles, *Memoir of Mrs. Ann H. Judson*, 3rd edn (London: Wightman and Co., 1830), p. v.
7. Midgley, p. 345; Alison Booth, *How to Make It as a Woman: Collective Biographical History from Victoria to the Present* (Chicago, IL: University of Chicago Press, 2004), pp. 2–3.
8. Joseph Fletcher, 'Introduction', in *Memoir of Mrs Stallybrass, Wife of the Rev. E Stallybrass, Missionary to Siberia*, ed. by Edward Stallybrass (London: Fisher, Son and Co., 1836), p. xv. Midgley has found similar references to the inspirational nature of the Judson and Newell biographies in her survey of female missionary memoirs, pp. 344–5.
9. Margaret Wilson, review, quoted in John Wilson, *A Memoir of Mrs Margaret Wilson of the Scottish Mission, Bombay* (Edinburgh: John Johnstone, 1840), p. 611.
10. Ibid., p. 616.
11. Midgley, *Women Against Slavery: The British Campaigns 1780–1870* (London: Routledge, 1992), pp. 16–23; and 'From Supporting Missions to Petitioning Parliament: British Women and the Evangelical Campaign against *Sati* in India, 1813–30', in *Women in British Politics*,

1760–1860: The Power of the Petticoat, ed. by Kathryn Gleadle and Sarah Richardson (Basingstoke: Macmillan, 2000), pp. 74–92 (pp. 75–7).

12 Linda Peterson drew attention to the potential of Ann Judson's novel and active presentation for nineteenth-century religious women, 'Women Writers', in *Women and Literature in Britain 1800–1900*, ed. by Joanne Shattock (Cambridge: Cambridge University Press, 2001), pp. 209–30 (pp. 222–4).

13 Hall, *White Male and Middle Class*, pp. 84–9; Hall and Davidoff, pp. 179–92.

14 It was common for life stories of missionaries to be retold in various versions and editions. For example, Candy Gunther Brown demonstrates how John Wesley's *Life of Brainerd* was re-interpreted over subsequent editions in his *The Word in the World: Evangelical Writing, Publishing and Reading in America 1789–1880* (Chapel Hill, NC: University of North Carolina Press, 2004), pp. 93–4.

15 Booth, p. 23; this is a similar process as that noted by Christine Krueger in her study of Methodist women preachers, *The Reader's Repentance: Women Preachers, Women Writers and Nineteenth-Century Social Discourse* (London: University of Chicago Press, 1992), p. 10.

16 After 1860, fewer versions of Ann Judson's biography were published, but her fame did not entirely diminish. In 1866, her story was included in Lydia Howard Huntley's *Great and Good Women: Biographies for Girls*, and throughout the 1880s, 1890s and into the twentieth century, the prolific Emma Raymond Pittman wrote versions of her biography and included her in collective biographies of women missionaries.

17 Knowles, pp. 277–8.

18 Margaret Grierson, *American Biography: Or, Memoirs of Mrs. A. Judson and Mrs. M. L. Ramsay* (Edinburgh: Leith, 1831) pp. 282–3 [my emphasis].

19 Grierson, p. 17.

20 Linda Wilson, *Constrained By Zeal: Female Spirituality Amongst Nonconformists, 1825–75* (Carlisle: Paternoster, 2000), pp. 182–3; see also Sharon Marcus, *Between Women: Friendship, Desire, and Marriage in Victorian England* (Oxford: Princeton University Press, 2007), pp. 15, 63.

21 Grierson, p. 280.

22 E.M.I., 'Mrs Judson and Little Maria', in *Missionary Stories* (London: John Snow, 1843), p. 8.

23 Ibid., p. 7.

24 Clara Lucas Balfour, *A Sketch of Mrs. Ann H. Judson* (London: W. & F. G. Cash, 1854), p. 18.

25 Semple has likewise attributed the emphasis on women's emotional and communicative role in the mission field to gendered expectations that limited women's activities, 'Missionary Manhood: Professionalism, Belief and Masculinity in the Nineteenth-Century British Imperial Field', *Journal of Imperial and Commonwealth History*, 36 (2008), 397–415 (p. 403).

26 Balfour, p. 17. [Further references appear parenthetically in the text.]

27 'Life of Mrs Ann H Judson', in *Christian Biography* (London: RTS, c.1832), pp. 1–144 (p. 17); Grierson, p. 46.

28 Daniel C. Eddy, *Heroines of the Missionary Enterprise; or Sketches of Prominent Female Missionaries* (London: Hal, Virtue and Co., 1850), p. 35.

29 James Gardner, *Memoirs of Christian Females* (Edinburgh: John Johnstone, 1841), p. 89.

Part I: 1830–1870

30 While Wilson has noted a similarity in the language of resignation to describe Christian death in obituaries for both men and women, she also noted that significantly more obituaries of women dwelt on the virtues of a passive death, especially if the experience involved suffering, pp. 158–9.

31 Grierson, p. 6. [Further references appear parenthetically in the text.]

32 Balfour, pp. 35–40.

33 'Early Life of Mrs Judson' (Tract 363), *1st Series Tracts of the Religious Tract Society*, Vol. X (London: RTS, c. 1830), p. 8.

34 D. Bruce Hindmarsh sees a similar tendency in Medieval hagiographies of the Lives of the Saints, leading him to conclude that autobiography, rather than biography, is the true evangelical genre, *The Evangelical Conversion Narrative: Spiritual Autobiography in Early Modern England* (Oxford: OUP, 2005), pp. 346–7.

35 Midgley, 'Can Women be Missionaries', p. 345; Booth, p. 8. Claudia Nelson also notes that Margaret Grierson's fictional story *Lily Douglas* similarly avoids depicting female individuality, *Boys Will be Girls: The Feminine Ethic and British Children's Fiction 1857–1917* (New Brunswick, NJ: Rutgers University Press, 1991), p. 13.

36 Eddy, p. vii.

37 Looking specifically at the continued inclusion of the Judson wives in American collections, Booth comes to the same conclusion that the representations of the deaths of 'this self-immolating family' increase the narratives' 'proselytising effect', p. 166.

38 Eddy, p. 48.

39 *Memoirs of Female Labourers in the Missionary Cause* (Bath: n.p, 1839), pp. 6–11.

40 Jemima Thompson, *Memoirs of British Female Missionaries* (London: William Smith, 1841), p. 19.

41 Thompson, p. 14; Booth also notes this exaltation of what she calls 'delayed suicide' in the narratives of Ann Judson's life, p. 171.

42 This is a treatment recognised by Brown as being particularly common in the case of women's narratives, p. 94.

43 Semple points to an increasing elision of piety and femininity in the rhetoric of a number of contemporary advocates for women's increased role in missions, *Missionary Women: Gender, Professionalism, and the Victorian Idea of Christian Mission* (Woodbridge: Boydell, 2003), p. 6. Sue Morgan also refers to the 'feminisation of religion' in the nineteenth century, 'Introduction: Women, Religion and Feminism: Past, Present and Future Perspectives', in *Women, Religion and Feminism in Britain, 1750–1900*, ed. by Morgan (Basingstoke: Palgrave Macmillan, 2002), pp. 1–19 (pp. 1–2).

44 'Female Influence and Obligations' (Tract 340), *1st Series Tracts of the Religious Tract Society*, Vol. X (London: RTS, c. 1830), pp. 1–2. [Further references appear parenthetically in the text.]

45 John Wesley, *An Extract of the Life of the Late David Brainerd Missionary to the Indians* (Penryn: Cock, 1815), p. 275. See Introduction and Prologue for more discussion of the development of a gendered missionary discourse.

46 *Memoirs of Female Labourers*, p. 13.

47 In 1852, John Angell James published a series of sermons entitled 'Female Piety', in which he reinforced the domestic character of this religious femininity, see Wilson, p. 11.

48 Gardner, pp. 6–7.
49 Richard Knill, 'Introduction', in *Memoirs of Female Labourers*, pp. v–viii (pp. vi–vii).
50 Advertised at the end of *Memoirs of Female Labourers*.
51 Booth has noted that the variety of women's occupations honoured in collections blurred the line between the public and domestic spheres, pp. 136–37.
52 Grierson, pp. 10–11.
53 Clare Midgley was one of the first scholars to write about Thompson and her collection, 'Can Women be Missionaries', pp. 347–8.
54 Thompson, p. 29.
55 Thompson, p. 94.
56 Midgley suggests that the 'Preliminary Essay' was probably written by her uncle, founder of the SPFEE, the Baptist Wriothesley Noel, 'Can Women be Missionaries?', p. 346.
57 Twells, pp. 115–6; Midgley, 'Can Women be Missionaries?', pp. 346–51.
58 Thompson, pp. xxix–xxx. [Further references appear parenthetically in the text.]
59 Miss M.A.P, Letter 1 February, 1834, London, SOAS, MSS/SpecialSeries/biographical/Southseas/FBN 35.
60 Catherine Hall sees a similar prioritising of the missionary life over a husband in the case of Mary Anne Middleditch who wrote obsessively to a friend about her desire for a missionary life abroad, and, when writing to her parents about her impending marriage to a missionary, emphasised 'love of Christ [...] not of her husband to be', Hall, *White, Male and Middle Class*, p. 223.
61 Thompson, p. 7. [Further references appear parenthetically in the text.]
62 Though Talia Schaffer suggests that there were many non-romantic understandings of marriage in the nineteenth century, this deprioritising of love in marriage in favour of religious opportunity would seem to be more mercenary than simply disavowing dangerous romance, *Romance's Rival: Familiar Marriage in Victorian Fiction* (Oxford: Oxford University Press, 2016), pp. 7–10. See Introduction for further discussion.
63 Despite this seemingly conservative approach, Midgley suggests that by using the term 'female missionary', the SPFEE was being far less cautious than in its earlier publications, 'Can Women be Missionaries?', p. 356.
64 'Editorial', *The Female Missionary Intelligencer*, 1 (1854), pp. 1–15.
65 Not all mission societies encouraged women missionaries to remain unmarried; the Basel mission refused to enforce celibacy for its unmarried women missionaries, seeing marriage as an overriding female goal, Ulrika Sill, *Encounters in Quest of Christian Womanhood: The Basel Mission in Pre- and Early Colonial Ghana* (Leiden: Brill, 2010), p. 54.
66 Mrs Walton, Letter, 16 February 1859, *Occasional Papers*, 1 (March 1859), in *Ladies' Committee Occasional Papers* ([n.p.]: Wesleyan Methodist Missionary Society, 1900), p. 13; Mrs Male, Letter, 4 May 1859, *Occasional Papers*, 3 (September 1859), p. 38.
67 Mrs Walton, Letter, 16 February 1859, pp. 11–12.
68 Sill, p. 45.
69 'Editorial', *Occasional Papers*, 1 (March 1859), p. 4 [emphasis added].

80 Part I: 1830–1870

70 Mrs Sanderson, Letter, 19 July 1859, *Occasional Papers*, 4 (January 1860), p. 60.
71 Mrs Jenkins, Letter, 3 February 1859, *Occasional Papers*, 2 (June 1859), p. 23 [emphasis in original].
72 Mrs Walton, Letter, 16 February 1859, p. 11 [emphasis added].
73 Mrs Piercy, Letter, 2 May 1859, *Occasional Papers*, 2 (June 1859), pp. 44–5.
74 Mrs Batchelor, Letter, 23 February 1859, *Occasional Papers*, 2 (June 1859), p. 22.
75 Mrs Batchelor, Letter, 12 April 1859, *Occasional Papers*, 2 (June 1859), pp. 36–7. On Henry Venn and ideas of an indigenous church, see C. Peter Williams, *The Ideal of the Self-Governing Church: A Study in Victorian Missionary Strategy* (Leiden: Brill, 1990).
76 Mrs Batchelor, Letter, 23 February 1859, pp. 20–2.
77 Mrs Jenkins, Letter, 27 August 1859, *Occasional Papers*, 4 (January 1860), p. 56.
78 See, for example, Martha Vicinus, 'Introduction', in *Suffer and be Still: Women in the Victorian Age*, ed. by Vicinus (London: Indiana University Press, 1972), p. xi; see also Fiona Bowie, 'Introduction', in *Women and Missions*, ed. by Bowie et al., pp. 5–6.
79 Mrs Jenkins, Letter, 3 February 1859, p. 23.
80 Mrs Batchelor, Letter, 12 April 1859, pp. 35–36.
81 'Editorial', *Occasional Papers*, 1 (March 1859), pp. 4–5.
82 Mrs Sanderson, Letter, 19 July 1859, pp. 59–60.
83 A Missionary's Wife, Letter, *Occasional Papers*, 4 (January 1860), p. 52.
84 'Editorial', *Occasional Papers*, 1 (March 1859), p. 5; Mrs Sandserson, Letter, 19 July 1859, p. 60.
85 A Missionary's Wife, Letter, pp. 53–54.
86 Miss Wildish, Letter, 19 July 1860, *Occasional Papers*, 7 (November 1860), pp. 142–3.
87 Malini Johar Schueller has suggested that religious life could take in the excess of displaced sexual emotions of women who were unable to express these emotions any other way, 'Nation, Missionary Women, and the Race of True Womanhood', in *Messy Beginnings: Postcoloniality and Early American Studies*, ed. by Malini Johar Schueller and Edward Watts (New Brunswick, NJ: Rutgers University Press, 2003), pp. 155–74 (p. 163). While I disagree with this rather formulaic idea of displacement, it is certainly true that the framework and language of piety provided these women with an emotional life and a way of expressing the power of these emotions.
88 Mrs Griffith, Letter, 3 February 1859, *Occasional Papers*, 1 (March 1859), p. 10.
89 Reverend George Sykes, Letter, 17 July 1860, *Occasional Papers*, 7 (November 1860), pp. 138–9.
90 'Editorial', *Occasional Papers*, 7 (November 1860), p. 124.
91 Postcolonial feminist critics, following Gayatri Spivak's work, have acknowledged the practice of Victorian women 'speaking for' and appropriating native Others as 'helpless victims awaiting the [...] redress of their condition at the hands of their sisters in the metropole', and using this as a justification for their participation in imperial philanthropic movements, Spivak, 'Can the Subaltern Speak', in *Marxism and the Interpretation of Culture*, ed. Nelson and Grossberg, pp. 295–306; see also Antoinette Burton,

Burdens of History: British Feminists, Indian Women and Imperial Culture 1865–1915 (London: University of Carolina Press, 1994), p. 7; and Midgley, 'From Supporting Missions to Petitioning Parliament', in *Women in British Politics, 1760–1860*, ed. by Gleadle and Richardson, p. 86.

92 Mrs Polglase, Letter, 9 September 1858, *Occasional Papers*, 2 (June 1859), p. 26. [Further references appear parenthetically in the text.]
93 Mrs Batchelor, Letter, 23 February 1859, p. 21.
94 Jay, pp. 154–60; Michael Wheeler, *Death and the Future Life in Victorian Literature and Theology* (Cambridge: Cambridge University Press, 1990), pp. 27–32.
95 'Editorial', *Occasional Papers*, 2 (June 1859), p. 21.
96 Thompson, p. i.

2 Missionary Self-Sacrifice in the Domestic Sphere
The Tracts and Novels of Martha Sherwood, Hesba Stretton and Dinah Craik

Introduction

We have seen how women were publishing biographies of female missionaries from as early as the 1820s. The spiritual injunction of the missionary Ann Judson's original biographer, James Davis Knowles, that women should serve God's cause by circulating accounts of missionary activity, had helped to establish the new occupation of professional religious writing for women. By the 1820s, professional writing was also required as part of the domestic mission to civilise the British populace, which, like the foreign mission movement, stemmed from the late eighteenth-century religious revivals.[1] New religious publishing houses demanded more material for children, for use in British Sunday schools as well as in middle- and upper-class homes.[2] Memoirs of female missionaries could be repackaged for this juvenile audience and marketed alongside similar works about children who died good Christian deaths – indeed, these were often produced by the same writers.[3] Alison Twells has demonstrated that the foreign and domestic missions developed in parallel in the early decades of the nineteenth century.[4] This interconnection of domestic and foreign missions can be seen even more clearly in literature: women tract writers would have been taking part in both missions interchangeably, depending on the tract they were writing at the time.

Significantly for women writers, during the first few decades of the nineteenth century, the evangelical community gradually came to accept more fictional religious literature. Works of missionary non-fiction were joined on nursery and schoolroom shelves by fictional tracts for children, each encouraging child readers to live more Christian lives and take part in the foreign or domestic missionary movement. Women writers often published in both genres; for example, Martha Sherwood published non-fictional and fictional tracts to instruct children in the Church catechism, and Margaret Grierson, whose sketch of Ann Judson's life (discussed in Chapter 1) would have been suitable for children, was also a prolific writer of fiction for Sunday schools in America and Britain.[5] Publishers' practices of recommending an author on the basis of her other titles would have contributed to evangelicals' acceptance of all types of writing

DOI: 10.4324/9781003332961-5

from within their community. Penny Brown has suggested that, through its association with the Sunday School movement, even the novel began to gain respectability.[6] By the mid-century, novelists, such as Elizabeth Gaskell and Dinah Craik, could move back and forth between the mainstream and evangelical publishing worlds and could take advantage of religious publishing channels to expand their readership and supplement their income.[7]

Most importantly for our understanding of evangelical culture's influence on women and the developing ideology of femininity, the common authorship of tract fiction and spiritual memoir resulted in thematic similarity across works, especially in terms of the didactic messages being transmitted about the nature of the female missionary. As we saw in Chapter 1, a specifically feminine, self-sacrificing and passive form of female missionary character was becoming popular in the biography of the mid-century; and religious literature began to follow this pattern when depicting ideal domestic femininity. Indeed, in some ways, authors of fiction were more able to paint ideally feminine and sentimental female missionary characters, given they did not have to negotiate the inconvenient personality of a real biographical subject. Alongside biography's female missionary martyrs, religious tract fiction established a stock cast of somewhat one-dimensional characters, including the self-abnegating 'holy child' and governess, and it is these characters that this chapter will examine.

Scholars have generally interpreted the 'holy', or redeeming, child character as the product of Romanticism and sentimentalism, which influenced early children's literature, rather than of the evangelicalism which formed the more immediate context.[8] Meanwhile, scholarship on the governess character in nineteenth-century fiction has established her as a figure used almost exclusively for social critique. Mary Poovey argued persuasively that the governess's socially ambiguous position, as neither part of the family nor servant, not only threatened the creed of separate spheres but also demanded that governesses construct themselves as models of domestic, self-sacrificial femininity.[9] However, the religious basis of the domestic ideology that scholars see as leading to the governess's plight has been neglected in this area of study, which is surprising, given that many examples of governess fiction have strong religious themes and plots, and the character appeared so often in religious tracts.[10]

In fact, I argue that, in nineteenth-century fiction, the characters of the 'holy child' and governess are often domestic proxies of the female missionary. So, though the female missionary in the foreign mission field was rarely depicted literally in nineteenth-century fiction, tract writers (who often saw themselves as working within the domestic mission) were engaging in the debate about the nature of the female missionary through these proxies. For instance, in presenting a governess character torn between the expectations of her role (passivity and self-renunciation) and her experience of a strongly emotional, and religiously purposeful, selfhood, tract writers were involved in the same negotiations about religious female identity as women missionaries like the letter-writing Wesleyan wives. And in depicting the deaths of 'holy children', tract writers were also representing female missionary sacrifice – which had complex implications for them, as missionary writers.

Religious tract fiction had an enormous influence on the literature and culture of the Victorian period, as many scholars have shown. Brown has argued that its use of sentiment, alongside its development of fictional narrative and characterisation, influenced Victorian novelists, including Charles Dickens.[11] Moreover, Cutt's study of late-Victorian autobiographies revealed that tract fiction had an extremely wide readership: middle-class children were every bit as likely as working-class children to have read religious tract fiction.[12] Whatever their class or location, whether their reading habits were religious or secular, most young women in the Victorian period would have been, directly or indirectly, influenced by religious tract fiction and its presentation of missionary femininity.

This chapter explores some of the religious fiction young women would have encountered in the Victorian period. I start by examining fictional tracts by Martha Sherwood and Hesba Stretton (the pseudonym used by the writer Sarah Smith), to show how the 'holy child' character in these women's writing symbolically took on the role of the female missionary. I move on to explore the treatment of child and governess characters in Sherwood's tracts and novellas, and also in those of Dinah Craik, to demonstrate how these writers influenced the development of a literary form of missionary femininity for Victorian women to emulate.

Martha Sherwood and Hesba Stretton: Missionary Writing and the 'Holy Child' Character

As tract writers, both Martha Sherwood and Hesba Stretton were fulfilling the missionary duty they would have felt as Christian women at this time. Sherwood publicly associated herself with the missionary cause when, in a piece for *The Sunday at Home*, she wrote about her personal acquaintance with the famous missionary, Henry Martyn.[13] Evangelicals throughout the empire would have seen Sherwood and Stretton's tracts, especially those for the Religious Tract Society, as carrying out the same missionary work as Martyn's. These tracts were used widely in Sunday schools, and some, such as Sherwood's *The History of Little Henry and his Bearer* (1814) or Stretton's *Jessica's First Prayer* (1867), were bestsellers; their descriptions in publishers' catalogues and the attractive presentation of many of the editions show they were popular as prizes and gifts. The tracts were also used by missionaries overseas; Sherwood's *Little Henry* was translated into numerous languages, and Stretton notably met a missionary and a man from Liberia who knew her books.[14]

Two million copies of *Jessica's First Prayer* had been printed by the time of Stretton's death in 1911.[15]

Martha Sherwood started writing tracts during her time as a British army wife in India. Converted by one of the army chaplains, between 1805 and 1816, she carried out informal missionary work providing religious instruction to the children in the army camp.[16] Sherwood's experience of the mission field alerted her to the sinfulness of many of her countrymen; she was shocked by the conditions and the standard of behaviour in the military camp, where families lived together in communal rooms, and drunkenness, blasphemy and other immoralities were common.[17] She found the army children (who would have included the mixed-race children of privates and their Indian mistresses) ill-mannered, wild and godless. Even the civilian colonials she was aware of, despite being of a higher class, were frequently not leading Christian lives and were bringing up their children in the habits of religious infidelity, or leaving them to the care of non-Christian Indian servants. The stark 'heathen' environment of India, with its ever-present threat of death, highlighted the urgency of the Christian mission for Sherwood; however, she was aware that religious infidelity was equally persistent back home in Britain. Therefore, on her return from India, Sherwood continued her missionary work by writing religious tract fiction for children across the British Empire.

Hesba Stretton, although mostly now forgotten, was well-known in her day. Her background was evangelical: her father was at one time an apprentice with the evangelical publishing house, Houlston and Son (which published many of Sherwood's works), and her mother was a strict Methodist. Stretton herself qualified as a governess and taught in Sunday school. Living in Manchester, Stretton became a member of Reverend Alexander McLaren's congregation at the Union Chapel and came to a belief that it was the individual's Christian duty to bring about social reform.[18] This belief led to her working alongside Dr. Barnardo and Angela Burdett Coutts, investigating the conditions of the slums for the Society for the Prevention of Cruelty to Children.[19] As Suzanne Rickard has argued, Stretton used her writing as another way to carry out her missionary social work in this arena.[20] As she produced tracts set in gritty urban landscapes familiar to the children she was seeking to educate and convert, she exposed slum life to her adult readers and raised the profile of women's domestic mission work.

Martha Sherwood's writings are especially significant in that they provided the pattern that later tract writers followed. Scholars have noted that Sherwood's literary style, as well as influencing the Victorian novel, was important in improving the attractiveness of tracts, and developing the form to its full potential for educating and entertaining child readers. Scholars have also acknowledged how Sherwood's literary development of religious fiction in part stemmed from her evangelical religion; it was her desire to depict the vitality of a truly Christian life, along with her evangelical emphasis on the inner life of the child, that led to more lively and rounded child characters than those that had been found in children's literature up to this point.[21] Sherwood can also be seen as contributing to the development of the Victorian cult of domesticity and the domestic novel.[22] However, many of the settings of Sherwood's tracts are decidedly non-domestic – for example, schools and army camps – requiring missionary characters to domesticate them, which suggests that Sherwood saw domesticity as an important acquirement for civilisation, rather than an intrinsic trait of Victorian women. Indeed, Sherwood's unflinching representation of heathen environments and eschatological subject matter align her far more with missionary biography than the domestic novel. Significantly, as Brown has noted, Sherwood established the conventions for tract fiction's depiction of the redeeming child and their death.[23] These conventions, as we will see, were very similar to those of female missionary biography.

One of Sherwood's first, and most influential child characters appeared in her bestselling tract, *The History of Little Henry and his Bearer*. Beginning the tale as an orphan in India, 'Little Henry' is adopted by a worldly English woman, who becomes known as his 'mamma', although she neglects him and leaves him entirely to the care of his 'bearer', the Hindu servant Boosy. When a pious woman from England comes to visit his mamma, she finds Henry to be, to her dismay, a five-year-old unable to speak English, on the verandah with the servants, 'left among people who know not God'.[24] More than just ignorant of Christianity, Sherwood portrays Henry as inherently sinful: 'He did not consider a lie as sinful; nor feel ashamed of stealing' (p. 30). The visitor takes Henry from this state of original sin and converts him to Christianity. When she leaves him, he undertakes to convert his bearer. Most of the rest of the tale dramatises Henry's efforts to provide religious instruction to Boosy, as his health begins to fail. As he comes to the realisation that he is dying, his instruction gains in power and, on his deathbed, he converts his mamma and gains Boosy's agreement that he will give up his caste, and convert to Christianity.

Sherwood uses Henry's youth and his premature death to give pathos to her tale of a child missionary, as did those who wrote about the short lives and deaths of many missionary women.[25] Sherwood emphasises Henry's lack of real power, and the dangerous situation he places himself in, when Mr Smith, one of Henry's mamma's only Christian friends, describes his efforts with Boosy: 'A little creature, who eight years ago had not breathed the breath of life, is endeavouring to impart divine knowledge to the heathen' (p. 86). The magnitude of the task, and its difficulty – Henry is 'endeavouring' fruitlessly at this point – makes Henry seem in comparison even smaller and weaker. Mr Smith quotes from the Bible to further dignify Henry's work, using a verse commonly used when discussing female missionaries: ' "God hath chosen the weak things of the world to confound the things which are mighty," 1 Corinthians i. 27' (p. 86). Mr Smith also explains the reason why child (and women) missionaries should not aim to do more than read the Bible to converts: they

Figure 2.1 'His eye, as he passed the door, caught little Henry sitting on the mat...', *The History of Little Henry and his Bearer Boosy* (London: Houlston and Stoneman, 1854). © British Library Board. All Rights Reserved/ Bridgeman Images.

should not 'argue and dispute' because 'Satan [...] may put words into his mouth which may puzzle you; so that your faith may be shaken while his remains unchanged' (p. 95). Instead, they should trust to the 'Word of God' in the Bible and back this up with prayers – as, indeed, did the young woman who converted Henry.

It is in death, though, that Henry proves most powerful in converting others. Scholars have argued that literary depictions of child deaths were largely concerned with sentimentalising and blurring the reality of these tragic events for parents and children alike.[26] However, as we saw in Chapter 1, the deathbed scene was one of the most important parts of the female missionary narrative; writers suggested that depicting the missionary's passive suffering would inspire readers to convert and support the mission. Sherwood transposes this missionary scene into her children's tract with the same motive. In a manner reminiscent of the female missionary biographer J. D. Knowles, Sherwood self-consciously defends her focus on Henry's death:

> There are but few persons who love to meditate upon scenes of death, and too many are only able to view the gloomy side of them, instead of following, *by the eye of faith*, the glorious progress of the departing saint.
>
> (pp. 132–33)

Her defence is didactic, arguing that those who would criticise her are deficient in Christian understanding, and describing how the supernatural vision of evangelical belief can transform death into a triumphant act of transcendence on the part of the saint.[27]

Little Henry enacts a perfect Christian death: self-sacrificing and resigned, which is shown to inspire those around him. Mrs Baron, the woman who first converted Henry, in turn learns from him to resign herself to God's will:

> 'Oh my child! my dear, dear child' she said, 'I cannot bear it! I cannot part with you yet!' The poor little boy was affected, but he gently reproved her, saying, 'If you love me, you will rejoice because I go to my father'.
>
> (p. 129)

Sherwood ensures the emotion of a child's death, the anguish of those who love them, is fully communicated, while preserving the saintliness of the child's attitude towards the event. Boosy is so impressed by the event, and so 'sorrowful' that his 'little sahib' is dying, that he is taken out of himself, repeating Henry's prayer for his soul while 'scarcely knowing what he was doing' (p. 121), and exclaiming 'I wish I could believe in the Lord Jesus Christ!' (p. 123).

Henry also uses his dying state to influence Boosy and his mamma. When he first realises that he is dying, he uses this projected loss to add power to his conversion efforts: ' "O, I wish! I wish I could persuade you to love the Lord Jesus Christ!" And then Henry, getting up, went to Boosy, and sat down upon his knee, and begged him to be a Christian' (p. 79). The childishly affectionate action of sitting on his bearer's knee adds pathos to his simple plea that Boosy convert in order to follow him to heaven. Meanwhile, when Henry's mother visits him on his deathbed, something indescribable occurs. The event is characterised as intensely private – it is not dramatised – and the narrator reports:

> Nobody knows the particulars of their conversation [...]. She came out of his room with her eyes swelled with crying [...]. From that time she never gave her mind so entirely to the world as she had formerly done, but became a more serious character, and daily read little Henry's bible.
>
> (pp. 131–2)

Henry's death, his resignation, selflessness and (presumably) eloquent final words represent the ideal missionary sacrifice of self in the cause of effecting conversions.

Indeed, Sherwood suggests her character and his sacrifice will be responsible for many more conversions than those described in her tale, as she explicitly calls on her child readers to 'remember Henry L – and *go and do likewise.* Luke x. 37' (p. 138), with this Biblical instruction to take on a missionary role forming some of the last words of the tract. When describing Little Henry's conversations with Boosy about the Bible, Sherwood suggests that more informal missionaries, such as children or women, might be more suitable to convert those of the servant class:

> Often he would stop him to explain to him what he was reading; and very beautiful sometimes were the remarks which he made, and better suited to the understanding of his bearer than those of an older or more learned person would have been.
>
> (pp. 116–7)

In addition to the 'weak' being given the power to convert by God, the child's simple faith is shown to be most suitable for converting others.[28] Child readers are therefore encouraged that they can be missionaries in their own small ways at home – even if all that is possible for them is an influential Christian death.[29]

Over fifty years after Sherwood's *Little Henry*, Hesba Stretton produced a similar missionary child character in her bestselling *Jessica's First Prayer*. First published in 1866 in serial form for the *Sunday at Home*, this tract tells the story of little Jessica, an appealing but ignorant street urchin, who comes into contact with a religious coffee seller and chapel caretaker, Mr Daniel, from whom she learns about Christianity. After her conversion, she converts others through the perfect simplicity of her faith, especially on her deathbed.

Initially, little Jessica resembles child characters from Stretton's other urban tales, or indeed, Sherwood's Little Henry at the beginning of his tale: 'no better than a heathen we send missionaries to'.[30] As well as being called a 'heathen', Jessica's poverty associates her physically with less developed peoples and even animals; the tale starts with her looking at a coffee stall with 'a gaze as hungry as that of a mouse which has been drawn by famine into a trap', and attention is drawn to her 'two bare little feet curling up from the damp pavement'.[31] Her animal nature and her bare feet make her strange to young readers wealthy enough themselves at least to attend Sunday school and make donations of their pennies to the collection, but also designate her as a case for their pity and charity, recognisable from sermons about the 'poor savages' across the seas. More than poor, Jessica is ignorant of religious morality: the coffee stall owner Daniel finds her attitude to good and evil amusing, reflecting wryly, 'the child's notion of goodness. He made good coffee and the police left him alone!' (p. 20). She also seems to be inherently sinful; when Daniel tempts Jessica by dropping a penny on the floor, she instinctively steals it.

However, Jessica surprises Daniel by showing an innate sense of sin as, with tears of remorse, she returns the penny. He reflects that she might actually be more moral than him: 'I never could have done it myself' (p. 26). For Jessica is typical of Stretton's urchins, who, although they are ignorant heathens in need of missionaries, are also innately good and, once educated about Christ, quickly become more holy than those engaged in organised religion.[32] Men who act to save the children in these works are shown to be in need of the child's simple religion to balance their more hard-hearted and dogmatic efforts. Daniel not only pre-judges Jessica, he also shoos her away from the chapel, exclaiming:

> This isn't a place for such as you. It's for ladies and gentlemen; [...] they'd be shocked to see a ragged little heathen like you. [...] We couldn't do with such a little heathen, with no shoes or bonnet on.
> (pp. 33–5)

The irony of a 'heathen' (repeated by Stretton for emphasis) forbidden to enter the chapel which could save her, and the immediate juxtaposition of the middle-class congregation in 'rustling [...] silk dresses' (p. 36), is heavily enough drawn so that young people who had been paying attention to their Bible would understand Stretton's criticism. Indeed, in this tale and even more in Stretton's sequel, *Jessica's Mother* (also published in the *Sunday at Home* during 1866), the simplicity of a child's religion is not only seen as useful to convert those who might struggle with more theological discourse, but as a more effective route to salvation generally.[33] In *Jessica's Mother*, Daniel and Jessica's minister is punished for caring more about making intellectual sermons than asking about the state of his congregants' souls, when he suffers a stroke that leaves him unable to do more than teach 'a simple congregation simple truths' in a small country chapel.[34]

Jessica is more than an innately 'holy child', though – she is a female missionary. When she is struck down by illness, the depiction of her passive, uncomplaining acceptance of death follows the pattern of deathbed scenes in female missionary biography as much as Sherwood's *Little Henry*. Her sacrifice is shown to have an effect on the souls around her; while Daniel is afraid that Jessica will die, like Henry's friends and relations, he is made more afraid of his own likely fate, reflecting, 'You're more fit for heaven than I ever was in my life' (p. 81). Jessica's innocent spirituality shows him how his reliance on the forms of religion has allowed him to become avaricious, and her dying causes him to repent, especially as Jessica's 'final' words are focused on his salvation: 'Jessica, who was light-headed and delirious, but in the wanderings of her thoughts and words often spoke to God, and prayed for her Mr Dan'el' (pp. 84–5). In addition to this self-forgetfulness on her deathbed, Stretton stresses Jessica's self-negation to the point that it becomes clear that it is not Jessica herself who speaks to Daniel. Jessica quotes the minister: ' "But you know what the minister often says," murmured Jessica, "Here is love, not that we loved God, but that He loved us, and sent his Son to be the propitiation for our sins"' (p. 81). Even quotation does not fully explain how a dying child like Jessica, who still refers to Daniel as Dan'el, can pronounce 'propitiation'. It is more probable that, like female missionary characters in mid-century biographies, Jessica is being presented by Stretton as a vessel through which God is speaking.[35]

Interestingly, Jessica's behaviour during her illness is not altogether passive. Jessica's efforts to pray despite her obvious weakness are described with exaggerated pathos: 'she lifted her wasted fingers to rest upon the bowed head beside her, while she shut her eyes and shaded them with her other weak hand. "Our father," she said in a faint whisper' (pp. 89–90). The adjectives 'wasted', 'weak' and 'faint' emphasise Jessica's weakness as a female missionary and the passivity of her method of conversion. However, the over-description of Jessica's actions here is also caused by the need to depict the tension of power and weakness within the missionary character: one hand sentimentally shades her eyes, but the other hand rests upon the bowed head of her male convert, brought to a position of supplication in front of the diminutive female missionary. Also, the evangelicalism Stretton portrays is the 'religion of the heart', which was developing in the 1850s and 1860s through the dissemination of missionary and tract writings such as this.[36] While Sherwood's Henry reproves Mrs Baron for her emotional reaction to his imminent death, the importance of emotion within Christianity is stressed in *Jessica's First Prayer*. Daniel's greatest sin is the lack of feeling in his faith, which he admits in the extremis of the deathbed scene: 'I've heard it so often that I don't feel it' (pp. 81–82). Jessica's (and Stretton's) stress on the Christian message of love suggests female missionaries' ability to intervene in theology.

Figure 2.2 '"Our Father," she said, in a faint whisper', *Jessica's First Prayer*. © British Library Board. All Rights Reserved/Bridgeman Images.

The greatest departure in Stretton's tract from conventional depictions of female missionaries in the mid-century is that Jessica does not in fact die but is spared in order to continue her conversion work with Daniel and middle-class society. It is unlikely that Stretton contrived this happy ending simply as a concession for the sake of her young readers, who would have been used to child obituary literature.[37] More likely Stretton is arguing, like Jemima Thompson and the Wesleyan wives (see Chapter 1), that conversion work is more effective if the female missionary is allowed to continue her work rather than sacrificing herself. Jessica's acceptance of her death sentence is in fact conditional: 'Our Father [...] I asked you to let me come home to heaven; but if Mr Daniel wants me, please to let me stay a little longer' (p. 90). While she has little to lose in life, and everything to gain in heaven, she passively accepts death. When a new life becomes visible – that of continuing as Daniel's adoptive daughter and saviour, softening his heart and religion by providing him with a domestic, familial life – Jessica actively asks to be spared for this alternative life, and God's plan for her is hastily re-interpreted. This happy ending and home on earth for the female missionary, while running counter to the evangelical message of repentance and passivity as the means to salvation and rewards in heaven, creates a far more attractive version of the missionary for child readers than did Little Henry's headstone.

Both Sherwood and Stretton establish their child missionaries as symbolic female missionaries, possessing powerful agency, even (or especially) on their deathbeds. However, associating female missionaries with child obituary literature, while bringing meaning to a child's death in the form of heroic sacrifice, ran the risk of infantilising the missionary character. While, like Sherwood, Stretton marshalled the elements and effects of child obituary literature and female missionary biography for *Jessica's First Prayer*, her avoidance of death for her heroine was an important departure from the form and significant for the presentation of the female missionary in the later part of the nineteenth century. Meanwhile, Sherwood went on to develop another female missionary character alongside the 'holy child' missionary, that of the governess.

From 'Holy Child' to Missionary Governess

Sherwood's development in the direction of the realist novel has been seen as her abandoning evangelicalism in favour of making her work more literary;[38] however, many of her later stories continue to include religious elements, such as the female missionary narrative. In fact, Sherwood's experiments with literary form led to some of the most significant developments in the presentation of the female missionary, as can be seen in her governess novel *Caroline Mordaunt* (1835).[39] This work is predominantly a comedy; in picaresque fashion, it presents the (mis)fortunes of the eponymous character and narrator as she struggles to fulfil the position of governess to a number of difficult families.

However, the novel is also a religious Bildungsroman, in that it provides a narrative of the governess's conversion and subsequent missionary work. It also contains the story of a redeeming child, Emily, and ends with the capitalised message, 'GOD IS LOVE'.[40] The more novelistic techniques that Sherwood uses in this text enables her to adapt the female missionary narrative in a number of ways.

The story of the 'holy child' Emily conforms in most respects to the conventions of the redemptive child narrative as established by Sherwood in *Little Henry*. Like Stretton's Jessica, Emily preaches a simple, spiritual faith, which eventually converts Caroline:

> It was long before she could make me understand this simple truth, - for it is a simple truth, though never to be understood by the natural heart. [...] I had never before seen an instance of spiritual teaching of this kind. [...] I became an entire convert to her way of thinking.
> (pp. 161–3)

Again, like Jessica, the child saint is imbued with a divine spirit: the 'natural' heart cannot understand, let alone preach this message, and there is no evidence of religious training in Emily's background. At times, Emily is not even allowed human form in Caroline's recollection: 'This last fair creature was as a bright vision glancing for a few moments on the senses' (p. 145). More like a spirit from heaven than a human child, she is sent to convert Caroline and then return to her heavenly home.

It is in the character of the governess Caroline that we can see Sherwood's move towards a more developed characterisation of a female missionary character. While Emily is sacrificed, Caroline is not. After her conversion, Caroline takes on a missionary role towards her charges and, though she uses the story of her converting child saint in her method of conversion, this is a far more active method of converting than passive self-sacrifice. She also experiences fulfilling emotion and ends happily married to a clergyman. Unlike in most missionary texts, the subject's story is not just used to illustrate a call to missionary action, rather the emphasis is on the life and religious experience of Sherwood's heroine. The novel's first-person narration means that the emotions experienced by a female missionary are more clearly explored than ever before. Sherwood's bifurcation of the female missionary role, into the redemptive child Emily on one hand and Caroline on the other, enables her to retain the power of the child missionary's sacrifice while claiming an active and more developed subjectivity for her adult female missionary.

Strong emotions are a major part of Caroline's conversion, and these religious feelings are portrayed as fulfilling in their own way for the unmarried Caroline. The conversion relationship, between Caroline and Emily, is described in the most detailed episode of the entire novel. While Caroline narrates most of the story from a position in the future present, using hindsight and experience to draw out the lessons of her life, for this episode, the narrative slows, human drama and emotion take centre stage, and the distance between Caroline the narrator and Caroline the character narrows to produce a sense of emotional urgency.

The two are brought together at a school, when Emily's father offers to take her home, along with her favourite teacher to be her governess. Caroline is working at the school and is immediately chosen by Emily to accompany her home, because she knows that Caroline has been reading the Bible to children in her bed chamber:

> Opening my arms, the lovely child rushed into them, and yielded to a violent fit of tears; then recovering herself and clasping her hands with beautiful earnestness, she said, 'Then my prayer is granted, and I shall have you to love me, and to read the Bible to me'.
>
> (p. 141)

The outward expression of affection and other rational, controlled sentiments was approved of by evangelicals and was common in tracts.[41] However, there is almost an excess of feeling in this story; passionate love, and even the physical signs of this love between Caroline and Emily, saturate this section of the novel. Caroline and Emily are often in each other's arms, and there is even secret hand-holding in the family coach (p. 145). Emily's tears in the quotation above are described as 'violent', requiring her to recover herself. Possession characterises this relationship, from Emily's declaration 'I shall have you to love me', to the moment the child expires in Caroline's arms as '*my* lovely one' (p. 165, my emphasis). The relationship also leads to dispossession on Caroline's part, of herself and wits; she notes that the child's claiming of her 'to love me', and the manner of this claiming, left her disordered, unable even to read, the child had so 'thrown my mind' (p. 142). Caroline's attachment to Emily is described as exceptional, as she later says 'no child of my own, ever since, has been dearer to me than was that lovely one' (p. 143). And the child's last words are to her governess rather than her relations (p. 165). Being part of a conversion creates a bond stronger than that of blood between the girl and the woman, and they possess each other in this fulfilling relationship.

Because Sherwood is clear that Emily is a child saint, a vessel for God to work through, the passion instilled by Emily the child in Caroline the woman is given greater solemnity and status: it is love for God, elicited by and bestowed through his vessel, dictated by His plan for Caroline's salvation and future work. The lack of agency here on Caroline's part is seen through the reversal of roles – the child becomes the teacher – and her experience that 'my heart had been drawn forcibly toward her' (p. 143), suggesting she had no choice but to follow. The power of this episode entirely changes Caroline's character and imbues her with an active missionary spirit to go forth and convert others to God in her role as a missionary governess.

As we can see, then, Sherwood's governess stories could be just as religious as her early tracts for children. Moreover, Sherwood's development of narrative technique in *Caroline Mordaunt* led to interesting characterisations of the female missionary, in that she was able to split, or double, the female missionary character. She displaced the sentimental emotion of the deathbed onto the child missionary character and portrayed the governess enjoying a far less self-sacrificing and more emotionally fulfilling missionary life. However, the emotional charge of the text remained rooted in the death of the 'holy child', reflecting the struggle to portray the female missionary life in Victorian fiction without including this sort of sacrifice – whether it was displaced from the female missionary, as in Sherwood's work, or avoided at last minute, as for Stretton's little Jessica. If this was the case among tract writers, how, then, did more mainstream, 'literary' writers, such as Dinah Craik, deal with the self-sacrificial female missionary character who was infiltrating mid-century representations of ideal femininity?

Dinah Craik's Governesses and Heroic Missionary Sacrifice

Although she was overlooked for most of the twentieth century, Dinah Craik was a popular writer in her own time and one who was praised by contemporaries for her 'high character' and 'moral influence'.[42] While Craik's upbringing was somewhat turbulent – her dissenter father was in and out of prison and the asylum during her early childhood – her mother was a 'staunch Anglican', and Craik's writing was sufficiently religiously orthodox for evangelical audiences.[43] She wrote for the Religious Tract Society and, by the end of the century, like Stretton and Sherwood, her works were widely available as Sunday school prizes.[44]

Even when writing novels, Craik was explicit that the woman writer had a missionary role. In her 1850 novel *Olive*, through the persona of a confident, third-person narrator, Craik expresses her interpretation of the missionary purpose of the novelist:

> Authors, who feel the solemnity of their calling, cannot suppress the truth that is within them. Having put their hands to the plough, they may not turn aside, nor look either to the right or the left. They must go straight on, as the inward voice impels; and He who seeth their hearts will guide them aright.[45]

In her anachronistic, Biblical expression, Craik here strikingly resembles nonconformist female preachers, as she characterises her writing as an inescapable, solemn calling to express God's truth.[46] Her reference to the 'inward voice' suggests an evangelical understanding of the conscience as an aspect of the Holy Spirit, prompting the novelist to communicate 'the [Godly] truth within' her. Though the simplicity of her language seems to approach the banal – 'nor look either to the right or the left' – this is in fact a reference to the book of Samuel, where one of David's men, Asahel, refuses to turn and fight those on either side, and instead runs straight into the spear of Abner.[47] Craik, then, while employing the accepted agricultural metaphor of ploughing for her missionary work (suggesting noble toil and faith in the harvest), is also mobilising the imagery of militant Christianity and martyrdom for women writers. Her fervour is in part a self-defence against evangelical critics, who she fears will accuse her of irreverence for using the novel for spiritual purposes. She depicts the positions of these critics as untenable within their own moral framework, when she rhetorically demands, 'human life without God! Who will dare tell us we should paint *that*?'.[48] Sally Mitchell has argued that, in *Olive*, Craik was demonstrating how female novelists could use the 'spiritual authority' granted them by virtue of their gender to respond to the religious doubt of novels in the 1840s.[49] I would add that Craik's governess stories of the 1850s show that the female figure of spiritual authority that Craik developed for governesses and novelists was highly inflected by the mid-century female missionary character.

In her stories, *The Half-Caste* (1851) and *Bread Upon the Waters* (1852), Craik follows Sherwood's example and uses the governess as a domestic proxy for the female missionary. Craik's works, though, explored the missionary woman in far more psychological depth than was possible in tract form. Using first-person narration for both stories, Craik attempts to imagine how her governess heroines can inhabit the self-sacrificial missionary role in a way that would allow them the agency, authority, and even the heroism, of female missionaries such as Mrs Judson, as well as the emotional fulfilment that Sherwood's work suggested was possible. However, as I will show, the psychological realism of her stories also reveals how aspiring to the heroic self-sacrificing nature of the female missionary could be highly challenging for mere mortal women.

In terms of their basic plots, *The Half-Caste* and *Bread Upon the Waters* are very similar. Both stories have heroines (Cassandra in *The Half-Caste* and Felicia in *Bread Upon the Waters*) who embark upon governess work that quickly takes on a missionary flavour. Their charges Zillah and Therese are both in some way foreign, and must be educated, civilised and converted to become suitable English wives. This education work involves diligent labour, devotion and even acts of heroism on the part of the governesses. While their charges marry, the governess heroines sacrifice any hopes for marriage themselves, ending instead as dependants in others' families, taking comfort in compensatory relationships with others' children. As Mitchell has argued, these stories attempt to adapt the form of the novel to tell stories based not on love and marriage for the central character, but instead on resignation and self-sacrifice for the sake of others.[50] In other words, Craik was endeavouring to adapt the form of the novel to tell the female missionary's story of her life and work.

The first of Craik's stories, *The Half-Caste*, is perhaps most successful in portraying the positive, fulfilling aspects of a female missionary's vocation. While there is a conventional narrative of love and marriage within this story, and a plot full of twists and secrets, it is the process of Zillah's conversion that actually structures the tale, and the relationship between convert and missionary that provides its emotional heart.

The faith of Craik and her heroine Cassandra that the 'half-caste', 'heathen' Zillah can be converted is part of Craik's engagement with mid-century missionary discourse. Zillah's initial appearance is not encouraging:

> With some surprise I found her a half-caste girl – with an olive complexion, full Hindu lips, and eyes very black and bright. She was untidily dressed, which looked worse since she was almost a woman; though her dull heavy face had the stupidity of an ultra stupid child.[51]

Cora Kaplan has noted how Craik's Zillah resembles Charlotte Brontë's Bertha in *Jane Eyre*;[52] she is also similar to the village school children that Jane Eyre teaches as part of her preparation for a possible missionary future with St John Rivers. 'Heathens' are described as physically different from missionaries, their heavy, lumpen stupidity emphasising their savage animality in contrast to their civilisers' more cerebral humanity. In Zillah's case, the miscegenation of her heredity is linked with the implication that her birth was also illegitimate.

However, it turns out that this rumour of Zillah's illegitimacy is untrue: Zillah is in fact an heiress whom the family are trying to keep in a state of ignorance in order to gain her fortune when she comes of age. In the same way, her racial difference is also chimerical and can be overcome by education and conversion. It is her villainous family who take a racist approach to her nature; they treat her like a member of the servant class, and Zillah's uncle's description of her makes use of contemporary racialist ideas: 'her modicum of intellect is not greater than generally belongs to her mother's race' (p. 340). In contrast, Cassandra resolves to educate her equally, alongside her cousins, and is rewarded for her faith by Zillah developing into a perfect English wife.

Cora Kaplan and Juliet Shields have drawn attention to the scientific and social dialogue about race in the 1840s and 1850s, both arguing that Craik's work argues against the racism that was becoming established by polygenist race theorists such as Robert Knox.[53] Craik's description of Zillah certainly draws more on developmental thinking about civilisation and race, in that she is depicted more as a child who can grow up, rather than an animal that is irredeemably Other. Importantly, in voicing her opposition to polygenist racial theory in this text, we can see that Craik was specifically drawing on missionary discourse that, necessarily, held that the races were all part of the same Family of Man, as a basis to believe in the possibility of their salvation.[54] This discourse, which would largely have been taken for granted by Sherwood and her audience, was necessary for the continuation of the mission movement, and for the noble work of female missionaries. Therefore, Craik is affirming her evangelical commitment to monogenist racial theory and the mission movement, through her narrative of a governess's faithful working towards her 'heathen' charge's conversion.

Although Cassandra uses racial ideas in her judgement of the girl's character, like missionaries, she focuses more on the sins that can be remedied: Zillah is overly passionate, lazy and always untidy. Cassandra's faith in Zillah's ability to convert is supported by Providence; when Zillah's life is threatened by illness, Cassandra nurses her back to health, noting that 'Poor Zillah did not die. She was saved for Heaven's strange purposes' (p. 346). For heaven to save a heathen is strong evidence that the girl could be saved in soul as well as body. Ultimately, Cassandra is proved right, and the effects of Zillah's conversion even appear as physical changes. After the crisis of her illness is past, Cassandra reflects that Zillah 'looked almost pretty and the light of the August moon so spiritualised her face' (p. 348). The August moon symbolises that it is nearly harvest-time for Cassandra's 'good seed', and the fact that Zillah has become 'quite pretty' implies that the conversion activity is beginning to bear fruit. Eventually, after proving her conversion by nursing Cassandra when she falls ill, Zillah is described as having grown up 'beautiful in mind as well as in body' and is seen as an equal – her face alongside that of Cassandra's in the mirror – or sometimes a 'daughter', of whom Cassandra says she is 'proud' (p. 362). Only Zillah's eyes remain as indicators of her previous heathen otherness, but these are now described as 'Oriental' (p. 362) and attract Mr Sutherland to become her husband. Cassandra, the missionary governess, has successfully educated, civilised and converted her 'half-caste' 'heathen' charge.

In addition to displaying faith in the female missionary's task of conversion, Craik portrays her heroine as experiencing a fulfilling life as a missionary, enjoying her professional work and success. For example, Cassandra refers to her nursing of Zillah in a way that stresses the professional and effective nature of her work. Though Kaplan notes that Craik saw nursing as an example of 'moral heroism',[55] it came to form a highly professional part of women's work in the mission field. Though expressing pride in missionary work was in tension with the expected self-effacement of the missionary, Craik's Cassandra, like professional missionaries in the field, finds ways to do this. She makes use of little phrases that suggest a complex relationship between the power of God and the power of the missionary, and even elide these two powers. When Zillah is saved from illness, Cassandra states that 'under Heaven, my care had saved her' (p. 348). Though heaven here has a part to play, the syntax of the sentence leaves the relationship between heaven and Cassandra's actions ambiguous.

Cassandra's most active and heroic missionary work is depicted in an episode where she saves Zillah from temptation, in the shape of a possible elopement with her cousin. Cassandra is certain that the situation is grave: Zillah's soul hangs in the balance, and this incident is portrayed by Craik with dramatic detail. The battle for Zillah between her cousin and her governess is depicted as an almost physical struggle, with Cassandra having to bravely face down the soldier cousin and his accomplice. Cassandra emerges as a heroic woman, who triumphs through her own power; she knows that 'the sole hope must lie in my own presence of mind, my influence over Zillah and my appeal to her sense of honour and affection' (p. 358). These things are all her powers, rather than heaven's, and stress her own agency in the salvation of Zillah. It is only when she has been successful and the crisis is over, that she thanks heaven. The resilience and strength of Cassandra in this episode is reminiscent of Knowles's heroic Mrs Judson.

In addition to professional fulfilment, Cassandra is also depicted as enjoying emotionally fulfilling relationships with young people in her care. More prominently, she enjoys an emotional conversion experience with Zillah, which is very like the conversion relationship of Sherwood's Caroline and Emily in *Caroline Mordaunt*. As well as taking pains in the classroom, Cassandra 'lures' Zillah into conversations in her bedroom at night. The language Cassandra uses refers to religious conversion: she wants to 'awaken' something in Zillah, and she wants to 'get at the girl's heart' rather than her mind (p. 343). The effect of this is that Zillah begins to develop a moral consciousness centred on her governess: 'This seemed her only consciousness of right or wrong – pleasing or displeasing me. At all events it argued well for my influence over her and her power of being guided by the affections' (p. 343). This use of emotional influence to convert recalls Clara Balfour's description of the ideal female missionary. Though it is Zillah rather than Cassandra who is rewarded with marriage to Mr Sutherland, Craik attempts to portray this as a happy ending for Cassandra too. Cassandra's first-person narration stresses the fulfilment she enjoyed in her missionary role of governess and concludes with her happiness that she now lives as a dependant in the Sutherland family home, helping to look after Zillah's daughter.

In many ways, *The Half-Caste* perhaps paints rather too rosy a picture of the inner life of a missionary governess. In particular, Craik does not fully explore her emotional experience of self-sacrifice, especially when it came to romantic love. In her *Bread Upon the Waters*, published a year later, this can hardly be said to be the case. In this story, Craik focuses in even greater detail on the governess missionary herself, and her inner life. While *The Half-Caste* glosses over the day-to-day difficulties of the governess, these struggles are part of a reformulation of the heroic female missionary character in *Bread Upon the Waters*, as Craik explores the character's suffering, sacrifice and nobility. This was probably in part because the story was produced to raise funds for the Governesses' Benevolent Institution, which would have been pleased with Craik's characterisation of their oft-maligned profession as heroic missionary work.[56]

Craik again establishes the missionary context of her tale by confronting her governess heroine Felicia with a foreign charge. Felicia is at first afraid of the half-French Thérèse, who is 'A very big girl [...] taller than myself, and with twice as much spirit. She really frightened me with her fierce black eyes and her foreign manner'.[57] Again, the suggestions of savagery lurk in the descriptors 'big' and 'fierce'. Another aspect of this text that establishes a missionary connection is its form. While *The Half-Caste* is similar to Sherwood's tract-like novel, *Caroline Mordaunt* in its first-person narration from a future of secure happiness, the form of *Bread Upon the Waters* recalls missionary biography. The story is told through the extracts of a fictional diary, with the present-day Felicia acting as editor as she comments on, and explains, her past-self's words and adds information to her story. As with missionary biography, the immediacy of the diary or letter form adds to the effect of psychological realism, encouraging the reader's sympathy.

Unlike Cassandra, and in a departure from the dominant female missionary character, Felicia finds the sacrifices of her profession very difficult. Even the choice to become a governess in the first place is seen as a sacrifice. Following her widowed father's remarriage, Felicia feels compelled by her conscience to leave home, as her father's second wife is exerting an immoral influence on her younger brothers. She therefore makes the moral choice to sacrifice her comfortable domestic life, including her social status and her hopes of marriage to family friend Mr Redwood, and becomes a governess to support herself and her brothers. Craik depicts Cassandra as feeling the sacrifice of living as a governess keenly. In her diary, Felicia often refers to having lost her social position and admits that asking for her salary is painful for her pride. She finds the work to be hard; at times, she compares her situation to wearing heavy chains. Like missionaries, she misses society and suffers feelings of loneliness. (Interestingly, at this time in her life, substitute relationships, such as the one between governess and pupil, do not satisfy her need for companionship.) In fact, the depth of her suffering over a period of two years is portrayed as so unimaginable that it is impossible to represent; Craik's older and wiser narrator explains that she burnt her journal entries for those years because one who can

> Weed his life, or his life's outward evidence, of all gloomy, erring and hurtful memorials, is as much bound to do it, as he is bound to root out from his garden, all things that might prove painful or injurious to those that come after him.
>
> (p. 47)

Like the missionary biographer J. D. Knowles, Craik's narrator is aware that the full depiction of religious crisis could be spiritually harmful to readers.

Nevertheless, Craik's preservation of the evidence of struggle shows her faith in the power of even fictional biography for teaching the heroism of missionary sacrifice. In the same way that the early missionaries Ann Judson and Harriet Newell were seen in their biographies wrestling with their decisions to make the sacrifice of becoming a female missionary, the depiction of Felicia's heroic struggle, and her older self's passive resignation to God's will, enables Craik to paint the missionary governess's sacrifice as more noble because of its difficulty. Eventually, Felicia seems to revel in the nobility of her profession, describing a governess's life as one in which 'every governess has it in her power to make herself and [...] all her fraternity, reverenced and honourable in the sight of the world' (p. 56). And Felicia's old love interest Mr Redwood rhetorically asks:

> And what is more honourable than a governess when she is a lady by birth, or at least by education. [...] What more noble than a woman who devotes her whole life to the sowing of good seed, the fruitage of which she may never see?
>
> (pp. 54–6)

As is common in Craik's work (for example, in her more famous *John Halifax, Gentleman*), nobility and honour are seen to stem from morality rather than social class or riches. A representative of the Governesses' Benevolent Institution similarly uses the language of honour in an appendix to Craik's story, when referring to 'the undeserved – nay, the honourable poverty' of governesses, caused by their 'self-forgetfulness'.[58] But it is also significant that Redwood applies the missionary metaphor of sowing good seed to governesses; both missionaries and governess are seen to selflessly sacrifice their lives for this cause.

The most difficult, and heroic, sacrifices Felicia makes in *Bread Upon the Waters*, though, are of any chance of love and marriage. Craik's first governess novel, *The Half-Caste* avoided dealing with this topic, as it tried to construct a new kind of novel that eschewed the love and marriage plot. Cassandra never admits to being in love with Mr Sutherland, so the sacrifice involved in her eventual single state is left ambiguous. While Kaplan suggests that the union of races in some way compensates for Cassandra's loss, Mitchell regards the 'substitute maternity' offered as the heroine's compensation as curious.[59] Formally, the avoidance leads to inconsistencies in narrative style. Initially, Cassandra's inner life is described in detail; however, from the point at which Zillah becomes the romantic heroine, Cassandra's narrative voice is more distanced, as she relates how she reacted to this turn of events with pious resignation. Craik cannot continue with her full portrayal of her character's subjectivity in all its affective experience, and instead returns to the 'flat' characters and techniques of moral didacticism.

The emotional and formal difficulties of eschewing love and marriage are more obvious in *Bread Upon the Waters*. At two points, the difficulty of sustaining a realist approach to psychic conflict produces ruptures in textual form: the diary breaks off, and the older, wiser narrator breaks into the story with moral reflections and explanations. The first break – the period of two dark years mentioned earlier – immediately follows a proposal of marriage from her employer. This temptation of a comfortable marriage leads to a night of soul searching. Turning to the words of her faith, Felicia reads the marriage service from the Prayer Book and realises that she cannot accept the proposal as she still has feelings for Redwood. Felicia's, and Craik's, interpretation of Christian marriage places great importance on romantic love. To marry without love, Felicia believes, would perjure herself 'in the sight of Heaven' and would be a case of sacrificing her soul for the sake of social status. Therefore, Felicia refuses to 'enter the married state with a lie upon my soul' (p. 46). The designation of a marriage of convenience as immoral, because loveless, challenges some contemporary views of marriage, including those of female missionaries who married simply because of organisational expectations. In this episode, Craik praises single governesses or missionaries who do not take the easy way out (for their morality as well as their nobility), but cannot depict the full emotional consequences of such a moral choice.

The second break in the narrative is even more marked and follows the most emotionally difficult sacrifice on Felicia's part: that of Redwood, with whom Felicia is brought back into contact. His speech about governesses convinces her that he admires her nobility and work, and this, along with the direction of the plot, sets up expectations of a romantic reward for Felicia. Felicia's style of diary writing, her interpretation of the direction of events and her inability to avoid expressing her excitement and hopes, at this point threatens to re-direct Craik's novel towards a traditional conclusion of love and marriage. Indeed, Felicia has to stop herself from writing about her hopeful anticipation: 'As for me, I shall meet –' (p. 68). Throughout the novel, the focus on Felicia's interiority challenges Craik's control of her fictional subject and moral message. Mostly, Craik steers her text away from romantic conclusions by using textual breaks and editorial clarification (such as was found in spiritual biography). However, at this point, where the reader expects narrative closure and would find it quite unsatisfactory for the young Felicia to simply resign her romantic hopes, Craik resorts to desperate measures: in a terrible swing accident, Craik lames her heroine, which, Felicia insists, makes marriage out of the question. Though Redwood feels he is duty-bound to propose anyway, Felicia likewise feels duty-bound to refuse, and to end her days, like Cassandra, as a content dependant in her brother's family. This unexpected ending has been seen as necessary for the purposes of the Governesses' Benevolent Institution, which supported governesses when they could no longer work.[60] However, the melodramatic violence of laming her heroine at this point suggests an awareness on Craik's part that the self-sacrifice required of female missionaries – and, by extension, all ideal Christian women – was impossible to portray in psychologically realistic and correctly Christian fiction; as scholars have suggested, Felicia's, and Craik's, unspoken emotional frustration is externalised as a physical crippling.[61] To some extent, as a missionary author, this violence of Craik against her main character also points to an unconscious displacement of sacrifice from herself, such as we have seen in the writings of women missionaries like the Wesleyan wives.

Both Craik's governess stories, through their use of psychological realism, constantly promise to uncover the affective experience of the female missionary in her act of sacrifice. In the end, though, they abandon psychological realism in favour of moral didacticism, portraying the female missionary as heroically self-sacrificing, finding fulfilment only in feelings of professionalism and compensatory relationships with substitute families. Only the avoidance of emotional exploration in *The Half-Caste* and the violence that erupts in *Bread Upon the Waters* hint at an unconscious unease or rebellion in Craik, against the requirement of female missionary self-sacrifice. As will be discussed in the next chapter, it was this rebellion that Charlotte Brontë had made explicit in her own governess story *Jane Eyre* for which she was famously castigated.

Conclusion

As she had been adapted in the tracts of Sherwood and Stretton, and later in the novellas of Dinah Craik, the female missionary figure had entered the world of fiction, becoming part of the cultural material that novelists such as Charlotte Brontë and Elizabeth Gaskell would explore and interrogate in their works. The quiet adjustments and adaptations of female missionary conventions by the women writers discussed in this chapter resulted in women characters of greater subjectivity than were emerging from mid-century female missionary biography. Suggestions of emotional fulfilment in the female missionary life, along with sometimes ambivalent presentations of self-sacrifice, complicated the image of the female missionary in the mid-nineteenth century. This had far-reaching consequences for the ideology of missionary femininity, and for the role of the woman writer.

Notes

1 See Alison Twells on the domestic mission and its roots, *The Civilising Mission and the English Middle Class, 1792–1850: The Heathen at Home and Overseas* (London: Palgrave Macmillan, 2009), pp. 25–34, 39–49, 53–8. Penny Brown has also noted that women could justify their writing for children as part of this mission, *The Captured World: The Child and Childhood in Nineteenth-Century Women's Writing in England* (London: Harvester Wheatsheaf, 1993), pp. 41–2.
2 Nancy Cutt, *Mrs Sherwood and Her Books for Children: A Study* (London: Oxford University Press, 1974), pp. 24–81.

3 As we saw in Chapter 1, where the anonymous 'Authoress' of *Memoirs of Female Labourers in the Missionary Cause* (1839) was advertised in that text as also having produced a collective memoir of child death: *Early Religion Seen in the Peaceful Happy End of Thirteen Young Children, who Lived and Died in the Lord*.
4 Twells, pp. 78–9, 84–104.
5 See, for example, Sherwood's non-fiction tract, *Conversations on the Shorter Catechism with the Scripture Proofs, for the Use of Children* (1824), and her more fictional *Stories Explanatory of the Church Catechism* (1822); see also, in addition to the biography attributed to her in Chapter 1, Margaret Grierson's *Lily Douglas: A Simple Story, Humbly Intended as a Premium and Pattern for Sabbath Schools* (1821).
6 Brown, p. 41.
7 Joanne Shattock, "Introduction', *The Works of Elizabeth Gaskell*, ed. by Joanne Shattock (London: Pickering and Chatto, 2005), Vol. 1, *Journalism, Early Fiction and Personal Writings*, pp. xxi–xxxiii (pp. xxiii–xxiv).
8 For example, see James Holt McGavran 'Introduction', in *Romanticism and Children's Literature in Nineteenth-Century England*, ed. by James Holt McGavran (London: University of Georgia Press, 1991), pp. 1–13 (pp. 2–4); Ross Woodman, 'The Idiot Boy as Healer', in *Romanticism and Children's Literature*, ed. by McGavran, pp. 72–95 (pp. 89–91); and Lynne Vallone, 'Women Writing for Children', in *Women and Literature in Britain 1800–1900*, ed. by Joanne Shattock (Cambridge: Cambridge University Press, 2001), pp. 275–300 (p. 279).
9 Mary Poovey, *Uneven Developments: The Ideological Work of Gender in Mid-Victorian England* (Chicago, IL: Chicago University Press, 1988), pp. 126–30. Following this, in her study on governess literature, Cecilia Wadso Lecaros insists that it is the governess's social position that is most important – despite acknowledging the existence of enough specifically religious governess fiction to form a sub-genre, *The Victorian Governess Novel* (Lund: Lund University Press, 2001), p. 221.
10 On the religious basis of separate spheres ideology, see Catherine Hall and Leonore Davidoff, *Family Fortunes: Men and Women of the English Middle Class 1780–1850* (London: Routledge, 2002), pp. 179–92. Interestingly, though Susan Zlotnick makes a connection between governesses and missionaries, she interprets both roles as almost entirely secular agents of imperialism, in 'Jane Eyre, Anna Leonowens, and the White Woman's Burden: Governesses, Missionaries and Maternal Imperialists in Mid-Victorian Britain', *Victorians Institute Journal*, 24 (1996), 27–56 (pp. 28–30).
11 Brown, pp. 41–3; see also Cutt, *Ministering Angels: A Study of Nineteenth-Century Writing for Children* (Wormley: Five Owls Press, 1980), pp. 19–20.
12 Cutt, *Ministering Angels*, p. xi. The argument for the enormous reach of tract fiction is also supported by Cutt's analysis of archival data from publishing houses such as Houlston and Son, *Mrs Sherwood*, pp. 24–36. Aileen Fyfe dates the widening of the RTS's audience to the middle classes to the point when the RTS began to publish more tracts in expensive book form, which, as Ann Thwaite notes, were given as gifts to middle-class children in addition to being awarded to working-class Sunday school scholars as prizes; Aileen Fyfe, 'A Short History of the Religious Tract Society', in *From 'The Dairyman's Daughter' to 'Worrals of the WAAF': The Religious Tract*

Society, Lutterworth Press and Children's Literature, ed. by Dennis Butts and Pat Garrett (Cambridge: Lutterworth Press, 2006), pp. 13–35 (p. 21); Ann Thwaite, 'What Is a Tract?', in *From 'The Dairyman's Daughter'*, ed. by Butts and Garrett, pp. 36–48 (p. 46).

13 *The Sunday at Home*, I (1854), p. 121.
14 Cutt, *Mrs Sherwood*, p. 13; *Ministering Angels*, p. 136.
15 Cutt, *Ministering Angels*, p. 136.
16 Cutt, *Mrs Sherwood*, p. 13, pp. 25–35.
17 Sherwood's *Stories Explanatory of the Church Catechism* provides a rich and realistic description of barracks life.
18 Cutt, *Ministering Angels*, pp. 119–25.
19 Patricia Demers, 'Mrs Sherwood and Hesba Stretton: The Letter and the Spirit of Evangelical Writing of and for Children' in *Romanticism and Children's Literature*, ed. by McGavran, pp. 129–49 (p. 131).
20 Suzanne Rickard, 'Victorian Women with Causes: Writing, Religion and Action', in *Women, Religion and Feminism in Britain, 1750–1900*, ed. by Sue Morgan (Basingstoke: Palgrave Macmillan, 2002), pp. 139–57 (pp. 146–7).
21 Cutt, *Ministering Angels*, pp. 19–20; Brown, pp. 41–3; Demers, 'Mrs Sherwood', in *Romanticism and Children's Literature*, ed. by McGavran, pp. 131–132.
22 Cutt, *Mrs Sherwood*, p. 41.
23 Brown, p. 50.
24 Sherwood, *The History of Little Henry and his Bearer*, 2nd edn (Wellington: Houlston and Son, 1815), p. 18. Further references to this work are given after quotations in the text.
25 Also, as Claudia Nelson notes, the bodily weakness of children (of both sexes) and women separates them from the world of masculine commerce and ties them to the idea of the spiritual, domestic 'Angel', *Boys Will be Girls: The Feminine Ethic and British Children's Fiction 1857–1917* (New Brunswick, NJ: Rutgers University Press, 1991), pp. 2–6.
26 Brown, p. 4; Michael Wheeler, *Death and the Future Life in Victorian Literature and Theology* (Cambridge: Cambridge University Press, 1990), pp. 44–5.
27 This is an example of theological blurring of language around death noted by Wheeler, pp. 27–30.
28 Scholars have noted how evangelical religion privileged the simplicity of children's, women's and indigenous converts' faith as it was believed to spring directly from their hearts and minds, in which the Holy Spirit was working. See Elisabeth Jay, *Religion of the Heart: Anglican Evangelicalism and the Nineteenth-Century Novel* (Oxford: Clarendon, 1979), p. 40; and Christine Krueger, *The Reader's Repentance: Women Preachers, Women Writers and Nineteenth-Century Social Discourse* (London: University of Chicago Press, 1992), pp. 60–2.
29 In holding out the missionary identity as one which children could take on, Sherwood was an influential part of a wider nineteenth-century evangelical education movement. For examples, see Eyre, *Mission and Reform, Nineteenth-Century Religion, Literature and Society*, ed. Naomi Hetherington, 4 Vols (Abingdon: Routledge, 2020), Vol. 2, pp. 233–46. Twells has also demonstrated how evangelical family practice, alongside children's literature, worked to instil a missionary identity in Victorian children, *The Civilizing Mission*, pp. 89–98.

30 Hesba Stretton, *Pilgrim Street: A Tale of Manchester Life* (London: R.T.S, 1867), p. 25.
31 Stretton, *Jessica's First Prayer* (London: RTS, 1867), pp. 11–2. Further references to this work are given after quotations in the text.
32 This treatment of children is reflective of evangelicalism's mid-century evolution away from the Calvinist tenet of original sin, but it also reflects the missionary theory of the Scottish evangelical, Thomas Chalmers, who believed that all mankind, even 'savages', possessed a 'natural virtue' that made conversion possible. See Brian Stanley, 'Christianity and Civilization in Evangelical Mission Thought, 1792–1857', in *Christian Missions and the Enlightenment*, ed. by Brian Stanley (Richmond, VA: Curzon, 2001), pp. 169–97 (pp. 179–80).
33 Nelson describes Jessica as the 'unconscious center' of the Christian community in this story, in comparison to the 'insignificant' Daniel and minister, pp. 18–9.
34 *Jessica's Mother* (London: RTS, n.d.), p. 115.
35 See, for example, Grierson, *American Biography: Or, Memoirs of Mrs. A. Judson and Mrs. M. L. Ramsay* (Edinburgh: Leith, 1831), p. 10.
36 Rickard notes Stretton's particularly New Testament faith in love and compassion, 'Victorian Women with Causes', in *Women, Religion and Feminism*, ed. by Morgan, p. 150.
37 Cutt, *Ministering Angels*, pp. 19–20.
38 Cutt, *Mrs Sherwood*, pp. 84–92.
39 This was not Sherwood's first governess story. As Cutt has noted, Sherwood also re-wrote Sarah Fielding's 1749 collection of stories, *The Governess: Or Little Female Academy*, evangelising Fielding's text by replacing most of the fairy stories with tract-like moral tales. See Cutt, *Ministering Angels*, p. 11. Interestingly, in this work, Sherwood begins to emphasise the 'holy child' aspects of one of the pupils, and the missionary nature of the governess, but does not sustain this characterisation through to the end of the text.
40 Sherwood, *Caroline Mordaunt; or, The Governess* (London: Darton and Clark, 1853), p. 214. Further references to this work appear after quotations in the text.
41 Vallone talks of tract writers engaging in an 'economy of tears', 'Women writing for Children', in *Women and Literature*, ed. by Shattock, p. 279; see also Emma Mason's discussion of Felicia Hemans' inclusion of feeling and 'affection' (as opposed to passion or enthusiasm) in her religious poetry, *Women Poets of the Nineteenth Century* (Tavistock: Northcote, 2006), pp. 37–47.
42 Sally Mitchell, *Dinah Mullock Craik* (Boston, MA: Twayne, 1983), p. i.
43 Karen Bourrier, *Victorian Bestseller: The Life of Dinah Craik* (Ann Arbor, MI: University of Michigan Press, 2019), pp. 5, 8–21.
44 Mitchell, pp. 2–5.
45 Dinah Craik, *Olive*, in *Olive and The Half-Caste*, ed. by Cora Kaplan (Oxford: Oxford University Press, 1999), pp. 1–331 (p. 224).
46 See Krueger on this aspect of early non-conformist female preachers, pp. 52–3.
47 II Samuel 2. 18–23. Krueger has also noted that female preachers engaged in an 'ethos of simplicity' as a discursive strategy for combatting prejudice, pp. 60–2.
48 Craik, *Olive*, pp. 223–4.

49 Mitchell, p. 31.
50 Ibid., p. 24.
51 Dinah Craik, *The Half-Caste*, in *Olive and The Half-Caste*, ed. by Kaplan, pp. 333–72 (p. 337). Further references to this work are given following quotations in the text.
52 Kaplan, 'Introduction', in *Olive and The Half-Caste*, ed. by Kaplan, pp. xxiii–xxiv.
53 In a nutshell, polygenists believed that racial differences were a result of races' differing points of origin and were therefore innate and immutable, while monogenists believed that all races had a common origin and that any racial differences could be overcome by increasing levels of civilization. See Kaplan, 'Introduction', in *Olive*, ed. by Kaplan, pp. xiv–xxiv, and Juliet Shields, 'The Races of Women: Gender, Hybridity, and National Identity in Dinah Craik's *Olive*', *Studies in the Novel*, 39 (2007), 284–300 (pp. 284–6).
54 On this missionary discourse, see Jane Samson, 'Ethnology and Theology: Nineteenth-Century Mission Dilemmas in the South Pacific', in *Christian Missions and the Enlightenment*, ed. by Brian Stanley (Richmond: Curzon, 2001), pp. 99–122. Twells has pointed to the widespread support of missionary activity among the Victorian public to argue that the influence of Knox's views has been overstated by many historians, pp. 178–204.
55 Kaplan, 'Introduction', in *Olive*, ed. by Kaplan p. xiii.
56 The Governesses' Benevolent Institution was set up in 1841 to raise the living standards and status of governesses through the provision of support services such as an employment bureau, a college, a savings bank, temporary accommodation and a retirement home.
57 Craik, *Bread upon the Waters* (Leipzig: Bernhard Tauchnitz, 1865), p. 29. Further references to this work are given following quotations in the text.
58 M.E.L, 'The Governesses' Benevolent Institution', in Craik, *Bread upon the Waters*, pp. 87–96 (p. 91).
59 Kaplan, 'Introduction', in *Olive*, ed. by Kaplan, p. xxiv; Mitchell, p. 25.
60 Mitchell, p. 26.
61 Elaine Showalter, *A Literature of Their Own: British Women Novelists from Brontë to Lessing* (Princeton, NJ: Princeton University Press, 1999), p. 23; Melissa Edmundson, 'Introduction', in Dinah Craik, *The Half-Caste*, ed. by Edmundson (Ontario: Broadview Editions, 2016), pp. 9–37 (p. 28).

3 Novel Approaches to Missionary Sacrifice
Charlotte Brontë and Elizabeth Gaskell

Introduction

In Chapter 2, we saw that the common Victorian heroine of the governess was often a domestic recasting of the female missionary. We now turn to perhaps the most famous and influential governess novel, Charlotte Brontë's 1847 *Jane Eyre*. The critical attention received by this novel since the 1970s makes it difficult to read out of the context of second-wave feminist interpretations and postcolonial reclamations.[1] And it might seem surprising to think about this novel in the tradition of female missionary biography – after all, contemporary readers were far from seeing it as a missionary text – on the contrary, they called it 'godless'.[2] However, as is well-known, Charlotte Brontë came from a religious background, and *Jane Eyre* provides evidence of her engagement with the evangelical missionary culture of the mid-nineteenth century. Taking the novel's missionary narrative literally enables us to see Brontë engaging with the debate about Christian womanhood as it was playing out in female missionary biography and women's tract fiction of the time.[3] We can also see her exploiting the more heroic aspects of the missionary to provide a strong identity for her heroine – and for herself as an author – while ultimately rejecting that which had been key to mid-century admiration for the character: the characteristic of self-sacrifice.

However, this was not the end of the story for this novel and its author. Much has been written about the myth that grew up around the Brontë sisters, largely as a result of Elizabeth Gaskell's biography of Charlotte.[4] Despite Brontë's rejection of the self-sacrificial female missionary identity in *Jane Eyre*, when the time came for her to be memorialised, the involvement of her friend Ellen Nussey, combined with Gaskell's own concern to rehabilitate her fellow novelist, led to Brontë being, paradoxically, reclaimed and mythologised in the tradition of female missionary martyrs.

This chapter begins by discussing the presence of the missionary movement in Brontë's life. It then presents a new reading of Brontë's *Jane Eyre*, focusing on the missionary plot and characterisation as well as demonstrating its rejection of the self-sacrificial elements of the female

DOI: 10.4324/9781003332961-6

missionary heroine. The chapter goes on to explore Ellen Nussey's efforts to influence Gaskell's biographical presentation of Charlotte and Anne Brontë, so that they could be interpreted as female missionary martyrs. Finally, I show how Gaskell's use of female missionary traits in her characterisation of Charlotte Brontë was preceded by her use of these when writing her novel *Ruth*, to argue that even the Unitarian Mrs Gaskell was influenced by the narrative of the self-sacrificial female missionary, and used the character to shore up her reputation for respectability.

The Missionary Movement in Brontë's Life

In explaining Brontë's religious influences, much has been made of her aunt's subscription to the *Methodist Magazine,* with some scholars suggesting Charlotte's work references this publication's stock of moral tales and characters.[5] However, Charlotte would have encountered such tales and characters in a range of religious periodicals and tracts, along with stories from the mission field and memoirs of Christian lives. Charlotte's father, the Reverend Patrick Brontë, is likely to have sometimes taken the *Christian Observer*, which included dispatches from the mission field, and Charlotte was at one point a subscriber to the London Society for Promoting Christianity Amongst the Jews.[6] Scholars have also pointed to the biography of the missionary Henry Martyn as the influence for *Jane Eyre's* St John Rivers; Cunningham asserts that Charlotte would have read this memoir at the Keighley library.[7] It would be surprising, though, if she had not also encountered there one or more versions of Ann Judson's memoir. She was certainly reading regularly within this genre; Elisabeth Jay notes that Charlotte recommended certain spiritual biographies to her friend Ellen Nussey.[8] And Charlotte's time at Miss Wooler's school would have provided additional exposure to this sort of literature.

The evangelicalism preached by Patrick, which would have formed the culture of the parsonage, was an early, intellectual form of the faith, suspicious of too much enthusiasm.[9] This is the evangelicalism that characterised Knowles's original biography of Ann Judson, and which inspired Judson herself. However, at Miss Wooler's, under the influence of the Dewsbury clergymen, the Brontë sisters encountered a more hardline and emotionally demanding mid-Victorian evangelicalism.[10] This more extreme form of evangelicalism encouraged people to become painfully aware of their sinful natures, and their souls' likely damnation, so that they turned to Christ and his Atonement as the only means of salvation. Young people especially experienced this pressure, which was often described in conversion accounts, such as those that appeared in the biographies of Ann Judson and Harriet Newell.[11] Encountering this extreme evangelicalism drove Anne Brontë to religious crisis, and there is evidence that Charlotte was brought to the same state of subjection, as I will discuss later in this chapter.

Most significantly, as scholars have noted, Charlotte received a marriage proposal from Nussey's clergyman brother Henry, who later considered becoming a missionary and has been seen as another model for St John Rivers.[12] This relationship made the possibility of life as a missionary wife – which was always imaginatively available to Charlotte and other women like her – a little less theoretical. But Charlotte was already involved in what Alison Twells has termed missionary philanthropy, as a facet of nineteenth-century women's missionary domesticity.[13] In *Shirley*, women's missionary fundraising is described with familiarity:

> It ought perhaps to be explained in passing, for the benefit of those who are not 'au fait' to the mysteries of the 'Jew-basket' and 'Missionary basket,' that these 'meubles' are willow-repositories, of the capacity of a good-sized family clothes-basket, dedicated to the purpose of conveying from house to house a monster collection of pincushions, needle-books, card-racks, work-bags, articles of infant-wear, &c. &c. &., made by the willing or reluctant hands of the Christian ladies of the parish, and sold per force to the heathenish gentlemen thereof, at prices unblushingly exorbitant. The proceeds of such compulsory sales are applied to the conversion of the Jews, the seeking up of the ten missing tribes, or to the regeneration of the interesting coloured population of the globe.[14]

While Charlotte gave this satirical description from behind the persona of *Shirley*'s narrator, and felt able to refer to 'silly Jew-basket work' in a letter to Ellen Nussey, her relationship with missionary philanthropy was not uncomplicated.[15] Another letter betrays her feelings of guilt around not contributing to the basket: 'What did your sister Anne say [...]? I hope she was too much occupied [...] to think of it'.[16] For Brontë, the 'Jew-basket' represents her culture's demand that women sacrifice parts of their life (their time and care) to the missionary cause, and her ambivalence concerning that demand.

Brontë's exposure to missionary culture gave her an understanding of how mid-century literature's characterisation of the female missionary – and her domestic proxy, the governess – was emphasising feminine self-sacrifice above all other traits for women to emulate. However, as we shall see, she also knew that there were other characterisations possible for the missionary woman and writer.

Reading the Female Missionary Narrative in Brontë's Novels

Brontë's *Jane Eyre* (1847) and *Villette* (1853) contain situations and characters with which readers would be familiar from missionary writings. *Jane Eyre* even follows the narrative form of female missionary biography and, in its first-person narration, recalls the early memoirs that extracted from missionaries' diaries. Indeed, subtitling *Jane Eyre* 'An Autobiography' echoes J. D. Knowles's use of the term to describe his original biography's inclusion of Ann Judson's own words, which had resulted in a rich and complex portrait of the female missionary's religious belief, work and sacrifice.[17] The result of first-person narration in *Jane Eyre* provides a similarly complex insight into the female missionary figure. Brontë shows how her governess heroine experiences intellectual and theological confidence in her missionary role, and enjoys some of the emotional fulfilment described by Martha Sherwood and Dinah Craik. However, Brontë's uncompromising psychological realism makes explicit the conflicts that were suppressed in earlier female missionary writing, and leads to an ultimate rejection of the self-sacrificial aspects of the female missionary character as she was depicted in the mid-century. In addition, in her subversion of the tropes of female missionary biography – especially as they were being used in tract and popular fiction – Brontë exposes the limits of missionary femininity for Victorian women.

Brontë's Missionary Governess

Like Sherwood and Craik, Brontë uses the governess and school teacher as domestic proxies for the female missionary. Indeed, although the roles are domestic, the situations of *Villette* and *Jane Eyre* are definitively missionary. *Villette's* Lucy Snowe carries out her lonely labours in the apostate field of Roman Catholic Belgium, while Jane Eyre takes on the heathen environment of Thornfield. Here, Jane's charge Adèle is irredeemably French and foreign: she sings unsuitable, 'bad taste' songs; she dances (always a bad sign for evangelicals); and Rochester states that 'coquetry runs in her blood, blends with her brains, and seasons the marrow of her bones'.[18] Rochester himself is unrepentantly fallen and sinful, engaging in the behaviour of an oriental king as he sequesters his first wife and attempts to install Jane as his second wife or concubine.[19] Later, Jane's stay at the village of Morton can be seen as a second missionary posting. Home missions were often used as training grounds for potential overseas missionaries, and part of the reason that St John Rivers deploys Jane in the village school is to prepare her for a life in the overseas mission field as his wife. Those ministered to by home missions were often described in the same language as the heathen served by foreign missionaries;[20] Brontë exemplifies this in her portrayal of Jane's new charges, when Jane calls them 'heavy looking, gaping rustics' (p. 385) and is dismayed that teacher and students 'have difficulty in understanding each other's language' (p. 378), as if they are of another race. Portraying the otherness of Jane's Morton natives as physical and linguistic associates them even more with the sorts of peoples encountered and described by missionaries.[21]

As well as using missionary settings and characters, *Jane Eyre* follows the form of missionary life writing. Female missionary biography told the story of its subject as a progression of stages: a childhood of small sins; conversion; a 'calling' to the mission; ministry in the field; and a good Christian death. When Brontë was writing *Jane Eyre*, much female missionary life writing of the 1840s treated childhood very quickly, reducing the life leading up to conversion to the generic. It also avoided describing the spiritual struggles of the female missionary around her calling, marriage and sacrifice, prioritising instead the female missionary's (passive) death.[22] Religious fiction by Sherwood, Stretton and Craik had inserted far more emotion into this spare story, especially surrounding conversion, but seldom departed from the convention of depicting the missionary character's death as one of passive self-sacrifice.

Following the depictions of female missionaries' early lives, the child Jane has faults of temper that are cured through religious education and conversion. Her heroines at Lowood, Helen Burns and Miss Temple, are of the missionary type; the character of Helen is directly influenced by the converting child saints of religious tracts and magazines, and Miss Temple is a missionary governess. Under their influence, the young Jane can be seen to undergo a form of conversion. In a familiar inversion, Jane herself becomes a governess and, at Thornfield, she is seen to be quickly successful in civilising, if not converting, her charge Adèle; Rochester notes when he returns from his initial absence from home that she 'has made much improvement' (p. 127). Jane also influences Rochester with her evangelical piety – so much so that he calls her his 'good angel' (p. 332), whom he cannot do without.

While most fictional versions of the missionary governess portray her work with children, Brontë does not focus much on Jane's work with Adèle. Instead, Jane's evangelical conversations with Rochester form the heart of her novel. As Mary Poovey noted, audiences were scandalised at the idea of a young woman having conversations about a man's dissipation, because it implied that women had knowledge of such things; Elizabeth Rigby, in her famous review, specifically criticised Jane's knowingness.[23] Victorian respectability required that women should be able to reform rakes like Rochester through the influence of their innocence, which required them, paradoxically, to be ignorant of sin.[24] However, female missionaries, such as Ann Judson, often had to encounter challenging cases of sin and heathendom in the mission field. Missionary biographies by the mid-century brushed these sorts of encounters under the carpet, replacing detailed description of missionary work with rhetoric that suggested the female missionary's domestic Christian influence was enough to convert any who came into contact with it.[25] In choosing Rochester for Jane's conversion efforts, and dramatising their encounters, Brontë is challenging social hypocrisy and returning the female missionary character to her origins in the redoubtable Mrs Judson.

In a similar manner, rather than summarising her female missionary's ministry using the mid-century rhetoric of 'spiritual influence', Brontë presents Jane's theological conversations with Rochester in detail. This dialogue shows that, though she may be rather controversial in her choice of convert, Jane's methods are exemplary in their pious self-effacement. For example, she consistently warns Rochester against depending on others such as herself for his salvation:

> 'Sir,' I answered, 'a Wanderer's repose or a sinner's reformation should never depend on a fellow-creature. [...] if anyone you know has suffered and erred, let him look higher than his equals for strength to amend, and solace to heal.
>
> (p. 229)

This speech is certain and secure in its accordance with early evangelical religious teaching: that no one could achieve salvation through their own efforts, without the help of God and the Holy Spirit. Here, Brontë is making a religious argument against women being thought of as angels who could reform their husbands by their own actions or influence. At the same time, she points to a problem at the heart of Craik's reformulation of missionary work as self-fulfilling (a tendency that was beginning to be seen in female missionary newsletters): that within evangelical Christianity it is sinful for a missionary to be overly satisfied with her own agency. Jane's traditional missionary trait of self-abnegation corrects this tendency as she passes responsibility and credit to God – though she continues to confidently act as Rochester's theological guide.

Jane's flight from Thornfield, before she immerses herself in home mission work at Morton, represents the spiritual crisis and temptation around the calling to missionary work that is described in many early missionary biographies – including Knowles's *Memoir of Ann Judson* – but which tended to disappear from the thinner biographies of the mid-century. This act of leaving Rochester, fleeing temptation to preserve her soul, was the one aspect of Jane's agency of which contemporary readers approved.[26] It is an ideal sacrifice of human love in the cause of religious duty, which can be likened to St John Rivers's renunciation of his 'human weakness' (his love for Rosamund) and the real-life missionary Henry Martyn's of his love Lydia Grenfell. Mary Ellis Gibson suggests that Martyn's story was particularly popular with women writers because of his construction of self-sacrifice as heroic.[27] That Brontë also understood this sort of missionary sacrifice as spiritual heroism can be seen in her emotional poem, 'The Missionary':

> Smouldering, on my heart's altar lies
> The fire of some great sacrifice,
> Not yet half quenched [...]
> My life-long hope, first joy and last,
> What I loved well, and clung to fast;
> What I wished wildly to retain,
> What I renounced with soul-felt pain;
> What–when I saw it, axe-struck, perish–

>   Left me no joy on earth to cherish;
>   A man bereft–yet sternly now
>   I do confirm that Jephtha vow:
>   Shall I retract, or fear, or flee?
>   Did Christ, when rose the fatal treeBefore him, on Mount Calvary?
>   'Twas a long fight, hard fought, but won,
>   And what I did was justly done.[28]

Those making this sacrifice of the heart are compared with Jephtha, who sacrificed his daughter, and with Christ himself. Though female missionaries wouldn't usually have such a sacrifice to make – Gibson observes that Brontë is unusual in voicing female desire in this context[29] – the original memoirs of Ann Judson and Harriet Newell did give voice to their concerns about the missionary marriage and whether this involved a sacrifice of romantic love as well as familial.[30]

With hindsight, Jane and Rochester attribute her act of sacrifice to God (as it is this which leads to Rochester's salvation). And Jane describes how her resolve to leave Thornfield was strengthened by 'a voice within me', and how 'conscience' instructed her in the words of the Sermon on the Mount: 'you shall, yourself, pluck out your right eye; yourself cut off your right hand' (p. 313). The inner voice of conscience could be understood within evangelicalism as an incarnation of the Holy Spirit, aiding Christians in their duty.[31] This, and Jane's involuntary call for God's help (pp. 320–1), enable her to resolutely 'renounce love and idol', in favour of duty and the true God, in whom she avers she trusts, and encourages Rochester to do the same (p. 333).

Freed of her 'mere human love / mere selfish yearning',[32] Jane goes on to epitomise the ideal female missionary in her work at Morton. She civilises her rustic farm pupils to such an extent that, as Gibson has noted, she can be seen as a more successful missionary than St John Rivers himself.[33] It is her work here that convinces St John that she has the vocation for the role of missionary wife, as he tells her she performed 'well, punctually, uprightly, labour uncongenial to your habits and inclinations; [...] with capacity and tact: you could win while you controlled' (p. 425). To 'win' the hearts of the heathen is part of the passive influence that missionary writers celebrated. Likewise, Jane's sacrifice in performing unpleasant work, her sharing of her new fortune and giving up her own study to assist his, leads St John to characterise her as 'docile, diligent, disinterested, faithful, constant' (p. 425), all adjectives common in mid-century writings about the ideal female missionary.

Ultimately, Jane's biggest success as a missionary is her conversion of Rochester. Rochester's speech on her return is one that many missionaries would have been happy to hear, as he re-interprets the novel's plot as one of divine Providence:

> My heart swells with gratitude to the beneficent God [...] He sees not as man sees, but far clearer: judges not as man judges, but far more wisely. I did wrong: I would have sullied my innocent flower – breathed guilt on its purity: the Omnipotent snatched it from me. [...] Of late, Jane – only of late – I began to see and acknowledge the hand of God in my doom. I began to experience remorse, repentance; the wish for reconciliation to my Maker. I began sometimes to pray: very brief prayers they were, but very sincere.
>
> (pp. 470–1)

Rochester's address of Jane in the middle of this passage, while avoiding attributing agency to her, connects her with his turn to Christianity and the change of mood, from an Old Testament religion of a vengeful and punishing God, to a far more New Testament, evangelical creed of remorse, repentance and reconciliation. Rochester associates these aspects of religion with Jane, and they are prefigured in one of their earliest conversations, when he speaks of the poison that is remorse and she replies that 'repentance is said to be its cure' (p. 142). In that conversation, Rochester emphasised the concept of 'reformation', suggesting the dependence of rakes on women to reform them. Conversely, in the later passage above, reformation is replaced with 'reconciliation' – a process that demands mutual effort on both sides. This is a highly reflective treatment of the intricacies of conversion, which privileges an emotional, co-dependent relationship.

Indeed, although *Jane Eyre* follows the form of missionary biography, Brontë's reflective treatment of missionary work and conversion signals her independence from the established rhetoric of the form. More than this though, as I will go on to demonstrate, her subversions of the tropes of female missionary writing – especially what it had become in the hands of tract writers – reveal her sceptical awareness of evangelical culture's increasing expectation that all women would emulate the self-sacrifice of female missionary martyrs.

Subverting the Mid-Century Female Missionary Narrative

Significantly, Jane rarely feels the satisfaction in her professional work that Dinah Craik describes in her governess novels. Though she is proud of her ability to work, and clear that her work at Lowood School was for a 'noble and useful institution' (p. 87), she nonetheless feels that there is something else, something even more noble, that she should be engaged in. The school in Morton, likewise, does not bring feelings of fulfilment, but rather of social humiliation:

> I felt – yes, idiot that I am – I felt degraded. [...] I was weakly dismayed at the ignorance, the poverty, the coarseness [...] But let me not hate

and despise myself too much for these feelings: I know them to be wrong – that is a great step gained. To-morrow, I trust, I shall get the better of them partially; [...] In a few months, [...] the happiness of seeing progress [...] may substitute gratification for disgust.

(p. 378)

This display of spiritual struggle aligns Jane's story with that of heroic missionaries such as Henry Martyn. When thinking of his missionary future, Martyn expresses his religious self-criticism in a very similar manner to Jane, writing: 'the thought that I must be unceasingly employed in the same kind of work amongst poor, ignorant people, is what my proud spirit revolts at. [...] At these times I feel neither love to God nor man'.[34] Brontë's portrayal of her heroine's struggle with missionary work exposes the emotion repressed in mid-century portrayals of female missionaries, as she uses the first-person voice and suddenly switches to the present tense, giving the reader the sense they are directly accessing Jane's thoughts in real time, or perhaps in a diary. Jane's emotional honesty shows that not all teachers can find fulfilment in the idea of the nobility of hard work and suffering; all she can do is hope for feelings of 'gratification' and 'happiness' if she proves successful.

Brontë also explores whether relationships between missionaries and converts can really prove as emotionally fulfilling as tract writers were suggesting. In a re-writing of the religious school story, Brontë depicts Jane enjoying a certain amount of fulfilling emotion in her relationships with her teacher Miss Temple and the missionary-child Helen, but these relationships do not have the power of those of, for example, Sherwood's work. Indeed, Miss Temple specifically represses strong emotion; as Jane notes, there was much about her that 'precluded deviation into the ardent, the excited, the eager: something that chastened the pleasure of those who looked on her and listened to her, by a controlling sense of awe' (p. 76). Although they engage in a conversion relationship of sorts, it is not emotionally satisfying enough for the ravenous Jane. And although Miss Temple is somewhat successful in converting Jane to a creed of self-renunciation, her influence lasts only as long as they are together at Lowood. Once she leaves, Jane finds that her mind

> had put off all it had borrowed of Miss Temple – [...] she had taken with her the serene atmosphere I had been breathing in her vicinity – [...] now I was left in my natural element; and beginning to feel the stirring of old emotions.
>
> (p. 88)

The suggestion that a conversion could be taken on superficially, and sustained only temporarily, is a great challenge to the evangelical conversion stories. Moreover, Brontë's depiction casts doubt on the idea that a female missionary can reliably succeed at getting at the heart of a convert.

Even the death of the 'holy child' Helen Burns lacks the power to convert Jane. Though her surname, Burns, brings to mind sacrificial, self-immolating death, Helen's actual death challenges the idea that such sacrifice should form the emotional heart of a missionary story. Outwardly, Helen's resigned passing conforms to the pattern of child deaths in religious tracts. She has childish faults enough to make her seem real and to have something to atone for; she bears her illness, like her unjust classroom punishments, in the way of Christ and the martyrs; and she uses her last words to attempt to convert Jane:

> I believe; I have faith: I am going to God. [...] I rely implicitly on his power, and confide wholly in his goodness: [...] I am sure there is a future state; I believe God is good: I can resign my immortal part to him without any misgiving. God is my father; God is my friend: I love him; I believe he loves me.
>
> (p. 85)

The repetition and the simplicity of the language recalls catechism and aligns her with the simple evangelical faith of 'holy child' characters (see Chapter 2). However, it is strange that the last words of Helen, who till now has burnt brightly in intellectual eloquence, are so devoid of passion or poetry. This may be the reason she is so unsuccessful with Jane, who, far from being converted at Helen's deathbed, still questions of Heaven: 'Does it exist?' Though Jane describes experiencing 'inexpressible sadness' and the 'impression of woe' (p. 73), tears – the tract writers' currency of redemption[35] – do not flow. Moreover, Jane is dubious about Helen's suggestion that suffering a lack of human affection must be endured, in order to be rewarded after death. And she still thinks it hard to have to sacrifice life, which even at Lowood she finds 'pleasant' and believes will hold 'sensations and excitements [...][for] those who had courage to go forth into its expanse' (p. 88). Despite her affection for the 'holy child', Jane is immune to her influence, rejecting her example of passivity and aspiring instead to courageously 'go forth' like a missionary into the field.

Most significantly, when Jane becomes a governess, she does not experience an emotional conversion relationship with Adele. Jane's dissatisfaction at Thornfield is usually linked with her 'dark double' Bertha, whose laugh Jane hears as she restlessly paces the battlements.[36] However, Jane's discontent should also be linked with her repudiation of what she calls the 'cant' and 'humbug' of her culture's depictions of children and the belief that teachers have a 'duty' to 'conceive for them an idolatrous devotion' (pp. 113–4). It is her admission that she has only cool feelings for Adele that immediately precedes her description of restless rebellion. In *Villette*, Brontë goes even further in her attack on the idea that governesses should experience fulfilling emotional relationships with their charges. In a somewhat horrific perversion of Sherwood's school story trope, Lucy is left alone during the summer holiday with a child who, rather than being a holy agent of redemption, she sees only as 'a sort of cretin', with a warped body and mind and a 'propensity' to 'evil'.[37] Brontë was clear: in her experience, the expectation that women could find sufficient fulfilment in their schoolroom work and relationships was fantasy.

Rejecting Self-Sacrifice

The main aspect of the female missionary narrative that Brontë rejects in *Jane Eyre* is that of passive self-sacrifice. Refusing to emulate the martyrdom of missionaries such as Harriet Newell, unlike Dinah Craik's spinster governesses, Jane declines to sacrifice her chances of romantic love or her life.

Jane's most powerful rejection of self-sacrifice is her famous refusal to become the wife of the missionary St John Rivers. Elisabeth Jay has, correctly, interpreted her rejection as a powerfully liberating, feminist, refusal to submit herself to this life.[38] It is important to be clear, though, exactly what Jane is refusing. She is not refusing the nature of the work. Given Brontë's likely familiarity with the strong women and wives of female missionary biography, it is unconvincing to suggest, as Cunningham does, Jane's refusal to become a missionary wife is a symbolic criticism of women's limited role in the mission.[39] In fact, Jane is very tempted when Rivers describes the work she would do:

> My work, which had appeared so vague, so hopelessly diffuse, condensed itself as he proceeded, and assumed a definite form under his shaping hand. [...] Of course [...] I must seek another interest in life to replace the one lost: is not the occupation he now offers me truly the most glorious man can adopt or God assign?
>
> (pp. 425–6)

The purpose, occupation and glory of the female missionary life attract Jane. She is pleased to have been recognised by Rivers as worthy of this occupation and proud of her ability to work in such a way that she can describe herself as the 'weapon' in Rivers's soldier-missionary hands. And she agrees to go with him, as a sister, a 'comrade' or a 'fellow-soldier' (p. 430).

What Jane refuses is the position of missionary *wife*, and a loveless marriage, even in the cause of the mission. Jane asks herself:

> Can I let him complete his calculations – [...] go through the wedding ceremony? [...] receive from him the bridal ring, endure all the forms of love (which I doubt not he would scrupulously observe) and know that the spirit was quite absent?
>
> (pp. 426–7)

This was a dilemma implicit in the arrangement of marriages between missionary men and appropriate partners, and which many religious women such as Brontë could find disturbing.[40] The metaphor Brontë employs here, of the forms and spirit of religion, suggests that Jane is perhaps a better evangelical than Rivers. Jane explains herself to the reader in terms of 'sense': 'my sense, such as it was, directed me only to the fact that we did not love each other as man and wife should; and therefore it inferred we ought not to marry' (p. 427). Here she positions the simplicity and common sense of evangelical faith against the complex intertwining of social, religious and sexual considerations that are clearly clouding Rivers's judgement. Jane recognises the baser instincts causing confusion in Rivers, when she pronounces him to be only 'a man, erring as I' (p. 428).

Jane is also refusing to be carried away by religious enthusiasm. In response to Rivers's final attempt to coerce her into accepting his proposal, Jane experiences the auditory 'vision' of a supernatural calling:

> Religion called – Angels beckoned – God commanded – life rolled together like a scroll – death's gate opening, shewed [sic] eternity beyond: it seemed, for the safety and bliss there, all here might be sacrificed in a second. The dim room was full of visions.
>
> (p. 441)

However, this calling, to something she instinctively rejects, is not to be trusted, and is in fact to be resisted. It is also temporary: the auditory vision changes, so that she hears Rochester calling her and runs instead to him and the fulfilment of her romantic desires. This perverting of such a stock example of God's continuing involvement in the world was probably received by many as one of the most heretical elements of Brontë's novel. It is consistent, though, with the novel's rejection of the place of emotion in evangelical conversion, especially in the female missionary narrative. Indeed, Brontë characterises the scene as one of dangerous religious enthusiasm; Jane narrates that her state of mind at this moment was 'excited', and confidently asserts that to have yielded would have represented a lack of 'judgement' (pp. 441–2). Brontë's recall of earlier evangelical values with this word, in contrast to the Methodist excitement and supernaturalism of the 'calling' invoked by Rivers, paints Jane as the more moderate, orthodox Christian.[41]

In rejecting Rivers's proposal, Jane is also refusing to sacrifice her life. She knows a missionary destiny at this time is premature death; when she is considering the idea, she rationally 'counts the cost' as missionaries were instructed to do: 'I feel mine is not the existence to be long protracted under an Indian sun. [...] If I go to India, I go to premature death' (p. 426). She does not reject missionary sacrifice out of hand, though; she only rejects it for herself unless, like tract fiction's heroine, little Jessica, there is nothing left to lose. Moreover, at the end of the novel, Jane writes an account of Rivers's missionary life and death in a way that suggests admiration of his dedication and sacrifice:

> Firm, faithful and devoted; full of energy, and zeal, and truth, he labours for his race [...] The last letter I received from him, drew from my eyes human tears, and yet filled my heart with Divine joy: he anticipated his sure reward, his incorruptible crown.
>
> (pp. 476–7)

Brontë's choice to end her novel with this fictional missionary memoir and the last words of Rivers's final letter has struck many readers. As scholars have noted, the ending effectually associates both Jane and Brontë with missionary sacrifice, and the apocalyptic, evangelical worldview it epitomised.[42] In this way, Rivers's anticipated death also acts as a displaced sacrifice: he provides the good evangelical death and emotional satisfaction required by the missionary narrative – while Brontë's heroine stays in good health.

There are other displaced sacrifices in the novel. At Lowood, it is Helen, rather than Jane, who fulfils the sacrificial 'holy child' role required in missionary tract fiction, and at Thornfield, though Jane suffers, it is Bertha who is finally sacrificed.[43] Bertha's status as Other, her racial characteristics heavily drawn by Brontë, recalls the heathens whom missionaries went to save, but her actions in the fire, as she stands above what she must intend to be her husband's funeral pyre, also call to mind the Hindu practice of sati, which missionaries often described as a justification for their cultural intervention. Through using a servant character to report the incident to Jane, Brontë is able to indulge her violent streak, describing Bertha's death in the detail that characterised missionary accounts:

> She was standing, waving her arms, above the battlements, and shouting out till they could hear her a mile off: I saw her and heard her with my own eyes. [...] I witnessed, and several more witnessed Mr Rochester ascend through the skylight on to the roof: we heard him call 'Bertha!' We saw him approach her; and then, ma'am, she yelled, and gave a spring, and the next moment she lay smashed on the pavement. [...] Dead as the stones on which her brains and blood were scattered.
>
> (p. 451)

The repeated 'witnessed' is here partly to exonerate Rochester – Bertha was not pushed – but also suggests the religious 'witnessing' of evangelicals in their writings of deathbed scenes.[44] Bertha's sacrifice that night results in Jane's freedom, and Jane's retelling of these violent acts liberates her further in that she can be the narrator of sacrifice, rather than its example.

Brontë as Female Missionary Writer: Re-writing Her Life Story

Reading her novels through the prism of missionary literature, it is evident that Brontë saw in the female missionary a potential role model for strong female characters, confident in their religious knowledge and practice. Meanwhile, she vehemently rejected the idea that missionary work and relationships could be fulfilling enough for women like herself, refusing to allow her characters to conform to the self-sacrificing ideal that was beginning to dominate in cultural depictions of female missionaries.

Of course, as has been argued, the female missionary was also a model for women writers, who could see themselves as carrying out the mission by writing moralistic fiction.[45] And Brontë herself used a missionary persona in her preface to the second edition of *Jane Eyre*, in which she addresses those she aims to convert:

> I turn to another class; [...] I mean the timorous or carping few who doubt the tendency of such books as 'Jane Eyre': in whose eyes whatever is unusual is wrong; whose ears detect in each protest against bigotry – that parent of crime – an insult to piety, that regent of God on earth. I would suggest to such doubters certain obvious distinctions; I would remind them of certain simple truths.[46]

Her association with the figure of the missionary is augmented by her claim to martyrdom, as she accepts that she will suffer her people's hatred of 'him who dares scrutinize and expose' (p. 4) their sins. Rather than passively suffering like an ideal female missionary though, Brontë goes on to align herself within the 'working corps' (p. 4) of Thackeray, whom she sees as a fellow missionary. Like him, she sees herself as seeking to 'restore rectitude to the warped system of things' (p. 4) and harnesses the power implicit in the role of missionary to preach her own theological truth. Indeed, her tone is highly confident as she makes her argument in short, bold assertions: 'Conventionality is not morality. Self-righteousness is not religion' (p. 4). She insists that it is society's incorrect, partial Christianity that has led to misinterpretations of her novel, accusing readers of confusing bigotry with piety. In calling her critics 'doubters' and emphasising 'simple truths', she manages to align her novel with true religion.[47]

Despite Brontë's identification with a strong, non-gendered or masculine missionary identity, and her rejection of female self-sacrifice in her novels, when it came to immortalising her in a biography, her friends worked hard to associate Brontë with the more popular feminine missionary martyr. To Victorians who knew her as a controversial, coarse, woman writer, this might have sounded like a tall order. However, following the publication of Elizabeth Gaskell's *The Life of Charlotte Brontë*, Christians in Britain and America experienced a reversal of opinion. Charles Kingsley wrote to Gaskell that he regretted his earlier prejudice and promised that he would 'now read carefully and lovingly every word she has written'.[48] Meanwhile, religious publishers in America pressed Brontë's friend Ellen Nussey for more reminiscences, more letters, to display Charlotte's 'inner life' and further reveal her 'heroic', 'suffering' and self-sacrificing 'womanhood'.[49] Charlotte's biographers had done their work well.

Elizabeth Gaskell and Ellen Nussey's Collaboration

The role Elizabeth Gaskell played in mythologising Charlotte Brontë through her biography has been much discussed.[50] However, the extent to which this biography was in many ways a collaboration with Charlotte's friend Ellen Nussey, and the particular effects of this, has been insufficiently examined. As Jay notes, the 'narrative line' of Gaskell's biography was provided by the 'four hundred or so' letters Charlotte had written to Ellen over their lives, and scholars are agreed that it was thanks to Nussey that Gaskell was asked to write the biography by Charlotte's family.[51] Despite this, Nussey has either been reduced to a minor character in the story of the biography, or castigated for providing a biased version of Charlotte and enabling the publication of her letters against the wishes of Patrick Brontë and Arthur Nicholls.[52] In fact, I argue that Nussey wielded significant influence over Gaskell's *Life*, moulding it in the tradition of female missionary biography.

Nussey was particularly involved in the mission movement. She shared missionary memoirs with Charlotte, attended meetings and pestered the Brontë sisters for items for the 'Missionary basket'.[53] So, when Nussey envisaged the memoir she wanted Gaskell to write, she probably had something like a female missionary biography in mind. Happily for Nussey, this vision dovetailed neatly with Gaskell's desire to present her fellow novelist as a respectable woman – and in this way to present women's writing as a moral, missionary endeavour.

The correspondence between Nussey and Gaskell reveals the extent of their collaboration, and the friendship that developed through their shared endeavour. In addition to providing Gaskell with Charlotte's letters, Nussey hosted Gaskell at her home twice in 1855 and visited Gaskell in early 1856. Nussey was on hand to assist the biographer, answering queries and providing advice on handling sources. Personally, Gaskell was touched by Ellen's fondness for her daughter Marianne and wrote warmly of their visits to one another: 'I think with much pleasure of my two half-days with you [...] Dear Miss Nussey I am so glad we have begun to know each other!'[54] At the point of publication, the collaboration soured somewhat; a letter from Nussey to Gaskell's publishers expresses her dissatisfaction that Gaskell had not taken enough of her suggestions on board: 'Mrs G considered the work so exclusively her own she was [not] disposed to alterations'.[55] To a certain extent, however, this

Figure 3.1 Portrait of Ellen Nussey, Brontë Society *Transactions* (1898). © British Library Board. All Rights Reserved/Bridgeman Images.

distancing of herself from Gaskell's first, controversial, edition, was performative. Correspondence between Nussey and Gaskell continued until Gaskell's death in 1866, suggesting that their friendship was not irrevocably damaged.

Despite Gaskell's independence in many aspects of the biography, Nussey's influence remains, and many evangelical readers would have recognised the tropes of female missionary biography in the presentation of this otherwise unconventional heroine. Nussey was concerned to present Charlotte as a properly converted evangelical; an exemplar of feminine domesticity; and a female missionary martyr. Although not always fully realised, Nussey's efforts to present Charlotte this way are still evident in the final text.

Narrating Charlotte's Religious Life

One of the most important aspects of a missionary biography was the missionary's conversion narrative. Nussey was in an ideal position to present Charlotte as experiencing the religious crises concomitant on evangelical conversion, as she herself had been instrumental in facilitating them. Juliet Barker criticises Nussey for encouraging Charlotte's morbid religious reflections at a time when her solitary situation made her vulnerable.[56] However, urging friends to consider the state of their souls was a way that evangelical women practised their religion, in the sincere faith that they could help their friends find salvation.[57] Reading Charlotte's more religious letters to her friend Ellen – sometimes out of the suggested chronological sequence – provides evidence of this conversion relationship and process.[58]

In 1836, Charlotte's letters imply that Ellen had started the conversion process, by asking 'kind, gentle, friendly questions'.[59] These questions led Charlotte to reflect on the gulf between her professed Christianity and her lack of faith:

> I know the treasures of the Bible I love and adore them. I can see the well of life in all its clearness and brightness; but when I stoop down to drink of the pure waters they fly from my lips as if I were Tantalus.[60]

Ellen's subsequent letter must have persisted in religious solicitude, as it prompted an emotional response in Charlotte, writing back to her '*dear, dear E.*':

> I am at this moment trembling all over with excitement after reading your note, it is what I never received before – it is the unrestrained pouring out of a warm, gentle, generous heart. [...] I will no longer shrink from answering your questions. I do wish to be better than I am.[61]

At this point, she casts off restraint and her subsequent letters to Ellen (until the spring of 1837) express the extreme emotions of partially glimpsed salvation combined with the self-flagellation that usually came of becoming aware of one's sinful nature and inability to attain true holiness:

> I hope, I trust, I might one day become better, far better, than my evil wandering thoughts, my corrupt heart, cold to the spirit, and warm to the flesh will now permit me to be. [...] My eyes fill with tears when I contrast the bliss of such a state brightened by hopes of the future with the melancholy state I now live in, uncertain that I have ever felt true contrition, wandering in thought and deed, longing for holiness which I shall <u>never, never</u> obtain.[62]

On reading these expressions of religious crisis, Ellen (and fellow evangelicals) might be reminded of Harriet Newell bemoaning her 'cold, stupid heart!' and inability to 'fly away from this clod of earth and participate in the holiness and pleasures of the saints within the veil'.[63]

In February 1837, Ellen would have been comforted by a letter from Charlotte that seemed to express the dawnings of religious conviction. Charlotte described a process in which she moved from feeling rebellious about being separated from Ellen, to understanding that it must be an act of God to keep her from loving Ellen, as the one who had aided her conversion, more than God: 'it must be because we are in danger of losing sight of the Creator in idolatry of the creature'. This process continued with her praying for the ability to resign her will to that of

God, and culminated in: 'a sweet, placid sensation' [...] How happy I was, how bright and glorious the pages of God's holy word seemed to me'.[64] Although Charlotte mourned that this 'foretaste' passed away, even a temporary experience of the peace and happiness of full religious conviction would be celebrated by evangelicals as evidence of a pious soul's progress to salvation.

Nussey made sure to share all these intensely personal letters with Gaskell, presumably hoping that Gaskell would present them in a way that made Charlotte's conversion narrative clear. However, perhaps because Gaskell was a Unitarian, to which sect continual conversion was an alien concept, the letters were not set out or explained in a way to make this narrative explicit. One of the most melancholy letters from the early phase of Charlotte's conversion was wrongly dated by Gaskell and separated from the other religious letters by the famous correspondence with Southey. The letter that suggested a positive resolution to Charlotte's religious crisis was also separated from the religious correspondence by Branwell's letter to Wordsworth, suggesting that Gaskell was more concerned with creating dramatic tension around the siblings' initial engagements with the literary world than she was with telling an evangelical narrative.

In addition to scattering the letters and their conversion narrative, Gaskell was selective when it came to publishing anything expressing Charlotte's sense of sinfulness. She cut a particularly telling passage from one of the October 1836 letters, when Charlotte breaks off from describing the influence of her friend to express her feelings of worthlessness:

> It is from religion that you derive your chief charm and may its influence always preserve you as pure, as unassuming and as benevolent in thought and deed as you are now. What am I compared to you? I feel my own utter worthlessness when I make the comparison. I'm a very coarse common-place wretch![65]

This omission was likely to avoid dwelling on Charlotte's conviction of her sinful nature, something that was characteristic of spiritual biographies but would have been distasteful to Gaskell's Unitarianism.[66] (A later letter, in which Charlotte repeated her fears of damnation, is also omitted.)[67] Gaskell would also have wanted to avoid presenting Charlotte's own admission of 'coarseness' – a charge from which she was aiming to clear her.

Ultimately, instead of stressing the seriousness of Charlotte's religious reflections, Gaskell pathologises them as symptoms of ill-health, referring to Charlotte's behaviour at this time as 'betokening a loss of healthy balance in either body or mind'.[68] In a later edition, she went further, insisting that in her own experience of Charlotte, she was 'free from religious depression when in tolerable health' (p. 443). The only clue that Gaskell gives that this melancholy and despondency might be interpreted differently, is her repeated comparison of Charlotte's words in these letters with the evangelical poetry of Cowper (pp. 107, 108).

Nussey and fellow evangelicals felt that there was more that Gaskell could have done to present Charlotte as appropriately religious. In 1871, Nussey wrote an article for the American *Scribner's Monthly*, entitled 'Reminiscences of Charlotte Brontë', in which she defended her decision to make Charlotte's letters available to the American publication *Hours at Home*, which had serialised these between June and October 1870:

> It has been said to me, 'Why do you not defend your friend's memory from the oft-made charge of irreligion?' [...] A series of events seemed to call, and to call so repeatedly, I could no longer refuse or delay to set about giving, as a tribute of justice to herself, a few more of her own words, the words of her *heart* and *feelings*, as they were elicited by the common accidents and incidents of daily life. The doing of this involves some sacrifice; but to shrink from possible annoyance or discomfort when duly called upon in defence of one we have loved is indeed to be cowardly and craven-hearted. [...] It is hoped the few more letters now given will not fail to show with deep truth that her religion, though it did not manifest itself in phraseology and shibboleth, yet existed in a higher and better sense, finding its expression in the thought and action which springs from trustful, obedient faith [...] Daily she was a Christian heroine, who bore her cross with the firmness of a martyr saint.[69]

In this introduction, Nussey takes on the character of an early female biographer of a woman missionary, depicting her own task as one of heroic sacrifice as she is 'called' to present an exemplary 'martyr saint' to the public. She emphasises the importance of using Charlotte's own words, stressing that these expressed her feelings, which were evidence of faith to evangelicals. And she presents Charlotte as a paragon of domestic piety, manifesting her faith in the dutiful actions of a woman's daily life. This is what she had hoped Gaskell would achieve with the biography, and her continual efforts to publish more of her friend's correspondence – at financial and legal risk to herself – suggest she believed that Gaskell had not fully succeeded.[70]

Even if Nussey did not believe Gaskell had done enough, *The Life* did not completely fail to rehabilitate Charlotte as a Christian. As Gaskell retained most of the text of Charlotte's letters from this time, evangelical readers would have seen, even without explanation, enough clues to convince them that Charlotte was at least not irreligious. Though they may have regretted that Gaskell had not presented Charlotte's conversion didactically enough for younger readers, they would have recognised the elements of female missionary biography in the inclusion of the more serious and emotional of Charlotte's letters to her friend.

Presenting Charlotte's Missionary Domesticity

One aim in which Gaskell and Nussey were united, was that of presenting Charlotte as an example of domestic self-sacrifice. Their earliest correspondence shows how their aims aligned. Nussey wrote to Gaskell:

> When I think of my dear friend as in her every day life and that it will be your endeavour to depict her in her every day charms I cannot but rest assured that aspersion must be silenced for ever. [...] she should be example of life and duty as indeed she deserved to be.[71]

And on receiving Charlotte's letters, Gaskell agreed: 'I am sure the more fully she, CB the <u>friend</u> the <u>daughter</u> the <u>sister</u> the <u>wife</u> is known – and known where need be in her own words – the more highly will she be appreciated'.[72]

In the same way that Nussey wanted to show Charlotte's piety in daily life, as Jay has noted, Gaskell wanted to celebrate her fulfilment of domestic duties, as she bore her loveless life of spinsterdom.[73] When Gaskell wrote to Lady Kay Shuttleworth about her disapproval of Brontë's novels, she insisted that Charlotte only expressed her cravings for self-fulfilment in her novels, while in life she patiently endured:

> The difference between Miss Brontë and me is that she puts all her naughtiness into her books, and I put all my goodness. [...] I am sure she works off a great deal that is morbid *into* her writing, and *out* of her life. [...] her life sounds like the fulfilment of duties to her father, to the poor around her, to the old servants [...] I am sure I could not have borne [...] her life of monotony and privation of anyone to love [...] I shall look up to her strength and (outward if you will) patience with wonder & admiration.[74]

Gaskell here imbues Charlotte's carrying out of domestic tasks, and sacrifice of fulfilment in life, with a heroic nobility, and she continues this in the biography.

Notably, Gaskell's biography domesticated Charlotte in the same way that female missionary biographers feminised their subjects; Charlotte is portrayed as a dutiful daughter, engaging in domestic tasks.[75] Moreover, Gaskell expands on her comment to Lady Shuttleworth, when she narrates the visits Charlotte made to the poor in Gaskell's company and emphasises their feminine nature:

> In all these cottages, her quiet presence was known [...] and she knew what absent or ailing members of the family to inquire after. Her quiet, gentle words, few though they might be, were evidently grateful [sic] to those Yorkshire ears. Their welcome to her, though rough and curt, was sincere and hearty.
>
> (p. 414)

This is a perfect example of female philanthropic, or missionary, visiting, which was a highly respectable extension of a woman's domestic duties. Twice Gaskell stresses that she was a 'quiet' presence, rather than an active proselytiser, and the effect is of a feminine influence being dispersed among the rough Yorkshire natives.

Another way Gaskell domesticated Charlotte was by focusing on her marriage, and imagining the transformative effect she believed this might have had on her friend.

> Henceforward the sacred doors of home are closed upon her married life. We, her loving friends, standing outside, caught occasional glimpses of brightness, and pleasant peaceful murmurs of sound, telling of the gladness within [...] we thought of the slight astringencies of her character, and how they *would turn* to full ripe sweetness in that calm sunshine of domestic peace.
>
> (p. 422, my emphasis)

The marriage did not last long, though, and Charlotte's letters of this time are not exactly brimming with enthusiasm for the married state. She writes ambivalently about how her time is no longer her own and expresses lukewarm feelings of respect and gratitude for her husband. Gaskell, however, instructs us to read these as 'low murmurs of happiness' (pp. 422–3). She also suggests that a woman's married life is (conveniently) out of the scope of biography, kept behind those 'sacred doors'. In this way, Charlotte's unfeminine identity as an author and literary celebrity in the public sphere disappears from view and is redeemed by her final destiny as a married woman, returned to the private sphere of the home.

Charlotte as Self-Sacrificing Missionary Martyr

Nussey's final aim – that Charlotte should be presented in the biography as a female missionary martyr – was successfully achieved by presenting her sister Anne's martyrdom and linking this with Charlotte. Gaskell was likewise keen to use the example of Anne's religiously motivated writing to redeem Charlotte's novels by association.

While Charlotte's novels were difficult to defend, her sister Anne's writing could be portrayed as inspired by a religious mission. As scholars have noted, Anne's most controversial novel *The Tenant of Wildfell Hall* fits the genre of temperance literature.[76] As this literary form contributed to evangelical campaigns to improve society's morals and manners, it can be seen as a form of domestic missionary writing. Despite the fact that this literature involved writing about distasteful subjects, women were encouraged to write temperance tales, as it was believed they could most affectingly depict the violent effects of the sin of drink on the domestic sphere.[77] Novelist Sarah Stickney Ellis was well-known and respected for her temperance fiction and was also involved in the London Missionary Society. Gaskell and the Brontës had their own links with the temperance movement: William Gaskell, while engaging in domestic mission work in Manchester, published a volume of verses entitled *Temperance Rhymes*, which depicted scenes of intemperance in working-class families, and Patrick Brontë started a temperance society in Haworth in 1834.[78]

Anne herself situated *The Tenant of Wildfell Hall* within the genre of temperance literature. Following the practice of Stickney Ellis, Anne used an explanatory preface to expound upon the necessity of portraying the realities of intemperance as a means to combat it.[79] In defending her novel against accusations of coarseness, Anne presented herself as duty-bound to write about this subject and explicitly invoked God as her inspiration: 'when I feel it my duty to speak an unpalatable truth, with the help of God I *will* speak it'.[80] When Charlotte wrote her 'biographical notice' of her sisters, she encouraged readers to believe that Anne was motivated to write her coarse novel out of a painful feeling of religious duty. Gaskell made sure to quote this notice in the biography: 'She brooded over it till she believed it to be a duty to reproduce every detail [...] as a warning to others. She hated her work, but would pursue it' (pp. 267–8). Anne is portrayed as a missionary-like martyr, sacrificing her comfort, happiness and reputation to circulate an authentic account of societal sin.

Moreover, the homelife of the Brontës is presented by Gaskell like something out of temperance fiction, with Anne and Charlotte emerging as domestic martyrs of intemperance. Despite the risk of legal action, Gaskell included the lurid details of Branwell's affair with his employer's wife: how she, 'bold and hardened' (p. 205), seduced Branwell even in front of her children, and how Branwell drank to drown his feelings of guilt and remorse. Gaskell defended her presentation of this material using the terms of temperance literature, aligning herself with this respectable form of missionary writing:

> The story must be told. If I could, I would have avoided it [...] but it is possible that, by revealing the misery, the gnawing lifelong misery, the degrading habits, the early death of her partner in guilt – the acute and long-enduring agony of his family – to the wretched woman [...] there may be awakened in her some feelings of repentance.
> (pp. 204–5)

So that the reader cannot misconstrue her motives she declares somewhat excessive regret (indeed, perhaps she protests too much) that she must reveal this titillating scandal in order to tell a cautionary temperance tale. And, as temperance stories condemned drunkenness specifically for the violence it did to the Victorian family, Gaskell's mobilisation of this genre within the biography further encourages the reader to see Charlotte as a martyr of domestic intemperance.[81] Moreover, because the story of this novelist was being told by a woman writer who so clearly wrote for religious reasons, Charlotte's writing could be assimilated within the context of self-sacrificial female missionary writing by writers such as her sister and biographer.

Of course, the martyrdom of the missionary writers Charlotte and Anne could not be completely established without 'witnesses' of their deaths. These were an essential element of spiritual biographies, stressing the subject's passive resignation to God's will, as well as any suffering they endured. They detailed the subject's last words, and often suggested that the subject experienced some kind of vision of their assured salvation, which enabled them to expire happily.[82] However, the description of Charlotte's death that Gaskell had obtained for the biography was troubling, in that it did not meet the criteria of a good evangelical death. According to her father and husband (Nussey had not been present), Charlotte was 'delirious', and her last words to her husband could be interpreted as a protest against God's will: ' "Oh! [...] I am not going to die am I? He will not separate us, we have been so happy" ' (p. 427). Readers might be reminded of the heretical lesson the young Jane Eyre drew from Brocklehurst's stories of the deaths of sinful children: ' "I must keep in good health and not die" '.[83]

Luckily, Nussey had been an eyewitness to Anne's much more pious death in Scarborough and had written about it soon after, following the pattern of evangelical death witnesses. As we have seen, it was a common device among missionary biographers to present more problematic missionary deaths alongside the exemplary deaths of converts, so that readers experienced the good effects of a good Christian death scene and associated this with the missionary they were reading about.[84] Nussey would have been keen to engineer this effect for the readers of Charlotte's biography.

Nussey tantalisingly, in a self-deprecating manner, mentioned her written account of Anne's death to Gaskell, insisting that she had only written it as a private document as part of her Christian practice:

> A few notes pencilled in my pocketbook shortly after our return from Scarboro – I brought the pocket book in my hand as we sat at work the evening you were here, thinking at the moment I would read to you what I had written but I had not courage to execute my purpose. The record of those few days is very slight and I am conscious very feebly portrayed [...] little did I think of any eye but my own ever viewing the remembrance I then recorded in my book.[85]

Of course, Gaskell asked her for a copy. Her author's sense that it was 'very desirable to have it from an eye-witness', for literary purposes, dovetailed with the desire of evangelical audiences to have eyewitness accounts of deaths, for their assurance of the departed's salvation.[86]

Nussey's account demonstrated that Anne's death fulfilled all the requirements of the good evangelical death. She writes that Anne 'evinced the pious courage and fortitude of a martyr' and was cheerful, grateful and happy to the end, with both Charlotte and Ellen in awe of the obvious religious turn of Anne's mind: 'It was plain that her thoughts were driven by the imposing view before her to penetrate forwards to the regions of unfading glory' (pp. 293–5). With this statement, Nussey portrays Anne as being halfway between life and death: her vision able to supernaturally penetrate the veil of mortality and catch a glimpse of heavenly regions. When the moment of Anne's death finally came, Nussey reports: 'calmly and without a sigh [she] passed from the temporal to the eternal'. Ellen indicates that Anne's 'faith never failed' and that her last words were for Charlotte (p. 295). Her stressing of Anne's filial regard here links Charlotte to her sister's perfect performance of Christian piety, enabling the audience to therefore associate Charlotte with a good Christian death.

In providing her written account of Anne Brontë's death to Gaskell in the way that she did, Nussey ensured Gaskell would publish it in its entirety. Indeed, because of its personal and immediate nature, Nussey's account acts as the emotional and religious heart of the narrative of Charlotte's life. Nussey had had such an influence on the writing of *The Life of Charlotte Brontë* that, although Gaskell did not consciously construct her biography as a female missionary memoir, any reader familiar with the genre would have been able to read it in this context. Paradoxically, the enduring image of the woman writer that had so rebelliously rejected missionary self-sacrifice in *Jane Eyre* was that of a martyred, missionary writer.

Elizabeth Gaskell's Self-Sacrificial Heroines

For many reasons, Gaskell was predisposed to include Nussey's female missionary discourse within her biography of Brontë. As scholars have noted, Gaskell was concerned to establish the writing as a legitimate, respectable occupation for women.[87] More exactly, she wanted to ensure that she could maintain her respectability as a missionary writer, writing about moral issues. Just four years before she produced her characterisation of Charlotte Brontë she had presented the public with another controversial heroine in her novel *Ruth*: a fallen woman, who nevertheless ended up resembling a female missionary martyr. The novel challenged readers' preconceptions of fallen women by portraying the eponymous heroine sympathetically, as capable of redemption, and ends with Ruth dying after taking on the self-sacrificial missionary role of a nurse during a typhus epidemic. Following this novel's publication, Gaskell also found the language of missionary martyrdom useful in dealing with the public's response. At this time, it seems that Gaskell was cloaking her potentially radical missionary writing in the material of acceptably feminine, self-sacrificing missionary heroines.

Scholars have been struck by Gaskell's vacillation between a strong, preacher-like identity and domestic self-effacement. Christine Krueger rightly sees her as a social reformer in the tradition of female preachers, and Matus states that she used the realist novel to religiously critique society.[88] However, Gaskell was initially reluctant to put her name to her novels, and her letters show her torn between what she saw as her duty to write novels of purpose and her inclination to a conventional domestic life. Chapple suggests that, as a Unitarian, Gaskell would have been affected by the legacy of society's disapproval of Unitarian dissent and points out that, in response to this disapproval of their religious beliefs, most Unitarians conformed to social mores where they could.[89] As we have seen, Gaskell had been concerned to present Brontë's feminine, domestic side as part of a similar bid for respectability. However, Gaskell wanted more than to be simply *perceived* as respectable, and for that reason, she needed to reconcile her zeal for missionary writing with the aesthetic of domestic, self-sacrificial femininity.

Gaskell's Mission and Unitarianism

Though Unitarians had traditionally stood back from the enthusiasm of the early foreign missionary movement, by the mid-nineteenth century, they were committed to the domestic mission as a way to bring about social progress, and as a way to claim a middle-class identity; Unitarian women could also see missionary philanthropy as an extension of their domestic duties.[90] Gaskell wrote of her writing as a God-given, missionary activity: as Elisabeth Jay has noted, she wrote to a friend that she believed her art was acceptable as it was her way of 'advancing the kingdom of God'.[91] She believed her earliest work *Mary Barton*, with its controversial handling of the tensions between factory owners and workers, could only do good: 'Surely there is no harm in directing the attention to the existence of such evils. [...] What I wrote so earnestly and from the fullness of my heart must be right'.[92] This faith in her mission helped her deal with the inevitable criticism.

Gaskell's supporters praised her for her self-sacrifice in her writing about unpalatable subjects. The politician Richard Cobden wrote to the Manchester Unitarian Julie Schwabe:

> I read Mrs Gaskell's Ruth before I left Town, and I blessed her as I closed the book for her courage and humanity. It cannot be a successful <u>novel</u> for works of fiction are never so unless they be read by the <u>young</u>; and Ruth will be considered dangerous company for unmarried females even in a book. But the good and brave authoress knew all this when she wrote it and therefore is there the greater merit due to her.[93]

Cobden sees Gaskell as consciously sacrificing any hope of commercial success, writing solely for the good it would do society.

Gaskell's letters show that she felt martyred by the public's reception of *Ruth*. She wrote to a friend: 'the only comparison I can find for myself is to St Sebastian tied to a tree to be shot at with arrows'.[94] Gaskell's self-identification with a martyred saint, responsible for converting a number of souls, brings Gaskell into line with female missionaries, and the women who wrote about them. Comforted by her hope that *Ruth* would do some of the good she had intended, Gaskell accepted her fate with the passive resignation of a missionary martyr: '[it] must be endured with [...] as little inward pain as I can [...] I have no doubt that what was meant so earnestly *must* do some good'.[95]

Writing 'Ruth' as a Tale of Self-Sacrifice and Social Redemption

Writing *Ruth* was a radical, missionary act. The novel calls out the lack of Christianity in society's treatment of fallen women and advances the controversial suggestion that these women could redeem themselves within their own communities, rather than through death or emigration.[96] To lessen the apparent radicalism of her story, Gaskell portrays Ruth carefully – as she did Brontë – so that she emerges as an ideal female missionary. Significantly, Gaskell's novel does allow glimpses of the more heroic identity possible for women missionaries (and writers), especially within the context of Christian Socialism. Ultimately, however, Ruth dies, and her self-sacrificial death effectively neutralises the anxiety that might have been induced by the novel's fallen-woman missionary heroine and its radical woman writer.

Gaskell uses a number of strategies to evoke the public's sympathy for Ruth. First, as has been noted, Ruth is as sympathetic a version of the fallen woman as could be drawn;[97] 'young, and innocent, and motherless', Ruth is taken advantage of by the dissolute gentleman Mr Bellingham.[98] She is not inherently degraded, though, and, once alerted to the sinful nature of her actions, shows herself to be capable of reformation. The one aspect of Ruth's fallen state that makes her less socially redeemable is something over which she had no control: she has a bastard child, the 'badge of her shame' (p. 119). Given this complication, there is additional work to do to ensure Ruth's redemption, and, to effect this, Gaskell turns her into a self-sacrificing missionary heroine.

Indeed, once she has left her seducer, Ruth's story is highly consistent with missionary narratives. She experiences an emotionally painful conversion, in which she recognises the error of her ways. As the minister Mr Benson reads from the Bible during Ruth's first time in his chapel:

> Ruth's heart was smitten, and she sank down; and down, till she was kneeling on the floor of the pew, and speaking to God in the spirit, if not in the words of the Prodigal son [...] bowed down and crushed in her sorrow.
>
> (p. 154)

Once aware of her sin, Ruth becomes a highly Christian character, happily carrying out her duties as governess in the Bradshaw family and mother to her child. When Bellingham reappears and offers her a future with him, first as his mistress, then as his wife, she refuses both offers, sacrificing a comfortable future for the cause of her soul and her son's:

> Evil would it be for him if I lived with you. I will let him die first! [...] if there were no other reason to prevent our marriage but the one fact that it would bring Leonard into contact with you, that would be enough.
>
> (pp. 301–3)

When Ruth's sin is discovered, she isolates herself from the world, sacrificing any hope of social acceptance or fulfilment, and takes on the life-threatening work of a hospital nurse during a typhus epidemic. This role is far more missionary than medical, and Ruth fulfils the character of the ideal female missionary. An old woman describes her, 'singing psalms the night through. Low and sweet, low and sweet, they tell me – till many poor things were hushed, though they were out of their minds' (p. 430). Rather than engaging with sin directly, it is Ruth's gentle, feminine Christianity that spreads a holy influence over the community, bringing Christianity to the apostate working classes, who 'had not heard psalms this many a year' (p. 430). The working-class community bless her as an embodiment of Christianity.

In Ruth's final act of self-sacrifice, she nurses Bellingham, succumbs to the fever and dies. Gaskell's description of Ruth's death is highly similar to those of female missionaries in biographies. She is passively resigned on her deathbed, displaying 'no outrage or discord even in her delirium' (p. 447). The nature of her illness even turns her into a form of the 'holy child': Gaskell writes that her 'open, unconscious eyes' revealed 'a sweet, childlike insanity within' (p. 448). However, at the end, she is able to recover her senses enough to perform a good evangelical death:

> Suddenly she opened wide her eyes, and gazed intently forwards, as if she saw some happy vision, which called out a lovely, rapturous, breathless smile [...] 'I see the Light coming,' said she. 'The Light is coming,' she said. And raising herself slowly, she stretched out her arms, and then fell back, very still for evermore.
>
> (pp. 447–8)

Her mourners, already awed by her self-sacrifice, are now assured of her salvation by her last words and the impression of her supernatural 'vision' of 'the Light'.

In the same way the example of female missionary martyrs was intended to influence readers to be better Christians, Ruth's self-sacrifice causes characters in the novel to resolve to be more forgiving, and less prejudiced by society's ideas of sin. The Anglican housekeeper Sally makes a distinction between the world's religion and that of the angels, as she repents: 'I was not kind to you [...] No! I never was kind to you, and I dunnot think the world was kind to you [...] but you are gone where the angels are very tender to such as you' (p. 452). And Mr Bradshaw, the novel's embodiment of a rigid, 'respectable' religion, such as Calvinist Methodism, feels 'anxious to do something to testify his respect for the woman who, if all had entertained his opinions, would have been driven into hopeless sin' (p. 458), implying that he now believes that, despite her initial sin, there is hope that Ruth is saved. These repentances are glimmers of hope in Gaskell's novel, that an ideal female missionary can convert others to a more humane religion, and change society for the better.

Despite Gaskell's concern to render Ruth as an ideal example of self-sacrificing missionary femininity, her portrayal of her heroine is, in some aspects, radical. These aspects betray Gaskell's Unitarian faith and interest in Christian Socialism, as well as reflecting her own identification, as a writer, with a more heroic female missionary persona.[99] Significantly, in the logic of the novel's plot, Ruth's death is not actually necessary. In the eyes of her community, her work as a nurse is enough to redeem her sin. The working classes bless her, and even Mr Bradshaw has been convinced: after the crisis of the typhus epidemic has passed, his daughter communicates to Ruth that Mr Bradshaw wishes to lend her his holiday home in Wales, as 'papa has been quite anxious to show his respect for you' (p. 432). In this way, Gaskell theoretically removes the requirement for female missionaries to be entirely self-sacrificing, which would have sat uncomfortably with her Unitarian faith. Rather than believing that Christ died as the substitute for mankind in a sacrifice demanded by God, Unitarians rejected such Atonement theology and its resultant demand for Christians' continued penance.[100] So, we may well ask, with Elizabeth Barrett Browning and Charlotte Brontë, just why Ruth had to die?[101]

In part, Ruth's death was necessary as part of Gaskell's re-writing of the female missionary character. Importantly, Ruth death is not entirely passive. Her sacrifice is instead actively heroic, in that she makes an informed choice to take on the work that would in all probability lead to her death; she assures Mr Benson, 'I have thought, and I have weighed. But through the very midst of all my fears and thoughts I have felt that I must go' (p. 425). She resolves to follow this strongly 'felt' missionary calling with the 'stillness' and 'solemnity' (p. 425) respected in early-century biographies of male and female missionaries. This sacrifice as a conscious choice resembles Gaskell's action of publishing *Ruth*. It also brings her into alignment with military heroes, as the conclusion of the novel sees her being memorialised with a hero's tombstone by Mr Bradshaw and 'the first stone-mason in town' (p. 458).

Not only is Ruth's death a heroic missionary act in the service of achieving conversions, though, it effects real social redemption, in the manner of Christ. Unitarians saw Christ's martyrdom as an expression of divine love, reconciling man to God, which, in its implications, was similar to the humanistic theology followed by many Christian Socialists.[102] In effect, further atonement was not necessary, but plenty of work was required to reconcile Victorian society's inhumane practices with Christ's example. While other women writers often compared their heroines' lives to that of Jesus – Craik's *Bread Upon the Waters* is inscribed to 'A woman, the daily record of whose life resembles that of Him'[103] – Gaskell goes further in creating Ruth as an incarnation of Christ. Sally repeatedly refers to Ruth as her 'lamb', and at her funeral, Mr Benson reads from Revelations (7. 14–17): 'These are they which come out of great tribulation, and have washed their robes, and made them white in the blood of the Lamb [...] For the Lamb which is in the midst of the throne shall feed them' (p. 457). Ruth is the Lamb, whose death symbolically washes future fallen women clean of their sins, on earth as in heaven. Such close identification with Christ would be acceptable to Unitarians, given their anti-Trinitarian belief in Jesus's humanity. However, Jay has noted that Gaskell's visual iconography in *North and South*, depicting Margaret in the position of Christ, when she is felled by a stone at a workers' demonstration, was 'daring', in the context of Victorian society more generally.[104] If it was daring to portray the relatively innocent Margaret as Christ, then depicting the fallen woman Ruth as the saviour most Victorians believed to be the son of God was highly radical.

Despite allowing her version of the female missionary character a heroic role of social redemption, in the final analysis, Ruth's death effectively neutralises much of the novel's radicalism. While the novel's story of Ruth's life and work suggested a radical social agenda on the part of its missionary writer, the conclusion brings the focus back to the self-sacrificial female missionary and her good death. Gaskell, largely, was able to maintain her respectability as a woman while pursuing her missionary duty as a writer, but her heroine had to be sacrificed.

Conclusion

Despite Charlotte Brontë's rejection of the self-sacrificial elements of the missionary identity for women, the image of the woman writer that emerged from this period was heavily associated with missionary martyrdom. In the same way that Gaskell neutralised the radical potential of her heroine *Ruth* to preserve her own respectability as a woman writer, she and her collaborator Ellen Nussey minimised Brontë's strong missionary voice by focusing on the self-sacrificial element of her life and strongly associating her with her sister's missionary writing and martyr's death. The woman writer who emerged from Gaskell's biography, who became a model for Victorian women writers, was one mediated by the missionary context, and who, like female missionary martyrs, had to write selflessly, as part of a painful duty to work to save the world. Writing in this persona allowed Gaskell some freedom to write radically about social problems, but it further ingrained self-sacrifice as a requirement for women writers as well as missionaries. As the next chapters will show, this had a particular influence on the feminist writers of the latter part of the century and the construction of the New Woman.

Notes

1. For example, those of Gilbert and Gubar in their *The Madwoman in the Attic: The Woman Writer and the Nineteenth-century Literary Imagination* (New Haven, CT: Yale University Press, 1979); Elaine Showalter in *A Literature of Their Own: British Women Novelists from Brontë to Lessing* (London: Virago, 1982); and Gayatri Chakravorty Spivak, 'Three Women's Texts and a Critique of Imperialism', *Critical Inquiry*, 12:1 (Autumn 1985), 235–61 (p. 244).
2. Mary Poovey, *Uneven Developments: The Ideological Work of Gender in Mid-Victorian England* (Chicago, IL: Chicago University Press, 1988), pp. 132–5.
3. Winter Jade Werner has recently demonstrated Brontë's engagement with specific missionary ideas in *Missionary Cosmopolitanism in Nineteenth-Century British Literature* (Columbus, OH: Ohio State University Press, 2020), pp. 109–42.
4. See Lucasta Miller's *The Brontë Myth* (London: Jonathan Cape, 2001); Elisabeth Jay, 'Introduction', in Elizabeth Gaskell, *The Life of Charlotte Brontë*, ed. by Elisabeth Jay (London: Penguin, 1997), pp. ix–xxxii; and Pamela Corpron Parker's 'Elizabeth Gaskell and Literary Tourism', in *Literary Tourism and Nineteenth Century Culture*, ed. by Nicola J. Watson (London: Palgrave Macmillan, 2009) pp. 128–38.
5. Talley, '*Jane Eyre's* Little-known Debt to *The Methodist Magazine*', *Brontë Studies*, 33 (2008), 109–19 (pp. 112–5).
6. Charlotte Brontë, letter 21 December 1839, repr. in *The Letters of Charlotte Brontë*, ed. by Margaret Smith, 3 Vols (Oxford: Clarendon, 1995), I, p. 201.
7. Cunningham, ' "God and Nature Intended You for a Missionary's Wife" ' in *Women and Missions*, ed. by Bowie, pp. 96–7.
8. Jay, 'Introduction', in Gaskell, *Life*, ed. by Jay, p. xiv.
9. Juliet Barker, *The Brontës* (New York: St Martin's Press, 1994), pp. 4–11.
10. Barker, pp. 282–3.
11. Boyd Hilton refers to extreme evangelicals as 'revelling in pain as though it were a mark of grace', *The Age of Atonement: The Influence of Evangelicalism on Social and Economic Thought, 1795–1865* (Oxford: Clarendon, 1988), p. 10.
12. Barker believes that Brontë conceived the character, and wrote the poem 'The Missionary', while staying with Ellen and Henry Nussey, p. 451.
13. Twells, *The Civilizing Mission and the English Middle Class, 1792–1850: The Heathen at Home and Overseas* (London: Palgrave Macmillan, 2009), p. 84.
14. Charlotte Brontë, *Shirley*, ed. by Jessica Cox (London: Penguin, 2006), pp. 108–9.
15. Letter, 20 November 1840, *Letters*, ed. by Smith, I, pp. 232–6 (p. 233).
16. Letter, 17 March 1840, *Letters*, ed. by Smith, I, pp. 211–3 (p. 212).
17. See Prologue.
18. Charlotte Brontë, *Jane Eyre*, ed. by Margaret Smith (Oxford: Oxford University Press, 1998), p. 146. Further references are given after quotations in the text.

138 Part I: 1830–1870

19 Cunningham also notes the oriental allusions surrounding Rochester in '"God and Nature Intended You for a Missionary's Wife"', in *Women and Missions*, ed. by Bowie, pp. 99–100.
20 Twells, p. 7.
21 Missionaries almost obsessively described the physical appearance and languages of the peoples they were trying to convert, believing that certain appearances and linguistic traits indicated kinship with Biblical races and the likelihood of conversion. See Jane Samson, 'Ethnology and Theology: Nineteenth-Century Mission Dilemmas in the South Pacific', in *Christian Missions and the Enlightenment*, ed. by Brian Stanley (Richmond, VA: Curzon, 2001), pp. 99–122 (pp. 113-7); and Rachael Gilmour, *Grammars of Colonialism: Representing Languages in Colonial South Africa* (Basingstoke: Palgrave Macmillan, 2006), pp. 103–4.
22 See Chapter 1.
23 Poovey, p. 135; Elizabeth Rigby (Lady Eastlake) '*Vanity Fair* and *Jane Eyre*', *Quarterly Review*, 84 (December 1848), (153–185).
24 Siv Jansson argues that Anne Brontë's *Tenant of Wildfell Hall* engages with this cultural belief, '*Tenant*', in *Women of Faith in Victorian Culture*, ed. by Hogan and Bradstock, pp. 31–47 (pp. 35–9).
25 See Chapter 1.
26 See, for example, Rigby, pp. 164–6.
27 Mary Ellis Gibson, 'Henry Martyn and England's Christian Empire: Rereading *Jane Eyre* through Missionary Biography', *Victorian Literature and Culture*, 27 (1999), 419–42 (pp. 421–3).
28 Charlotte Brontë, 'The Missionary', *Poems by Currer, Ellis, and Acton Bell* (London: Aylott and Jones, 1846), pp. 157–63 (pp. 158–9).
29 Gibson, p. 433.
30 See Prologue.
31 Elisabeth Jay, 'Women Writers and Religion: "A Self Worth Saving, a Duty Worth Doing, and a Voice Worth Raising"', in *Women and Literature in Britain 1800–1900*, ed. by Joanne Shattock (Cambridge: Cambridge University Press, 2001), pp. 251–74 (pp. 265–7).
32 Brontë, 'The Missionary', p. 158.
33 Gibson, p. 433.
34 Quoted in Margaret Grierson, *Labourers in the East* (Edinburgh: William Oliphant, 1830), p. 134.
35 Lynne Vallone, 'Women Writing for Children', in *Women and Literature*, ed. by Shattock, pp. 275–300 (p. 279).
36 Gilbert and Gubar, pp. 348, 360.
37 Charlotte Brontë, *Villette*, ed. by Tony Tanner (London: Penguin, 1985), pp. 227–9.
38 Jay, 'Women Writers and Religion', in *Women and Literature*, ed. by Shattock, p. 267.
39 Cunningham, '"God and Nature Intended You for a Missionary's Wife"' in *Women and Missions*, ed. by Bowie, pp. 97–8.
40 As we saw in Chapter 2, Dinah Craik invoked the Book of Common Prayer to argue that Christianity precluded women marrying a man they could not love.
41 Jay has outlined how moderate evangelicals often distinguished themselves from the enthusiasm of Dissenters in *Religion of the Heart: Anglican*

Evangelicalism and the Nineteenth-Century Novel (Oxford: Clarendon, 1979), pp. 18, 104.
42 Mary Wilson Carpenter, *Imperial Bibles, Domestic Bodies: Women, Sexuality, and Religion in the Victorian Market* (London: Ohio University Press, 2003), p. 138; Cunningham, '"God and Nature Intended You for a Missionary's Wife"' in *Women and Missions*, ed. by Bowie, p. 103.
43 Spivak drew attention to how Bertha's self-immolation consolidates Jane as heroine, in an example of what she terms the 'epistemic violence of imperialism', p. 244.
44 Jay, *Religion of the Heart*, pp. 154–5. See also Chapter 1.
45 See Chapter 2.
46 Charlotte Brontë, 'Preface' (1847), in *Jane Eyre*, ed. by Margaret Smith, pp. 3–5 (pp. 3–4). Further references are given after quotations in the text.
47 This language also recalls the 'ethos of simplicity' that Krueger identifies in early Methodist women preachers, pp. 60–2.
48 Charles Kingsley, Letter, 14 May 1857, Elizabeth Gaskell Manuscript Collection, University of Manchester Library, MS 730/58.
49 'Unpublished letters by Charlotte Brontë', serialised in *Hours at Home: A Popular Monthly of Instruction and Recreation*, Vol XI (New York: Charles Scribner and Co, May 1870–October 1870), pp. 101–10 (p. 101); Ellen Nussey, 'Reminiscences of Charlotte Brontë', *Scribner's Monthly*, 2 (May 1871), pp. 18–31 (p. 18).
50 Jay reminds us that Gaskell's Charlotte is, after all, an 'imaginative creation', 'Introduction', in Gaskell, *Life*, ed. by Jay, p. xxvii; meanwhile, Lucasta Miller has explored the afterlife of this creation in her *The Brontë Myth* (London: Jonathan Cape, 2001), pp. 26–58; and Juliet Barker has attempted to dismantle the myth in her biography, *The Brontës*.
51 Jay, 'Introduction', in Gaskell, *Life*, ed. by Jay, p. xiv; Miller, p. 59.
52 Joan Bellamy, 'Mary Taylor, Ellen Nussey and Brontë Biography', *Brontë Society Transactions*, 21, 7 (1996), pp. 275–83 (pp. 276–8); Juliet Barker, 'Saintliness, Treason and Plot: The Writing of Mrs Gaskell's *Life of Charlotte Brontë*', *Brontë Society Transactions*, 21 (1994), pp. 101–15 (pp. 105, 109–11).
53 Ellen Nussey, Pocket Diary, 25 June 1844, Harry Ransom Center, University of Texas in Austin, Nussey Collection 1.6.
54 Letter, [20 October 1855], University of Manchester Library, JGS 30/4. Though the source dates this letter as 'Jan 86', Chapple and Pollard more convincingly date it as 20 October 1855, *The Letters of Mrs Gaskell*, ed. by J. A. V. Chapple and Arthur Pollard (Manchester: Mandolin, 1997), pp. 873–4.
55 Nussey, Letter, n.d., University of Manchester Library, JGS 30/4.
56 Barker, *The Brontës*, pp. 283–5.
57 See Prologue.
58 I have mainly relied on Smith's authoritative edited collection to piece this together, but my reconstruction of the conversion narrative, combined with evidence from Gaskell's biography, and Nussey's publication of the letters elsewhere, have led me to believe that Smith's sequencing of the letters is occasionally incorrect.
59 Brontë, Letter, 10 May 1836, *Letters*, ed. by Smith (pp. 143–4).
60 Ibid.

61 Letter, quoted in Gaskell, *Life*, ed. by Jay, p. 108. Though Margaret Smith dates this as 1837, both Gaskell and Nussey (in her own publication of the letters) date it as 1836, and the excitement expressed would seem to signal the beginning of an intimate conversion relationship.
62 Letter, 5 and 6 December 1836, *Letters*, ed. by Smith, I, pp. 155–6 [this letter is wrongly dated in Gaskell's *Life*].
63 Newell, Diary, 3 March 1811, quoted in Leonard Woods, *Memoirs of Harriet Newell*, p. 70.
64 Letter, February 1837, *Letters*, ed. by Smith, I, pp. 164–5 (p. 164).
65 Letter, [?October 1836], *Letters*, ed. by Smith, I, pp. 152–3 (p. 153). The cut passage is indicated by an ellipsis in Gaskell's *Life*, p. 109.
66 See John Chapple, 'Unitarian Dissent' in *Cambridge Companion to Elizabeth Gaskell*, ed. Jill Matus, pp. 164–77 (p. 165).
67 Printed in 'Unpublished letters by Charlotte Brontë', *Hours at Home*, pp. 109–10. This letter is also absent from Smith's collection, as the *Hours at Home* letters are deemed unreliable. It may be that Nussey or the editors of this publication fabricated parts of the letters attributed to Brontë, which, in itself, would testify to how concerned they were to establish a more religious mythology around her.
68 Gaskell, *Life*, p. 106. Further references to this work are given in the text.
69 Nussey, 'Reminiscences of Charlotte Brontë', *Scribner's*, p. 18.
70 In addition to publishing letters and reminiscences in American periodicals, Nussey attempted to produce her own volume of collected letters – the infamous Horsfall Turner publication – which became the subject of legal wrangling and was eventually withdrawn from publication. Most of the volumes were pulped, but a couple remain, including one in the British Library.
71 Nussey, Letter, n.d., University of Manchester Library, JGS 30/4.
72 Gaskell, Letter, 6 September 1855, University of Manchester Library, JGS 30/4.
73 Jay, 'Introduction', in Gaskell, *Life*, ed. by Jay, pp. xii–iii.
74 Gaskell, Letter, 7 April 1853, in *The Letters of Mrs Gaskell*, eds. J. A. V. Chapple and A. Pollard, pp. 227–30 (pp. 228–9).
75 Miller stresses this aspect of the biography, pp. 61–2, 72–3; Nicola Watson also suggests that Gaskell details the domestic routine of the Parsonage in order to separate Brontë from her authorial persona of Currer Bell, in *The Literary Tourist: Readers and Places in Romantic and Victorian Britain* (Basingstoke: Palgrave Macmillan, 2006), p. 118.
76 See Marianne Thormählen, ' "Horror and Disgust": Reading *The Tenant of Wildfell Hall*', *Brontë Studies*, 44 (2019), 5-19.
77 Amanda Claybaugh, *The Novel of Purpose: Literature and Social Reform in the Anglo-American World* (London: Cornell University Press, 2007), pp. 87–8.
78 Barbara Brill, *William Gaskell 1805–1884: A Portrait* (Manchester: Manchester Literary and Philosophical Publications, 1984), pp. 45–51; Henrietta Twycross Martin, 'The Drunkard, the Brute and the Paterfamilias: The Temperance Fiction of the Early Victorian Writer Sarah Stickney Ellis', in *Women of Faith*, ed. by Hogan and Bradstock, pp. 6–30 (p. 23).
79 Twycross-Martin, 'The Drunkard', in *Women of Faith*, ed. by Hogan and Bradstock, p. 24.

80 Anne Brontë, 'Preface to the Second Edition', *The Tenant of Wildfell Hall*, ed. by Herbert Rosengarten (Oxford: Oxford University Press, 1992), p. 4.
81 Miller notes how the presentation of the Brontë sisters as victims of domestic adversity has endured, Miller, p. 72.
82 Jay, *The Religion of the Heart*, pp. 154–60; Michael Wheeler, *Death and the Future Life in Victorian Literature and Theology* (Cambridge: Cambridge University Press, 1990), pp. 27–32.
83 Brontë, *Jane Eyre*, p. 33.
84 See Prologue and Chapter 1.
85 Nussey, Letter, n.d., University of Manchester Library, JGS 30/4.
86 Gaskell, Letter, [December 1855], *Letters of Mrs Gaskell*, ed. by Chapple and Pollard, p. 877.
87 Jay, 'Introduction', in Gaskell, *Life*, ed. by Jay, pp. xi–xiii.
88 Christine Krueger, *The Reader's Repentance: Women Preachers, Women Writers, and Nineteenth-Century Social Discourse* (Chicago, IL: University of Chicago Press, 1992), p. 16; Matus, 'Introduction', in *Cambridge Companion*, ed. by Matus, pp. 2–3.
89 Chapple, 'Unitarian Dissent', in *Cambridge Companion*, ed. by Matus, pp. 164–77; also see Ruth Watts, 'Rational Religion and Feminism: The Challenge of Unitarianism in the Nineteenth Century', in *Women, Religion and Feminism in Britain, 1750–1900*, ed. by Sue Morgan (Basingstoke: Palgrave Macmillan, 2002), pp. 39–52 (p. 41).
90 Twells, pp. 5, 84; see also Kathryn Gleadle, *The Early Feminists: Radical Unitarians and the Emergence of the Women's Rights Movement* (Basingstoke: Macmillan, 1995), p. 6, pp. 90–106.
91 Quoted in Jay, 'Introduction', in Gaskell, *Life*, ed. by Jay, p. xii.
92 Letter, [late 1848], *Letters of Mrs Gaskell*, p. 67.
93 Richard Cobden, letter, 21 March 1853, University of Manchester Library, Eng MS 730/25.
94 Gaskell, Letter, January 1853, *Letters*, pp. 220–1.
95 Ibid., p. 221.
96 As Alan Shelston describes, Gaskell had helped a fallen woman in Manchester access the support of a charitable emigration society so was well aware of this possible solution, though she does not choose it for Ruth, 'Introduction', in Elizabeth Gaskell, *Ruth*, ed. by Alan Shelston (Oxford: Oxford University Press, 1998), pp. vii–viii.
97 Ibid., pp. xiii–xv.
98 Gaskell, *Ruth*, ed. by Shelston, p. 56. Further references to this work are given in the text.
99 Gaskell corresponded with the Christian Socialists, Charles Kingsley and F. D. Maurice, explicitly about *Ruth*, Kingsley, Letter, 25 July 1853, University of Manchester Library, Eng MS 730/57; Maurice, Letter, 17 February 1854, Eng MS 731/65. She also encouraged her acquaintances in industry to distribute Kingsley and Maurice's pamphlets to their workers, letter, [c. 20 February 1850], *Letters of Elizabeth Gaskell*, pp. 104–5.
100 Chapple, 'Unitarian Dissent', in *Cambridge Companion*, ed. by Matus, pp. 164–77 (pp. 164–5).
101 Elizabeth Barrett Browning, Letter 16 July [1853?], University of Manchester Library, Eng MS 130/9; Shelston, 'Introduction', in Gaskell, *Ruth*, ed. by Shelston, p. xix.

102 Chapple, 'Unitarian Dissent', in *Cambridge Companion*, ed. by Matus, pp. 164–5.
103 Dinah Craik, *Bread Upon the Waters* (Leipzig, Bernhard Tauchnitz, 1865), p. 3.
104 Jay, 'Women Writers and Religion', in *Women and Literature*, ed. by Shattock, p. 252.

Part II
1880–1900

4 Missionaries of the New
Sarah Grand, Olive Schreiner and Margaret Harkness

Introduction

The New Woman writers emerged in the turbulent decades of the 1880s and 1890s, when the stability of middle-class society was being threatened not only by radical movements such as feminism and socialism but also by a loss of religious certainty following progressive scientific and philosophical inquiry. Mike Kissack and Michael Titlestad express well the 'sense of bereavement' caused by agnostic thought and evident in the literature of the period.[1] However, I would argue that the extent of secularisation in this period has been exaggerated. As Elisabeth Jay observes, evangelicalism's specific beliefs and practices became less dominant among the middle classes and appear less in literature, however, evidence would suggest that religion did not disappear in this period, but rather evolved.[2] Peter d'Arcy Jones has pointed out that the death of agnosticism's champion Charles Bradlaugh, in 1893, slowed the progress of secularisation significantly.[3] It has also been acknowledged that the so-called secular movements of feminism and socialism were often inspired by religious belief.[4] Moreover, at the same time as supposedly secular arguments about degeneration, empire and socialism were taking place, the Salvation Army was working in the slums of London, and university-educated, progressive middle-class men and women were negotiating social problems from their own, often religiously influenced, slum settlements and mission houses.[5] Though many of the New Woman activists and writers engaged in a secular feminism, a significant number were still inspired by religious ideas and beliefs – and, I argue, by the character and narrative of the female missionary.

Generalising about the 'New Woman' of the 1880s and 1890s is inadvisable; she was both a real, cultural phenomenon – a feminist activist or writer – and a fictional construct, representing aspirations or fears about modern women and their increasing freedoms in terms of education, employment and sexuality.[6] Moreover, the New Woman activists and writers were not distinct groups – most New Woman writers were also activists – nor were they part of a united feminist movement.[7] Scholars have considered Sarah Grand and Olive Schreiner alongside radical

DOI: 10.4324/9781003332961-8

feminists or socialists, such as Mona Caird, Beatrice Webb and Eleanor Marx, but also with New Woman writers such as George Egerton, Thomas Hardy and Oscar Wilde.[8] Scholars have tended to start from secularist assumptions, focusing on the New Woman writers' radical feminism;[9] however, feminist scholars have been concerned by the latent conservatism at the heart of some New Woman writings, for example, Grand's espousal of eugenics and support of the goals of the social purity movement.[10] I argue that the feminism of many New Woman writers has to be understood as part of their religious belief. Moreover, the elements of radicalism and conservatism in their writing stem, in part, from the paradoxes inherent in the female missionary narrative, which still exerted an influence on religious women.

The three women writers examined in this chapter came from religious backgrounds and, I argue, saw their social causes of feminism and socialism as religious missionary movements. While Sarah Grand attacked organised religion – she once referenced an American newspaper's claim that English women's degradation was due in part to 'the tyranny of a heartless, political Church'[11] – in her writing, her feminism emerges as intertwined with a religious philosophy that fit within the broad church of Victorian evangelicalism; furthermore, Grand's writing shows a striking continuity with earlier female missionary writers. Olive Schreiner was born into the extreme religion of Calvinist missionary parents in South Africa.[12] Although her work in the 1880s and 1890s largely deals with agnosticism, it is also shot through with religious imagery, and a missionary faith in the future resolution of doubt and injustice in the world, which sustained and comforted many of her feminist readers.[13] Though the journalist and novelist Margaret Harkness has been less studied, it is known that she was the daughter of an Anglican clergyman.[14] While scholars have suggested that Harkness turned to Christian Socialism and the Salvation Army during her crisis of faith, I argue that her work shows instead the power of the female missionary narrative for reconciling spiritual and social turmoil.[15]

The feminist writing of Grand, Schreiner and Harkness, like that of other New Woman writers, engaged in the contemporary debates around sexual and marital reform, especially concerning the Victorians' sexual double standard, which had been dramatically exposed in the debates surrounding Josephine Butler's campaign to repeal the Contagious Diseases Act. Grand's writing explicitly referred to Butler's campaign and engaged with the social purity movement; her novels dramatically depict the consequences for middle-class women of unregulated male sexual behaviour and female sexual ignorance. Schreiner's work, contrastingly, more closely echoes Mona Caird's feminist writing, which championed female sexual liberation. And Harkness follows Schreiner in imagining alternatives to marriage for women. Despite their differences, I argue that all three writers portray the 'New Woman' in their fiction as a missionary, and her feminist cause as a deeply religious 'redemptive mission', using the language and tropes of female missionary writing.[16] Like earlier missionaries, they were especially concerned with the problems of self-sacrifice for women. Though their focus on the self-immolation of their female heroines has troubled scholars looking for a more positive feminism, I argue that in their use of this defining trope of the female missionary narrative, New Woman writers most powerfully expressed an understanding of feminism, especially at this time of uncertainty, as courageous.[17]

Schreiner and Harkness's feminist writings also encompassed socialist themes. Scholars have noted that socialism at this time comprised disparate and diverging groups; while many socialists were concerned with working scientifically for systemic social change, others took a more spiritual, visionary approach, such as those involved, like Schreiner, in 'The Fellowship of the New Life', which was based on millenarian religious beliefs in a better future.[18] At the same time, the Christian Socialist movement placed a belief in the Incarnation and Divine Immanence at the centre of their work, which led to a collapsing of distinctions between sacred and secular.[19] And General Booth's missionary Salvationism also evolved to place an emphasis on ameliorating material social conditions as important for bringing about God's Kingdom on Earth.[20] Schreiner and Harkness engage with these currents in social work as they communicate the New Woman's utopian mission to bring about a better world through breaking down class and sexual difference.

The writers discussed in this chapter used new forms of writing to communicate their message.[21] Schreiner's novel *The Story of an African Farm* and her shorter 'dream' pieces can be seen as examples of modernist experimentation but are also reworkings of older forms of parable, spiritual biography and devotional vision writing.[22] Meanwhile, Grand established herself as one of the foremost writers in the new women's magazine market, developing this form both to preach her polemics but also to create the character of the New Woman missionary.[23] Finally, Harkness adapted the traditional novel by using her journalistic experience, including reportage-style description, while also using the themes and tone of sentimental religious or socialist tracts.[24] These forms, combining the old and the new, embody the position of the New Woman, at once on the shores of modernity yet reaching back to the earlier female missionary narrative in sometimes conservative but often radical ways.

This chapter starts by examining Sarah Grand's writings to demonstrate how she constructed herself in a female missionary role, and the feminist cause as a religious one, as well as exploring her novel *The Heavenly Twins* for how she and her New Woman characters deal with the issue of female missionary sacrifice. I then explore Schreiner's allegories in *Dreams* and her novel, *The Story of an African Farm* to identify the female missionary tropes in her utopian philosophy. Finally, I consider Margaret Harkness's engagement with missionary narratives in her Salvation Army novel *Captain Lobe* or *In Darkest London*.

Sarah Grand and the New Woman Missionary

One of the most revolutionary of the New Woman writers, Sarah Grand arguably coined the term 'New Woman'. She also famously unveiled the Victorian sexual double standard and the dangers of venereal disease in her highly controversial and successful novel *The Heavenly Twins* (1893).[25] Before this, she had left her husband and started a new life as a professional writer, creating her New Woman self in the expanding periodical press as 'Madame Sarah Grand'. She and her writing were at once radical and yet comfortingly domestic; for example, she displayed a feminine fondness for fashion.[26] Grand also defended her writing about taboo subjects as morally important for the future health and well-being of the nation.[27] In later life, Grand embraced orthodoxy and the establishment, taking on the role of Lady Mayoress of Bath alongside mayor Cedric Chivers. In this capacity, she gave a speech about *The Heavenly Twins* in which she insisted that her work should be seen within orthodox Christian belief.[28] Notwithstanding the radicalism of her writing, the serious moral purpose of her work aligns her with female missionaries, and the tropes of female missionary discourse were integral to her construction and presentation of the New Woman mission.

While many scholars see Grand as a heroic, pioneer New Woman for her writing about radical feminist concerns, her more conservative, social purity feminism has troubled them.[29] Ann Heilmann has seen Grand's portrayal of women as superior beings, taking responsibility for the future of society, as unfortunately tied to the essentialism of social purity feminism, and Angelique Richardson has pointed out that her eugenic, determinist point of view led to a conservative view of gender and class differences as biologically inherent.[30] Generally, Grand has been accused of inconsistent views and feelings: the old and the new at odds with each other as her radicalism was checked by instinctive conservatism. Interestingly, Beth Sutton-Ramspeck links Grand with a feminism that based its power for transforming society on domestic femininity and the extension of maternal power.[31] Meanwhile Heilmann allows for her ideological division by suggesting that Grand enjoyed the 'indeterminacy of her shifting positions', deploying the rhetoric of female higher morality and engaging in a performance of fashionable femininity at will.[32]

Rather than seeing her as caught between radicalism and conservatism, I argue that Grand was acting in the tradition of nineteenth-century evangelical women and authors such as Charlotte Brontë and Elizabeth Gaskell: she was attempting to educate women as to their religious duty and society's crimes against Christianity and, in doing so, was taking on a public role (see Chapter 3). Like these earlier women, Grand could see herself as a missionary, and her progressive feminist causes as not only compatible with, but in fact central to the evangelical mission to realise God's plan for mankind. Grand's 1880s and 1890s version of the feminist missionary writer was perhaps more obviously radical, though, as she was speaking out against women's injuries in Britain and was less constrained by organised (male) religion. Facing the difficulties of a controversial public role, Grand drew on the established, feminine, self-sacrificing female missionary character, as well as the more forthright, militant female missionary type, to construct herself and her characters. Like women missionaries in the field, I argue that she drew strength and authority from both these constructions, piously believing in the moral and self-sacrificial crusade of women, yet enjoying her activity and agency as a radical writer-missionary.

Missionary Self-Fashioning

In the Foreword to the 1923 edition of *The Heavenly Twins*, Grand explicitly associates her writing with the religious act of converting what she terms the Old Woman to the New Woman mission, making the point that the dubious reputation of her novel actually won people over to her cause whom it had before been impossible to 'capture and convert'.[33] This idea of conversion enables a conception of the Old and New Woman as not at all distinct species and suggests the potential of the Old Woman to become an advocate for the New Woman's cause. In the Foreword, Grand tells a number of short autobiographical anecdotes (which may or may not have been true), including one about meeting, at the appropriately feminine occasion of a tea party, a 'delightful grandmother of the conservative Victorian type' (p. 398). It transpires, though, that this Old Woman is an enthusiastic convert to Grand's cause, and the speech attributed to her by Grand provides a doctrinally correct instruction for how to react to *The Heavenly Twins*:[34]

> I resent the state of ignorance in which we were kept, and the way in which we were deceived about matters which so intimately affected our well-being and the well-being of the whole human race. I am ashamed of myself and of every woman who allowed herself to be [...] deceived, and not only allowed it, but preferred to be kept in ignorance [...] With the children to think of too! the poor darling little sufferers whom it was our duty to protect and defend!
> (pp. 397–8)

Grand attributes this woman's 'awakening' to her novel, which enabled her to fully understand the importance of the mission. In a way reminiscent of the selflessness of missionaries in leaving their old lives, this woman moves from her own account, to Woman more widely, and the human race. This engagement with the future of the human race as part of a woman's religious duty, both in the abstract, and in the shape of a more tangible duty towards her children, echoes the spiritual biographies that linked female missionaries with pious mothers and daughters (see

Chapter 1). Finally, the direct victims of the current system, whom the mission will save, are ringed round with sentiment – those 'poor darling little sufferers' – to increase the sense of wrong and appeal affectively to a domestic feminine sympathy.

In this narrative, Grand paints herself as an ostensibly self-effacing, passive female missionary. Through ascribing the polemical speech to the converted Old Woman, she can represent herself as a conciliatory, even-tempered martyr who has been redeemed by time. She reacts to the convert's tirade and a comment about how people treated her personally with saintly forbearance and a parable-like aphorism, 'the mills of God grind slowly' (p. 398), which depicts her as a vessel for God's work. She similarly disclaims her own agency in her writing, and stresses its Godly provenance. She claims that she did not choose the subject of her novel, or even to write at all. She describes the production of the novel in the same way that female missionaries justified their religious 'calling' and religious women writers defended their foray into publishing:

> I did not choose my tool; it was given to me. I did not [...] choose the *motiv* of this book; the *motiv* chose me. I broke silence [...] on the impulse to speak [...] on the urgency to write which comes to the writer who has something to say. The Zeitgeist determined my subject matter [...] sooner or later the thoughts and feelings of the inarticulate, seeking expression, select a medium, and I happened to be the medium on whom the ideas in the air laid hold.
>
> (pp. 400–1)

Like female missionaries, Grand's mission was 'given to' her, chosen for her and impelled her to speak. Linda Wilson has argued that religious women could see it as a responsibility to go against society in the service of their religion; like these women, Grand was 'constrained by zeal' to 'break silence' and the social restrictions to follow her Godly mission.[35] Instead of using the language of a Christian God here, she uses ideas from transcendentalism, such as the 'Zeitgeist', and quotes Emerson as saying that women are more susceptible to ideas in the air (p. 400). The ideas of this religious philosophy and those of Spiritualism (suggested by Grand's use of the word 'medium') are easily appropriated by Grand into the traditional idea of the female missionary or preacher as vessel for God's word, and the essentialist idea of women as especially suited for this role of moral communicator (which we have seen was common in female missionary writing as well as in social purist discourse). Grand finally uses an unmistakable and explicitly religious term for her inspiration, attributing the first line of her novel to 'what the Quakers call "a pointing"' (p. 401), so that there can be no doubt that her writing is sanctioned by God.

More radically, Grand sets herself up as a missionary of a new religion. She attributes the Old Woman's chosen ignorance to the old, mistaken religion of organised Christianity: the Old Woman believed that she was being pious in equating husband and father with God. Whereas, the New Woman is 'the modern religious woman' (p. 399), who has learned to rely on her conscience – which evangelicals often interpreted as an embodiment of the Holy Spirit – in place of organised religion.[36] Grand also deploys the powerful narrative of heroic martyrdom. In this scene, a character suggests that a monument should be erected to her, 'built of the stones they threw at the author for writing the book' (p. 399), which further establishes Grand as self-sacrificing – stoned by unbelievers. Grand even associates herself with Christ's martyrdom when she says, 'They are forgiven for that; they knew not what they did' (p. 399). This casting of herself as Jesus and analogising her bad press with the crucifixion is a striking suggestion of how Grand saw herself and the New Woman mission. Like the earlier female missionaries, Grand was very able to find and exploit the radical possibilities and authority inscribed within the language of religious sacrifice.

Grand is clear that it was her religious commitment to active missionary work, expressed in the language of personal conversion, that most empowered her. Grand attributes her awakening to an example of female suffering: 'a beautiful Irish girl' who became disfigured by disease after only two years of marriage.[37] Grand uses this girl in the same way that female missionaries like Ann Judson used examples of 'heathen' women to invoke feelings of universal sisterhood and awaken women to the mission.[38] Grand uses the pronoun 'we' in her journalism to include other women in the New Woman mission, which she says 'forces us out of our apathy'.[39] Though British middle-class women were not subject to such barbaric practices as their Eastern sisters, Grand insists that they too are victims – of 'brutal' treatment and what she terms 'that horror' (p. 404), meaning venereal disease transmitted to them by their immoral husbands.

Grand also describes being inspired by another New Woman missionary: Josephine Butler, whom she became aware of when she heard 'eminent men' (p. 318) maligning her and her campaign to repeal the Contagious Diseases Acts. Grand speaks of Butler in religious terms as 'one of the greatest [...] saints who ever lived' (p. 317), and effectively adds to the tradition of writing female hagiography for the inspiration of future workers. Grand writes how she herself was inspired to become a missionary in imitation of Butler: she was seized with the conviction that 'it was time someone spoke up' and that she 'would not shirk it'.[40] Being 'seized with' conviction is similar to how she passively describes her writing as being 'inspired' by a 'calling', but the language of having a duty to speak and act that cannot be 'shirked' suggests a far more active missionary piety. Even more powerfully, she uses military images that recall the language of the Wesleyan missionary wives when she imagines herself as 'some knight of old' who would 'stand by' other women missionaries such as Josephine Butler against male attack with the authority here of a Christian crusade (p. 318).

Grand's Inspirational New Woman Missionary

In her less autobiographical writing, Grand explored a number of different types of New Woman characters, some of whom were visions of the future, while others were transitional figures.[41] One of her more ideal versions of the character appears in 'The New Aspect of the Woman Question' as a figure resembling a female missionary from biography. She is depicted as set above society, passively 'sitting apart in silent contemplation all these years' until she 'proclaimed for herself what was wrong [...] and prescribed the remedy'.[42] Grand is drawing on the idea of the aesthetic beauty of passive piety to depict the New Woman missionary as attractive, yet, in fact, this character is highly radical. Contemplation is a religious activity, and the idea of the New Woman missionary as silent, yet sure, approaches the 'still small voice' of God that Elijah eventually hears.[43] The movement from passivity to 'proclaiming' and 'prescribing' for society continues this construction of woman as prophet, endowed with religious authority.

In 'The Undefinable', a short story often interpreted as being about female artistry, Grand introduces another radical New Woman missionary, who arrives at the home of a decadent male artist to provide him with a new model/muse and, in the process of modelling for him, manages to convert him to the Godly cause.[44] Scholars have convincingly interpreted Grand here as 'saving' aesthetics from the influence of decadence, but they have not fully appreciated the religious language in which this is cast.[45] In fact, the New Woman missionary in this story is powerfully associated with Christ. At one point, she arrives 'just as [the artist] was about to step into [his] carriage'.[46] As Richardson notes, the image that the narrator gives of Lot's wife, as the artist turns away from the carriage, back into the house, was often used as a warning for those who would not mend their sinful ways, even as the Apocalypse approached; it soon becomes clear that not only is the New Woman a missionary, she is in fact a messianic vision of the Second Coming.[47] There are two moments of conversion in the story, which are achieved by the two faces of Christ, or the two ideals of the female missionary. The first is the woman's passive, 'indescribable grace [...] evidence of strength in reserve' and 'a certain quietude [...] emanating from her forcibly' (p. 131), which creates serious, religious feelings of gravity, gladness and responsibility in the artist, yet is also, like many conversions, associated with a strong, 'exquisite sense of pleasurable emotion' (p. 131). This emotional conversion experience leads the painter directly to extol, in the manner of a convert to the New Woman cause, 'the glorious womanhood of this age of enlightenment' (p. 132), explicitly naming it as divine.

The second conversion moment gives the female missionary the power of masterly proclamation and associates her even more strongly with the Messiah, as she declaims:

I am the woman who stood at the outer door of your studio and summoned you to judge me; the same whom, in your spiritual obscurity, you then found wanting. Rend now that veil of flesh, and look! Who was at fault?

(p. 134)

The idea of the New Woman as the stranger at the door recalls Matthew 25, 'I was a stranger and you invited me in' (25:35), and makes the case for the divine within the human: 'whatever you did for one of the least of these brothers and sisters of mine, you did for me' (25:40). The Godly identity of the New Woman is emphasised by the physical reactions that the painter experiences; he describes himself *obeying* 'like one electrified' and his admission of guilt to her demand 'Who was at fault?' 'bursts' from him 'involuntarily' (p. 134). The experience of the divine is an almost out-of-body experience, in which his 'vision is clouded; [he] saw nothing but mist' and which 'consumes' him with emotion and creativity – the New Woman is in effect allowing him a glimpse of the possible future. Her demand that he 'rend [...] that veil of flesh' refers to both the moment when Jesus's death caused the curtain of the Temple to be 'rent in twain' (Matthew 27:51) and the scriptural exegesis of this event as making possible a new way to reach heaven: 'through the veil, that is to say, his flesh' (Hebrews 10:20).[48] Grand's message is that men who judge the New Woman are sinfully not recognising her as the embodiment of Christ on earth, and those who oppose her cause are wilfully remaining in ignorance, rather than taking the way that will bring about Christ's Kingdom on Earth.

Despite the divinity of this New Woman, Grand does not idealise her; she is another interim New Woman missionary figure, who is 'an impossible mixture of incongruous qualities' (p. 130), struggling with her flaws. In all her writings, Grand admitted the transitional nature of the New Woman and allowed her to be human, 'unlovely' and 'full of faults'.[49] It was in her novels, though, that she was most able to portray the difficult experience of being a New Woman missionary, such as the lengthy, painful process of conversion, and the psychological impact of wrestling against society. As I will show in the next section, Grand's most famous novel *The Heavenly Twins* is full of such missionary characters, who heroically sacrifice conventional lives to follow their necessary and difficult vocation to bring about a new world.

Grand's New Woman Missionary Narrative and The Heavenly Twins

Grand was insistent that Christianity was a significant presence in *The Heavenly Twins*, as she explained in a speech she gave as Mayoress of Bath at a 1928 Josephine Butler Centenary. Though she recalled hearing that Butler had criticised this novel, saying 'There is no God in that',

Grand insisted that this was a common misreading of her novel and that it should be impossible to miss God's presence in it. To prove this, she drew her audience's attention to the device of the cathedral bells in her novel, which repeatedly play a line from Mendelssohn's *Elijah*; Grand felt that these bells were 'the haunting thing in the book'.[50] Most scholars, however, have continued to ignore this aspect of the novel, in their focus on the more secular themes of sexual disease and marriage reform. Though Heilmann has recognised that Ideala, the eponymous heroine of the Grand novel which precedes *The Heavenly Twins* in a trilogy, is a 'quasi-religious' character, she does not fully acknowledge the missionary nature of characters such as Evadne, Mrs Orton Beg and Angelica in *The Heavenly Twins*.[51] These characters are all depicted as converts and missionaries – some more successful than others – and their narratives show that they are inspired and sustained in their New Woman work by the religious conviction communicated by Grand's cathedral bells.

The novel is made up of three linked coming-of-age narratives, focusing on the contemporary feminist questions about marriage, sexual disease and women's sexual innocence. But these narratives also often strongly resemble the female missionary narrative of conversion, followed by a Providential 'call', leading to sacrifice in the course of difficult missionary endeavours. Though she does not fully commit herself to New Woman missionary activity, Evadne Frayling learns the responsibility inherent in women's marriage choices and feels compelled to enforce celibacy in her own marriage as part of the mission to reform men. Meanwhile, the theoretical feminist Angelica Hamilton-Wells, following a cross-dressing dalliance, is brought to a religious conversion, which leads her to sacrifice romance in favour of New Woman activism. Finally, Edith Beale's story is that of a sacrificial convert. An archetypally innocent young woman, her ill-advised marriage causes her to be infected with syphilis, lose her sanity and then her life. How Grand concludes her heroines' stories – Edith's terrible death, Evadne's lack of effective feminist action and Angelica's punishment for sexual transgression – has troubled previous scholars.[52] Seeing these plots, though, as reworkings of female missionary narratives reveals Grand's understanding of the feminist missionary character and her sacrifices and suffering at the hands of modern society.

Grand begins her novel with a Proem, which introduces Grand's device of the cathedral bells' chime. The bells are an aspect of her novel that departs from realist style to enable the inclusion of the supernatural, the Godly, within the novel and as part of the New Woman mission. In this, Grand follows the practice of early female missionary writers and novelists, who included God's presence in the form of Biblical quotations, supernatural visions, and by depicting the experience of prayer. Grand makes it impossible to ignore her haunting chimes, as, whenever she

♪ *Musical notation:* He, watch-ing o- ver Is - ra - el, slumbers not, nor sleeps.

Figure 4.1 'He, watching over Israel, slumbers not, nor sleeps'. Stave of music from Mendelssohn's *Elijah*, as used by Sarah Grand in *The Heavenly Twins*. Image author's own.[53]

refers to them, she includes within the text the physical stave of notated music from *Elijah* that is ascribed to them.

The stave breaks the text and forces the reader to contemplate not just the words that appear under the stave, but the message as a whole – combined with the invoked power of religious music – as part of the feminist message of the novel. *Elijah* was very popular at the end of the nineteenth century; Sir George Grove wrote in 1896 that the oratorio 'has taken its place, if not on a level with "The Messiah", very near it'.[54] And Grand suggests that readers, on 'hearing' the bells will, like many of her characters, involuntarily continue the musical phrase, 'carrying the running accompaniment, as well as the words and the melody, on to the end' (p. xxxix). Readers would therefore have been able to follow the line which Grand includes in the text, 'He, watching over Israel, slumbers not, nor sleeps', with that which succeeds it in the oratorio: 'Shouldst thou, walking in grief, languish, He will quicken thee'.[55] The words reassure activists that while they struggle, if they have faith in God, they will be supported. The oratorio continues to underline this promise through repeating the message that 'He that shall endure to the end, shall be saved' and enjoining listeners to 'rest in the Lord' and 'wait patiently'. Readers might also recall the psalm from which the first line was taken, which promised God's assured protection from harm, especially to those 'going out', which missionaries would have understood as a special message directed at them.[56]

As well as a comfort, the bells are a call to arms; Elijah was enabled to overthrow kings and wreak God's own vengeance before being carried away to Heaven.[57] The psalm from which Mendelssohn took the second line of his phrase invokes a militaristic, Biblical struggle: 'Though I walk in the midst of trouble, thou wilt revive me: thou shalt stretch forth thine hand against the wrath of mine enemies, and thy right hand shall save me'.[58] The potentially violent power of God that could be turned against the enemies of the righteous is dramatically evoked in the oratorio with choral and orchestral tone painting of the earthquakes that accompanied God's appearance to the prophet, and a vigorous chorus summarising Elijah's subsequent holy warfare. Through asking her readers to 'play' the complete phrase in their heads, Grand ensures that, every time this musical stave appears in the novel, these associations of promised support in the militant and holy New Woman struggle will be recalled. The final paragraph of the Proem explains that the bells' purpose in the novel is to call people to missionary work: 'for every one a special hour would come, when they would be called, and then left to decide' (p. xlvii). When Grand interrupts her prose at key points in the novel with the chime, she signals the New Woman concerns that are part of the religious mission and dramatises the calling and conversion of her characters to the cause.

Evadne's story is the first to follow the Proem, and follows the form of a female missionary biography. Immediately after the bells of the Proem have chimed their missionary calling, Evadne is presented, looking out at the world 'inquiringly' (p. 3), as if in search of such a sign. Her narrative begins with her moral and intellectual development, and her seriousness following her awakening to the realities of the world recalls the piety of newly-converted missionaries. She realises that a woman's decision to marry is a far more significant one than she had originally believed; marrying an immoral man is not just injurious to the woman, but to the whole of society: ' "Marrying a man like that, allowing him an assured position in society, is countenancing vice, and" she glanced round apprehensively, then added in a fearful whisper – "*helping to spread it*" ' (p. 79). Her assurance in the rectitude of her conscience enables her to resist society's beliefs about how women should act within marriage, effectively countering with the social purity activists' authoritative language of eugenic reproduction.[59] She presents her arguments forcefully to her aunt, Mrs Orton Beg, demanding that she converts for the sake of the next generation:

> You set a detestably bad example. So long as women like you will forgive anything, men will do anything. You have it in your power to set up a high standard of excellence for men to reach in order to have the privilege of associating with you.
>
> (p. 79)

As well as converting her to the truth of social purity theory, Evadne is calling on her aunt to become a female missionary: to keep men to a high standard of morality through her moral influence.

Evadne's efforts to convert her aunt are accompanied by the chiming of Morningquest's bells. Though mostly ignored by scholars, Orton Beg is, like the grandmother in the 1923 Foreword, another of Grand's sympathetically drawn Old Women: 'the best sort of woman [...] the purest minded, the highest principled, the most devoted'.[60] Orton Beg is portrayed as a spiritual person, living 'for the life to come entirely', exerting the passive religious influence of pious women that enables her visitors to 'rise into the ecstasy of the higher life [...] with the desire to go forth and do great deeds of love' (pp. 69–70). However, she is depicted as slumbering while the bells chime, 'mechanically' repeating

Missionaries of the New 157

and extending the musical phrase, before she 'awoke with a start' (p. 71). This awakening is repeated when Evadne arrives to shatter her peace with the New Woman message. The bells ring again during this interview, the stave of music intrudes into the room, associating Evadne's insistence that she is morally compelled to leave her disreputable husband with the religious mission.

While Evadne's narrative includes this episode of conversion and strong missionary activity, she fails to commit to a New Woman missionary career. She abandons her principles by agreeing to live with her husband and by promising him that she will not get publicly involved in feminist activism. Her missionary work takes the form of merely setting 'an example' (p. 343) and exerting a passive influence. When Edith Beale's death convinces her that this was not enough, she spirals into depression. Scholars' disappointment with Evadne as a modern feminist is understandable; however, such difficulties with faith were often included in the female missionary narrative. In this tradition, Evadne's struggles with her missionary identity, along with her sacrifice of health, can be included powerfully as evidence of heroic New Woman martyrdom.

Conversion to the New Woman mission is portrayed as a sacrifice. Orton Beg's awakening is depicted sympathetically as a painful thing. She dislikes hearing 'anything unsavoury' (p. 78) and expresses her conversion as a loss, telling her niece that

> Every word that you say seems to banish something – something from this room – something from my life to which I cling. I think it is my faith in love – and loving. You may be right, but yet – the consequences! the struggle, if we must resist!
>
> (p. 80)

The New Woman life will be one of harsh truths and resistance. It is clearly 'easier to submit [...] disagreeable to know' (p. 80). Orton Beg's former religion allowed her to avoid the 'torture' of thinking about sin and to leave 'the inexplicable' to God (pp. 80–1). In her journalism, Grand insisted in the same way that her choices required sacrifice on her part; she describes herself as 'shrinking' from her task, and suffering, Christ-like, for the sake of the rest of humankind: 'there should be one person to do whatever there was to be done, and to save the others as much as possible'.[61] Ultimately, the language of this suffering sacrifice leads to a rhetoric of heroism rather than passive self-immolation. Grand declares: 'we go forth at his bidding to deliver his message; but let no one shame himself by saying that we do not suffer in the going'. The suffering becomes a badge of honour, reflecting their heroic service in the holy New Woman mission.[62] The authority within this rhetoric gives women strength to contemplate the fight and, following the death of Edith Beale, Orton Beg is able to write strongly 'we must alter all this', before going off to campaign with Evadne's New Woman friends (p. 349).

The novel suggests, though, that the most problematic sacrifice that a New Woman has to make is that of romantic love and marriage. Love is shown to be impossible once a New Woman has sacrificed her comfortable innocence. Orton Beg has to give up his feminine faith in 'love – and loving' (p. 80), and the marriages of Evadne and Angelica Hamilton-Wells are characterised as contracts, in which the female missionaries can outline their scope of influence and action: Evadne demands a marriage of celibacy, and Angelica realises that the most rational path open to her is to marry a suitable man with whom she can live freely, even – or perhaps especially – if she does not love him. Her proposal to Mr Kilroy is, 'Marry me and let me do what I want' (p. 321), its lack of romantic vocabulary demonstrating her sacrifice of that possibility. As we have seen, women missionaries often went into unromantic marriages in order to access the mission field; while missionary writing tended to minimise the sacrifice entailed in these unions, and the implications for women missionaries' femininity, novels could explore how women might have experienced such a situation. In *The Heavenly Twins*, Angelica's marriage of convenience and her resistance of femininity are shown to lead to tragedy.

The volume of the novel which follows the relationship of Angelica (disguised as 'The Boy') and the Tenor has been examined as an exploration of cross-dressing and Victorian sexuality.[63] The episode fulfils a number of functions in Grand's narrative, though. The relationship is, first, an admission that the sacrifice of romantic marriage can lead to New Women feeling unfulfilled. It also shows Grand's regret that equal, honest relationships between the genders are impossible until society is reformed through the New Woman mission. Angelica explains that the 'charm' of the relationship she is able to have with the Tenor when she is disguised as the Boy lay in the 'benefit of free intercourse with your masculine mind undiluted with your masculine prejudices with regard to my sex' (p. 458).

Most importantly, however, this episode is instrumental in Angelica's conversion to Christianity and her commitment to the religious New Woman mission. The Tenor approaches their relationship like a female missionary or a character in tract fiction: he intends to use intimacy to convert the Boy, 'to influence him in some worthy direction' (p. 385). He encourages the Boy's nocturnal visits so that he can lead him 'by example principally, but also by suggestion' (p. 403). Angelica at this point is struggling against the calling of religion; the narrator mentions twice how she hates the chime of the bells – for her, it is 'cruel as eternal damnation' (p. 436) – and she reacts strongly to any evidence of 'the Tenor's simple piety' (p. 414), that influential trait so admired in female missionaries. For evangelicals, this struggle would have been a positive sign, and the Tenor certainly feels that in quieter times, when his relationship with the Boy is intimate and familial – 'almost paternal' – they experience spiritual joy together; when 'grey glimpses of the old cathedral [...] set his whole poetic nature quivering [...] joy sanctified by reverence', there are suggestions that the Boy is 'in harmony' with this experience (p. 405).

The Tenor also encourages Angelica not to see social problems as evidence of the absence of God, but as causes to which feminine religion can provide solutions. When they first meet in the square at night, Angelica reacts with 'repugnance' (p. 375) when she sees a prostitute. The Tenor, in contrast, sings the litany to himself, then calls to all the forms of God – 'Pater de coelis Deus […] Fili Redemptor mundi […] Spiritus sancte Deus' – and finally to 'Sancta Maria' (pp. 372–5). His singing, most significantly when he calls to the female influence of the Virgin, brings about an emotional reaction in the prostitute, who is seen to reflect on her life and call on God to 'pitié de moi!' [sic] (p. 375). The girl's presence in the square, juxtaposed with the Tenor's singing and the bells' repeated chime, leads Angelica to the positive step of religious questioning: 'Do you believe it?' (p. 376). As the Tenor affirms his faith, it is united with feminist action, as Grand shows an unidentified lady – probably Angelica's religious aunt Fulda – speak with the prostitute and take her to the Sisters of Charity. Earlier in the novel, when Angelica asks the heroine of Grand's earlier novel, Ideala (who is presented as a family friend of Angelica's) where 'the true spirit of God is' (p. 267), Ideala answers that the spirit of God is within women – or more precisely, the New Woman. Though the Catholic priest reacts to this as heresy, the claim is only really radical in its association with feminism – otherwise, it falls within the tradition of specifically female piety, seen in female missionary writing throughout the century.

Finally, like a female missionary, the Tenor makes the ultimate sacrifice in the course of his conversion work, and it is this which leads Angelica to take up her religious New Woman mission. Most scholars have interpreted the death of the Tenor and the return of Angelica to her husband as punishments for their transgressions.[64] Grand's violent ending of the relationship is certainly a reminder that relationships of this sort between men and women are at this point impossible and that the New Woman must gain fulfilment only through her mission. More importantly, though, the sacrificial death of the Tenor is the crisis that brings Angelica to her full conversion. Angelica realises that this man has continually sacrificed himself in the cause of her salvation:

> To see the 'Boy' eat and be happy was all he asked, and if hunger pinched him, he filled his pipe and smoked till the craving ceased […] no-one else had ever sacrificed anything for her sake, no one else had ever cared for her as he had cared.
>
> (p. 517)

In his sacrifice, the Tenor resembles Christ himself; when he encounters the Boy in the square, he is singing the 'Agnus Dei' – he 'finds himself' singing it 'involuntarily', it supernaturally 'possesses' and 'haunts' him (p. 372) – and this associates him with Christ as the sacrificial lamb.[65] Angelica herself recognises him as one who is instrumental in bringing about God's plan when she names him 'Israfil'; as well as the angel of song, Israfil is the angel in Islam who blows the final trumpet to signal the resurrection, or the Christians' second coming.[66] The Tenor's conversion work and final sacrifice are part of God's plan to create Angelica as one of the New Women who will reform the world. Fulda explicitly interprets the Tenor's death this way to Angelica, confronting her with her duty as a New Woman:

> Angelica smiled disagreeably, 'You are insinuating that he died for me to save my soul' [...] Her aunt took no notice of her sneer. 'Oh, not for you alone,' she answered earnestly, 'but for all the hundreds upon whom you, in your position, and with your attractions, will bring the new power of your goodness to bear.
>
> (p. 535)

In the hour between the chimes of the Morningquest bells, which Fulda explicitly suggests are calling her 'specially – this moment' (p. 357), Angelica struggles to become Fulda's religious, serious New Woman. The discourses of eugenics and decadence appear to offer her a way to avoid conversion; she argues, 'I inherit bad principles from my ancestors [...] I was born bad, and delight in my wickedness', and the narrator describes how she 'threw herself into her easy chair, crossed one leg over the other so as to display a fair amount of slender foot and silk-clocked stocking, as it is the elegant fashion of the day to do' (pp. 536–7). At the end of the hour, though, Angelica abandons these excuses and alternative constructions of womanhood and hears the bells' chime with 'a new significance' (p. 540). The Tenor's sacrifice has enabled her to give up her own desires and become satisfied with the New Woman's mission of fulfilling work and the promise of a better world for women in the future.

Perhaps the most haunting sacrifice in Grand's novel, though, is that of Edith Beale, whose story is used to inspire feminist work. Like the victims of sati, whose deaths are repeatedly presented by female missionaries, Edith's death accuses the society that allows women to be so sacrificed. Grand has Edith voice this accusation on her deathbed, telling her father, husband and the parish doctor: 'You, who represent the arrangement of society which has made it possible for me and my child to be sacrificed in this way. I have nothing more to say to any of you' (p. 300). The episode presents a perversion of the ideal religious woman's deathbed performance. Indeed, God, in the form of the bells' chime, is absent in Edith's death scenes; the chime sounds once 'portentously' (p. 293) before the scenes and then is conspicuous by its absence – only the word of God in the form of the Bible is invoked, and that is literally thrown in man's face when Angelica hurls it at Menteith and breaks his nose. Edith does not passively submit to death. Rather than making prayers, she shouts accusations. In place of pious beauty, she presents an ugly countenance: 'There were deep lines of suffering upon it, and her eyes glittered feverishly, but otherwise she was gray, and ghastly, and old' (p. 300). Edith's is no beautiful, saintly death. Her death is the work of man rather than God, and it inspires the novel's New Woman characters to go forth in Grand's religious New Woman mission.

Grand's reworking of missionary tropes and narratives enabled her to present herself and the New Woman mission in the heroic rhetoric of Christian self-sacrifice. The struggles of her novel's characters show them to be only more courageous in their giving up of conventional lives and love. Interestingly, like Brontë, Grand manages to avoid ever fully sacrificing her feminist characters, instead creating a Christ-like New Man who is willingly martyred for the New Woman cause. As we shall see, this New Man figure appears also in the work of Schreiner and Harkness, alongside their more agnostic versions of the New Woman missionary.

Olive Schreiner: Mission and Sacrifice

As the daughter of missionaries, Schreiner's childhood would have been steeped in evangelical culture, and she would have witnessed firsthand the lives of female missionaries.[67] Although she famously lost her Christian faith in childhood, the influence of aspects of the female missionary identity and narrative can be seen in her development of a personal form of religious belief, encompassing her feminism and socialism, and in her writing.[68] In this section, I examine her early works, *The Story of an African Farm* (1883), and her allegorical dream pieces (written in the 1880s), for their treatment of the New Woman and the female missionary narrative.

Working from her own admission that she became a freethinker as a child, scholars have tended to define Schreiner as an agnostic and have explored the extent to which she was influenced by more secular Victorian philosophies, such as Comtean positivism.[69] However, her novel *African Farm* has been seen as a series of ironic inversions of Comte, suggesting that such a secular science did not provide Schreiner with a solution to her metaphysical struggles.[70] It must be remembered that agnosticism is not the same as atheism; agnostic freethinkers of this time had recourse to other forms of faith. Heywood suggests Schreiner embraced G. H. Lewes's version of positivism, which additionally included the world of dream, myth and religion.[71] And many scholars have found elements of Emersonian transcendentalism in her writing.[72] Carolyn Burdett has argued that Schreiner found modern hope to replace her religious faith Spencer's evolutionary *First Principles*;[73] significantly, Spencer included in this the category of the 'Unknowable', which allowed for the continuing existence of mystery and the hope of future revelation within Victorian science.[74] Berkman points out that this belief that, in the future, metaphysical questions would be solved, doubts resolved, and 'ultimate Truth' revealed, lay at the heart of 1880s and 1890s Freethought.[75] Freethinkers had not given up on the possibility of a Revelation, and Schreiner's doubts did not preclude her New Woman mission being inspired by a similar religious belief in a better future for humankind as displayed by Grand.

The utopianism still present in freethinking agnosticism was linked, for Schreiner, with other progressive movements of the period. In London in the 1880s, she became involved with the Fellowship of the New Life, which was an idealist group of socialist artists who stressed collectivism and men and women's fellowship, in opposition to the individualism, personalism and egoism of capitalism.[76] Like other members of this group, Schreiner could think of herself as an artist working in the socialist mission to bring about a more moral world.[77] For Schreiner, this meant using her writing to communicate a feminist message, urging society to reform.

As we shall see, the combination of her missionary Christian background and her utopian, feminist social vision led Schreiner to create New Woman fiction that renewed the female missionary narrative and allowed her to identity with aspects of the female missionary character.

Schreiner's Self-Sacrificial Feminist Missionaries

Schreiner's collection of dream fragments and allegories, published as *Dreams*, communicate a belief in a better future to be achieved through women's work and sacrifice, as part of a religious mission given to them directly from God. The works are strongly Christian in their allegorical forms and Biblical language. Elisabeth Jay has pointed to the influence of religious texts in the recurring images of wine presses and the catechistic form of the dialogue, and has argued that Schreiner's marketing of *Dreams* was a missionary-like act for the feminist cause, in that she hoped to 'awaken' rich readers who might have some power to bring about change.[78] More than this though, in many of the 'Dreams', Schreiner presents herself and the New Woman as missionaries working to realise a Christian vision of a better world.

In 'I Thought I Stood', the female narrator imagines herself going to heaven in order to 'arraign [her] brother, Man' because he has 'taken [her] sister, Woman, and has stricken her, and wounded her, and thrust her out into the streets'. She demands that the kingdom be transferred to her because man 'is not worthy'.[79] The present, real-world situation between man and woman is seen here to be going against God's law, requiring action to save the kingdom from its fallen state. God refuses the narrator's request, pointing out that it is her duty to help her sister. Feminist activism on behalf of fallen women, such as Schreiner engaged with in London and South Africa, is therefore seen as a religious duty. When the narrator returns, this time with her sister, God gives the women a clear instruction to become missionaries: though they ask for divine intervention, for God to speak to man, or to give them a message for him, God interrupts and says 'Go, take the message down to him! [...] Upon your hearts it is written; take it down to him' (p. 32). The message of the New Women is therefore constructed as a religious message, and the writing of New Women texts becomes a missionary activity.

The missionary activity of the majority of the female narrators and characters in these stories is that of sacrifice. Though Heilmann finds Schreiner's emphasis on such sacrifice defeating for feminism, I would argue that Schreiner was aware of the powerful effect depictions of female missionary self-sacrifice could have, and invokes the power of feminine suffering in service of her feminist mission.[80] The female narrator in 'I Thought I Stood' has to risk her 'pure' hands (p. 31) and go down into the mire to help her fallen sister; their work is also arduous, leaving them 'very tired' (p. 31). Burdett and Heilmann have noted that the allegorical form allowed Schreiner to express emotion, but I would suggest that neither fully acknowledged how important it was for Schreiner to include such feeling in her work.[81] The reluctance of the female characters to take up their martyrdom in the cause of gaining a better future for women betrays how painful self-sacrifice was to Schreiner, but also establishes the heroism of New Woman feminists. In 'Three Dreams in a Desert', the heroine has to give up love of man in order to become a pathfinder to a better world for the human race, which will only be reached once women have been advanced to equal status with men. The intensity of feeling caused by this is embodied in the woman's cry of '*Oh, I am alone. I am utterly alone!*'.[82] What remains with the reader is the woman's heroic fortitude as she 'grasped her staff' and set off to dedicate herself in the very slow progress of making a track to the edge of the river, so that one day women might build a bridge with their bodies and, eventually, cross over.[83]

Great heroism is necessary for the allegorical missionaries of *Dreams* because Schreiner's doubts mean that there is no longer a clear millenarian vision of the Second Coming being brought about by God's servants spreading the gospel to gain salvation for all, and no faith that there will be reward for their sacrifice in the hereafter. The aim of the New Woman missionary must be to carry out work for the redemption of future generations; there is no certain redemption for her.[84] Nevertheless, Schreiner adapts the vision of the hereafter implicit within female missionary sacrifice narratives to retain a form of sustaining faith. She notably dedicates *Dreams*:

> To a small girl-child,
> who may live to grasp
> somewhat of that which for us
> is yet sight, not touch.[85]

Her vision of the future is doubly deferred – the girl child of the future still might not even grasp it – so it is the hope itself, which almost takes the form of a prayer, in which Schreiner and her readers can take comfort. While her female characters might not experience the bringing about of heaven on earth themselves, they have hope that their self-sacrifice will lead to an improvement in the human world for women in the future. Certainly, the popularity of Schreiner's work, especially with the later suffragettes, would testify to the presence in the allegories of a hopeful faith in redemption that could sustain her heroic feminist missionaries.[86]

The Heroic Self-Sacrificial New Woman Missionary in The Story of an African Farm

The full implications of the replacement of a faith in reward after death with faith in a more general redemption of humankind in the future are played out in Schreiner's novel *The Story of an African Farm*. Allegories of the New Woman missionary's experience in an agnostic world are presented alongside the tragic story of a New Woman heroine in an attempt to create a narrative to sustain missionaries of the New Woman cause.

As many scholars have noted, this novel is largely about the loss of faith, and two chapters at the centre of the novel deal specifically with this metaphysical crisis: 'Times and Seasons' and 'Waldo's Stranger'.[87] Though these chapters are often discussed as if they were unrelated to the plot of the New Woman character Lyndall, the chapters of loss and confusion immediately precede the grown-up Lyndall's reappearance at the farm, which forcibly suggests that, as in *Dreams*, the future of the world, including the survival of faith, is tied to the fate of women. The allegorical form of these chapters means their lessons can be applied as much to the New Woman writer or reader as to the male characters associated with them; indeed, the Hunter's story was able to be republished as a standalone allegory in Schreiner's *Dreams*.

These allegorical chapters demonstrate what remains in Schreiner's philosophy to sustain faith in the New Woman mission. 'Time and Seasons' describes a relatively traditional struggle with faith, experienced by many Christians in the nineteenth century.[88] It details the movement from primitive belief; to taught Calvinism; to the rejection of this for a more Victorian, 'God is Love' type theology; and finally, to doubt: 'Now we have no God. [...] now he has flitted away from us, and we see what he was made of – the shadow of our highest ideal, crowned and throned. Now we have no God'.[89] Schreiner creates a modern allegory in this chapter: there is a lack of specificity as she breaks from particular characters and places to attribute this metaphysical crisis to a universal 'we'. Moving quickly through chronological time, Schreiner portrays the movement from faith to disbelief as a natural growing up; the sections roughly correspond to stages in a child's development, which has led scholars to read the chapter as championing the progress of positivist philosophy and to read the allegory of the Hunter, immediately following, as the next stage in the process towards scientific rationalism.[90] However, there is a temporal setting to this allegory – there is no God 'now' – which, in a narrative of progress, suggests the possible existence of a future where these doubts are resolved.

Scholars have suggested that Schreiner posits either transcendentalism – the One, the Oversoul – or scientific positivism as the route out of metaphysical crisis.[91] However, I would argue that Schreiner instead reaches for the Christian narrative of the female missionary when she immediately follows 'Time and Seasons' with her allegory of the Hunter. Schreiner never fully breaks with the terms of reference of evangelical Christianity and its literature, and this allegory takes place in a primitive world, containing lands of symbolic darkness such as 'the land where it is always night' (p. 128), and characters such as Wisdom and Knowledge who direct the Hunter's quest for the elusive silver bird, Truth (pp. 124–5). The Truth that the Hunter seeks, is God by another name; likewise, the Hunter's quest, like that of the female missionary, demands the Christian virtues of patience, hard work, suffering and self-sacrifice as he has to leave his home, journey through the Land of Negation and Denial, and engage in a life's work building a stairway up the mountains to where Truth will be found. As well as resembling modern science's incremental progress towards knowledge, the Hunter's is a heroic, and religious, missionary narrative.[92]

Like Schreiner's New Woman missionaries in *Dreams*, the Hunter is required to renounce everything in his search for God and the promised world to come; even the comforting lies of traditional Christianity must be sacrificed. The lies in this tale are represented by beautiful birds, including one named 'Reward after Death' (p. 125). This last tenet of faith notably supported female missionaries through their sufferings, enabling them to die passively, with the conviction that they were saved for the hereafter. To labour for the conversion of the world, for the improvement of conditions for all classes and races in the future, with no such reward for oneself, is a far greater sacrifice. The Hunter expresses the emotion involved in giving up his last treasured bird, 'Immortality':

> 'Oh, my beautiful, my heart's own!' he cried, 'May I not keep you?'
> He opened his hands sadly.
> 'Go, he said. 'It may happen that in Truth's song one note is like to yours; but *I* shall never hear it.'
> Sadly he opened his hand, and the bird flew from him forever.
> (p. 128) [italics in original]

The repetition of 'sadly', the second time moving the adverb to the beginning of the sentence for emphasis, augments the 'forever' and the impassioned, protesting question to give an impression of the cost to the Hunter and the absolute irrevocable nature of his sacrifice. His only hope is for when mankind has found Truth, that this unknown future thing might approach the beauty of the past religion – but he is clear that he will never know it and the stressed '"*I* shall never hear it"' contains the bitterness of his sacrifice. This is the case for the New Woman – her efforts are all for those who will come after, with no hope that she herself will share in the successes of this new world.

Like the New Woman heroine in 'Three Dreams in a Desert', despite the cost, the Hunter chooses to persevere with his mission of building a stairway – another bridging structure – to enable future generations to proceed further towards the goal. His declaration of intent is made 'bravely' and, when he almost despairs, although he utters a 'wild cry', he gains control over himself and silently, stoically works on for years through blood and pain (p. 131). In Christian terms, he sees his 'salvation' in this work (p. 131) and, when beset by the Echoes of Despair, he utters a rhetorical speech that recalls the missionary's situation:

> Have I torn from my heart all that was dearest; have I wandered alone in the land of night; have I resisted temptation; have I dwelt where the voice of my kind is never heard, and laboured alone, to lie down and be food for you, ye harpies?
>
> (p. 132)

The Biblical language here, with the anachronistic 'ye' and 'dwelt', contains the idea of labouring bravely alone, with faith in one's own conscience, for a supernatural cause. Most significantly, the difficulty of the sacrifices entailed in the mission serves to enhance the Hunter's missionary heroism.

Schreiner gives the dying Hunter the only comfort she envisages as possible for New Woman workers and reports his death like that of a missionary, granting him a supernatural vision of the world to come, which leads him, in his triumphant final words to express a conviction that his mission was not in vain:

> 'Where I lie down worn out other men will stand, young and fresh. By the steps that I have cut they will climb [...] They will never know the name of the man who made them [...] but they will mount, and on *my* work; they will climb, and by *my* stair! [...] And no man liveth to himself, and no man dieth to himself [...] My soul hears their glad step coming,' he said 'and they shall mount! They shall mount!' He raised his shrivelled hand to his eyes.
>
> (p. 133)

Schreiner allows the Hunter's soul to outlive his shrivelled, worn-out body: while she says that his eyes would no longer be able to see, his soul is enabled to 'hear' as he experiences a supernatural aural 'vision' of the success to come. Though there is a tension here between self-renunciation, in that no-one will put his name to his contribution, and pride in his work, the Hunter is able to reconcile this through the words of the Bible: 'none of us liveth to himself', meaning the work is for a larger cause than self-aggrandisement, but, equally, 'no man dieth to himself' – the submersion of self in life allows one to ascribe meaning to death and to exult in one's achievement through sacrifice.[93] This metaphysical comfort is held out to Schreiner's New Woman workers in their sacrifices, even in a world of uncertain faith.

It is immediately after the allegory of the Hunter that, in the novel, Schreiner's New Woman heroine Lyndall reappears on the farm. Now grown up and worldly wise, it becomes clear that Lyndall has experienced existential crisis. When Waldo expresses his growing atheism, 'there is nothing worth doing. The universe is so large, and man is so small –' he is interrupted by Lyndall's injunction:

> We must not think so far; it is madness, it is a disease [...] it is a poison, not a food. If we live on it it will turn our blood to ice; we might as well be dead. We must not, Waldo; I want your life to be beautiful, to end in something. You are nobler and stronger than I [...] and as much better as one of God's great angels is better than a sinning man.
>
> (p. 184)

Lyndall has followed his thoughts and can reproduce the train such atheism would take. She includes herself in the injunction 'We must not', showing that she herself has risked this stultifying state of existence. For the New Woman missionary, the loss of the old religion is dangerous, as it is the loss of energising passion – atheism turns 'blood to ice', life to death – whereas a continuing reference to greater beings – God and his great angels – can inspire nobility and a life's work or mission. The threatening nature of agnosticism for missionaries such as Lyndall is further articulated by Waldo's Stranger:

> A time of danger, when the old slips from us, and we have not yet planted our feet on the new. We hear the voice of Sinai thundering no more, and the still small voice of reason is not yet heard.
>
> (p. 135)

Like Grand, Schreiner references Elijah, who found the Lord not in the earthquake, but in a 'still small voice',[94] to represent the voice of the New Woman, speaking on after the thundering of the patriarchy (the Old Testament's voice of Sinai) has dwindled to nothing.

The child Lyndall especially personifies the 'still small voice' in *African Farm*, when she quietly, almost passively, exerts her will for the good of herself and others. When Em is beaten and the two are locked in their room, her behaviour is described as calm and determined as she deliberately and methodically breaks the glass window, attempts to cut through the wooden shutter and finally tries to burn it down. At every failed attempt, Em is described as wailing, blubbering and howling, while Lyndall speaks 'quietly' if at all, is described as 'quite quiet for a time' (p. 58) and suppresses any outburst of frustration through biting her lip. She explains, rationally, that 'I never heard that howling helped anyone' (p. 59). Most effectively, she is able to stop Tant Sannie beating Em through simply laying 'her small fingers on the Boer-woman's arm', her 'clear eyes and [...] quivering white lips' (p. 57) communicating more than screams would have done. And her simple commands and statements to Bonaparte and Tant Sannie, in their quiet deliberateness, have the power to give her temporary authority over her elders: 'Move!' she says to Bonaparte, 'and he, Bonaparte the invincible, in the hour of his triumph, moved to give her place' (p. 57). In her self-assertion, she resembles Jane Eyre.[95] Indeed, she can be seen as another reworking of the 'holy child' character of evangelical tract fiction; less sentimental, her clear possession of power associates her even more strongly with Christ, the original Holy Child. In this way, Schreiner, like Grand, portrays the young New Woman as a Messiah.

In the same way that Grand's New Woman characters are often shown to fail, and disappoint feminist scholars, the grown-up Lyndall fails as a New Woman missionary.[96] She is aware of the mission, but experience has defeated her strength. When confiding in Waldo, she depicts herself as Moses, unable to carry her people to the Promised Land:

> To see the good and the beautiful [...] and to have no strength to live it, is only to be Moses on the mountain of Nebo, with the land at your feet and no power to enter. It would be better not to see it.
>
> (p. 162)

While not favoured by earlier female missionaries, the identification with Moses is perfect for Schreiner's New Women: they are to do the work that will enable their descendants to enter the Promised Land, while they die on the plains of Moab.[97] Lyndall, however, finds her sacrifices more difficult than Schreiner's allegorical women in *Dreams* and is unable to experience them as a source of power or satisfaction. Unlike female missionaries in biographies, Lyndall's character expresses regret at having become a missionary in the first place and for her sacrifices.

The sacrifice of love and of female passion demanded by the New Woman and the social purity movement is seen in Schreiner's portrayal of Lyndall's struggles and eventual demise as an almost impossible price to pay for progress. Lyndall attempts to sacrifice love by running away from London and her lover, and proposing a contractual marriage to Gregory Rose, similar to that made by Grand's Angelica. Lyndall sets out her terms:

> What I am saying is plain, matter-of-fact business. If you are willing to give me your name within three weeks' time, I am willing to marry

you; if not, well. I want nothing more than your name. That is a clear proposal is it not?

(p. 199)

However, as a human, failing New Woman missionary, Lyndall abandons her principles and run away to the Transvaal with her lover. While she attempts to carve out a rational agreement with him that will keep her free, the image of her shrinking once the arrangement is made stresses the continuing inequality of heterosexual relationships: she is described as having 'a weary look', 'a worn look' (p. 206), 'her shoulders were bent; for a moment the little figure had forgotten its queenly bearing and drooped wearily' (p. 207). For the reader is now quite aware that Lyndall is a 'fallen woman'; the narrative hints that she is already pregnant, and she refers to having had a sexual relationship with her lover – having put herself in his power and liking 'to experience [...] to try' (pp. 205–6). Lyndall is no longer the proud New Woman, and droops and shrinks to a child, without the power to 'resist' (p. 207).

Lyndall's death contrasts starkly with the deaths of female missionaries in biography. Like a pious female missionary, she mostly suffers in silence, only once imploring God to stop her suffering, which, in fact, draws attention to the body in pain and adds pathos to the image of the suffering missionary: ' "I do not ask for [...] all things I have longed for," she cried; "only a little freedom from pain! only one little hour without pain! Then I will suffer again" ' (p. 242). This is where the similarity with female missionary deathbed scenes ends, though, and her long, drawn-out death makes harrowing reading. When she is made aware that she is dying, she cannot die happily, accompanied by visions of heaven; the Christian duty of preparing someone for death is, in a dramatic reversal, named by her doctor as the 'Devil's work'. Lyndall is seen by Gregory, 'her body curled up, and drawn close to the wall' in an attitude of despair (p. 243). Though scholars have struggled to see nobility in Lyndall's death, the extent of her degradation stresses the tragedy of a promising feminist missionary being sacrificed in this way by a patriarchal society.[98] As she portrays the dying Lyndall looking into her own eyes in the mirror, Schreiner telescopes the life of her missionary:

> It had been a child's face once, looking out above its blue pinafore; it had been a woman's face, with a dim shadow in the eyes, and a something which had said 'We are not afraid, you and I; we are together; we will fight, you and I'.

(p. 252)

In this way, Lyndall and the reader are reminded of her childhood power and potential, and her efforts to be a militant woman missionary, as well as her still strong sense of self. Moreover, Lyndall's awareness of her failure and impending death, and her continuing lack of faith in any afterlife, shows what it really means to sacrifice the comforting promises of Christian faith. The dramatic tragedy in Lyndall confronting her failed self in this way is heightened by the understanding that, for her, there is nothing else outside her suffering self – no God – to look to for comfort. Despite this, she courageously faces her oncoming death with the steadiness of a martyr: 'The dying eyes on the pillow looked into the dying eyes in the glass; they knew that their hour had come' (p. 252). The condition of religious doubt in which they have to, as women, struggle and perhaps fall, demands of New Women even greater courage.

Interestingly, Lyndall's suffering sacrifice leads to the advent of Schreiner's 'New Man' character. Lyndall's fiancé Gregory Rose takes on a new role and makes sacrifices in his turn when he disguises himself as a nurse and takes on the character of a woman. Scholars have understood Gregory – named after a fourth-century Cappodocian Father, who helped to reconcile the Church following the Arian heresy – as the reconciliatory figure of the 'New Man';[99] to bring about a better world, Schreiner suggests that not only do women need to be raised in status, but men need to develop more feminine, moral characteristics.[100] In this way, Schreiner's modern theories actually revisit the gender ambiguity central to the earliest conceptions of the female missionary character, who was able to draw on the characteristics of military, masculine martyrdom and take inspiration from the figure of Christ in both his manly and feminine guises.[101] In his role of nurse, Gregory is, like a female missionary, self-sacrificing, especially as he cannot express himself and his love to Lyndall. In his missionary acts of caring, nursing and witnessing at Lyndall's deathbed Gregory is able to make that sacrifice of self which Schreiner, like Brontë before her, saw was impossible for women to make heroically in a context where such sacrifice would only be interpreted as a natural feminine capacity.

Significantly, Gregory only shares Lyndall's sacrifices – Schreiner does not transpose sacrifice away from the female missionary. Indeed, her New Women missionaries are denied all fulfilment but that which can be found in sacrifice, and all hope except in a better future for other women and society. However, through this formulation, Schreiner exalted the figure's courage and bravery to inspire the cause of feminism.

Margaret Harkness, New Woman Missionaries and the Salvation Army

For many years, Margaret Harkness appeared only in the margins of studies of the fin de siècle, as the cousin of Beatrice Webb and friend of Olive Schreiner. However, recent work has given her social work and writing greater prominence. As a professional writer living in London in the 1880s and 1890s, she was to all intents and purposes a 'New Woman', and she wrote about topics of concern to radical women of the period.[102] She also came from a religious background, however, and the legacy of Christianity can be seen within her novels, especially her 1889 novel, *Captain Lobe* (republished as *In Darkest London*), which I will examine in this section.

Scholars have mostly examined Harkness as a socialist novelist, concentrating on her portrayal of the London slums.[103] Lynne Hapgood has noted how Harkness's life and work can specifically give an insight into how women of the time experienced some forms of socialism.[104] Likewise, Eileen Sypher and Seth Koven have drawn attention to her importance in a history of the experience of female workers in the slums.[105] Scholars have also commented on Harkness's experimental style, which uses journalistic and social investigative techniques, even incorporating material from her own newspaper articles.[106] However, although it is a novel about social problems, *In Darkest London* is not a socialist novel, and its intertwining of social concerns, agnosticism and Salvationism has led scholars to differing conclusions as to Harkness's own philosophy.[107]

Harkness's Philosophy and the New Woman Missionary

As with Schreiner, Harkness's socialism was connected with her inclusive feminism, which was concerned with the suffering of the working class and disabled people as well as women. Also like Schreiner, Harkness was involved in the same confident, utopian socialism of 1880s London.[108] She embraced empirical social science and cross-class activism: fact-finding in the slums, supporting the Match Girls' Strike and working as part of the London Dockers Strike Committee in 1889. However, as scholars have noted, by the 1890s, the socialist community had lost much of its optimism and inclusiveness. Deborah Epstein Nord points to the suicides of Amy Levy and Eleanor Marx, as evidence for the tenuousness of independent women's lives in these days; political socialism didn't help these women and, by the end of 1889, Harkness had finally broken with her socialist circle and was looking elsewhere for inspiration for her own vision of feminism.[109] Christian Socialism, with its focus on Christ's humanity, had some influence on her thinking, as did the similarly Incarnation-inspired Salvationism of General Booth's Salvation Army. However, as Hapgood has noted, the materialist emphasis of both these movements by the late nineteenth century could leave adherents spiritually unfulfilled.[110]

The Salvation Army was certainly a source of fascination for Harkness; Biderman suggests it was the Army that inspired her, in her novel *In Darkest London*, to explore an 'amalgamation of Christianity and socialism'.[111] Similarly, Fishman, relying on her reaction to the first Salvation Army hostel in 1888, notes her positive belief that Salvationism and Socialism could work together.[112] However, Sypher and Ross, while acknowledging Harkness's approval of the Army and their practices, remind us that Harkness was never actually an adherent of the Salvationist religion.[113] Though many scholars have been convinced of her agnosticism due to her ridiculing of organised religion, I argue that her work, like Schreiner's, in fact returns to Christian beliefs for their ability to express the uncertain faith of feminism and socialism at the fin de siècle.[114] Like Schreiner, Harkness came from a Christian background: her father was a clergyman who disowned her when she moved to London and took up the cause of socialism.[115] Though her contribution of two historical tracts on the Assyrians and Egyptians for the RTS was probably motivated by financial need, they do show excellent knowledge of Biblical history;[116] it is possible that her study in this direction led to her religious doubt and freethinking. I argue that for Harkness, struggling with religious doubt and disappointed with the socialist movement, any hope of a future solution of social problems was based not only on the practices of the Salvation Army, but also on the Christian beliefs surrounding the female missionary and her narrative. Writing in the 1890s, she explicitly praised Schreiner's missionary allegory of the Hunter; this feminist missionary narrative, such as was being explored in the works of Schreiner and Grand, provided her with an alternative to contemporary socialist discourses and a sustaining sense of her own mission to bring about a better world.[117]

In the manner of female missionaries, Harkness employed a strategy of humility in her writing. Her work as author and editor of journalistic series on the East End was often not credited.[118] Her RTS tracts were also published semi-anonymously, under the gender-neutral name of M. E. Harkness, and her novels were published under the pseudonym John Law. The tracts are written in an objective academic style very unusual in a female-authored tract; there is no storytelling or addressing of the reader and no obtrusive narrator. No trace of the writer's own opinions can be found, and the introduction by a clergyman does not even mention the writer's qualifications for writing such tracts. This style of writing and publishing, in its self-effacement in favour of objective presentation, suggests that, like earlier female missionaries, Harkness believed herself to be a vessel through which truths could be expressed.

Like other New Woman writers, Harkness lived and worked for her missionary cause. In a similar manner to settlement workers in London at this time, she lived among the poor in the East End and, as a journalist, she worked to expose the obscene poverty and suffering in the London slums.[119] The renaming of her novel *In Darkest London* – an allusion to both Stanley's *In Darkest Africa* and Booth's *Darkest London and the Way Out* – certainly suggests that Harkness and her publishers were 'drawing a parallel' between the East End and Africa, but, more than this, the new title also associated the author with the tradition of missionaries who wrote accounts of benighted populations in the foreign and domestic mission fields.[120] The methodology of the social investigator in the slums and the style in which results were published was almost identical to methods being used by missionaries in their anthropological studies. However, Harkness departs from the tendency of such early sociologists to construct causal narratives in their writing to explain the slums and to scientifically classify the poor as 'deserving' or 'undeserving' characters.[121] Moreover, the differing classes, religions and genders of her novels' most positively drawn missionary slum workers suggest that for Harkness, as in evangelical tradition, an individual's faith would be more important than anything else to the mission to improve social conditions.

In Darkest London: Salvation Army Lasses and New Woman Missionaries

In Darkest London was originally published in serial form as *Captain Lobe* over the course of 1888. Making the hero of the novel the Salvation Army worker Captain Lobe, who first appeared in Harkness's earlier work *City Girl*, suggests that the missionary characters of the Salvation Army are Harkness's main interest in this novel. Certainly, in addition to Lobe's work in the East End, Harkness extensively presents the Army's slum sisters' missionary work as a possible solution to social problems. And Lobe's romantic interest, Ruth, is portrayed as a convert to Salvationism, working towards becoming a missionary herself. However, in addition to these Salvation Army missionaries, Harkness also presents a New Woman character who, while not an adherent to Salvationism, sees the Army's missionaries as portraying another, more abstruse, yet more valuable, social mission, which perhaps comes closer to that which Harkness was labouring for.

The novel presents the East End as full of a confusing array of slum workers and their philosophies, many struggling with agnosticism, doubt and feelings of failure in the face of the continual suffering of the poor. Alongside her depiction of the Salvation Army's practices, she also has her New Woman character present an evaluation of the approach of Salvationism versus Socialism, finally rejecting both. Harkness also includes aspects of the political feminist discourse through her working-class character Jane Hardy, who has educated herself on the Woman Question. However, the East End that Harkness presents is not simply a realistic portrayal of the space where theories and practices were tested – it is also a place where the supernatural elements of the world emerge in the shape of the religious prophesies of the Salvation Army, the dreams of converts, and Captain Lobe's disturbing visions of hell.[122] This environment cries out for female missionary characters, inspired by a new formulation of feminist, socialist Christianity.

The Salvation Army's female slum saviours are most obviously missionary characters. They are depicted in ways that recall the self-writing of missionary women like the Wesleyan wives. They are matter-of-fact, active missionaries, who describe their treatment by slum dwellers laconically – when showing her bruises, one states, 'some of the people are very rough'.[123] The women draw strength from their vocation and from their inclusion in an 'army'. The military language of early missionaries is encouraged and given legitimacy as Harkness is now able to depict such women as true soldiers; they 'bombard' (p. 47) the public houses with the Salvation Army's magazine, *The War Cry*, and take heart from their songs. Their mission gives them the confidence to confront sinners; one of them walked 'straight [up] to an old man [...] and asked, "Have you made a start yet? [...] The time is short. You are getting an old man. It's time to make a start"' (p. 42). This confident injunction to one of a 'savage-looking set of men' (p. 40) in a thieves' kitchen is striking. They see themselves and the world as part of a religious drama, which will end with the Day of Judgement, and the rich living near the slums being accused by God: '*I* was hungry, and ye gave Me no meat' (p. 41) – a reference to the same Biblical passage used by Sarah Grand in her 'Undefinable'. Speaking for God, and prophesying the Day of Judgement in this way shows the slum saviours' authority.

Significantly, though, it is not the slum saviours' Salvationism that Harkness is advancing as the cure for the slums' social ills. She gives voice to criticisms of the Salvation Army through her New Woman character, who explicitly rejects Salvationism; she rejects the Army's belief in hell as a 'terrible doctrine' and explains that the belief in any sort of afterlife is an impediment to working earnestly to change social conditions (p. 69). The New Woman also criticises the Army for not imitating Christ's charity, telling Lobe: '[i]f Christ were to walk down the Whitechapel Road this evening ... he would feed the hungry men and women' (p. 67). Harkness presents the early version of the Salvation Army in this novel, and its doctrine is one of Atonement evangelicalism, holding that the conversion of the poor is more important than the amelioration of their material needs.[124] In the chapter 'Slumdom', Harkness's slum saviours refuse to give to the poor, saying 'you must give up your sins; then God will send you food' (p. 50). One of the starving men counters this lesson with a doctrine that evokes Incarnation ideas:

> The Bible calls God a father, and no father would starve his son for sinning. He would give him food first, and speak about his sin afterwards ... don't come here to talk of salvation to a man like me. I'm hungry.
>
> (p. 50)

Though the next chapter is a continuation of 'Slumdom', Harkness ends this chapter with this critique of Salvationism, giving the hungry sinner the last word.

What Harkness, and her New Woman character, praise in the Army's female missionaries is their ability, and courage, to go among the poor, demonstrating an inclusive social mission similar to that of the Christian Socialists and settlement workers, based on Christian love and comradeship.[125] Harkness presents them as treating the working classes, and being treated in return, with respect and kindness: a woman who had treated them badly while drunk gives them flowers as a peace offering; a man defends them in a pub, saying 'they are the only folks that come among us. They have been good to my missus' (p. 59). When the New Woman is dying, she resolves to leave all her money to them, twice calling them 'our nineteenth-century heroines' (pp. 254–6). This mission of love is also expressed by Captain Lobe, whose simple, explicit admission 'I love my people' (p. 163) causes him to struggle with the Army's order that he must leave them.

For, inherent in Harkness's missionary narratives is the requirement of self-sacrifice. David Glover has convincingly argued that the self-sacrifice of the Army is seen as a necessary corollary to 'a heartless politics'.[126] Of course, self-sacrifice was also one of the most powerful aspects of the female missionary narrative, which Schreiner's work had especially reformulated for New Women. Harkness's Captain Lobe is sufficiently androgynous to be interpreted as a female missionary. He is often portrayed as nervous and delicate, usually adjectives that describe a woman of poor health rather than a man. He lives piously, according to the mission's rules, on a scant amount of money, surviving on potatoes and tea. This, combined with his active life with the Army – he is often shown in this novel walking the length of the East End – causes him to suffer in his self-sacrificial mission:

> Such meagre fare is apt to affect the spirits: and lying there on the sofa, the captain felt both mentally and physically exhausted. He was slightly made, and delicate. The life he led took the strength out of him.
>
> (p. 17)

Harkness utilises tropes of feminine delicacy for sentimental effect in this novel, drawing on the tradition of feminine, suffering female missionaries of mid-century biography, explored in Chapter 1. Harkness would also have been encouraged by Salvation Army discourse, which rejected masculine physical strength in favour of non-violent spiritual power, to see these acts of loving self-sacrifice as a particularly feminine religious practice.[127] The description of the would-be slum saviour, Ruth, follows a consistent formula of religious imagery in this novel: her forehead is an ivory tablet on which only truth could be written, her hair is golden, halo-like. The idea of such a delicate, golden-haired young woman sacrificing herself in the slums is enough to make Lobe turn pale.

However, Harkness creates a new aesthetic when Ruth loses her beauty after contracting smallpox. The recovered Ruth's reaction to her scarred face is aligned with her sacrifice and forbearance in her slum work, making her new appearance beautiful in the heroic holiness it implies. Her scarred face is also a mark of strength, that she is a survivor. Similarly, Lobe's nervousness is not always portrayed as weak femininity: it is also connected with energy. He is always moving, acting, and it is through the Salvation Army that he is able to put this dynamism to work and feel that he has achieved his vocation. He believes in saving the souls of the poor from hellfire, and the power of this Christian belief is awesome to Harkness, who contrasts it with the lack of belief and inaction of general society. In one of her narratorial interruptions, she is explicit in this judgement:

> People who *really* believe in hell do not indulge in the morning paper, or join a circulating library; they would imagine it un-Christlike to leave sinners to perish while they themselves enjoyed clubs, concerts, dinner-parties, crushes, and other entertainments [...] A Salvation blood-red vest reminds men of other things than pipes and tennis.
>
> (p. 19)

Lobe's sympathy is here reinterpreted by the narrator as coming from 'a fire fed by self-sacrifice' (p. 18). This sort of sacrifice suggests an active martyrdom, rather than the usual passivity associated with feminine self-sacrifice, and is depicted as a powerful weapon.

Harkness's New Woman character is also notable for her self-sacrificing female missionary nature. Like Grand's New Women, she has sacrificed the possibilities of conventional comforts, love and marriage in her refusal to be blind to the situation of humanity. Instead of living a West End life, she is shown visiting the poor and, when she comes to Lobe's lodging, she refuses to sit, insisting instead on looking out of the window at the slums (p. 54). In addition to giving up conventional comforts, like Schreiner's New Woman, she also feels that she must sacrifice religious belief in order to achieve her purpose. She suggests to Lobe that a slum worker's belief in God must be sacrificed or 'they would be so blinded by the glory of His presence, that they could not do His work on earth' (p. 56). Her privileging of earthly work necessarily repudiates any belief in immortality or reward after death; her mission is to heighten the urgency of social change 'in order that all may have, during their short span of life, a chance of happiness' (p. 57). At the heart of Lobe and the New Woman's discussions is a tension between the evangelical Army's belief in hell and Atonement, and the humanitarian, Incarnation-based approach of the New Woman, which resembles that of settlement workers.[128]

Though the New Woman describes herself as agnostic, Harkness is able to cast her agnosticism within the Christian mission 'to prepare for His Second Advent' (p. 56). As in Schreiner's work, this second coming is more a belief in the earthly world's future. The New Woman describes this future to the slum character 'Napoleon the midget'; her only comfort for him is that, if he comes back again after death, the world will have changed:

> Social conditions are becoming different. Barriers are breaking down, and classes are amalgamating. By the time you come back all men will be brethren. Young men will be ashamed of their strength, if it makes them despise midgets; young women will not shrink away, if it makes you look unhappy. People will put you first then, if you come

into the world handicapped. For love will be strong, even down here in Whitechapel; and this earth will be heaven.

(p. 58)

'You' in this speech becomes an inclusive, hypothetical future person. They will not find reward in this future but are able to find comfort in their faith that current social work will prove redemptive. Emphasis on 'classes' and 'barriers' suggests that it is the work of gender-inclusive socialist movements that will bring about this vision of the future, which itself is clearly based on Christian Socialist beliefs, focusing on the brotherhood of man and the power of Christian love.[129]

Like Schreiner's Lyndall, the sacrifice of the agnostic woman is given greater poignancy because she does not die in satisfied certainty of rewards in heaven. Her farewell letter to Lobe is confused, containing the confession of a sin, a recounting of a dream and a consideration that 'Perhaps, after all, my God, and the God of my father, are not so very different' (p. 182). She comes to this conclusion through her belief in love and the probable coming of 'all that St. John, the Apostle of Love, foresaw in the Book of Revelation' (p. 182). Her dream also sets her on the side of God, against society, as he demands, as Harkness in her work continually demands, 'Is it nothing to you, O nineteenth-century Christians, that men starve and drink, that women in despair kill their infants?' (p. 182). In her concern and sacrifices for these things, the woman has proven her Christianity – a New Woman, Socialist Christianity – which, in its contrast to society's Christianity, and its prompting to mission work, is portrayed as a better, truer religion.

Despite the power of the self-sacrificial narrative made use of in the story of the New Woman character, Harkness does not sacrifice all her female missionaries. While her New Man, Captain Lobe, willingly sets off for an uncertain future in Australia, Ruth remains at home. This suggests that the Salvation Army marriage of man and woman working together as missionaries was not convincing to Harkness. And, indeed, *In Darkest London* continually focuses on relationships among women rather than between women and men, matter-of-factly depicting women engaging in passionate 'mateship'.[130] *In Darkest London* opens with a seemingly inconsequential meeting of Lobe and two women; though he is attempting to recover 'Patty' to the benevolent home, she and her female friend will not be parted, her friend repeating 'I can't bide without Patty' (p. 12). Lobe cannot understand this relationship; however, Harkness implies that this relationship, which suggestively inspires a 'titter' in the hospital, is highly important and sustaining to the girls.

It is the working-class, anti-capitalist, pro-woman Jane Hardy that is the most promising female missionary in this novel, as she forms a friendly partnership with Ruth. Jane exposes Ruth to the realities of the slums and through their friendship – and presumably Ruth's religious influence – Jane herself becomes less jealous and bitter. While Harkness criticised the settlement workers' pretentions to cross-class relationships, this friendship enables both women to work to campaign against and ameliorate the suffering of other women in other classes.[131] A form of Christian, female, socialism enables Harkness to challenge or at least adapt eugenic theories. Indefinitely deferring the marriage of the weak, feminine Lobe and Ruth is eugenically prudent, but rather than simply suggesting that these weak specimens should not breed, Harkness attaches Ruth to the stronger Jane. Jane recognises that Ruth is 'one of those people who cannot stand alone, who must fall to the earth if they have nothing to keep them upright' (p. 199). For Lobe, Ruth's holy looks suggest that God will work through her and give the weak vessel the strength required for mission work. The alternative future, though, that exists in the ending of *In Darkest London* is that, radically, Jane, as a 'hardy' specimen of a woman, will take on the job of propping up Ruth and that the incorporeal crossing of these natures and classes will result in a stronger race of women in the future.

It is also Jane who recognises Captain Lobe as the androgynous New Man when, in the last line of the novel, she states that Lobe 'isn't a man – he is a woman' (p. 200). The positive characteristics of Captain Lobe – or 'Love' – are based on the female missionary aspects of the Salvation Army's religious practice. Harkness's novel is ambiguous, but possible solutions to social problems emerge in her presentation of androgynous missionary self-sacrifice, cross-class female relationships and religious forms of feminism and socialism.

Conclusion

The work of religious New Woman writers shows that the female missionary character and narrative continued to be important in women's self-construction and understanding of social issues even in the turbulent, agnostic decades of the 1880s and 1890s. Women writers and readers could find strength and comfort in the narrative of self-sacrifice and faith in the future presented by the missionary figure. Also, in eliding the female missionary and the New Woman, these writers were able to reimagine the feminist movement as prophesied by Christianity, as the force that would bring about the New World envisioned in Revelations. Moreover, like earlier women writers, the feminists' construction of their work as a pious mission led them to adapt the nineteenth-century novel and create new forms of art to express the very different narrative of their lives lived for a cause.

However, it cannot be denied that by focusing so much on the female missionary seriousness and self-sacrifice of their New Woman heroines, these writers ensured that such tropes would survive in women's writing into the twentieth century. Rather than avoiding sacrifice for their New Women, they tend to extend its requirement to their New Man characters, suggesting, perhaps, that when men become more womanly, especially in their capacity for sacrifice, women will be able to abandon their roles as the sole martyrs of the world and enjoy more equal, fulfilling relationships.

It is tempting to see the sacrificial, female missionary narratives of religious New Woman writers as an unfortunate branching off from the secular progress of feminism and feminist writing. These were not the only turn-of-the-century feminist women to follow religious role models, though. As we will see in the next chapter, teachers and students at the new women's colleges were also adapting female missionary ideas and rhetoric to sustain them in their new experiences.

Notes

1 Mike Kissack and Michael Titlestad, 'Olive Schreiner and the Secularization of the Moral Imagination', *English in Africa*, 33 (2006), 23–46 (pp. 23–4); see also Elaine Showalter, *Sexual Anarchy: Gender and Culture at the Fin De Siècle* (London: Bloomsbury, 1991), pp. 4–5.

2 Elisabeth Jay, *Religion of the Heart Anglican Evangelicalism and the Nineteenth-Century Novel* (Oxford: Clarendon, 1979), pp. 11–2.

3 Peter d'Arcy Jones, *The Christian Socialist Revival 1877–1914: Religion, Class, and Social Conscience* (Princeton, NJ: Princeton University Press, 1968), p. 3.

4 Lucy Bland has argued that social purity feminists combined terms of morality and religion with biological terms to define their position, Bland, *Banishing the Beast: English Feminism and Sexual Morality 1885–1914* (London: Penguin, 1995), p. 48; also, Ann Heilmann describes the New Woman movement as expressing 'a new spirituality', Heilmann, *New Woman Strategies: Sarah Grand, Olive Schreiner, Mona Caird* (Manchester: Manchester University Press, 2004), p. 2. On religious thought and feeling in socialism, see Livesey, *Socialism, Sex, and the Culture of Aestheticism in Britain 1880–1914* (Oxford: Oxford University Press, 2007), pp. 6–9; and Stephen Yeo, 'A New Life: The Religion of Socialism in Britain, 1883–1896', *History Workshop*, 4 (1977), 5–56 (pp. 8–23).

5 For an understanding of the place of religion in settlements and philanthropy, see Seth Koven, *Slumming: Sexual and Social Politics in Victorian London* (Princeton, NJ: Princeton University Press, 2004); Nigel Scotland, *Squires in the Slums: Settlements and Missions in Late Victorian London* (London: Tauris, 2007); and Ellen Ross, 'Introduction', in *Slum Travellers: Ladies and London Poverty, 1860–1920*, ed. by Ellen Ross (Berkeley, CA: University of California Press, 2007), pp. 1–39.

6 See Sally Ledger, *The New Woman: Fiction and Feminism at the Fin De Siècle* (Manchester: Manchester University Press, 1997), p. 1–3; and Gail Cunningham, *The New Woman and the Victorian Novel* (London: Macmillan, 1978), pp. 9–10.

7 Deborah Epstein Nord, '"Neither Pairs Nor Odd": Female Community in Late Nineteenth-Century London', *Signs*, 15 (1990), 733–54 (pp. 733–4).

8 See Ledger; Heilmann; Livesey; and Angelique Richardson, *Love and Eugenics in the Late Nineteenth Century: Rational Reproduction and the New Woman* (Oxford: Oxford University Press, 2003). Grand and Schreiner's short stories

also appear together in collections with those of male writers such as Hardy and Wilde, in *Women Who Did: Stories by Men and Women 1890-1914*, ed. by Angelique Richardson (London: Penguin, 2002) and *Daughters of Decadence: Women Writers of the Fin De Siècle*, ed. by Elaine Showalter (London: Virago, 1993).

9 Heilmann, p. 2; Ledger, p. 6; Cunningham, p. 17.

10 See Richardson, *Love and Eugenics*, p. 7; and Heilmann, 'General Introduction', in *Sex, Social Purity and Sarah Grand*, ed. by Ann Heilmann and Stephanie Forward, 4 vols (London: Routledge, 2000), I, pp. 1–15 (p. 3).

11 Grand, 'Foreword to *The Heavenly Twins* 1893–1923' (1923), repr. in *Sex, Social Purity and Sarah Grand*, ed. by Heilmann and Forward, I, pp. 397–408 (p. 408).

12 For a brief biography, focusing on Schreiner's religious experiences, see Elisabeth Jay, 'Introduction', in *Dreams: Three Works by Olive Schreiner*, ed. by Elisabeth Jay (Birmingham: Birmingham University Press, 2003), pp. ix–xxviii (pp. x–xv); also see Joyce Avrech Berkman, *The Healing Imagination of Olive Schreiner: Beyond South African Colonialism* (Amherst, MA: University of Massachusetts Press, 1989).

13 Heilmann, *Strategies*, pp. 129–30.

14 Harkness's life and work have begun to receive the attention they deserve. See Lynne Hapgood, ' "Is This Friendship?": Eleanor Marx, Margaret Harkness, and the Idea of a Socialist Community', in *Eleanor Marx*, ed. by John Stokes (Aldershot: Ashgate, 2000), pp. 129–43; and Flore Janssen and Lisa C. Robertson (eds), *Margaret Harkness: Writing Social Engagement 1880–1921* (Manchester: Manchester University Press, 2018).

15 Hapgood, 'Is This Friendship?', in *Eleanor Marx*, ed. by Stokes, p. 139; Koven, p. 167.

16 Bland, p. xix.

17 Notably to Heilmann, who sees it as evidence of Schreiner's 'residual allegiance to authoritative discourses [...] of woman-sacrifice', *Strategies*, p. 123.

18 Livesey, p. 45.

19 Boyd Hilton, *The Age of Atonement: The Influence of Evangelicalism on Social and Economic Thought 1785–1865* (Oxford: Clarendon, 1988), p. 5; Jones, pp. 86–7.

20 Yeo, p. 13.

21 See especially, Heilmann, *Strategies*, p. 3; Richardson, 'Introduction', in *Women Who Did*, ed. by Richardson, pp. xxxi–lxxxi (pp. xlviii–li).

22 Elisabeth Jay has also noticed the Biblical rhythms of these pieces and has also noted that the structures of questions and answers recall the Catechism, 'Introduction', in *Dreams*, ed. by Jay, p. xvii.

23 Heilmann, 'General Introduction', in *Sex, Social Purity and Sarah Grand*, ed. by Heilmann and Forward, pp. 4–5.

24 This form has been noticed by critics: see Koven, p. 167; R. A. Biderman, 'Introduction', in Margaret Harkness, *In Darkest London*, ed. by R. A. Biderman ([n.p.]: Black Apollo Press, 2003), pp. 7–10 (p. 9).

25 Heilmann, 'General Introduction', *Sex, Social Purity and Sarah Grand*, ed. by Heilmann and Forward, p. 8; also see Showalter, *A Literature of their Own*, pp. 205–7.

26 Grand, 'Foreword', repr. in *Sex, Social Purity and Sarah Grand*, ed. by Heilmann and Forward, p. 404.

Missionaries of the New 181

27 Richardson, *Love and Eugenics*, pp. 126–8.
28 'The Heavenly Twins: Bath Mayoress Tells Their Story – Josephine Butler Centenary' (1928), repr. in *Sex, Social Purity and Sarah Grand*, ed. by Heilmann and Forward, I, pp. 317–20 (p. 319).
29 Ledger, p. 6; Cunningham, pp. 2–3.
30 Heilmann, 'General Introduction', in *Sex, Social Purity and Sarah Grand*, ed. by Heilmann and Forward, pp. 2–3; Richardson, *Love and Eugenics*, p. 7.
31 Sutton-Ramspeck, *Raising the Dust: The Literary Housekeeping of Mary Ward, Sarah Grand and Charlotte Perkins Gilman* (Athens, OH: Ohio University Press, 2004), pp. 2–4.
32 Heilmann, *Strategies*, pp. 3–7; and 'General Introduction', in *Sex, Social Purity and Sarah Grand*, ed. by Heilmann and Forward, pp. 4–5.
33 Grand, 'Foreword', in *Sex, Social Purity and Sarah Grand*, ed. by Heilmann and Forward, p. 397 [Further references to this edition – full details given above – appear parenthetically in the text].
34 Richardson points out Grand's didactic tendency of directing her reader in *Love and Eugenics*, pp. 118–9.
35 Linda Wilson, *Constrained by Zeal: Female Spirituality Amongst Nonconformists, 1825–75* (Carlisle: Paternoster, 2000), pp. 10–1.
36 Elisabeth Jay, 'Women Writers and Religion: "A Self Worth Saving, a Duty Worth Doing, and a Voice Worth Raising"', in *Women and Literature in Britain 1800–1900*, ed. by Joanne Shattock (Cambridge: Cambridge University Press, 2001), pp. 251–74 (pp. 265–7).
37 'The Heavenly Twins: Bath Mayoress Tells Their Story ', in *Sex, Social Purity and Sarah Grand*, ed. by Heilmann and Forward, p. 318. [Further references to this edition – full details given above – appear parenthetically in the text].
38 Midgley describes this strategy in 'From Supporting Missions to Petitioning Parliament: British Women and the Evangelical Campaign against *Sati* in India, 1813–30', in *Women in British Politics, 1760–1860: The Power of the Petticoat*, ed. by Kathryn Gleadle and Sarah Richardson (Basingstoke: Macmillan, 2000), pp. 74–92 (pp. 77–9).
39 Grand, 'The New Aspect of the Woman Question' (1894), repr. in *Sex, Social Purity and Sarah Grand*, ed. by Heilmann and Forward, I, pp. 29–35 (p. 32).
40 Grand, 'Foreword', in *Sex, Social Purity and Sarah Grand*, ed. by Heilmann and Forward, p. 404.
41 Richardson has suggested that in her short fiction and journalism, Grand was able to circumvent the requirements of realism to depict ideal, or unchanging snapshots of the species of New Woman, rather than the flawed, human women required by the realist novel.
42 Grand, 'The New Aspect of the Woman Question', in *Sex, Social Purity and Sarah Grand*, ed. by Heilmann and Forward, p. 30.
43 I Kings 19. 12.
44 Showalter, 'Introduction', in *Daughters of Decadence*, ed. by Showalter, p. xvi.
45 Richardson, *Love and Eugenics*, pp. 127–8; Richardson, in her edition of 'The Undefinable', notes three Biblical references, but this hardly scratches the surface of the religious message of the story, *Women Who Did*, ed. by Richardson, p. 406.

46 Grand, 'The Undefinable', repr. in *Women Who Did*, ed. by Richardson, pp. 115–36 (p. 122). [Further references to this edition – full details given above – appear parenthetically in the text].

47 Richardson, *Women Who Did*, p. 406.

48 Incidentally, Charles Spurgeon used this same pair of verses together in an 1888 sermon at the Metropolitan Tabernacle, Spurgeon, 'The Rent Veil', www.spurgeon.org/sermons/2015.htm> (accessed 8 August 2013).

49 Grand, 'The New Woman and the Old' (1898), repr. in *Sex, Social Purity and Sarah Grand*, ed. by Heilmann and Forward, I, pp. 69–76 (pp. 70–3).

50 '*The Heavenly Twins*: Bath Mayoress Tells Their Story', in *Sex, Social Purity and Sarah Grand*, ed. by Heilmann and Forward, p. 319.

51 Heilmann, *Strategies*, pp. 52–4.

52 Heilmann, 'General Introduction', in *Sex, Social Purity and Sarah Grand*, ed. by Heilmann and Forward, p. 8; Richardson, *Love and Eugenics*, pp. 101–2; Showalter, *A Literature of Their Own*, pp. 206–7.

53 Grand, *The Heavenly Twins* (Ann Arbor, MI: University of Michigan Press, 1992), p. xliii. [Further references to this edition appear parenthetically in the text].

54 George Grove, 'Foreword', in F. G. Edwards, *The History of Mendelssohn's Oratorio 'Elijah'* (London: Novello, 1896), p. iii.

55 Mendelssohn, *Elijah* (Boston: Oliver Ditson, n.d.), p. 23. http://openlibrary.org/books/OL25407757M/Oratorio_libretto_Elijah (accessed 26 September 2012).

56 Psalm 121.

57 Mendelssohn, *Elijah*, pp. 24–8.

58 Psalm 138.

59 Bland, pp. 229–30.

60 Grand, 'Foreword', in *Sex, Social Purity and Sarah Grand*, ed. by Heilmann and Forward, p. 399.

61 '*The Heavenly Twins*: Bath Mayoress Tells Their Story', in *Sex, Social Purity and Sarah Grand*, ed. by Heilmann and Forward, p. 319.

62 Grand 'The New Woman and the Old', in *Sex, Social Purity and Sarah Grand*, ed. by Heilmann and Forward, p. 76.

63 Richardson, *Love and Eugenics*, pp. 104–5; Heilmann, 'General Introduction', in *Sex, Social Purity and Sarah Grand*, ed. by Heilmann and Forward, pp. 7–8.

64 Heilmann, 'General Introduction', in *Sex, Social Purity and Sarah Grand*, ed. by Heilmann and Forward, p. 8; Richardson, *Love and Eugenics*, pp. 101–2.

65 Julie Melnyk has noted how Christ featured in women's theological writing: as suffering a model of feminized man and a preview of an androgynous life to come after the Apocalypse, 'Introduction', *Women's Theology in Nineteenth-Century Britain: Transfiguring the Faith of their Fathers*, ed. by Julie Melnyk (London: Garland, 1998), pp. xii–xviii (pp. xvi–xvii).

66 Evelyn Dorothy Oliver and James R. Lewis, *Angels A to Z*, 2nd edn (Canton MI: Visible Ink Press, 2008), p. 202. books.google.co.uk/books?isbn=1578592127 (accessed 28 July 2013).

67 Berkman, pp. 16–21; Jay, 'Introduction', in Schreiner, *Dreams*, ed. by Jay, p. x.

68 Jay, 'Introduction', in Schreiner, *Dreams*, ed. by Jay, p. xv.

69 Berkman, pp. 12–3; Cherry Clayton, 'Militant Pacifist: Olive Schreiner Rediscovered', in *The Flawed Diamond: Essays on Olive Schreiner*, ed. by Itala Vivan (Coventry: Dangaroo, 1991), pp. 40–54 (p. 43).
70 Carolyn Burdett, *Olive Schreiner and the Progress of Feminism: Evolution, Gender, Empire* (Basingstoke: Palgrave, 2001), pp. 30–2; Christopher Heywood, '*The Story of an African Farm*: Society, Positivism and Myth', in *The Flawed Diamond*, ed. by Vivan, pp. 26–39 (pp. 26–32).
71 Heywood, 'Society, Positivism and Myth', in *Flawed Diamond*, ed. by Vivan, p. 27.
72 Jay, 'Introduction', in Schreiner, *Dreams*, ed. by Jay, p. xix; Kissack and Titlestad, p. 33.
73 Burdett, pp. 24–8.
74 Aileen Fyfe, *Science and Salvation: Evangelical Popular Science Publishing in Victorian Britain* (London: University of Chicago Press, 2004), p. 3.
75 Berkman, pp. 51–2.
76 Livesey, pp. 44–68; see also Wim Tigges, 'A Feminist Mirage of the New Life: Utopian Elements in *The Story of an African Farm*', in *The Literary Utopias of Cultural Communities 1790–1910*, ed. by Maguérite Corporaal and Evert Jan Van Leeuwen (Amsterdam: Rodopi, 2010), pp. 189–208 (pp. 189–90).
77 Livesey, p. 4.
78 Jay, 'Introduction', in Schreiner, *Dreams*, ed. by Jay, pp. xvii–xix.
79 Schreiner, 'I Thought I Stood' (1890), repr. in *Dreams*, ed. by Jay, pp. 31–2 (p. 31). [Further references to this edition – full details given above – appear parenthetically in the text].
80 Heilmann, *Strategies*, p. 126.
81 Burdett, pp. 78–9; Heilmann, *Strategies*, p. 120.
82 Schreiner, 'Three Dreams in a Desert' (1887), repr. in *Dreams*, ed. by Jay, pp. 16–21 (p. 20). [italics in original]
83 Schreiner, 'Three Dreams in a Desert', in *Dreams*, ed. by Jay, p. 20.
84 Burdett argues that the allegories are mainly concerned with the New Woman's renunciation, pp. 79–80.
85 Schreiner, *Dreams*, in *Dreams*, ed. by Jay, pp. 1–46 (p. 2).
86 Heilmann, *Strategies*, pp. 129–30.
87 Berkman, p. 46–52; Burdett, p. 18; Kissack and Titlestad, pp. 28–33.
88 Berkman notes that John Galsworthy recommended the novel to a friend troubled with religious doubt, p. 43.
89 Olive Schreiner, *The Story of an African Farm*, ed. by Joseph Bristow (Oxford: Oxford University Press, 1992), p. 113. [Further references to this edition appear parenthetically in the text].
90 Berkman, p. 24.
91 Kissack and Titlestad, p. 29; Jay, 'Introduction', in Schreiner, *Dreams*, ed. by Jay, p. xix; Berkman, p. 24.
92 Burdett, p. 24.
93 Romans 14: 7.
94 II Kings 19. 12.
95 Lerner, 'Olive Schreiner and the Feminists', in *Olive Schreiner and After: Essays on Southern African Literature in Honour of Guy Butler*, ed. by Malvern van Wyk Smith and Don Maclennan (Cape Town: David Philip, 1993), pp. 67–79 (p. 71).

184 Part II: 1880–1900

96 Burdett, p. 31; see also Lerner, 'Olive Schreiner and the Feminists', in *Olive Schreiner and After*, ed. by Smith and Maclennan (London: David Philip, 1983), pp. 67–79 (p. 75).
97 Deuteronomy 34. 1–5.
98 Lerner, 'Olive Schreiner and the Feminists', in *Olive Schreiner and After*, ed. by Smith and Maclennan, p. 75; Heywood, 'Society, Positivism and Myth', in *Flawed Diamond*, ed. by Vivan, p. 34.
99 Burdett, p. 37; Heywood, 'Society, Positivism and Myth', in *Flawed Diamond*, ed. by Vivan, p. 34; Tigges, 'A Feminist Mirage', in *Literary Utopias*, ed. by Corporaal and Van Leeuwen, p. 199.
100 Berkman, pp. 136–40; Lerner, 'Olive Schreiner and the Feminists', in *Olive Schreiner and After*, ed. by Smith and Maclennan', pp. 76–7; also, see again Melnyk on the androgynous Christ in women's theological writings, 'Introduction', *Women's Theology in Nineteenth-Century Britain*, ed. by Melnyk, pp. xvi–xvii.
101 See Prologue and Chapter 1.
102 Koven, p. 166.
103 Fishman unapologetically uses her novels as historical source material Fishman, *East End 1888: A Year in a London Borough Among the Labouring Poor* (London: Duckworth, 1988), pp. 115–8.
104 Hapgood, 'Is This Friendship?', in *Eleanor Marx*, ed. by Stokes, pp. 141–2.
105 Eileen Sypher, *Wisps of Violence: Producing Public and Private Politics in the Turn-of-the-Century British Novel* (London: Verso, 1993), pp. 17–20; Koven, pp. 199–202.
106 Koven, p. 167; Sypher, p. 112.
107 Hapgood, 'Is This Friendship?', in *Eleanor Marx*, ed. by Stokes, pp. 129–30.
108 Hapgood has sketched her involvement with many of the leading socialists of the day, Hapgood, 'Is This Friendship?', in *Eleanor Marx*, ed. by Stokes, pp. 130–6.
109 Hapgood, 'Is This Friendship?', in *Eleanor Marx*, ed. by Stokes, pp. 133–4; Nord, p. 737.
110 Hapgood, 'Is This Friendship?', in *Eleanor Marx*, ed. by Stokes, pp. 187–90.
111 Christian Socialism is a term often used in association with Margaret Harkness, but so far there has been no thorough study exploring her engagement with the various branches of this religious philosophy.
112 Fishman, pp. 257–9.
113 Sypher, p. 115; Ross, 'Margaret Harkness', in *Slum Travellers*, ed. by Ross, pp. 89–90 (p. 90).
114 Sypher, p. 114.
115 Ross has usefully drawn attention to the influence of Church of England philanthropy on many women who entered on slum work in this period, 'Introduction', in *Slum Travellers*, ed. by Ross, p. 4.
116 Sypher, p. 107.
117 Margaret Harkness [John Law], 'Olive Schreiner'. *Novel Review*, May 1892, pp. 112–6 (p. 112).
118 Koven, pp. 166–7.
119 Koven provides a valuable introduction to her journalism, pp. 166–7.
120 Andrzej Diniejko, 'Margaret Harkness: A Late Victorian New Woman and Social Investigator', Victorian Web. www.victorianweb.org/gender/harkness.html (accessed 20 December 2012).

121 Ruth Livesey has identified this tendency in social reformers in 'Reading for Character: Women Social Reformers and Narratives of the Urban Poor in Late Victorian and Edwardian London', *Journal of Victorian Culture*, 9 (2010), 43–67 (pp. 47–53).
122 In this way, Harkness is extending the mythological or nightmarish depictions of the East End that other late nineteenth-century writers, such as journalist Arthur Mee or novelists Mrs Humphrey Ward and Robert Buchanan, were producing; see Hapgood, 'Is This Friendship?', in *Eleanor Marx*, ed. by Stokes, p. 187.
123 Margaret Harkness, *In Darkest London*, ed. by R.A Bilderman ([n.p].: Black Apollo Press, 2003) p. 40. [Further references appear parenthetically in the text].
124 Yeo, p. 13.
125 Scotland, pp. 17–24.
126 David Glover, *Literature, Immigration and Diaspora in Fin-de-Siecle England: A Cultural History of the Aliens Act* (Cambridge: Cambridge University Press, 2012), pp. 70–2.
127 Lauer, 'Soul-Saving Partnerships', in *Masculinity and Spirituality in Victorian Culture*, ed. by Bradstock, pp. 196–8.
128 For discussion of the tensions between these two beliefs at this time, see Yeo, p. 13; and Scotland, pp. 17–24.
129 Jones, pp. 86–8.
130 Koven, p. 218.
131 Koven, pp. 258–9.

5 Women, Religion and Power
University Women's Missionary Writing

Introduction

The extension of women's higher education in the late nineteenth century has often been understood as part of a secular narrative of feminist advancement, with scholars criticising the more religious principals of women's colleges for holding conservative, 'anti-feminist' views.[1] However, the majority of women's higher education colleges – like those for men – were set up on religious foundations and, as Laura Schwartz has shown, even conservative religious ideas could create in these colleges a kind of feminist ethos.[2] Moreover, as will be demonstrated in this chapter, it was often the female missionary role, as embraced by many in religious colleges, that provided the basis for women to take on identities of authority and to build a strong corporate identity among college students and graduates.

While it was concerned with improving conditions and opportunities for women, the women's higher education movement was not formally aligned with the campaign for women's suffrage. The first women's colleges opened in London in the 1840s, prior to the organised suffrage movement: Queens College was founded by Christian Socialists Charles Kingsley and Frederick Denison Maurice to provide better education for governesses, and Bedford College was founded for similar reasons by the Unitarian Elizabeth Jesser Reid.[3] And while Emily Davies was well-known for her feminist views, when, in 1869, she set up her women's hall in Hitchin near Cambridge (which became Girton College), like other women principals, she took care to avoid associations with the suffrage movement.[4] Cambridge's other women's college Newnham (founded in 1871) espoused conservative ideas about women's nature and less ambitious goals for their educational achievement. Similarly, Oxford's Anglican colleges Lady Margaret Hall (LMH) and St Hugh's, founded in 1879 and 1886, were known for their conservative approach to women's education, as expressed by LMH's principal and founder of St Hugh's, Elizabeth Wordsworth.

Indeed, the women's colleges carried out their mission to improve women's educational opportunities by using what have been understood

DOI: 10.4324/9781003332961-9

as paradoxically conservative arguments, based on women's essentially moral nature; and they protected their institutions by demanding their students' adherence to high standards of feminine behaviour.[5] There was undeniably strong opposition to women's higher education in the late nineteenth century. The 'Girton Girl' caricature that emerged in the popular press represented contemporary fears about sexual anarchy and the degeneration of the race prompted by the advancements of women.[6] And opponents repeatedly alleged that women engaging in university study faced medical risks, such as infertility, brain damage and mental breakdown.[7] As Martha Vicinus has argued, women who wanted to take part in higher education required a strong alternative discourse to sustain them in their endeavours;[8] although, as a secular, second-wave feminist, she is not keen on the religiosity of the discourses many of the women principals chose.[9] However, I argue that many of the so-called conservative discourses used by college principals had radical implications in terms of women's role in the world and often resembled those in favour of female missionaries. Arguments based on women's morally superior, domestic nature were made to justify their authoritative work to reform society, and it was argued that it was women's responsibility to educate themselves for this work.[10] Meanwhile, the women of Westfield College in London developed a unique female missionary rhetoric, which combined militant evangelical belief with 'muscular Christian' college ethos and strong emotion to sustain their graduates going out into the world.[11] Despite opposition, the movement for women's higher education was successful, making slow but steady progress;[12] and the figure of the Girton Girl was countered by the missionary-influenced 'Sweet Girl Graduate', as popularised by writers such as L. T. Meade.

This chapter is largely based on a case study of what was probably the most explicitly missionary of the women's colleges: Westfield College, founded in London in 1882 and led by the evangelical Anglican, Constance Maynard. Westfield aimed to turn out graduates who were committed Christians, and many of its early students went on to be missionaries. Historical accounts of the college, especially those based on student recollection, only tell us so much;[13] students remembered that Maynard ensured her college conformed to evangelical standards of behaviour, but mostly recall their experience of college life in the same way as most female students in others of the new female higher education colleges: cocoa parties, debates and clubs.[14] My research in Westfield's archives revealed a more specific institutional discourse, co-created by a community of women, through the language and form of their writings. Maynard's diaries provide insight into her negotiations of the female missionary role, while her correspondence with alumnae develops an empowering female missionary rhetoric that jettisoned the tropes of self-sacrifice in favour of militant, nationalist confidence. Meanwhile, the college's students used female missionary culture to sustain their collegial women's community and reinvigorate the struggling genre of women's college newsletters – so that Westfield's college magazine, *Hermes*, recalls the earlier form of the female missionary newsletter.[15] Of course, Westfield was not the only women's college sustained by female missionary activity. My research in the archives of LMH and Royal Holloway showed that most women's colleges supported the University Women's Settlement in the London borough of Southwark; many went on to found their own college settlements;[16] and students often formed societies to support foreign missions, as well as going on to work in missions when they graduated.

I start this chapter by considering the influence of the first principals of the women's colleges, especially that exerted by the explicitly missionary Constance Maynard at Westfield, as expressed in her private writings and those for her students. I go on to explore how missionary culture helped form feminist communities in women's colleges, both in the form of clubs and newsletters. I end this chapter by suggesting how women's missionary college culture influenced women's missionary culture more widely at the turn of the century, by examining the work of graduates in settlements and missions.

Constance Maynard and the Missionary College Principal

Constance Maynard believed it was her mission to lead a women's college with religion at its heart; her aim was to spiritually support young women as they developed their intellectual capacity so that they would graduate to become Christian workers in education, social work and the mission. She knew from her own experience that Christianity in the late nineteenth century was under threat from the forces of secularism and that the influence of religion in education was waning. Her writings reveal how her own evangelical Christianity provided her with a strong missionary identity that sustained her pioneering work as a college principal and which she could model and transmit to her students.

Religious and Educational Experiences

Maynard came from a highly conservative background; her parents espoused a strict, old-fashioned Atonement evangelicalism that had not evolved into the more emotional religion of the mid and late century. Maynard's family life was one where children were highly restricted and supervised: daughters were mainly kept at home; social visits or holidays, even with family, were tightly controlled; friendships could be vetoed; marriage was not to be thought of before the age of thirty – when Maynard received a surprise proposal when she was twenty-one, her mother refused it on her behalf. Maynard struggled to incorporate her experiences of religion, love and beauty within her parents' religion; she found an outlet for her more emotional Christianity at her boarding school, Belstead, under the tutelage of the headmistress, Mrs Umphelby

Figure 5.1 Photograph of Constance Maynard and her staff at Westfield College, 1888. Maynard is in the centre; standing behind her are (left to right) Anne Wakefield Richardson and Mabel Theodora Beloe, and seated in front of her are Josephine Willoughby and Frances Grey. Image provided by Queen Mary University of London Archives.

(known as 'Mamie') who taught a more Incarnation-based evangelicalism. However, Maynard's school days came to an abrupt end when her parents decided that she had no need for further formal education.[17]

Despite this conservative background and truncated schooling, Maynard became one of Emily Davies's pioneering first women students in Cambridge. She acquired parental permission for her three-year college career incrementally, in the way of a favourite daughter, rather than through active rebellion. Her father was more puzzled than concerned about this new interest and, though her mother at first granted permission for only one year, Maynard continued her studies to completion, taking the Moral Sciences Tripos.[18] Following her university education, she took up teaching roles at Cheltenham Ladies' College; St Leonard's School in St Andrews, where her friend Louisa Lumsden was headmistress and Maynard's relative Lewis Campbell was on the management committee; and her old school, Belstead. Her teaching activity was sanctioned by her parents largely because it came at a time of some temporary financial difficulties, and presumably the connections of these institutions with friends and family made this employment more palatable. It was through taking on a family role – that of keeping house for her brother – that she was later able to live in London, where she enjoyed opportunities of studying at the Slade Art School as well as taking part in the religious activity and social work going on in London in the 1880s: working at her brother's Evangelical Coffee House at Wimbledon, marching with the Salvation Army and engaging with a number of other London missions and churches.[19]

Maynard had suffered the challenges of secularism firsthand. As a young woman, on holiday with her brother in Germany, she encountered German 'freisinnig' – freethinking – ideas, which contributed to the religious doubt she believed was often experienced by young people.[20] And as a student at Girton, she was dismayed at the irreligious aspect of the college and lack of moral guidance.[21] Even her beloved Belstead disappointed her when she returned as a teacher, as she noted a lack of rigour in the religious instruction provided, reflecting that the students 'do not make first class Christians; the cross is not pressed on them'.[22] These experiences led to her belief that the right kind of religious instruction was necessary in women's educational institutions and her growing conviction that it was her vocation to provide this.[23]

Personal Writings and Missionary Identity

Maynard's own writings provide the best evidence of her understanding of her missionary identity. They are preserved alongside and within the Westfield College archive, in a way that challenges the usual definitions of public and private. The college archive contains the formal records and documents that appear in any such institution's archive, such as committee reports, administrative correspondence and student records; however, it also preserves Maynard's personal correspondence with her alumnae. Meanwhile, the Maynard archive includes a number of diaries dedicated to the day-to-day business of her college – the 'brown books' – alongside her spiritually reflective (and revealing) 'green book' diaries and the unpublished (epic) manuscript of her autobiography. Though some of the 'green book' diaries contain material of an intensely personal nature, Maynard's methodical maintaining and labelling of the diaries suggests that she intended them to be used as source material for potential biographers; like early missionary writers and publishers before her, Maynard's anticipation of the usefulness of her personal writings trumped any regard for privacy.[24] And, indeed, soon after Maynard's death, ex-student Caroline Firth carried out the anticipated task, compiling a somewhat hagiographic biography, which quotes liberally from Maynard's personal papers. However, unlike early female missionary writers, Maynard had also decided, in 1925, to write her own life story for publication, unmediated by compilers or editors.[25] Not only did Maynard consider her narratives of spiritual struggle to be edifying for young women following her, she was also aware of herself as an important figure in the public history of women's higher education.[26] Linda Peterson has suggested that it was becoming more common by the late Victorian period for women to produce memoirs of professional careers, however, I would suggest that Maynard's confidence in this respect stemmed more from her understanding of herself in a female missionary role.[27] In any case, subsequent leaders of the college shared Maynard's understanding of the importance of Westfield's story and continued to maintain a detailed record of its development; a register of students was later updated to include alumnae destinations and specifically recognised their contributions to education and the evangelical mission.

To reveal Maynard's sense of her missionary identity, I rely mainly on the 'green book' diaries. Maynard's autobiography is useful for understanding her hindsight interpretation of her mission at Westfield, however, this is coloured by her painful remembrance of suffering during the later Westfield years, inevitable feelings of failure, and her attempts to understand her past actions using twentieth-century theories of Freudian psychoanalysis.[28] Given this, I have chosen to rely on the 'green book' writings that describe Westfield College's ethos as it was being invented.

Of course, like the letters and diaries of female missionaries before her, Maynard's diaries cannot be read as spontaneous or authentic transmissions of inner thoughts and feelings. When Maynard started the diary as a six-year-old child, she was writing for a specific audience; the very first words are: 'Mother, I'm going to tell you all about myself'.[29] While the ultimate aim of such a diary was communion with God, it is clear that this parental mediation affected expression, long after scrutiny had ceased. Maynard's voice in the diary is often self-conscious. She frequently appears to be writing for an imagined reader, to whom she is offering advice and example, in the same way missionaries like Ann Judson wrote accounts of their conversions and spiritual progress for the use of others, as we saw in the Prologue. And, in the same way that female missionaries often depicted themselves as simply vessels for God's words and work, despite their active agency in the field, Maynard is sometimes uncharacteristically self-effacing in her accounts of her work.[30]

In 1880, Maynard writes self-consciously about overcoming the inhibitions of the spiritual record, so that her diary will be more open, not necessarily to her family, but certainly to God and posterity:

> The only way is to put down exactly what you *do* feel [...] and not step out of your way for one instant into what you *ought* to feel and then, though your drawing may be anything but beautiful, it is of value as a study. It was in 1872 I threw off restraint and honestly tried this.[31]

Although addressed to a reader, Maynard's expressed belief in her authenticity is borne out by the diaries following this date of 1872. Her candour is sometimes quite striking when she uses the diary to explicitly work through struggles, including each step of painful logic or casuistry. There are often movingly contradictory entries where she clearly struggles to reconcile her impulses and instinctive beliefs with God and her avowed religion. Such early attempts to incorporate her sometimes painful experiences into her missionary discourse, as the female missionary biographers Knowles and Woods incorporated the difficulties of Harriet Newell and Ann Judson, provide the germs of the later Westfield discourse.[32]

Many of Maynard's struggles as a religious educational pioneer she experienced in common with other religious principals of women's colleges, such as Elizabeth Wordsworth at LMH, Annie Moberly at St Hugh's and Matilda Bishop at Royal Holloway. These women found themselves in an especially difficult and lonely situation. On the one side, they were opposing their conservative Christian friends and family in their campaign for women's higher education, and on the other side, they were fighting the secular tendency of higher education, often against women who might have been their feminist sisters and mentors.

Maynard knew that her family disapproved of her plan for a college; she wrote in her diary, in 1880, that they had suggested that 'to turn out wise and aggressive labourers would be worse than failure'.[33] She also feared, like many women at the time, that her work in higher education could be seen as selfishly rejecting family duties in favour of self-aggrandisement.[34] Laura Schwartz, in her study of Elizabeth Wordsworth, the first principal of LMH and founder of St Hugh's, noted that Wordsworth's Anglo-Catholic family and friends, including the writer Charlotte Yonge, were very much against women learning for the sole purpose of academic achievement, and only supported her work because they knew she would ensure LMH encouraged women to study for the right reasons – to develop talents given by God so that they could better carry out woman's mission in the world. Wordsworth also argued that it was the Church's duty to support colleges like hers, as, without them, religious young women looking for intellectual fulfilment would be 'lured away' by secular institutions.[35]

On the secular front, as Vicinus has noted, Constance Maynard clashed with her intimate friend and colleague Louisa Lumsden over how far religion should be encouraged in progressive girls' schooling, which was one factor leading to her departure from St Leonard's.[36] Maynard was also anxious about how her old college principal, Emily Davies would react to her proposed college, especially after her scheme was attacked at an 1882 meeting of Girton alumnae, where she reports Lady Stanley sneered at the college's presumed 'piety'.[37] Maynard understood that many in the vanguard of advancing female education found the inclusion of religion in higher education an unwelcome influence on young women. She and other religious women principals often had to remain firm against secular encroachments; when she was discussing taking on the leadership of the new Royal Holloway College, she reluctantly had to refuse because the committee would not agree to her desire for religious tests for staff.[38]

And though Matilda Bishop then took on the principalship of this college under the committee's conditions, she felt compelled to resign when they insisted on allowing separate worship for non-conformists in the college chapel.[39]

Maynard's account of setting up Westfield emphasises how she fought a concerted campaign to realise her vision of a religious higher education college for women. She held meetings with those sympathetic to her cause and made speeches at evangelical and philanthropic women's conferences.[40] By thus publicly positioning herself as interested in a principal's role in a religious college, she was recommended to Ann Dudin Brown, who had resolved to set up a missionary preparation college for women. While this opportunity met Maynard's religious criteria (Brown wanted a college like Mary Lyon's Mount Holyoke missionary training school in Massachusetts, and others on the committee were committed to a focus on conversion), Maynard had to fight to ensure the college would also aim for high academic standards and status. She won, and the resulting Westfield College was designed to be as academic as the existing university colleges for women – indeed, at her insistence it was based in London where students could be awarded degrees – while also focusing on converting and preparing its students for active, useful lives as highly qualified missionaries, teachers and other workers.

To sustain herself in her campaign for her religious women's college, it was important for Maynard to understand her actions within the terms available to active religious women. Like Elizabeth Wordsworth, she could see herself as working to defend Christianity against secularism and helping to further women's mission in society. However, she lacked the explicit support of the Anglican Church, which was often made manifest at LMH and Royal Holloway when bishops, royals and even the Archbishop of Canterbury attended special events and spoke approvingly of their progress.[41] Instead, due to her lower-church, evangelical religious affiliations, Maynard was able to understand her work powerfully as a mission, with herself as a missionary, following a Godly 'calling', engaging in a religious military campaign and pursuing an exciting, fulfilling life's work.

Maynard explicitly associated herself with the same vocation as missionary men and women, and her diaries show her negotiating missionary tropes and identities to understand and justify her active, public role. When she went to see the missionaries off to the Congo, in October 1882, she wrote with excitement that she was 'Yes, really off, on the same kind of work'.[42] She is clear throughout the diaries that her work is a calling from God rather than her own choice, suggesting a continuity with the belief that missionary women were mere vessels, carrying out God's will. Through 1880 and 1881, when the college was tentatively becoming a possibility, she refers to herself as an 'instrument' to be prepared by God and talks almost passively of her decision: 'I [...] thought "Now shall I take it?" and the answer came, "Yes, it would be a good thing'.[43] Once the future becomes less tentative, though, her prose becomes more active; it is she who collects the audience for her conference, she who writes the report and she who gains the support of, among others, Emily Davies, Josephine Butler and Lord Shaftesbury. However, when she is offered the post of principal, in May 1882, both self-congratulation and pious self-effacement jostle for dominance in the diary entry:

> Success is so *very* nice, so very pleasant [...] when [...] we saw the grand sight of the presentation of degrees in Burlington House, the world of hard work and of ambition into which I am throwing myself came before me vividly. It is not a direct choice, never – I could find simpler ways than this. It is that these things are and will be and it is not for me to hold aloof.[44]

It is difficult to know whether Maynard fully believed in her rhetoric of self-abnegation, or if she was performing the evangelically correct behaviour instilled in her by her upbringing for a hypothetical audience. The belatedness of the self-abnegation and the emphasis on her own actions in the months preceding suggest that she is reverting here to the conventions of the existing discourse, perhaps because she is experiencing a tension between her excitement at the prospect of meaningful activity and her understanding of herself as subject to God's will.

In her private writings, Maynard also engaged with the problem of missionary suffering and sacrifice. It was a daunting prospect to become one of the first female heads of a higher education institution, and when Maynard took on the role, in May 1882, she admitted to relieving her fears of a lonely future with a fit of weeping.[45] Generally, though, while Maynard spoke of her life's work as hard and lonely, this was less in order to stress pious suffering and sacrifice, in the way of mid-century female missionary biographers, and more to elevate her mission and her abilities above others. When, in 1881, it was suggested she should take over the role of headmistress of her Christian finishing school, Belstead, she wrote that she was called 'to something harder, sterner, to the unruly swell of the great tide, to the rising flood of the world's best efforts in education'.[46] Her self-confident faith even enabled her to speak of her work as superior in its success and difficulty to the enterprises of men. In her autobiography, she emphasises the fruitless sacrifice of those male missionaries to the Congo – 'not one survived two years' – and suggests that her brother's mission among 'warm-hearted miners and fishermen' with a 'nice pleasant coffee house attached' was less demanding than her own.[47]

Indeed, when she writes of her struggles against family and society in her diaries, it is not to the language of self-abnegation that she turns, but rather to the language of missionary militancy; like the Wesleyan wives, at these points, she uses stirring rhetoric and elevates her situation to one of spiritual combat. For example, in June 1881, she writes:

> I would like to fly high, to attack the very top, storm the very citadel within, to shew [sic] my brothers that *nothing* is too strong if we have the Lord with us, and that after very patient, skilful obedient working, we may shout for the Lord hath given us the city![48]

The passion of this passage and its metaphorical location of herself and her 'brother' missionaries within a Biblical world is quite startling. Maynard casts herself as an avenging angel – flying high to attack and storm targets – such as the captain of the Lord's host appearing to Joshua before the storming of Jericho, which is called to mind through her quotation from this chapter: 'Shout; for the Lord hath given you the city' (Joshua 6:16). Through this simultaneous casting of herself as avenging angel, missionary and prophet (Joshua), she imagines herself as a leader of righteous humanity, showing her brothers not only that as a Church with the support of God they will be triumphant, but also outlining how they will achieve this. It is notable that she does not only call for patience and obedience, but also for skilful working, which can be seen as her consistent aim: she was determined to produce workers for the Church who had been developed intellectually and professionally as well as spiritually. Though the city is given by the Lord, the active role Maynard advocates can be seen clearly in the strength of the verbs she piles on top of one another – by the time she reaches 'storm' she not only disposes with adjectives but also with 'to', and one can almost imagine the quickening of her pen on the paper as she speeds to her exultant conclusion.

This imagining of her struggles in terms of a Biblical war is common in Maynard's writing and is the most striking evidence of continuity with earlier missionary discourse – both male and female. The image of an active struggle with Heathendom suggests a battle that has been continuous since the time of the Old Testament, and the sort of fantastical example of this practice in the example above is common when Maynard writes about her work. The transposition of such terms onto the everyday political tussles of women's education can seem overly dramatic, but is consistent with the evangelical practice of piously living religion in everyday life. Watson has pointed out that the roots of this idea of Christian life as lived in a form of 'siege warfare' go back to Bunyan in the seventeenth century.[49] Writing these passages also stirred Maynard to action and helped her justify her ambitions, in the same way that earlier female missionaries were inspired by the texts of Ann Judson and David Brainerd.

To defend her militant fervour, Maynard at one point quotes Wilson Carlile, later founder of the Church Army, who told her in 1880 that, as Christians, they must all be 'aggressive'.[50] This religious licence clearly helped Maynard in the unfeminine behaviour of negotiating with boards and individuals to get what she wanted. Although her 1881 campaign to become principal of the stately and imposing new Holloway College failed, she expressed it in very acquisitional terms:

> I wanted it, every brick of it for the Lord and His blessed service. In some 50 years I wanted all England to be looking gratefully at those walls as the birthplace and training school of some of the noblest of its mothers, its teachers and its missionaries [...] This time it is pure aggression on my part.[51]

She also wrote about her ambition for her college to be able to acquire degrees for its students in militaristic terms: in 1880, she termed the London BA degree 'the fairest field in all England' – invoking the idea of a battle or the mission field. Though she phrases her question 'why should this not be the ostensible raison d'etre of a Christian College?' as a simple, rhetorical one, it would actually have been regarded as unreasonable by many of her contemporaries.[52] Not only would awarding degrees be stealing a march on the other women's colleges (the Oxford and Cambridge colleges could not award degrees until the twentieth century), but Maynard was in the vanguard of those stressing intellectual development as important preparation for evangelical mission work. Maynard's identification with such a militant missionary identity gave her remarkable confidence as an early woman principal, which would be necessary to achieve her ambitious aims for Westfield's students.

Maynard's Missionary Practice

Despite the newness of the position of college principal, many of the practices Maynard employed to convert her students to a more devout evangelicalism displayed continuity with those used by earlier women missionaries and were associated with Christian femininity. Like other religious college principals, she sometimes took on a maternal role in relation to her students, and also made use of the intimacies of Victorian female friendship to initiate emotional conversions in her students. However, as a woman in a position of authority, she also developed new strategies well-suited to the new environment of a modern women's college community. All these practices contributed to the missionary discourse of Westfield and the missionary identity modelled for her students.

Many of the early women's college principals presented themselves as families, deploying familial metaphors in their descriptions of themselves, which seemed to make higher education for women more acceptable to middle-class families, and to some principals of colleges themselves.[53] Elizabeth Wordsworth reportedly preferred the college to be 'family-sized'; in 1905, when it had expanded considerably from its early beginnings, she took four students to live with her in a private house, where she could have more domestic influence over them. However, maternal influence was not always – or often – of the ideal, feminine, Angel of the House variety. Students from her house described Elizabeth Wordsworth's influence in terms of an upper-class, High-Church Victorian mother: domestic life with her was surprisingly formal, and she attempted to regulate their manners, clothes and church attendance.[54]

Maynard's understanding of the maternal role was similarly formal. Her upbringing had reflected early evangelicalism's rejection of Romantic conceptions of the innocent child in favour of the belief that children, like all human beings, were born in a state of depravity and must be aided in their battle against their flawed natures. Evangelical mothers were educated about their heavy responsibility: selfish family love, or the indulgence of sentimental feelings, popularised in the late eighteenth century, was to be avoided in favour of a strict regime of monitoring and regulation.[55] Maynard found the repression required as part of this evangelical-mother role difficult, as she experienced strong emotional attachment to her first charges. During the first term, she writes most evocatively of her maternal instinct as she re-creates the scene in which she had to explain to her students why worldly amusements such as dancing and parties were forbidden:

> On Saturday, last night, late when I came up I found them a little riotous: they invited me to F. Synge's room, blew out my candle, made me sit down and begged me to 'talk to them' [...] All the latent mother in me wakes when I sit thus close to them but it would have been a poor earthly mother indeed, and I was saved in time and spoke decidedly and truly [...] [Margaret's] sweet fresh face was on my knee in the dim firelight and we talked long and quietly of what it was to forsake these things for the Lord's sake [...] Master, Counsellor, Guide, take and reform this poor heart to *any* pattern that will make it the best of mothers to these sweet, fresh, whole young lives.[56]

The scene is reminiscent of Sherwood's governess stories, in which students and teachers were portrayed in intimate, familial positions as they taught each other religious truths (see Chapter 2). However, while Maynard is tempted by a 'latent' instinct to be an indulgent mother to her students here, she sees this as something to be resisted as 'poor' and 'earthly'. She believes she must consciously choose to be a good Evangelical mother – 'the best of mothers' – 'saved' by God for this purpose. Though she credits God with saving her here, she seems also to take pride in describing how she resisted temptation and spoke 'decidedly and truly', in the manner of a good, authoritative evangelical parent.

Maynard was able to transcend ideas of domestic femininity usually associated with mothers, paradoxically through her adoption of the high-status role of the evangelical parent. Jay has noted that in evangelical households, the father did not maintain exclusive power over the family and, in the case of family prayers, the mother could literally take his place.[57] The kind of responsibility assumed by Maynard and other evangelical mothers is also that of a clergyman's for his flock. Even in the emotional passage above, Maynard can be seen rejecting family imagery, turning to a God who is 'master' and 'counsellor' rather than 'father', and focusing on her religious mission. Indeed, Maynard describes the form of mothering required by her role as one of public service parenting:

> In their different spheres both youth and maiden are flattered, courted, praised and their heads turned in every possible manner. The Lord does not thus spoil His little children [...] Truly I think we can hardly do enough for them during the years when temptations are so many.[58]

Maynard's college family is more like the family of the Church and is similarly expansive and inclusive – a corporate 'we' acting to protect God's children from the temptations put in their way by the world and even their parents. In this way, Maynard can be seen to have divorced the rhetoric of family and parenting from its usual association with the female condition, relying instead on more masculine and religious authorities to justify her spiritual leadership. Scholars have suggested that a number of women social reformers used a maternal rhetoric to claim new roles for themselves in state policy.[59] What they do not fully acknowledge, though, is that rhetoric such as Maynard's detaches the parental role from the domestic sphere, placing it firmly in the institutional realm.

There were of course elements of evangelical motherhood – and other female relationships – that could be both useful for missionary practice and emotionally fulfilling. We have seen how women missionaries described female relationships as formational of their religious practice, and how writers such as Sherwood and Craik depicted women teachers enjoying intimate, mother-daughter-type relationships with their students as part of conversion narratives. Similarly, Nadia Valman has shown how, in Grace Aguilar's work, the mother's gradual conversion of her child can be experienced as 'an ecstatic exchange'.[60] Furthermore, evangelical constructions of religious love challenged the biological family's primacy; members of a church not related to each other could appropriate emotional family feelings, not only using the language of family, but experiencing the ardour of love tied strongly to religious outcomes, such as bringing the 'son' or 'daughter' to a better understanding of God.[61]

Maynard believed that she could have a stronger influence on the young if she could excite feelings of love in them and has been, rightly, criticised for emotionally manipulating the young women in her care.[62] Certainly, Maynard actively set up scenarios that would ensure emotional reactions in her students, believing that these would lead to conversion. For example, in her end-of-year diary entry in December 1883, Maynard recalls an episode from the spring term, when she had concerns about the religious commitment of her student Margaret Brooke. Suspecting that Brooke was in love with her, she made her disappointment clear in a cold disciplinary speech and withheld any expression of her own love until Brooke came in penitent tears to Maynard's room:

> At night, late, I was conscious of someone close outside my door. I guessed but would not speak [...] I put out my light, and then came a low rap and in an instant more I had my arms round her, my love, my darling [...] she said [...] 'Oh, I couldn't, *couldn't* bear it [...]' and on my breast came the shower of her tears [...] Oh my dear heart, my sweet child, safe there in my arms she could not refuse comfort.[63]

Perhaps surprisingly, Maynard was not uncomfortable with her means of conversion, and was supported in her approach by religious publications and missionaries. By the middle of the century, *The Christian Observer* was encouraging both men and women in their conversion efforts to capitalise on states of grief and remorse and to use the withholding or granting of love, softening tears, embraces and kisses, to manipulate the emotions of their targets.[64] And, according to Maynard's diary, one of her friends, Annie MacPherson, who worked in the East End, passionately encouraged Maynard's approach, instructing her:

> If you have the power of slipping your hand into the arm of another by winning words and by the strong pressure of love, leading them to Jesus, do it, do it, do it just wherever your tact sees you can.[65]

Rather than using emotions cynically in the cause of conversion, there is evidence that women using love to convert also experienced feelings of love themselves. For example, an alumna of LMH described Elizabeth Wordsworth using intimacy to influence her students: 'religion meant much to her. She sometimes put her arms round one and said "Couldn't you go more often to Chapel?" Of course one said yes'.[66] The almost wistful way Wordsworth's request is made, suggests it is Wordsworth, rather than the student, who is as emotionally invested in this exchange. As scholars have noted, Maynard experienced love and passion as central to her own experience of religion.[67] With Brooke, she gained, for a time, almost perfect religious and romantic fulfilment; even in her remorseful autobiography, Maynard does not seem to regret this relationship: 'for it was restrained and lovely'.[68] Moments where the two discuss this self-restraint and the way their love must be part of their religious 'cause' are described in detail in both the diaries and the autobiography and usually end with Brooke in Maynard's arms.

Maynard describes other religious moments with young women in a way that suggests she experienced them as sensually and erotically fulfilling. For example, when she describes her involvement in prayer meetings – which she established as part of her missionary practice wherever she went[69] – she focuses on the way she and her female companions seem compelled to kiss at the close as the measure of a successful religious experience. Sharon Marcus has suggested that religious women reached for the language of seduction to describe religious encounters, as they experienced their love for God and female friends with equal intensity.[70] For Maynard, this language reflects not only the same sort of passion but her experience of the intertwinement of human and religious love. For example, she writes after the last and perhaps only successful prayer meeting at the Slade Art School:

> Best of all E Halse [...] now so heartfelt in her yearning after the Lord Jesus, that He should be indeed the one love of her heart [...] As we rose, we for the first time kissed each other. It will not die when I am gone.[71]

Rather than a performed, manipulative act, the kiss here is the direct result of a shared religious experience. The erotic charge is part of what Maynard sees as the authenticity of religious experience and convinces her that her prayer meeting has made a lasting impact.[72]

Maynard included her experience of passion within religion in her public, college work, connecting fulfilment in this meaningful, religious mission with emotional, even romantic fulfilment. She almost unconsciously connects life, work and love in her diary and prayers: 'I prayed earnestly "find my life, my love, my work, for me!"'.[73] More explicitly, she articulated the need for a companion to support her in her work: 'I did *so* want a kind arm round me and a "come, we will share it all" from a voice I could trust'.[74] The strength of this longing – 'Oh I did *so* want' – is arresting. In her autobiography, she expresses this longing in orthodox religious terms when she writes 'I wanted one life to stand beside me', using the Biblically significant term of 'standing' together, against the world.[75] However, at the time, she found no difficulty in asking God to '*satisfy*' her desires; Phipps has noted that she saw her fulfilling, passionate relationships as a 'gift' or reward from God for her work.[76] Certainly, her writings and actions show that she believed in fulfilment within the missionary life, and a fulfilling form of missionary marriage:[77] Maynard called Lumsden her husband when they worked together in Girton and St Leonard's and this notion was repeated, though reversed, with Brooke, who called herself Maynard's wife.[78]

Maynard's Missionary Correspondence

In addition to converting students through prayer meetings and in the domestic spaces of her college, Maynard continued to influence her flock through her correspondence with the more religious alumnae – many of whom became missionaries. The alumnae correspondence took the unusual form of a chain letter: Maynard would write a letter to the first student on a list, who read it and sent it on with one of her own to the next person on the list, who then added hers and sent the bundle to the next alumna. This continued until the letters came back to the original authors who replaced their own letters with new ones and continued to send the bundle round. In this way, all were involved in a correspondence 'ring', receiving each other's news from the field with the news of Westfield and Maynard. Old letters were sent back to Westfield for safekeeping and were later disseminated to a new generation of correspondents in a second ring, converting and sustaining the new recruits in the field. Maynard mostly referred to the correspondence as the Budget (a somewhat old-fashioned term for a packet of news) or the Ring. This method was perfect for busy, professional women, wishing to maintain contact with each other but having no time to copy whole letters, or even extracts, to numerous correspondents. The Westfield correspondence ring was therefore more efficient than traditional coteries or female missionary newsletters, yet equally effective in maintaining a sense of a virtual female missionary community.[79] The correspondence runs from 1887 onwards, beginning when the first students were graduating, which was also the time when Maynard's personal influence on the ground was being diluted by the expansion of the Westfield staff. Corresponding this way with the alumnae allowed Maynard, as the principal, to ensure that her influence had been felt and that the mission was continuing.[80]

Maynard's personality was a powerful force in keeping such a correspondence ring going, but it was when this personality was combined with the power of a religious college and a position of authority that it was really successful. Maynard had attempted a similar correspondence with the member of the prayer circle she had set up at Girton – the GPM, or Girton Prayer Meeting. However, that correspondence was more difficult to sustain, and almost failed because she was told 'there are only two or three [letters] one cares to read', meaning her own.[81] The tone of Maynard's Westfield correspondence is confident as she self-consciously constructs her public voice as the students' former college principal. If there are any spiritual difficulties to work through in the letters, Maynard is consistent in her views, using the form of the letter and the existence of a group of semi-inferior respondents, to conduct the argument in a measured, Socratic manner. Maynard also keeps the subject of the correspondence professional, in that she does not discuss her own problematic passions and relationships with her alumnae. While many of them would have been exposed to her methods of emotional conversion, she never explicitly encouraged this behaviour or encouraged its discussion on paper. Rather, she modelled a brisk confidence for her missionaries to emulate.

Indeed, in her correspondence, Maynard managed to continue the confident militarism of early missionary writings while avoiding the cultural insistence on sacrifice. While she may have struggled sometimes in her personal writings to embody a pious spirit of self-abnegation, and to understand her loneliness within the frame of missionary sacrifice, there is no trace of such struggles in the alumnae correspondence. She did not allow her students to be self-deprecating, demanding that they tell her all that they have been doing in the world, and at one point criticising them: 'you are altogether too diffident as to the value of your interest as expressed in letters'.[82] And in 1887, she calls for her alumnae to be soldiers: 'What is the use of our College if it does not turn out "soldiers and servants" waiting and working and living first of all for this end?'.[83] The soldier metaphor is continued in further letters as she describes the work of some of her alumnae who are 'really enlisted' in 'real "outpost sentinel posts"' and calls for them to be 'bravely held'.[84] In her construction of her students as an army – making her, of course, the general – Maynard was in harmony with Victorian evangelicalism's inclusion of manly, military heroes, such as Hedley Vicars and General Gordon, within its cultural discourse.[85] Maynard is also audacious, like the New Woman missionaries, in aligning herself and her alumnae with male religious figures, for example, naming Westfield's first missionary, Katherine Tristram, as the college's 'Prince of missionaries', whereas earlier missionaries would call themselves the servants of a rather more important Prince.[86]

When Maynard had to write about sacrifice, she re-imagined it, as had the New Woman writers, as a heroic act. Maynard does not include self-abnegating language or dramatic images of self-immolation in the student correspondence, and draws attention to the hardships of a missionary's life only to exaggerate their courage:

> I. Andrews' work is lonely and responsible too. Her home will be a few hundred miles to the S. of Mangalore and the young coffee planters [...] who are the sole English inhabitants, are v. wild. Drinking is in full force and many die of it [...] My cousin [...] went out there as a lad 5 years ago and kept a noble stand as a decided Christian, but the weight of loneliness, he says, becomes almost crushing after a time.[87]

Her missionaries are shown to be as brave, if not more so, than men engaged in a similar Christian 'stand'. While such a term might sound defensive compared with Maynard's more active language elsewhere, Watson has shown how 'holding' sentinel posts and 'standing' against the enemy have a longer tradition than the more aggressive terms of late nineteenth-century evangelicalism and in fact encompass ideas of active and noble sacrifice; he points out that 'the primary examples of "standers" are the martyrs [...] the saints who have been brave to the utmost'.[88] Martyrdom was envisioned for men as an active, heroic choice, and Maynard claims this laudable destiny for her alumnae.

Mainly, though, martyrdom was always only an eventual possibility for these missionaries, and Maynard suggests that it is more likely that they will enjoy an active and fulfilling religious service. For example, while in the 1890s Maynard describes Tristram's life as one of hard work, she more often stresses the positives, such as the fact that Tristram (and other female missionaries) can be pleased that they are following their true calling: 'nothing can be better than this, for His command is very plain and the way is open'.[89] There is almost a suggestion here that they are luckier than those at home who must find their calling in a less accepting, less open context. Even when Tristram has broken down through overwork and has to return home, Maynard's comment is that 'I know how greatly she enjoys a voyage'.[90] There is no mention at all of any sacrifice.

Indeed, Maynard seems to have refused to allow her students to take on the role of the martyr; on one occasion, she wrote:

> Pioneer work seems to creep from point to point till one is tempted to think that nothing has been done and it needs a brave spirit to go on in the face of such reflections. But cheer up! Such progress follows the law of a falling stone, it goes on, not with equal, but with increasing energy with the lapse of time.[91]

In this passage, Maynard can be seen using all the discourses at her disposal. The jollying tone of 'cheer up!' recalls the atmosphere of schoolgirl slang and sports; militaristic language is hinted at in her stress of the bravery needed in their work; and the way it is expressed – 'one is tempted' – reminds her students that she and the other alumnae have experience of this pioneer work and have themselves gone on, in the face of everything, to be successful. Most interestingly, she is also using a scientific allusion – 'the law of a falling stone'. Many at this time saw science as a threat to religion; Darwin's discoveries and new theories about the age of the earth had cast doubt on the Bible and had led many to become freethinkers. However, there were also evangelicals for whom scientific developments could be reconciled with faith.[92] Maynard encouraged her students to study botany, biology and physics, and her embrace of new forms of knowledge shows the ability of her college's religious philosophy to encompass secular subjects. Moreover, she used secular terms for her own purposes: in the quotation above, she alludes to a law of physics to suggest that women's pioneer work – and in their case, female missionary work – is an inevitable natural process, which will increase in power and success as time goes on. Maynard was not unique in this use of scientific terms within a religious discourse;[93] however, Maynard's ability to use scientific language consistently to communicate a religious message would have been inspiring to students whose faith might have been threatened by their intellectual development. This practice also effectively replaced the language of sacrifice for women missionaries with a far more up-to-date rhetoric.

In her alumnae correspondence, Maynard achieved a missionary narrative that was far more able than earlier female missionary writing had been to stress the personal power of the individual. In taking on the male missionary rhetoric of militancy, and figuring martyrdom as an active choice, she also crucially moved away from the idea of a separate, gendered discourse for female missionaries, claiming back, in effect, the terrain lost in the decades following Knowles's first biography of Ann Judson. Furthermore, her descriptions of female missionaries enjoying fulfilling lives had the power to inspire and sustain her college as a whole.

Missionary Culture and the Women's Colleges

As we shall see, missionary activity was occurring in most women's colleges. Where colleges differed, was in how fully religious mission was integrated into college culture.[94] The student records from Westfield's archive reveal how successfully they were influenced to take on missionary identities, especially by the college newsletter, which benefited from having a consistently engaging and content-rich subject in the mission. Study of other college newsletters suggests they similarly benefitted when the student body took on missionary causes, and languished when missionary activity was absent. Moreover, the newsletters supported the missionaries who graduated from women's colleges by continuing to include them in a virtual collegiate community.

Religious and Missionary Collegiality

The new women's colleges provided more women than ever before with the experience of communal, corporate living. However, collegiate feeling – an extensive intellectual, professional and social support that had long been available to men – had to be developed and nurtured. This was a process, which required college women to work out what should characterise their particular college spirit and sustain their community beyond the college gates.

Some colleges (and girls' schools) took on the secular culture of men's colleges and public schools. Competitive sport, college songs, newsletters, debates, clubs and schoolgirl slang have been identified by scholars as strengthening women students' sense of identity as well as binding students to their institutions.[95] It is questionable however, how far schoolgirl slang and college songs could support students who did not go on to further intellectual work. These elements of college identity seem to have tied students to life inside their institution and been constructed in defence against societal criticism, rather than as a positive alternative identity. And the need for some greater goal for a collegiate community to work towards is suggested by the number of women from higher education colleges who went to work in university settlement houses.[96]

Other colleges aimed at a religious, feminine version of collegiality, which, as time went on, developed to include appropriately feminine missionary activity. At its commemoration day in 1891, Royal Holloway had a number of Church and university representatives speak about the nature of women student and female collegiality they should be aiming to develop. Bishop Barry spoke on behalf of the Archbishop of Canterbury, arguing that 'the law of natural selection' determined men's and women's roles and that women's 'power and influence on the whole life of the country, as wives and mothers, was greater than any professional influence that the world could offer'. And, in his speech, the Vice Chancellor of Cambridge, Master of Trinity, Dr Butler, stressed that Royal Holloway students should aim to emulate the highest ideals of the men's universities and develop the angelic characteristics of 'sympathy', 'love of beauty [and] truth' and 'public spirit', which he described as a 'treasure above all words', recalling the Biblical description of a virtuous woman as being a treasure 'above rubies' (Proverbs 31:10).[97] Similarly, at the 1892 commemoration day, the Principal of Kings called for the women's college to develop a 'higher ideal' when it came to the collegiate 'tone of mind', rather than 'merely imitating the men'.[98] Meanwhile, at LMH and St Hugh's, Elizabeth Wordsworth and Annie Moberly were also disseminating a view that women had a distinctive contribution to make to the world, in line with the talents that God had granted them.[99] All these colleges went on to engage in missionary-type work, running settlements, a 'Waif and Stray' Society and clubs for factory girls, East End boys, and young servants. As will be seen in the next section, reports of this activity were disseminated throughout the colleges by their newsletters and magazines.

It is this feminine, religious collegiality that L. T. Meade emphasised in her 1891 novel *A Sweet Girl Graduate*, to counter the controversial 'Girton Girl' caricature. Her heroine Priscilla evinces 'extreme earnestness' and 'the sincerity of a noble purpose', which are nurtured by friendships which find fullest expression in their attendance at chapel together.[100] Moreover, Meade presents college education as preparing women for lives of service. The narrator states that the woman graduate's aim should be to become 'not learned, but wise; not to build up a reputation, but to gain character; to put blessedness before happiness, duty before inclination'.[101] Priscilla learns to avoid the selfishness of study for its own sake and changes her course of study, giving up her ambition for a degree in order to qualify quickly as a governess in order to support her family. This conclusion suggests that, at least for Meade, self-sacrifice continued to be important for many college women's missionary characterisation.

Westfield developed a religious, missionary collegiality from the start, in line with the vision of its first principal, Constance Maynard. Constance Maynard had seen that religious collegiality could be powerful for the evangelical mission. While Maynard was shocked at the secular nature of Girton, she recognised that if such institutions could be won over to the Christian side, colleges could do more than simply support young people in their faith – they could become valuable power-bases providing a stream of Christian soldiers for the cause.

Even before Westfield, she aspired to create a similar sort of society of women: 'a "Christian Education Union", an inner, really working, circle, of people with degrees, medical ladies, etc.'. This was her aim when she established the GPM, and she describes one meeting with typical zeal: 'We stood together in a larger ring than ever yet has met and I knew that Girton will not die but live and be a power in the future'.[102] Her conflation of the institution and the religious influence which she had implanted within it is clear here, as is the importance that she places on it as she describes it in terms of life and death. Unfortunately, without her presence and full attention, it was a fluctuating power at best. A college of her own, with a religious ethos in addition to the collegial aspect of enduring, supportive networks of educated and professional women, was the perfect solution.

Maynard's groups of religious women – both those imagined and those set up at Girton and Westfield – were referred to in language rich with imagery of circles and rings, which suggests women working in a non-hierarchical relationship, with collectively shared goals, unbroken support and influence radiating out from the centre. The GPM and Westfield groups were also held together by Maynard's 'ring' correspondence system, which reflected a new idea of a female group identity, with all the young women corresponding equally with each other rather than with particular friends. Maynard described it to her students as working 'on the time honoured principle of the Irishman's knife', meaning maintained and passed on, from one generation to another, suggesting ideas of inheritance and legacy. What was being passed on was in fact the college's core moral discourse, in the form of useful information, exemplars and a network of contacts in the professions, as Maynard described:

> How many of you would like to join a Correspondence Society? I have no name for it but the *thing* I understand very clearly, and I for one want to belong to it. There is quite a long list of you now out in the world [...] Now and then, especially when any change takes place, we want to have a little picture of what you are saying and doing and experiencing and striving after![103]

Maynard's implication here is that she will belong equally with the alumnae. She also communicates her expectation that her need to be kept informed of the work of her alumnae is shared by the collective of the college.

Implanting a collective religious mission into the heart of the potentially powerful college discourse was, for Maynard, not only the most politically opportune course of action but also an essential enhancement to give her students another empowering influence and a focus for their future lives. To a certain extent, this combining of college culture with religion was already at work in male public schools, through the use of militant hymns.[104] More powerfully, though, Maynard gave her students an explicit and specific religious purpose of the evangelical mission to enliven their college identity. In addition to the secular activities of the college, the students of Westfield were encouraged to take a common and active interest in the great cause of missionary work, which they could continue in any capacity once they had graduated. Maynard assumed that her alumnae understood this as the main objective of the college, as has been seen in her rhetorical question in the alumnae correspondence of June 1887: 'What is the use of our College if it does not turn out "soldiers and servants" waiting and working and living first of all for this end?'. Although she admitted it was difficult and that 'no other college has ever even attempted to carry out a union such as we propose', she persisted with her Correspondence Society in order to sustain her agents in the world and maintain their force.[105] The principal of Royal Holloway likewise saw her college's work with the Factory Girls' Club in Lambeth as having the potential to provide 'a strong bond of union between the different generations of our students'.[106]

The sites in which the impact of missionary collegiality can be seen most clearly are the college newsletters and the missions or settlements college leavers went on to found and work with (and which formed a large part of the content of college publications).

College Newsletters and Collegiate Missionary Activity

College publications were important to women's colleges from a relatively early point in their lives; Girton's college newsletter first appeared in 1882. Even Bedford College, which struggled to support collective activity at the college level, given its non-residential character, produced a magazine from 1886. Initially, though, there is an air of experimentation and pragmatism to the publications, as groups of college women started up various forms of magazines for differing audiences. LMH started in 1890 with *The Daisy*, its college magazine written by and for current students; it added *Fritillary*, a magazine co-edited with other Oxford women's colleges in 1896, and its alumnae association started its own newsletter in 1892. Royal Holloway's earliest publication, the 'College Letter', which ran from 1890, was designed more for alumnae than current students. Meanwhile, Westfield's *Hermes*, which ran from 1892 to 1997, was always a collaborative effort, including material by current students, tutors and alumnae, and similarly addressed to the whole college. In many ways, Maynard's alumnae correspondence was also a form of newsletter, although its circulation was more select. Indeed, she expresses the spirit of alumnae publications as she assures her correspondents of their continuing inclusion in the institution of Westfield when she writes: 'it is the Old students who are the real college you know'.[107]

Many of the early college publications show a lack of confidence in the ability of women's colleges to sustain them. Editors struggled to achieve the right tone, find appropriate material and subscribers and generally justify their papers' existence. Girton's college newsletter, which ran from 1882, reveals a self-doubt at the heart of the college in its early years.[108] In 1884, the newsletter's editors express their difficulties with the new literary form and their inability to create serious content:

> is it better to be dull or to be flippant? – to be neither is to be both [...] by avoiding a flat level of dullness, we instantly plunge into an abyss of flippancy, dragging the College in the mud after us.[109]

At LMH, before the Old Student Association publication was started, with its sustained interest in the college's settlement work, the college magazines were 'precarious' and always in danger of extinction.[110] With the support of nothing but a secular college culture, university-educated women and their publications were in danger of flailing in the mud rather than making their way in the world.

College publications with a greater sense of religious mission, in addition to having more to write about, played a clear and important role in binding the college community, including alumnae, together in a shared purpose. They were also influential in establishing their colleges' particular missionary cultures. This led to a more confident editorial voice. For example, in 1895, the student editor of Westfield's college newsletter *Hermes* made a strong call for students to expand Westfield's number of missionaries, writing – almost as stirringly as Maynard could – of how their college could turn out even more servants for God and how many opportunities there now were in the world:

> Should we not enlarge our conception of what we, as a College, can do to aid the cause of Christ in heathen lands. Some of our number have been honoured by the call to an active part in the struggle with Heathendom and from them comes the cry 'the harvest truly is plenteous, but the labourers are few! [...] There is ample room in the Bishop Poole school for another scholar; G.M. Walford wants teachers for her village schools; E. Brenton Carey has doubtless plenty of work for nurses at Karachi.[111]

There is an inclusivity in the Westfield ethos that can be seen in the language used by the student paper. The editor's idea of being able to do more 'as a College' underlines this and the students refer to 'us' and 'we' in their articles even though the paper was circulated beyond the current students to those in other women's colleges and to those who went before. In her alumnae correspondence, Maynard had also stressed the inclusivity of Westfield's mission, in that students can still partake of it 'even in the simplest sphere at home', through cultivating a missionary spirit.[112]

One way that college students engaged in a serious sense of religious mission was by supporting London settlements. Girton and Newnham began the University Women's Settlement in Southwark in 1887. Influenced by Mrs Barnett, it followed Toynbee Hall's approach, explicitly offering welfare, education, recreation and general elevation rather than conversion.[113] As I explored in Chapter 4, in the late nineteenth century, urban missions like university settlements or the Salvation Army became more aligned with the practices of secular philanthropy and less concerned with proselytising; the doctrine of Incarnation stressed how Jesus had cared for the bodies as well as the souls of the poor and sick, and advocated living amongst the poor and converting by example rather than preaching.[114] Despite the feeling among Anglicans that the Southwark settlement was 'irreligious', most colleges had students who went to live and work there.[115] However, in developing critiques of urban missions in their college newsletters, and by championing their own mission work, Westfield and LMH were raising strong corporate voices in contemporary theological debate.

The evangelical Maynard, of course, had strong views about the Southwark settlement's approach to saving the poor. In her alumnae correspondence in 1888, Maynard advanced her position and enlisted her alumnae onto her Atonement-based 'side' of the argument:

> It seems to be rather sinking away [...] the good done is so small, so transitory, so quickly swallowed up by the flood of opposing evil [...] they go on, giving pleasant evenings to some of their Pupil teachers in the Board schools [...] trying to give some of the children a few days country holiday and various other kind little things [...] yet do not touch in any permanent fashion the life and condition of the poor people at all.[116]

Maynard's derogation of the methods of the settlement – 'pleasant evenings', 'kind little things' – is typical of the evangelical disapproval of methods which focused on material rather than spiritual needs. It also makes the work of the settlement seem trivial in comparison with the religious seriousness of the poor's ungodly situation: they, and the settlement are sinking in a flooding swamp of evil. Maynard also suggests that the settlement workers are guilty of biological determinism, as she quotes certain women as saying that the work is, in fact, impossible, because of the nature of the poor: 'They say no lever is strong enough to lift a really drunken man and reform him'. The idea that anyone might be intrinsically different, unable to be saved, was strongly opposed by evangelical missionaries and their supporters. In a way that implies that she is preaching to the choir, Maynard reminds her students that all humanity has the potential to be saved and that any opposing view is actually blasphemous in that it diminishes God's power:

> My friends, would one have any heart to work at all, if one started from such a point as this? Would it not seem to spoil the whole of

our 'good tidings' if we thought even some of those who need it so sorely were shut out? Should we not feel that the divine weapons put into our hands were after all not *al*mighty [...] I thought of the noble work of the Salvation Army, plunging down into the thickest masses of these 'hopeless' cases and bringing up one after another in triumph, redeemed and set right.[117]

Maynard is here marshalling her favourite military images and almost preacher-like rhetoric to counter the views and methods of philanthropic settlements. Instead, she holds out the Salvation Army as a positive, reinforcing example of true salvation, to encourage her students to continue in their missions and their methods.[118]

LMH's publications were less critical of the Southwark settlement – as a High Church institution, the college saved its censure for Maynard's beloved Salvation Army. One student, in a review of *In Darkest London*, wrote using the corporate 'we': 'We may loathe the Salvation Army. We may detest its methods. But [...] we can hardly deny its results'.[119] And Edith Pearson, who became head of LMH's own settlement used the opportunity of critiquing Booth's methods to advance an Anglican approach that she calls on LMH students to take as a college:

Is there any reason why [The Church of England's] unequalled organization should not be used, and used as an irresistible weapon against this hideous evil, if only her members would realize their individual responsibility? [...] The remedy will be found when all who enjoy the advantages of education, refinement, and culture regard these as trusts to be used for the benefit of those less favoured, and will break down this class separation by giving real personal, loving sympathy.[120]

Like Maynard, Pearson uses military language in this extract – the Church is a weapon – and later calls for her fellow students to 'bravely face the facts'. Meanwhile, she insists that the Church should aim to reclaim the poor and not 'hand over large numbers of our people to those whom we feel to be in serious error'. Moreover, she notes that the Salvation Army's missionaries are usually lacking in education and culture, whereas LMH's students could 'use the intellect that has been cultivated by reading and thought, as well as the sympathies that have been developed through the tenderness of home and friendship', if, she pleads 'they will only respond to the call that just now is so urgent'.[121] This language of a missionary calling in LMH's *Daisy* strongly echoes that in Westfield's *Hermes*.

LMH's founding of its own settlement under the leadership of Pearson in 1897 occurred around the same time that the Old Students' Association newsletter was becoming established and was a project that took a prominent place in the pages of LMH's publications.[122] The editors referred to it as 'a dream [...] which has long been cherished by many among the old students'.[123] As well as an LMH possession, the settlement was a way the college played a role in winning ground from irreligious settlements for the Church of England. Moreover, it was reported that 'it would form a much stronger link between the members of Hall than the existing Old Students' Association, and still further increase the esprit de corps for which LMH was famous'.[124] This vision of missionary collegiality would seem to have been an objective almost as important as the missionary impulse.

Another way that college students and alumnae enjoyed a missionary purpose was by collectively following the work of their more adventurous missionary alumnae and through corporate sponsorship of converts. In the same way as LMH's student association newsletter appears around the same time as its settlement, Maynard started her alumnae letters just as Katherine Tristram had become a CMS missionary. This gave her an opportunity to bind her students to a spirit of collective mission and encourage her students to increase the number of missionaries out of Westfield:

> Miss Tristram will not write herself at this time. Her paper of application is sent into the CMS and she is sealed as a real missionary. Our first! – But not the last, no by some good score, or far more, not the last.[125]

Though this can only have been an aspiration of Maynard's, it is noticeable that she phrases it to her students as a prediction or prophecy that they and their successors must now fulfil. The image of 'some good score, or far more' of Westfield missionaries is also suggestive of an army, enlisting Westfield students in the military rhetoric of the female missionary discourse. Significantly, Tristram's acceptance as a missionary is a collective, Westfield achievement and Maynard uses the possessive 'our' to claim her from her employer, the CMS. It is also not a personal achievement of Tristram's, and she becomes common property of the college – Maynard writing on her behalf in the way of a female missionary biographer rather than letting her tell her own story.

When writing about their sponsorship of converts, there is an unfortunate element of appropriation in college students' language. For example, Royal Holloway referred to their 'college waif', or 'our waif', Rose Bowering, whom their society clothed and supported. When, like many who rescued working-class girls, the college decided for her that she should be trained for service, the college letter was self-congratulatory in that 'there could hardly be a better work for the College to do than thus to rescue a child from every sort of misery, and to bring her up to a happy and useful womanhood', suggesting that Bowering's success reflected more on them than on her.[126] At Westfield, Maynard and her students spoke about their 'ownership' of the so-called 'Westfield scholars' (converts in Tristram's school whom the Westfield students sponsored). Terms of possession and judgement appear constantly, such as when Maynard writes of 'our wicked Chika Ruth, who seems to be turning out well after all'.[127] In this way, Westfield approached their collective ownership of missionaries in the way of a collegiate family. Maynard's comments about 'Chika Ruth' are like those of a monitoring evangelical mother, and Tristram allows the students, in an article in *Hermes* in 1885, a glimpse into the conversion relationship their subscriptions have supported: 'It rejoiced one to see the change in her face, manner and life and to know how she witnessed when she went home for the holidays'.[128] Through taking responsibility for a student's conversion, Tristram is placing herself and, through appealing to their imagination, the Westfield students, in the position of joint evangelical parents to the erring, but improving child.

Interestingly, Maynard not only referred to Tristram's converts as Westfield's collective offspring, but also used this rhetoric for the non-human fruits of the college: of the new school St Katherine's, she writes: 'It is delightful to hear of St Katherine's. She is but three and a half years old, what a girl for her age! – well may we be proud of her. I love hearing about those children'.[129] Through this transformed feminine rhetoric, Maynard is able to stress how Westfield as an institution has been part of creating an object of pride as valid – or more so – as the numerous babies other graduates have presumably written to Maynard about. In this way, Maynard is also able to effusively support the professional endeavour of her alumnae.

The coverage of Katherine Tristram's missionary activities by Westfield College's newsletter, *Hermes*, demonstrates that Maynard's specifically confident missionary discourse, eschewing any rhetoric of self-sacrifice, was taken up by her students. Tristram herself – who was one of Maynard's earliest converts – wrote an article in 1895, which stressed how pleasurable she found her career:

> I could tell of so many brought out of darkness into light, though in some the light is still but dim. You can imagine what a joy it is to work among them, and how I am looking forward to going back to them and the work.[130]

The report of her homecoming by Westfield's student editors focuses on the exhibition she staged, including Japanese implements and objects d'art that she brought back with her, and clearly shows the lure of the exotic, exciting life of travel afforded a foreign missionary: 'Miss T, who had donned Japanese dress for the occasion, exhibited many interesting articles from Japan and explained many Japanese customs'.[131] When Royal Holloway's missionary alumna Miss Thornton came back from Japan to stay at her college, the College Letter reported a similar event.[132]

In contrast, a spirit of missionary martyrdom persists to some extent in the publications of LMH. The founding of their own settlement house is undertaken in part as a remembrance of the student Mary Eleanor Benson (daughter of the Archbishop of Canterbury), whose death in 1890 put an end to her charitable work in the slums of Lambeth. The Old Student Association newsletter reported the Bishop of Rochester's address about the founding of the settlement, which he made at a meeting during the college's 1886 Gaude, and about the college's martyr missionary:

> As an example of what [LMH] should have been desired to train none fitter to represent it could be imagined than Mary Eleanor Benson. Modern to her finger-tips, full of all the dash, I might say the mental smartness of modern life, with an understanding so quick as to be able to hold her own anywhere; but how much more there was, warm, deep affections, [...] deep and large thoughts of what the time required; and a fund of strong and wide charity for its people and their needs. Oxford knew one part of her, Lambeth knew another; it is not Lambeth the Palace of which I am speaking, but the streets and lanes of the "Great City". If LMH helped to form in a century ten souls such as hers it would I think be worth the doing.[133]

The bishop's characterisation of Benson, as an individual for emulation, insists that intellectual development and modernity should not be the sole aim of college women – they need in addition to devote themselves to the needs of the world and its people.

It was not only LMH's bishop patron who used this language of sacrifice. In a similar vein, the LMH newsletter reports critically on the level of comfort in the settlement house:

> At present it may be looked upon by some as almost too comfortable to be ideal; the idea of life in a slum with only a crust to eat is rather lost sight of [...] and there is a somewhat prosaic healthiness in the appearance of the residents as a whole.[134]

Though the tone is somewhat tongue-in-cheek, this report suggests at least some in the college believe in missionary asceticism and suffering. Certainly, alumni Eglantine Jebb, who went on to found Save the Children, is remembered for emptying her college room of luxuries – such as carpet and chairs.[135] And a more extreme case of martyrdom is connected with LMH's sister college St Hugh's, in the case of alumna Emily Wilding Davison throwing herself onto the course of the Grand National to be trampled to death in the mission for women's suffrage.[136] Certainly, in her posthumously published essay, 'The Price of Freedom', Davison characterised the militant suffragette as a religious martyr: 'To re-enact the tragedy of Calvary for generations yet unborn, that is the last consummate sacrifice of the Militant'.[137] Interestingly, this connecting of the feminist martyr with Christ, and the implication that there will be no reward other than that of knowing her death is sanctified by God and is to bring about a better world for future women, is reminiscent of the rhetoric of Olive Schreiner and Margaret Harkness.

Meanwhile, at Royal Holloway, a rhetoric of responsibility and usefulness was advanced. In 1891, the college letter reported that the Archbishop of Canterbury had instructed that the students 'must lay upon ourselves this considerable burden of responsibility' and that, enjoying as they did the luxury of higher education, 'we should ask what was the meaning of this splendour, and what use was there in it?'[138] Consequently, their philanthropic missionary activity was often referred to as a 'thank-offering'; in 1891, the College Letter reports that the vote taken on the college supporting a club for factory girls in Lambeth was 'almost unanimous' and that 'some of us felt that we, who by the liberality of others, do our work among surroundings of unique beauty and comfort and healthfulness, could find no more fitting thank-offering than such as work as this'. And the principal repeated the term in her speech at the commemoration day a year later.[139]

As time went on, college students became more independent from the influence of their specific institutions and developed more of a cross-institutional peer culture.[140] For example, as Westfield's *Hermes* developed, it became part of a wider context through its circuits of publication and dissemination. In addition to reporting news of other women's colleges, *Hermes* commented on wider university sector movements, such as the Temperance Movement and Women's Suffrage, and championed what it described as the 'effort [...] being made to affiliate Women's colleges with the Student Missionary Movement'.[141] With the help of their publication, the student body of Westfield constructed itself as a conscious and confident member of the university sector. Even though Maynard herself disapproved of the methods of the Student Volunteer Missionary Union (as it became), Westfield students were active in their conferences and organisation.[142] Meanwhile, in the early twentieth century, St Hugh's students became active in the Oxford branch of the Church League for Women's Suffrage, and Royal Holloway's newsletter reported of the founding of the college's Christian Union and its affiliation with the national body of the Christian Union.[143] Religious college feeling had empowered young women students in their new identities as college students; it then enabled them to see themselves as more than just members of a women's college and to engage in wider movements across universities and outside education altogether.

College Missionaries in the Field

It has been argued that women missionaries of this period – especially those of the CMS and SPG – were a 'new race'; while the official line was still that women did not take part in proselytising, in practice their increased responsibilities in education and medical work were instrumental in conversion.[144] The change in the nature of women missionaries has to be, to some extent, a result of Anglican mission societies recruiting a large number of women who had attended the new women's colleges.

Of the students at Westfield between 1882 and 1898, ten percent became missionaries abroad. If those carrying out other missionary and philanthropic work at home are added to this number – for example, those engaged in anti-opium work, working in 'soldiers homes', or the CMS training school – this brings the total to over twenty-five percent.[145] Westfield missionaries could be found in countries such as Japan, South Africa and the Sudan, to name but a few. Meanwhile, in 1893, LMHs Old Student's Association was reporting that: 'M Macleane has gone to a sisterhood at Graham's Town, South Africa. E Fletcher is now a professed All Saints' sister. [...] G.E.M Church has been appointed Head Mistress of the Girls' High School, Matura, Ceylon'.[146] Graduates were taking the missionary-inflected culture of their colleges around the world, planting it at the heart of their own colleges in the mission field.[147]

The influence of collegiate missionary rhetoric can be seen in the writings of late nineteenth-century missionaries, as college-educated women entered missionary organisations and engaged in missionary writing and publishing. The SPG's Women's Committee, started in 1866, was by the 1880s confident enough in its membership and the enduring interest in their work to launch its own periodical – the *Grain of Mustard Seed*. In its first issue, it proudly recounted how its growth did appear indeed to be as Matthew said: 'which indeed is the least of all seeds: but when it is grown, it is the greatest among herbs, and becometh a tree' (Matthew 13:32). By 1880, the committee had funds of £5,162, 95 teachers and a total of 2,880 pupils in its nineteen schools in India, Burma, Japan, Madagascar and South Africa.[148] In addition to providing the usual extracts from female missionaries' letters, *The Grain of Mustard Seed* in the 1880s was publishing well-constructed, polished articles written by its women members and editors. These included histories of their missions; reviews of publications, including those by geographical societies; and depictions of mission life. One of these articles, entitled 'Our Neighbours', strikes a self-assured tone, reminiscent of college newsletters, as it addresses its audience rhetorically: 'How shall I describe them? Noisy, dirty, quarrelsome. It would be impossible to live amongst them and not be amused, saddened, and shocked at what is going on about us'.[149] Overall, this publication shows that women missionaries in the late nineteenth century, thanks in part to their increased engagement in higher education, were confident enough to comment on male-authored studies, and to write in an entertaining fashion about themselves and their organisations as historically significant.

The specific influence of Westfield College's missionary rhetoric can be seen in the cases of Katherine Tristram and Margaret Brooke. Westfield's first foreign missionary, Katherine Tristram was recruited by the CMS to run an educational institution in Japan. As a professional missionary in her own right, her papers are easily found in the CMS archive. She and her work were also followed by the press; when she first went out to Japan, the *Gleaner* named her as 'their own' missionary, for whom they would raise funds that year.[150] And like women missionaries before her, Tristram sent extracts of her journals home in letters, which were often published.

For Tristram, the Westfield discourse enabled her to live a fulfilling professional life without sacrificing emotion and personal relationships. Her life as a missionary was balanced by a life at home full of family and friends and especially an intense friendship she continued with Miss Alice Hodgkin, an alumna of Westfield, through letters and on regular walking holidays together. She happily associated this relationship with her religion, writing: 'I am having a time of prayer and now a talk with you, how thankful I am that our union and friendship is so altogether in Him'.[151] This religious friendship, so reminiscent of Maynard's at their most successful, is a fitting tribute to Maynard's religious philosophy.

However, the context of the mission field starkly reveals that college women's assumption of authority and ability to reject notions of self-sacrifice was often based on the appropriation and sacrifice of native women. Women's construction of the 'heathen' woman as victim was important for their understanding of their own political agency.[152] Like the Wesleyan women, when writing about their missionary work, Westfield graduates continued to deploy the trope of transposed sacrifice which enabled the use of its emotional power while leaving them free to act.

The main influence Tristram took from Westfield was Maynard's practice of using personal influence and love for conversion. In her 1895 article for *Hermes* about the Westfield scholar, she describes watching this process between her students: 'Though she fought against it her love was drawn out for this friend, her heart was touched and changed and she became a Christian herself'.[153] Tristram is explicit in her writings about the deployment of 'loving kindness', and the power relation implicit in the familial language of Westfield's ownership of converts is revealed to be a far more power-laden strategy of appropriation when transposed to a foreign land and enacted between obviously unequal partners. Opportunities for conversion arose in more extreme conditions and involved subjects infinitely more vulnerable than Maynard's students. For example, in the aftermath of a major earthquake in 1891, Tristram travelled to the disaster zone to nurse the victims – and to proselytise. She writes:

> There are so many injured and they want doctors and nurses badly. It seems just the time to show them love and tell them of Christ as well as bringing them comfort to their poor suffering bodies.[154]

She is more candid about the vulnerability of her subjects than Maynard ever was, as this situation allows no other interpretation – the population being stripped of all resources by the earthquake. However, her seizing of the situation as an opportunity for proselytising seems almost gleeful – 'It seems just the time' – and nursing the victims' bodies appears to be a secondary consideration.

Moreover, in these letters, it is clear that Tristram has full power over the bodies of the Japanese, even using their pain as a tool for conversion:

> She was in such great pain and kept calling all the time on Buddha to help her. I told her today that there was One who really would help her, but she was too bad to bear more than a word or two.[155]

This focus on the bodies and deaths of converts recalls the Wesleyan wives' narration of native sacrifices. The power to seize such opportunities in the name of conversion, while compelling in the abstract in Maynard's letters, is deeply troubling for the modern sensibility when observed in action. While the ownership of converts was empowering for sponsors in England, it took on a different – at times macabre – aspect in Japan. Tristram was determined to hold on to the bodies of her converts: even in death she sued for possession of the cremated remains of her students.[156] This behaviour underlines how women missionaries could use the colonial context and the authority of the church to exert power over indigenous peoples. To an extent, like the Wesleyan wives, Tristram emancipated herself from the female missionary imperative to self-sacrifice through appropriating and sacrificing her converts in her place.

Former Westfield student Margaret Brooke went as part of a CMS mission to the Sudan after marrying her cousin Graham Wilmott Brooke. Like Tristram, Margaret seems to have been able to experience a missionary life that was fulfilled both professionally and personally; she worked in Africa alongside her husband until his death in 1892. Despite not having her own entry in the CMS archive, Margaret was in fact the author of Brooke's official journal for the majority of their married life in the Sudan. As secretary, she was also heavily involved in producing the newsletters that the mission sent back to England.[157]

Within mission history, the Sudan mission was significant and controversial. Its governance was premised on the need for European leadership, signalling a change of direction within the CMS from Henry Venn's vision of a self-governing church, and C. Peter Williams has seen Graham Brooke as instrumental in this change of direction. However, I would argue that Margaret, and her Westfield missionary culture, was a major influence on her husband and on the mission's ethos. Williams argues that the CMS were looking for university-educated missionaries, full of revival spirit, such as that fostered by the Keswick circle and Hudson Taylor's China Inland Mission movement, and suggests that Graham, with his family links to Keswick, was the ideal recruit.[158] However, Graham had not been to university and was in fact very newly converted. In 1886, around the time that Margaret left Westfield, Graham had returned from a scientific exploratory trip up the Niger when 'a great and very sudden increase of Spiritual light' came over him, changing his former concern with the temporal conditions in the Niger, to that of religious mission.[159] The timing suggests that Margaret could have been responsible for Graham's conversion.

The university-educated Margaret, full of Westfield's missionary spirit, was exactly the missionary the CMS was looking for. In her work in Sudan, Westfield's religio-military rhetoric inspired her and suffuses the mission's writings. In July 1890, in the journal, Margaret describes an editorial discussion over correspondence for publication in which it was agreed that these writings should be 'as powerful a weapon as possible'.[160] Graham comments in one of his letters home that the sentiments in one of the newsletters were certainly not down to him: 'the others were a good deal stronger than I was myself on the duty of not passing over [...] the most essential points to a true understanding of our position'.[161] This newsletter, co-authored by Margaret in September 1890, follows the practice of Maynard in that it stresses the challenges faced by the missionaries in order to make their battle more heroic:

> Perhaps the following notes of some actual experiences may give some notion of the battle as it really is fought [...] Let no-one suppose that the missionary [...] comes out to a simple, ignorant people whose hearts are speedily won by frankness and sympathy. On the contrary, from his first arrival he is watched with a keen distrust [...] completely veiled [...] by a clever assumption of childlike simplicity.[162]

Through an anthropological description of the African tribe, this piece seeks to enlighten its audience to the true nature of the subjects the missionaries are dealing with and thus elevate their mission. A newsletter from May 1890 stresses the heroism of the band of missionaries, in comparison with the rest of the church: 'to such a field, and to such a battle, all that can be mustered are four young men and two young ladies'.[163]

Margaret's missionary rhetoric could not, however, manage the idea of martyrdom. Her heroic and military tone is at odds with Graham's self-aware inclusion of sacrifice in the description of the mission's 'Principles and Object', which included a section entitled 'Counting the Cost':

> All volunteers for the Sudan mission are expected carefully to weigh the consequences [...] When they [...] are sent to the front [...] They must go forth altogether unarmed and face the full significance of the Master's words – 'I send you forth as lambs among wolves'.[164]

Although this passage refers to 'volunteers' and 'the front', suggesting a military metaphor, Brooke's soldiers are unarmed and unprotected other than by God. While Margaret writes that 'It might be God's will for the missionaries to glorify him by meekly enduring assassination', this is only an afterthought and remains hypothetical in contrast to the strident tone of the rest of the newsletter.[165] The Sudan mission failed just two years later, culminating in Graham Wilmott Brooke's martyrdom.

Conclusion

Margaret Brooke went on to work for the CMS in England, and Katherine Tristram died happily, in 1948, in Japan, where her school had been her life's work. While the foreign missionary field exposed its practical and moral limits, Westfield's missionary culture had certainly allowed both these women to follow their intellectual and spiritual ambitions into professional, influential and, at times, fulfilling, careers as missionaries.

More generally, as this chapter has shown, missionary culture was hugely influential on the development of women's college culture at the turn of the century. Missionary college principals such as Constance Maynard and Elizabeth Wordsworth established a religious collegiality in their communities, which inspired a serious generation of women students to lives of social service in addition to Christian mission. In turn, women's college culture influenced the character of missionary societies, institutions and publications as college-educated women took on increasingly important roles in the mission movement.

Notes

1 For example, see Valerie Sanders, *Eve's Renegades: Victorian Anti-Feminist Women Novelists* (Basingstoke: Macmillan, 1996), p. 6; Martha Vicinus, *Independent Women: Work and Community for Single Women 1850–1920* (London: Virago, 1985), pp. 8–9. For a more detailed historiography of women's education and a discussion of religion's place in it, see Angharad Eyre, 'Education', in *Women in Christianity in the Age of Empire: 1800–1920*, ed. by Janet Wootton (London: Routledge, 2022).
2 Laura Schwartz, *A Serious Endeavour: Gender, Education and Community at St Hugh's 1886–2011* (London: Profile Books, 2011), pp. 19, 38.
3 Ibid., p. 5. Incidentally, among the students who attended lectures at Bedford College was Dinah Mullock, later Craik, whose work is examined in Chapter 2.
4 Vicinus, pp. 134–43.
5 Carol Dyhouse, *Girls Growing Up in Late Victorian and Edwardian England* (London: Routledge, 1981), pp. 57–9; June Purvis, *A History of Women's Education in England* (Milton Keynes: Open University Press, 1991), pp. 114–5.
6 Richardson, 'Introduction', in *Women Who Did*, ed. by Richardson, pp. xxxvi–xxxviii; Viv Gardner, 'Introduction', in *The New Woman and Her Sisters: Feminism and Theatre 1850–1914*, ed. by Viv Gardner and Susan Rutherford (London: Harvester Wheatsheaf, 1992), p. 2; However, as Sally Ledger notes, scholars should be careful not to confuse this mythical woman with real university women of the time, *The New Woman: Fiction and Feminism at the Fin De Siècle* (Manchester: Manchester University Press, 1997), pp. 1–3.

7 Marth Vicinus, '"One Life To Stand Beside Me": Emotional Conflicts in First-Generation College Women in England', *Feminist Studies*, 8 (1982), 603–28 (p. 607).
8 Vicinus, *Independent Women*, pp. 6–8, 123–39.
9 For studies of religious vocation and the pioneering heads of girls' schools and women's colleges, see Joyce Senders Pederson, *The Reform of Girls' Secondary and Higher Education in Victorian England: A Study of Elites and Educational Change* (New York: Garland, 1987), pp. 174–5, 254–8; and Carol Dyhouse, 'Miss Buss and Miss Beale: Gender and Authority in the History of Education', in *Lessons for Life: The Schooling of Girls and Women 1850–1950*, ed. by Felicity Hunt (Oxford: Blackwell, 1987), pp. 22–38 (p. 28).
10 Schwartz, pp. 26–38; see also Lucy Bland, *Banishing the Beast: English Feminism and Sexual Morality 1885–1914* (London: Penguin, 1995), p. xix; and LeeAnne M. Richardson, *New Women and Colonial Adventure Fiction in Victorian Britain: Gender, Genre and Empire* (Gainesville, FL: University Press of Florida, 2006), p. 2.
11 On muscular Christianity in men's colleges, Norman Vance points to Thomas Arnold's work at Rugby school to 'substitute ethical (and religious) values for merely social qualities', *The Sinews of the Spirit: The Ideal of Christian Manliness in Victorian Literature and Religious Thought* (Cambridge: Cambridge University Press, 1985), p. 25; Similarly, J. R. Watson emphasises the importance of hymns in public school chapels in developing an ethos of 'spiritual warfare' in future colonial governors and soldiers, 'Soldiers and Saints: The Fighting Man and the Christian Life', in *Masculinity and Spirituality in Victorian Culture*, ed. by Andrew Bradstock, Sean Gill, Anne Hogan and Sue Morgan (Basingstoke: Macmillan, 2000), pp. 10–26 (p. 24).
12 Rita McWilliams-Tullberg, 'Women and Degrees at Cambridge University', in Vicinus, *A Widening Sphere: Changing Roles of Victorian Women*, ed. by Martha Vicinus (London: Methuen, 1980) pp. 117–45 (p. 135).
13 For examples, see C. B. Firth, *Constance Louisa Maynard, Mistress of Westfield College: A Family Portrait* (London: George Allen, 1949); Janet Sondheimer, *Castle Adamant in Hampstead: A History of Westfield College* (London: Westfield College, 1983); Queen Mary, University of London Archives, 'The Students' Experience of Westfield College'. www.qmul.ac.uk/library/archives/archive-galleries/the-students-experience-of-westfield-college/ (accessed 20 January 2022).
14 Perry Williams, 'Pioneer Women Students at Cambridge, 1869–81', in *Lessons for Life*, ed. by Hunt, pp. 171–91 (pp. 180–1).
15 See Chapter 1 for examination of such newsletters.
16 As scholars have related with regards to the settlements set up by the male colleges of Oxford and Cambridge, it was usually denominational differences that resulted in each college eventually having its own settlement house; see Seth Koven, *Slumming: Sexual and Social Politics in Victorian London* (Princeton, NJ: Princeton University Press, 2004), pp. 230–52; and Nigel Scotland, *Squires in the Slums: Settlements and Missions in Late Victorian London* (London: Tauris, 2007), pp. 166–7.
17 Firth, pp. 51–102; see also Pauline Phipps, *Constance Maynard's Passions: Religion, Sexuality and an English Educational Pioneer, 1849–1935* (Toronto: University of Toronto Press, 2015), pp. 6–7, 25–7.

18 Firth, p. 102.
19 Constance Maynard, Queen Mary, University of London Archives, Constance Maynard collection, CLM/1, 'Green Book' diary [hereafter cited as GB], 21 November–12 December 1880.
20 Maynard refers to this experience later when helping a family friend, GB, 5 August 1880.
21 Barbara Stephens, *Emily Davies and Girton College* (London: Constable, 1927), p. 288.
22 Maynard, GB, 31 December 1880.
23 Phipps notes how this vocation supported Maynard to meet her professional goals, p. 8.
24 See Prologue and Chapter 1.
25 Constance Maynard, Queen Mary, University of London Archives, Constance Maynard collection, CLM/6, Autobiography, 7 Vols, I, p. 1; Mary Kupiec Cayton draws attention to the mediation of women's published religious accounts by ministers and memoirists, 'Harriet Newell's Story: Women, the Evangelical Press and the Foreign Mission Movement', in *An Extensive Republic: Print, Culture and Society in the New Nation 1790–1840*, ed. by Robert A. Gross and Mary Kelley (Chapel Hill: University of North Carolina Press, 2012), pp. 408–16 (pp. 411–3).
26 Maynard, Autobiography, I, pp. 1–3.
27 Linda Peterson, 'Women Writers and Self Writing', in *Women and Literature in Britain 1800–1900*, ed. by Joanne Shattock (Cambridge: Cambridge University Press, 2001), pp. 209–30 (p. 210).
28 See Pauline Phipps for discussion of Maynard's engagement with Freud and other authorities to understand her desires, 'Constance Maynard's Languages of Love', *Women's History Review*, 25 (2016), 17–34.
29 Maynard, quoted in Firth, p. 1; Jay has noted the evangelical mother's practice of encouraging children in the habit of introspection, requiring them to keep a daily record of their thoughts, which was regularly scrutinised, *Religion of the Heart*, p. 149.
30 See Chapter 1.
31 Maynard, GB, 28 October, 1880.
32 See Prologue.
33 Maynard, GB, 31 December 1880.
34 Vicinus, *Independent Women*, p. 128.
35 Schwartz, pp. 20–31.
36 Vicinus, '"One Life"', pp. 610–2.
37 Maynard, GB, 22 October 1882.
38 Maynard, Autobiography, VI, pp. 56–95.
39 Royal Holloway College Archives, Royal Holloway, University of London, Egham, RHC AS/902/1–26, Royal Holloway College Letter, December 1897.
40 Maynard, Autobiography, VI, pp. 56–95.
41 Lady Margaret Hall Archives, Oxford, Old Students' Association Newsletter, 1896, pp. 12–8; Royal Holloway College Letter, December 1890, p. 5, and July 1891, pp. 2–10.
42 Maynard, GB, 29 October 1882.
43 Maynard, GB, 5 December 1880.
44 Maynard, GB, 17 May 1882.
45 Ibid.

46 Maynard, GB, 5 February 1881.
47 Maynard, Autobiography, VI, pp. 58, 80.
48 Maynard, GB, 27 June 1881.
49 Watson, 'Soldiers and Saints', in *Masculinity and Spirituality*, ed. by Bradstock et al, p. 10.
50 Maynard, Autobiography, VI, p. 23.
51 Maynard, GB, 30 October 1881.
52 Maynard, GB, 2 May 1880.
53 Vicinus, *Independent Women*, pp. 128–9; see also Lisa C. Robertson, ' "We Must Advance, We Must Expand": Architectural and Social Challenges to the Domestic Model at the College for Ladies at Westfield', *Women's History Review*, 25 (2016), 105–23 (pp. 108–12).
54 LMH Archives, Oxford, 'A Hundred Years of Hall Gossip', in *The Brown Book: Centenary Number* (1978).
55 Jay, pp. 54–6, 139; Nadia Valman, *The Jewess in Nineteenth-Century British Literary Culture* (Cambridge: Cambridge University Press, 2007), p. 101.
56 Maynard, GB, 5 November 1882.
57 Jay, p. 144.
58 Maynard, GB, 31 December 1880.
59 Seth Koven and Sonya Michel, 'Introduction', in *Mothers of New World: Maternalist Politics and the Origins of Welfare States*, ed. by Seth Koven and Sonya Michel (London: Routledge, 1993), pp. 1–42 (pp. 2–4).
60 Valman, p. 102.
61 This can be seen throughout the century, for example, in the missionary correspondence of Abigail Beighton, 1818–1821, London, SOAS, MS 380689, and that of Edith Lucas of the China Inland Mission, 1890–1891, London, SOAS, MS 380627.
62 Vicinus, ' "One Life" ', p. 612; Pauline Phipps, 'Faith, Desire, and Sexual Identity: Constance Maynard's Atonement for Passion', *Journal of the History of Sexuality*, 18 (2009), 265–86 (pp. 275–6).
63 Maynard, GB, 27 December 1883.
64 H. W., 'A Hint to Ministers and Others Who "Weep with Them that Weep" ', *Christian Observer*, January 1850, pp. 6–11.
65 Maynard, GB, 20 January 1881.
66 LMH Archives, Oxford, Courtney 3/1, Kathleen Courtney, Memoir.
67 Phipps, 'Faith, Desire, and Sexual Identity', p. 266.
68 Maynard, Autobiography, VII, pp. 18–9.
69 Constance Maynard, Autobiography, VI, p. 77.
70 Sharon Marcus, *Between Women: Friendship, Desire, and Marriage in Victorian England* (Oxford: Princeton University Press, 2007), p. 63.
71 Maynard, GB, 5 June 1882.
72 Naomi Lloyd also notes how religious acts were productive of erotic desire for Maynard, 'Religion, Same-Sex Desire, and the Imagined Geographies of Empire: The Case of Constance Maynard (1849–1935), *Women's History Review*, 25 (2016), 53–73 (p. 60).
73 Maynard, Autobiography, VI, p. 80.
74 Maynard, GB, 17 May 1882.
75 Maynard, Autobiography, V, p. 172.
76 Maynard, GB, 17 May 1882; Phipps, 'Faith, Desire, and Sexual Identity', p. 276.

77 In this incorporation of missionary work and fulfilling marriage, Maynard was not alone. The Salvation Army was also encouraging its members to work together in home and public, Laura Lauer, 'Soul-Saving Partnerships and Pacifist Soldiers: The Ideal of Masculinity in the Salvation Army', in *Masculinity and Spirituality*, ed. by Bradstock et al, pp. 196–9; Seth Koven also found that marriage was encouraged among settlement workers, *Slumming*, p. 200.
78 Marcus has likewise commented on what she sees as the 'mutation' of marriage at this time, which included the embracing of the form by female couples, Marcus, pp. 2–5.
79 Candy Gunther Brown has noted evangelicals' use of 'textual community' to sustain evangelical culture and faith, *The Word in the World: Evangelical Writing, Publishing and Reading in America 1789–1880* (Chapel Hill, NC: University of North Carolina Press, 2004), pp. 1–9.
80 Unfortunately, from the first few rings, only two letters from alumnae remain, and conclusions have to be drawn from Maynard's responses as to the nature of the letters from her missionaries, female activists, nurses and teachers.
81 Maynard, GB, 8 May 1881.
82 Maynard, Queen Mary, University of London Archives, Westfield College collection, WFD 26/1, Letter to alumnae, January 1894.
83 Maynard, Letter, 3 June 1887.
84 Maynard, Letter, 4 February 1888.
85 Watson, 'Soldiers and Saints', in *Masculinity and Spirituality*, ed. by Bradstock et al, pp. 18–9; Vance, p. 27.
86 Maynard, Letter, January 1894.
87 Maynard, Letter, 4 February 1888.
88 Watson, 'Soldiers and Saints', in *Masculinity and Spirituality*, ed. by Bradstock et al., p. 12.
89 Maynard, Letter, September 1891.
90 Maynard, Letter, September 1895.
91 Maynard, Letter, 23 January 1895.
92 At the centre of some scientific writing, there was a continued emphasis on the unknowable, and Aileen Fyfe has shown how evangelical popular science publications re-interpreted scientific evidence to make it conform to religious belief; Aileen Fyfe, *Science and Salvation: Evangelical Popular Science Publishing in Victorian Britain* (London: University of Chicago Press, 2004), p. 3.
93 Contemporary preachers that she went to hear used science for imagery and conceits; Stevenson Blackwood used basic economic and banking terms in his religious lecture 'Heavenly Arithmetic', and a Mr Haig Miller compared the Holy Spirit to a helium balloon, Maynard mentions that she became aware of these examples during her time in London 1881–1882, Autobiography, Vol. VI, pp. 60, 123.
94 The connection of missionary work and women's nineteenth-century colleges is an under-researched area; however, scholars have begun to study students' involvement in missionary work in America and at the beginning of the twentieth century; David Setran, *The College Y: Student Religion in the Era of Secularisation* (New York: Palgrave Macmillan, 2007), pp. 1–5; Nathan Showalter, *The End of a Crusade: The Student Volunteer Movement for Foreign Missions and the Great War* (London: Scarecrow, 1998), pp. 2–3.

95 Vicinus, *Independent Women*, p. 142.
96 Ellen Ross, 'Introduction', in *Slum Travellers*, ed. by Ross, p. 20.
97 Royal Holloway College Letter, July 1891, pp. 7–9.
98 Royal Holloway College Letter, July 1892, pp. 7–8.
99 Schwartz, p. 13. All these religious colleges can be seen deploying the arguments made by social purity feminists that women were morally superior to men and therefore had a specific role to civilize humanity; see Bland, p. 91.
100 L. T. Meade, *A Sweet Girl Graduate* (London: Cassell and Co., 1891), pp. 84–5, 288.
101 Ibid., p. 288.
102 Maynard, GB, 5 December 1880.
103 Maynard, Letter, 3 June 1887.
104 Watson, 'Soldiers and Saints', in *Masculinity and Spirituality*, ed. by Bradstock et al, p. 18.
105 Maynard, Letter, 3 June 1887.
106 Royal Holloway College Letter, July 1892, p. 3.
107 Maynard, Letter, January 1893.
108 Vicinus, *Independent Women*, p. 143.
109 *Girton Review*, December 1884, Oxford, Girton College Archives, GCCP, p. 7.
110 'A Hundred Years of Hall Gossip', *The Brown Book*, p. 38.
111 Queen Mary, University of London Archives, Westfield College collection, WFD/23/3, *Hermes*, 1895, p. 6.
112 Maynard, Letter, 23 October 1888.
113 Scotland, p. 156.
114 Scotland, pp. xii–xiii; Koven, p. 186.
115 Katherine Bentley Beauman, *The Lady Margaret Hall Settlement 1887–1997: A Century of Caring in the Community* (n.p.: The Friends of Lady Margaret Hall Settlement, 1997), p. 6; Scotland, p. 155.
116 Maynard, Letter, 31 May 1888.
117 Ibid.
118 Though General Booth's beliefs about slum missionary work changed to become more aligned with the Christian Socialist view of the importance of ministering to the poor's material as well as spiritual needs, at this time, the Salvation Army was still working on the basis of an Atonement evangelicalism, focusing first and foremost on conversion; Yeo, p. 13.
119 LMH Archives, Oxford, C. G. Luard, 'In Darkest England', *The Daisy*, 2 February 1891, pp. 7–8.
120 Edith Pearson, 'In Darkest England', *The Daisy*, 2 February 1891, pp. 7–8.
121 Ibid.
122 'A Hundred Years of Hall Gossip', *The Brown Book*, p. 42.
123 'The Gaude', Old Students' Association Newsletter, 1896, p. 9.
124 Ibid., pp. 22–3.
125 Maynard, Letter, 4 February 1888.
126 Royal Holloway College Letter, December 1890, p. 10; December 1891, p. 8; and April 1893, p. 3.
127 Maynard, Letter, 16 January 1893. As Winter Jade Werner notes, the missionary renaming of converts, often by donors from the metropole, demonstrated colonial tendencies towards paternalism and a desire to

Women, Religion and Power   225

overwrite indigenous cultural systems, *Missionary Cosmopolitanism in Nineteenth-Century British Literature* (Columbus: Ohio State University Press, 2020), pp. 120–1; Naomi Lloyd also identifies an imperial aspect in Maynard's missionary evangelicalism, pp. 56–66.
128 Katherine Tristram, in *Hermes*, 1895, p. 5.
129 Maynard, Letter, 20 October 1896.
130 *Hermes* (1895).
131 *Hermes* (1895).
132 Royal Holloway College Letter, p. 5.
133 'Address by the Bishop of Rochester', Old Students' Association Newsletter, 1896, pp. 12–8.
134 'The Settlement', Old Students' Association Newsletter, 1897, pp. 10–1.
135 Courtney, Memoir.
136 Schwartz, p. 40.
137 Emily Wilding Davison, 'The Price of Liberty', *Suffragette*, 5 June 1914, p. 129.
138 Royal Holloway College Letter, July 1891, pp. 9–10
139 Royal Holloway College Letter, December 1891, p. 6; July 1892, p. 3.
140 Setran has explained how the peer culture developed in American universities in this period was important for the 'lived religion' on campuses, p. 3; also, Susan C. Jarrett has described how newsletters in particular enabled emancipated black students in American colleges to develop their own official, intellectual voice, 'Classics and Counter-publics in Nineteenth-Century Historically Black Colleges', *College English*, 72 (2009), 134–59 (p. 142).
141 *Hermes*, 1894, p. 1.
142 Sondheimer, pp. 66–7.
143 Schwartz, p. 39; Royal Holloway College Letter, July 1900.
144 Deborah Kirkwood, 'Protestant Missionary Women: Wives and Spinsters', in *Women and Missions: Past and Present, Anthropological and Historical Perceptions*, ed. by Fiona Bowie, Deborah Kirkwood and Shirley Ardner (Oxford: Berg, 1993), pp. 23–41 (p. 36); Elizabeth E. Prevost, *The Communion of Women: Missions and Gender in Colonial Africa and the British Metropole* (Oxford: Oxford University Press, 2010), p. 4.
145 These figures have been arrived at through examining the Student Register 1882–1898, Queen Mary, University of London Archives, Westfield College collection, WFD/10/1/1.
146 'Old Students' Destinations', Old Students' Association Newsletter, 1893, pp. 10–1.
147 See Barbara E. Campbell's study of mission schools and colleges, *To Educate Is to Teach to Live: Women's Struggles Toward Higher Education* (New York: Women's Division, United Methodist Church, 2005).
148 Papers of the SPG, Bodleian Libraries, SPG-CWW, *Grain of Mustard Seed, or Women's Work in Foreign Parts*, May 1881, p. 3.
149 Mrs M. J. Farnham, 'Our Neighbours', *Grain of Mustard Seed*, July 1881, p. 22.
150 Katherine Tristram, Scrapbook, Birmingham University Library, CMS Acc104 F3.
151 Tristram, Letter, 'Extracts of Letters from K. Tristram to A.M. Hodgkin', Birmingham University Library, CMS Acc104 F4, 15 May 1892.

152 Antoinette Burton, *Burdens of History: British Feminists, Indian Women and Imperial Culture 1865–1915* (London: University of Carolina Press, 1994), pp. 30–1.
153 Tristram, in *Hermes,* 1895, p. 5.
154 Tristram, Letter, 4 November 1891.
155 Tristram, Letter, 19 November 1891.
156 A. M. Hodgkin, note, Birmingham University Library, CMS Acc104 F4.
157 Graham Wilmott Brooke, Letter, 21 April 1890, 'Letters of Graham Wilmott Brooke', Birmingham University Library, CMS Acc 82 F4/4.
158 C. Peter Williams, *The Ideal of the Self-Governing Church: A Study in Victorian Missionary Strategy* (Leiden: Brill, 1990), pp. 146–51.
159 'The Sudan Mission Band', *The Christian Worker,* April 1890, Birmingham University Library, CMS Acc 82 F4/6.
160 Margaret Brooke, Journal, 18 July 1890, Birmingham University Library, CMS Acc 82 F4.
161 Graham Brooke, Letter, 12 May 1890.
162 The Sudan Mission, *Monthly Leaflet,* September 1890, Birmingham University Library, CMS Acc 82 F4/8, p. 1.
163 The Sudan Mission, *Monthly Leaflet,* May 1890, p. 3.
164 Graham Wilmott Brooke and Rev. Robinson, *The Sudan and Upper Niger Mission of the CMS (Principles and Objects),* 17 January 1890, Birmingham University Library, CMS Acc 82 F4.
165 The Sudan Mission, *Monthly Leaflet,* May 1890, p. 4.

Conclusion

The female missionary character appeared early in the nineteenth century as the biographers of Ann Judson and Harriet Newell attempted to produce realistic, yet positive depictions of missionary women. The character that emerged was rich and complex, whose heroic mission-field narratives made for compelling reading. In her confident, religiously authorised action, her feminine piety and her courageous sacrifice of self for others, she represented a way for women to understand their own religious subjectivities; whether readers were destined for a domestic family life, or a more active missionary role, the female missionary and her narrative allowed for an expansive understanding of women's place in the world. Women writers especially were able to see themselves as missionary workers and, in this climate, became prolific producers of didactic fiction.

When the secularisation of domestic ideology led to a more restrictive view of woman's nature, some biographers of female missionaries began to close down the opportunities presented by the figure, emphasising her feminine and domestic characteristics. And, as she became an exemplar for domestic piety, women were encouraged to imitate her pious self-sacrifice too, which became seen as an essential female trait. It was to these cultural moves that the tracts of Sherwood and Stretton, and the novels of Charlotte Brontë, Dinah Craik and Elizabeth Gaskell responded. Drawing on representations of the female missionary in all her guises, these authors unveiled the paradoxes that women were being forced to live, and contested the characterisation of the missionary woman with their own radical alternatives.

As the writing of missionary women themselves had proven, the female missionary narrative could enable a militant, confident female activism while allowing women to understand themselves and their emotions through a framework that emphasised the importance of their lives and work. For women's writing, the female missionary narrative radically envisaged a plot for a woman's life that did not depend on romance and marriage and which valorised the emotions of religious female relationships. In ways that revolutionised the conventional form and plot of the nineteenth-century novel, women writers developed the

DOI: 10.4324/9781003332961-10

female missionary figure to better reflect the experiences of Victorian women. When, in the 1880s, secularisation threatened the basis of the figure that had authorised women's religious activity, the New Woman writers reinvigorated the female missionary narrative to become a powerful metaphor for feminism.

In the late nineteenth century, the expansion and professionalisation of women's roles in the mission led to an increase of women involved in the textual community of female missionary newsletters. The more advanced training of women missionaries in high schools, colleges and hospitals also involved women in a real collective identity. Some religious women principals took the opportunity to enshrine female missionary culture in the heart of the new women's colleges, which furthered the mission cause and provided women with an inspirational ideology to sustain them following graduation. These material conditions meant that female missionary culture, which had been communicated mainly through literature, now became part of the ethos of women's educational institutions and was disseminated through both concrete communities and virtual networks of women.

There were problems with the female missionary character and narrative, most notably, the imperative to self-immolation. The transposition of this sort of death to male characters by Brontë and the New Woman writers suggests a desire to include or embody the holy martyr's role, but also an awareness that representing women in this position would only further entrench self-abnegation as an essentially female trait. Meanwhile, though the notion of sacrifice could be ignored in the domestic environment of women's colleges, once graduates entered the mission field, potential martyrdom became a pressing problem. For missionary women in the field, ambivalence about martyrdom for themselves led them to exert power over converts, using literary techniques to narrate natives' deaths – rather than their own – as the central sacrifices of their female missionary narratives.

Despite these problems, at the turn of the century, the female missionary was continuing to exert a fascination on the public imagination in Britain. Missionary literature was flourishing, and 1900 saw new editions of James Gardner's *Heroines of Missionary Enterprise* and Emma Raymond Pitman's *Lady Missionaries in Foreign Lands*. Moreover, Ann Judson's story remained popular well into the twentieth century, with an edition of Pitman's biography *Ann H. Judson: The Missionary Heroine of Burma* being re-published in 1948. Judson's courage and dedication to the cause could still provide a relevant inspiration for women of this period, many of whom would have been active in the war effort or in bringing the new welfare state into being. The female missionary figure had come a long way from her beginnings in the original biographies of the early nineteenth century, and her evolution had been hugely important for women's writing and activism.

But what of the wider legacy of the female missionary? Recently scholars have begun to acknowledge the influence of religion on first-wave feminism. For example, some scholars have been struck by aspects of religion in suffragist writing, for example, in the work of the American Elizabeth Cady Stanton.[1] And it is well-known that suffragettes – and, later, the influential socialist and feminist Vera Brittain – were inspired and sustained by New Woman writers such as Olive Schreiner and what I have identified as her female missionary texts.[2] Further research might valuably explore how twentieth-century women's culture was influenced by the turn of the century's particularly religious missionary feminism. Certainly, as this feminism had been disseminated by schools and colleges, I would expect to see the female missionary's legacy in school and college fiction, for example, in the characterisation of female headmistresses by authors such as Elinor M. Brent Dyer, and in the informing rhetoric of women's voluntary organisations, such as the Girl Guides and the Women's Voluntary Service.[3] Some of us who were involved in Guiding in our youth might remember the tone of handbooks and magazines as one promoting worthwhile activity for young women, with a basis in a religious and global moral authority.

The inheritance of twentieth- and twenty-first-century women needs to be reviewed in light of the missionary nature of nineteenth-century feminism and women's writing. Though largely ignored till now, the female missionary character was a dominant influence on nineteenth-century women's culture. Her legacy ensured that many women up to the present day understood themselves as women, writers and feminists within a moral framework inspired by missionary femininity.

Notes

1 See Emily H. Mace, 'Feminist Forerunners and a Usable Past: A Historiography of Elizabeth Cady Stanton's *The Woman's Bible*', *Journal of Feminist Studies in Religion*, 25 (2009), 5–23; Kathi Kern, ' "Free Woman Is a Divine Being, the Savior of Mankind": Stanton's Exploration of Religion and Gender', in *Elizabeth Cady Stanton, Feminist as Thinker: A Reader in Documents and Essays*, ed. by Ellen Carol DuBois and Richard Cándida Smith (New York: New York University Press, 2007), pp. 93–110.
2 See Ann Heilmann, *Strategies*, pp. 129–30; Alan Bishop, ' "With Suffering and Through Time": Olive Schreiner, Vera Brittain, and the Great War', in *Olive Schreiner and After: Essays on Southern African Literature in Honour of Guy Butler*, ed. by Malvern van Wyk Smith and Don Maclennan (Cape Town: David Philip, 1993), pp. 80–92 (pp. 82–3). Also see Chapter 4.
3 The written minutes of their annual meetings to discuss voluntary work to aid the assimilation of European Voluntary Workers, which were circulated to the Ministry of Labour among other public bodies, do in fact contain what I would consider to be rhetoric inspired by the female missionary discourse, Ministry of Labour, 'Liaison with Women's Voluntary Services', London, National Archives, LAB 26/235.

Bibliography

Unpublished, Manuscript and Archival Sources

Bedford College Archive, Royal Holloway, University of London, Egham.
China Inland Mission (CIM) Archive, SOAS Library, London, Papers of Edith Lucas, MS 380627.
Church Missionary Society (CMS) Archive, Birmingham University Library, Papers of Graham Wilmott Brooke, CMS Acc 82; Papers of Katherine Tristram, CMS Acc 104.
Elizabeth Gaskell Manuscript Collection, University of Manchester Library.
Girton College Archives, University of Oxford.
Lady Margaret Hall Archives, University of Oxford, Old Students' Association papers; *The Brown Book; The Daisy*.
London Missionary Society Archive, SOAS Library, London, Correspondence of Thomas and Abigail Beighton, MS 380689; Papers of J. Bunby, MSS/SpecialSeries/biographical/Southseas/FBN 35; 'Domestic Memoir of Mrs Morrison', 1824, MS 380583.
The National Archives, London, Ministry of Labour files, 'Liaison with Women's Voluntary Services', LAB 26/235.
Nussey Collection, Harry Ransom Center, University of Texas at Austin.
Nusey, Ellen (ed.), *The Story of the Brontës: Their Home, Haunts, Friends, and Works, Part Second – Charlotte's Letters* (Bradford: Horsfall Turner, n.d.), British Library.
Queen Mary Archives, London, Papers of Constance Maynard, CLM; Westfield Collection, WFD.
Royal Holloway College Archives, Royal Holloway, University of London, Egham.
Society for the Propagation of the Gospel Archive, Bodleian Library, Oxford, SPG.
Wesleyan Methodist Missionary Society Archive, SOAS Library, London, WMMS.

Contemporary Periodicals Consulted

Christian Observer, 1830–1850.
Female Missionary Intelligencer, 1854, 1881.
Ladies Committee Occasional Papers, 2 Vols ([n.p.]: Wesleyan Methodist Missionary Society, 1900), 1859–1862.
The Sunday at Home, 1854–1857.

Primary Published Materials

A Missionary's Wife, 'Letter January 1860', in *Ladies' Committee Occasional Papers*, 2 Vols ([n.p.]: Wesleyan Methodist Missionary Society, 1900), I, pp. 52-4.
Balfour, Clara Lucas, *A Sketch of Mrs. Ann H. Judson* (London: W. & F. G. Cash, 1854).
Batchelor, Mrs, 'Letter 23 December 1858', in *Ladies Committee Occasional Papers*, 2 Vols ([n.p.]: Wesleyan Methodist Missionary Society, 1900), I, pp. 8-9.
——, 'Letter 23 February 1859', in *Ladies Committee Occasional Papers*, 2 Vols ([n.p.]: Wesleyan Methodist Missionary Society, 1900), I, pp. 20-2.
——, 'Letter 12 April 1859', in *Ladies' Committee Occasional Papers*, 2 Vols ([n.p.]: Wesleyan Methodist Missionary Society, 1900), I, pp. 35-37.
Brontë, Anne, 'Preface to the Second Edition', in *The Tenant of Wildfell Hall*, ed. by Herbert Rosengarten (Oxford: Oxford University Press, 1992), pp. 3-5.
Brontë, Charlotte, *Jane Eyre*, ed. by Margaret Smith (Oxford: Oxford University Press, 1993).
——, *Shirley*, ed. by Jessica Cox (London: Penguin, 2006).
——, *The Letters of Charlotte Brontë*, ed. by Margaret Smith, 3 Vols (Oxford: Clarendon, 1995).
——, 'The Missionary', in *Poems by Currer, Ellis, and Acton Bell* (London: Aylott and Jones, 1846), pp. 157-63.
——, *Villette*, ed. by Tony Tanner (London: Penguin, 1985).
Craik, Dinah, *Bread Upon the Waters* (Leipzig: Bernhard Tauchnitz, 1865).
——, *Olive*, in *Olive and The Half-Caste*, ed. by Cora Kaplan (Oxford: Oxford University Press, 1999), pp. 1-331.
——, *The Half-Caste*, in *Olive and The Half-Caste*, ed. by Cora Kaplan (Oxford: Oxford University Press, 1999), pp. 333-72.
Davies, Emily, letter, 12 June 1874, repr. in *Collected Letters 1861-1875*, ed. by Anne Murphy and Deirdre Raftery (London: University of Virginia Press, 2004), pp. 425-9.
Davison, Emily Wilding, 'The Price of Liberty', *Suffragette*, 5 June 1914, p. 129.
Dickens, Charles, *Bleak House*, ed. by Nicola Bradbury (London: Penguin, 1996).
'Early Life of Mrs Judson' (Tract 363), in *1st Series Tracts of the Religious Tract Society*, Vol. X (London: RTS, c. 1830).
Eddy, Daniel C., *Heroines of the Missionary Enterprise; or Sketches of Prominent Female Missionaries*. ed. by John D. D. Cumming (London: n.p., 1850).
'Editorial March 1859', in *Ladies Committee Occasional Papers* ([n.p.]: Wesleyan Methodist Missionary Society, 1900), I, pp. 3-7.
'Editorial November 1860', in *Ladies Committee Occasional Papers*, 2 Vols ([n.p.]: Wesleyan Methodist Missionary Society, 1900), I, pp. 124-39.
'Editorial June 1859', in *Ladies Committee Occasional Papers* ([n.p.]: Wesleyan Methodist Missionary Society, 1900), I, p. 21.
E.M.I., 'Ann Judson and Little Maria', in *Missionary Stories* (London: John Snow, 1843-44).
'Female Influence and Obligations' (Tract 340), in *1st Series Tracts of the Religious Tract Society*, Vol. X (London: RTS, c. 1830), pp. 1-2.
Firth, C. B., *Constance Louisa Maynard, Mistress of Westfield College: A Family Portrait* (London: George Allen, 1949).

Gardner, James, *Memoirs of Christian Females; With an Essay on the Influences of Female Piety* (Edinburgh: John Johnstone, 1841).
Gaskell, Elizabeth, *Life of Charlotte Brontë*, ed. by Elisabeth Jay (London: Penguin, 1997).
——, *Ruth*, ed. by Alan Shelston (Oxford: Oxford University Press, 1998).
——, *The Letters of Mrs Gaskell*, ed. by J.A.V. Chapple and Arthur Pollard (Manchester: Mandolin, 1997).
Grand, Sarah, 'Foreword to *The Heavenly Twins* 1893–1923' (1923), repr. in *Sex, Social Purity and Sarah Grand*, ed. by Ann Heilmann and Stephanie Forward, 4 Vols (London: Routledge, 2000), I, 397–408.
——, *Ideala*, ed. by Molly Younkin (Kansas City, MO: Vallancourt, 2008).
——, *The Heavenly Twins* (Ann Arbor, MI: University of Michigan Press, 1992).
——, '*The Heavenly Twins*: Bath Mayoress Tells Their Story – Josephine Butler Centenary' (1928), repr. in *Sex, Social Purity and Sarah Grand*, ed. by Ann Heilmann and Stephanie Forward, 4 Vols (London: Routledge, 2000), I, pp. 317–20.
——, 'The New Aspect of the Woman Question' (1894), repr. in *Sex, Social Purity and Sarah Grand*, ed. by Ann Heilmann and Stephanie Forward, 4 Vols (London: Routledge, 2000), I, 29–35.
——, 'The New Woman and the Old' (1898), repr. in *Sex Social Purity and Sarah Grand*, ed. by Ann Heilmann and Stephanie Forward, 4 Vols (London: Routledge, 2000), I, pp. 69–76.
——, 'The Undefinable', repr. in *Women Who Did: Stories by Men and Women 1890–1914*, ed. by Angelique Richardson (London: Penguin, 2002), pp. 115–38.
Grierson [Margaret], *American Biography: Or, Memoirs of Mrs. A. Judson and Mrs. M. L. Ramsay* (Edinburgh: Leith, 1831).
——, *Labourers in the East or Memoirs of Eminent Men who Were Devoted to the Service of Christ in India*, 3rd edn (Edinburgh: Oliphant, 1830).
——, *Lily Douglas: A Simple Story, Humbly Intended as a Premium and Pattern for Sabbath Schools* (Edinburgh: Leith, 1821).
Griffith, Mrs, 'Letter 3 February 1859', in *Ladies' Committee Occasional Papers*, 2 Vols ([n.p.]: Wesleyan Methodist Missionary Society, 1900), I, pp. 10–1.
Grove, George, 'Foreword', in, *The History of Mendelssohn's Oratorio 'Elijah'*, ed. by F. G. Edwards (London: Novello, 1896), p. iii.
Harkness, Margaret [John Law], *A City Girl*, ed. by Ian Fletcher and John Stokes (London: Garland, 1984).
——, *In Darkest London*, ed. by R. A. Bilderman ([n.p].: Black Apollo Press, 2003).
——, 'Olive Schreiner', *Novel Review*, May 1892, pp. 112–6.
Huie, James, *Records of Female Piety* (Edinburgh: n.p., 1841).
Huntley, Lydia Howard, *Great and Good Women: Biographies for Girls* (Edinburgh: n.p., 1866).
H. W., 'A Hint to Ministers and Others Who "Weep with Them that Weep"', *Christian Observer*, January 1850, pp. 6–11.
Jenkins, Mrs, 'Letter 3 February 1859', in *Ladies' Committee Occasional Papers*, 2 Vols ([n.p.]: Wesleyan Methodist Missionary Society, 1900), I, p. 23.
—— 'Letter 27 August 1859', in *Ladies Committee Occasional Papers*, 2 Vols ([n.p.]: Wesleyan Methodist Missionary Society, 1900), I, pp. 55–6.

Judson, Ann Hasseltine, 'Address to Females in America Relative to the Situation of Females in the East', in *Memoir of Mrs Ann H. Judson*, ed. by James Davis Knowles (London: Wightman and Co., 1830), pp. 321–4.

Knill, 'Introduction', in *Memoirs of Female Labourers in the Missionary Cause* (Bath: n.p., 1839), pp. v–viii.

Knowles, James Davis, 'Life of Mrs Ann H Judson', in *Christian Biography* (London: RTS, c. 1832), pp. 1–144.

——, *Memoirs of Mrs. Ann H. Judson*, 3rd edn (London: Wightman and Co., 1830).

'Lessons from Heathen Lands', in *Missionary Stories* (London: John Snow, 1843–4).

Lewis, Sarah, *Woman's Mission*, 10th edn (London: John Parker, 1842).

Longfellow, Henry Wadsworth, 'Retribution', in *The Belfry of Bruges and Other Poems* (London: George Slater, 1849), p. 32.

Meade, L. T., *A Sweet Girl Graduate* (London: Cassell and Co., 1891).

M. E. L., 'Governess's Benevolent Institution', in *Bread Upon the Waters*, ed. by Dinah Craik (Leipzig: Bernhard Tauchnitz, 1865), pp. 87–96.

Memoirs of Female Labourers in the Missionary Cause (Bath: n.p., 1839).

Mendelssohn, *Elijah* (Boston, MA: Oliver Ditson, n.d.), http://openlibrary.org/books/OL25407757M/Oratorio_libretto_Elijah (accessed 26 September 2012).

Nussey, Ellen, 'Reminiscences of Charlotte Brontë', *Scribner's Monthly*, Vol. 2 (May 1871).

Pitman, Emma Raymond, *Lady Missionaries in Foreign Lands* (London: S.W. Partridge, 1889).

Polglase, Mrs, 'Letter 9 September 1858', in *Ladies Committee Occasional Papers*, 2 Vols ([n.p.]: Wesleyan Methodist Missionary Society, 1900), I, pp. 26–7.

Queen Mary and Westfield College Archives, 'The Students' Experience of Westfield College', www.library.qmul.ac.uk/node/1307 (accessed 8 August 2013).

Rigby, Elizabeth (Lady Eastlake), 'Vanity Fair and Jane Eyre', *Quarterly Review*, 84 (December 1848), 153–85.

Sanderson, Mrs, 'Letter 22 October 1858', in *Ladies' Committee Occasional Papers*, 2 Vols ([n.p.]: Wesleyan Methodist Missionary Society, 1900), I, pp. 9–10.

—— 'Letter 19th July 1859', in *Ladies' Committee Occasional Papers*, 2 Vols ([n.p.]: Wesleyan Methodist Missionary Society, 1900), I, pp. 59–60.

Sargent, John, *Memoir of the Rev. Henry Martyn*, 4th edn (London: J. Hatchard and Son, 1820).

Schreiner, Olive, *Dreams*, repr. in *Dreams: Three Works by Olive Schreiner*, ed. by Elisabeth Jay (Birmingham: Birmingham University Press, 2003), pp. 1–46.

——, 'I Thought I Stood' (1890), repr. in *Dreams: Three Works by Olive Schreiner*, ed. by Elisabeth Jay (Birmingham: Birmingham University Press, 2003), pp. 31–2.

——, 'The Gardens of Pleasure', repr. in *Dreams: Three Works by Olive Schreiner*, ed. by Elisabeth Jay (Birmingham: Birmingham University Press, 2003), p. 13.

——, *The Story of an African Farm*, ed. by Joseph Bristow (Oxford: Oxford University Press, 1992).

——, 'Three Dreams in a Desert' (1887), repr. in *Dreams*, ed. by Elisabeth Jay (Birmingham: Birmingham University Press, 2003), pp. 16–21.

Sherwood, Martha, *Caroline Mordaunt; or, The Governess* (London: Darton and Clark, 1853).
———, *Conversations on the Shorter Catechism with the Scripture Proofs, for the use of Children* (London: Simpkin and Marshall, 1824).
———, *Stories Explanatory of the Church Catechism* (Wellington: Houlston and Son, 1823).
———, *The Governess: or Little Female Academy* (Wellington: Houlston and Son, 1820).
———, *The History of Little Henry and His Bearer*, 2nd edn (Wellington: Houlston and Son, 1815).
Spurgeon, Charles, 'The Rent Veil', 25 March 1888, www.spurgeon.org/sermons/2015.htm (accessed 8 August 2013).
Stallybrass, Edward (Ed.), *Memoir of Mrs Stallybrass, Wife of the Rev. E Stallybrass, Missionary to Siberia* (London: Fisher, Son and Co., 1836).
Stretton, Hesba (Sarah Smith), *Jessica's First Prayer* (London: RTS, 1867).
———, *Jessica's Mother* (London: RTS, n.d.).
———, *Pilgrim Street: A Tale of Manchester Life* (London: R.T.S, 1867).
Sykes, Reverend George, 'Letter 17 July 1860', in *Ladies Committee Occasional Papers*, 2 Vols ([n.p.]: Wesleyan Methodist Missionary Society, 1900), I, pp. 138–9.
Thompson, Jemima, *Memoirs of British Female Missionaries* (London: William Smith, 1841).
'Unpublished Letters by Charlotte Brontë', *Hours at Home: A Popular Monthly of Instruction and Recreation*, Vol. XI (New York: Charles Scribner and Co, May–October 1870).
Walton, Mrs, 'Letter 3 February 1859', in *Ladies Committee Occasional Papers*, 2 Vols ([n.p.]: Wesleyan Methodist Missionary Society, 1900), I, pp. 11–3.
———, 'Letter 16 February 1859', in *Ladies' Committee Occasional Papers*, 2 Vols ([n.p.]: Wesleyan Methodist Missionary Society, 1900), I, pp. 11–3.
Wesley, John, *An Extract of the Life of the Late David Brainerd Missionary to the Indians* (Penryn: Cock, 1815).
Wildish, Miss, 'Letter 19 July 1860', in *Ladies Committee Occasional Papers*, 2 Vols ([n.p.]: Wesleyan Methodist Missionary Society, 1900), I, pp. 142–3.
Wilson, John, *A Memoir of Mrs. Margaret Wilson, of the Scottish Mission, Bombay; Including Extracts from Her Letters and Journals, Etc* (Edinburgh: John Johnstone, 1840).
Woods, Leonard, *Memoirs of Mrs. Harriet Newell*, 2nd edn (London: Booth and Co., 1816).

Secondary Works

Barker, Juliet, 'Saintliness, Treason and Plot: The Writing of Mrs Gaskell's *Life of Charlotte Brontë*', *Brontë Society Transactions*, 21 (1994), 101–15.
———, *The Brontës* (New York: St Martin's Press, 1994).
Beaumann, Katherine Bentley, *The Lady Margaret Hall Settlement 1887–1997: A Century of Caring in the Community* ([n.p.]: The Friends of Lady Margaret Hall Settlement, 1997).
Bebbington, W. D., *Evangelicalism in Modern Britain: A History from the 1730s to the 1980s* (London: Unwin Hyman, 1989).

Bellamy, Joan, 'Mary Taylor, Ellen Nussey and Brontë Biography', *Brontë Society Transactions*, 21, 7 (1996), 275–83.
Berkman, Joyce Avrech, *The Healing Imagination of Olive Schreiner: Beyond South African Colonialism* (Amherst: University of Massachusetts Press, 1989).
Biderman, R. A., 'Introduction', in Margaret Harkness, in *In Darkest London*, ed. by R. A Biderman ([n.p].: Black Apollo Press, 2003), pp. 7–10.
Bishop, Alan, '"With Suffering and Through Time": Olive Schreiner, Vera Brittain, and the Great War', in *Olive Schreiner and After: Essays on Southern African Literature in Honour of Guy Butler*, ed. by Malvern van Wyk Smith and Don Maclennan (Cape Town: David Philip, 1993), pp. 80–92.
Bland, Lucy, *Banishing the Beast: English Feminism and Sexual Morality 1885–1914* (London: Penguin, 1995).
Booth, Alison, *How to Make It as a Woman: Collective Biographical History from Victoria to the Present* (Chicago, IL: University of Chicago Press, 2004).
Bourrier, Karen, *Victorian Bestseller: The Life of Dinah Craik* (Ann Arbor, MI: University of Michigan Press, 2019).
Bowie, Fiona, 'Introduction', in *Women and Missions: Past and Present, Anthropological and Historical Perceptions*, ed. by Fiona Bowie, Deborah Kirkwood and Shirley Ardener (Oxford: Berg, 1993), pp. 1–18.
Bradley Ian, *Call to Seriousness: The Evangelical Impact on the Victorians* (London: Cape, 1976).
Brill, Barbara, *William Gaskell 1805–1884: A Portrait* (Manchester: Manchester Literary and Philosophical Publications, 1984.
Brown, Candy Gunther, *The Word in the World: Evangelical Writing, Publishing and Reading in America 1789–1880* (Chapel Hill, NC: University of North Carolina Press, 2004).
Brown, Penny, *The Captured World: The Child and Childhood in Nineteenth-Century Women's Writing in England* (London: Harvester Wheatsheaf, 1993).
Burdett, Carolyn, *Olive Schreiner and the Progress of Feminism: Evolution, Gender, Empire* (Basingstoke: Palgrave, 2001).
Burton, Antoinette, *Burdens of History: British Feminists, Indian Women and Imperial Culture 1865–1915* (London: University of Carolina Press, 1994).
Butts, Dennis, 'Introduction', in *From the Dairyman's Daughter to Worrals of the WAAF: The Religious Tract Society, Lutterworth Press and Children's Literature*, ed. by Dennis Butts and Pat Garrett (Cambridge: Lutterworth Press, 2006), pp. 7–12.
Caine, Barbara, *Victorian Feminists* (Oxford: Oxford University Press, 1992).
Cayton, Mary Kupiec, 'Harriet Newell's Story: Women, the Evangelical Press and the Foreign Mission Movement', in *An Extensive Republic: Print, Culture and Society in the New Nation 1790–1840*, ed. by Robert A Gross and Mary Kelley (Chapel Hill, NC: University of North Carolina Press, 2012), pp. 408–16.
Chapple, John, 'Unitarian Dissent', in *Cambridge Companion to Elizabeth Gaskell*, ed. by Jill L. Matus (Cambridge: Cambridge University Press, 2007), pp. 164–77.
Claybaugh, Amanda, *The Novel of Purpose: Literature and Social Reform in the Anglo-American World* (London: Cornell UP, 2007).
Clayton, Cherry, 'Militant Pacifist: Olive Schreiner Rediscovered', in *The Flawed Diamond: Essays on Olive Schreiner*, ed. by Itala Vivan (Coventry: Dangaroo, 1991), pp. 40–54.

Culley, Amy, *British Women's Life Writing, 1760–1840: Friendship, Community and Collaboration* (Basingstoke: Palgrave Macmillan).

Cunningham, Gail, *The New Woman and the Victorian Novel* (London: Macmillan, 1978).

Cunningham, Valentine, '"God and Nature Intended You for a Missionary's Wife": Mary Hill, Jane Eyre and Other Missionary Women in the 1840s', in *Women and Missions: Past and Present, Anthropological and Historical Perceptions*, ed. by Fiona Bowie, Deborah Kirkwood and Shirley Ardner (Oxford: Berg, 1993), pp. 85–105.

Cutt, Nancy, *Ministering Angels: A Study of Nineteenth-Century Writing for Children* (Wormley: Five Owls Press, 1980).

———, *Mrs Sherwood and her Books for Children: A Study* (London: Oxford University Press, 1974).

David, Deirdre, *Intellectual Women and Victorian Patriarchy: Harriet Martineau, Elizabeth Barrett Browning* (London: Macmillan, 1987).

Demers, Patricia, 'Mrs Sherwood and Hesba Stretton: The Letter and the Spirit of Evangelical Writing of and for Children', in *Romanticism and Children's Literature in Nineteenth-Century England*, ed. by James Holt McGavran Jr (London: University of Georgia Press, 1991), pp. 129–49.

Diniejko, Andrzej, 'Margaret Harkness: A Late Victorian New Woman and Social Investigator', Victorian Web, www.victorianweb.org/gender/harkness.html (accessed 20 December 2012).

Dixon, Thomas, *From Passions to Emotions: The Creation of a Secular Psychological Category* (Cambridge: Cambridge University Press, 2003).

DuPlessis, Rachel Blau, *Writing Beyond the Ending: Narrative Strategies of Twentieth-Century Women Writers* (Bloomington, IN: Indiana University Press, 1985).

Eason, Andrew Mark, *Women in God's Army: Gender and Equality in the Early Salvation Army* (Ontario: Wilfrid Laurier University Press, 2003).

Edmundson, Melissa, 'Introduction', in Dinah Craik, *The Half-Caste*, ed. by Edmundson (Ontario: Broadview Editions, 2016), pp. 9–37.

Etherington, Norman, *Missions and Empire* (Oxford: Oxford University Press, 2005).

Eustace, Nicole, Eugenia Lean, Julie Livingston, Jan Plamper, William M. Reddy and Barbara H. Rosenwein, 'AHR Conversation: The Historical Study of Emotions', *American Historical Review*, 117 (2012), 1487–531.

Eyre, Angharad, 'Education', in *Women in Christianity in the Age of Empire: 1800-1920*, ed. by Janet Wootton (London: Routledge, 2022).

Findlay, George G., *The History of the Wesleyan Methodist Missionary Society*. 5 Vols (London: J.A. Sharp, 1921–24), p. IV.

Fishman, *East End 1888: A Year in a London Borough Among the Labouring Poor* (London: Duckworth, 1988).

Fyfe, Aileen, 'A Short History of the Religious Tract Society', in *From the Dairyman's Daughter to Worrals of the WAAF: The Religious Tract Society, Lutterworth Press and Children's Literature*, ed. by Dennis Butts and Pat Garrett (Cambridge: Lutterworth Press, 2006), pp. 13–35.

———, *Science and Salvation: Evangelical Popular Science Publishing in Victorian Britain* (London: University of Chicago Press, 2004).

Gardner, Viv, 'Introduction', in *The New Woman and Her Sisters: Feminism and Theatre 1850–1914*, ed. by Viv Gardner and Susan Rutherford (London: Harvester Wheatsheaf, 1992), pp. 1–14.

Gibson, Mary Ellis, 'Henry Martyn and England's Christian Empire: Rereading *Jane Eyre* through Missionary Biography', *Victorian Literature and Culture*, 27 (1999), 419–42.

Gilbert, Sandra M. and Susan Gubar, *The Madwoman in the Attic: The Woman Writer and the Nineteenth-Century Literary Imagination* (London: Yale University Press, 1979).

Gill, Sean, 'Heroines of Missionary Adventure: The Portrayal of Victorian Women Missionaries in Popular Fiction and Biography', in *Women of Faith in Victorian Culture: Reassessing the Angel in the House*, ed. by Anne Hogan and Andrew Bradstock (Basingstoke, Macmillan, 1998), pp. 172–85.

Gilmour, Rachael, *Grammars of Colonialism: Representing Languages in Colonial South Africa* (Basingstoke: Palgrave Macmillan, 2006).

Gleadle, Kathryn. *The Early Feminists: Radical Unitarians and the Emergence of the Women's Rights Movement, 1831–51* (Basingstoke: Macmillan, 1995).

Glover, David, *Literature, Immigration and Diaspora in Fin-de-Siecle England: A Cultural History of the Aliens Act* (Cambridge: Cambridge University Press, 2012).

Grimshaw, Patricia and Andrew May, 'Reappraisals of Mission History: An Introduction', in *Missionaries, Indigenous Peoples and Cultural Exchange*, ed. by Patricia Grimshaw and Andrew May (Eastbourne: Sussex Academic Press, 2010), pp. 1–9.

Hall, Catherine, *White, Male and Middle-Class: Explorations in Feminism and History* (Cambridge: Polity, 1992).

Hall, Catherine and Leonore Davidoff, *Family Fortunes: Men and Women of the English Middle Class 1780–1850* (London: Routledge, 2002).

Hapgood, Lynne, ' "Is This Friendship?": Eleanor Marx, Margaret Harkness, and the Idea of a Socialist Community', in *Eleanor Marx (1855–1898): Life, Work, Contacts*, ed. by John Stokes (Aldershot: Ashgate, 2000), pp. 129–43.

Heilmann, Ann, 'General Introduction', in *Sex, Social Purity and Sarah Grand*, ed. by Ann Heilmann and Stephanie Forward, 4 Vols (London: Routledge, 2000), I, 1–15.

——, *New Woman Fiction: Women Writing First-Wave Feminism* (London: Macmillan, 2000).

——, *New Woman Strategies: Sarah Grand, Olive Schreiner, Mona Caird* (Manchester: Manchester University Press, 2004).

Heywood, Christopher, '*The Story of an African Farm*: Society, Positivism, and Myth', in *The Flawed Diamond: Essays on Olive Schreiner*, ed. by Itala Vivan (Coventry: Dangaroo, 1991), pp. 26–39.

Hindmarsh, D. Bruce, *The Evangelical Conversion Narrative: Spiritual Autobiography in Early Modern England* (Oxford: Oxford University Press, 2005).

Hilton, Boyd, *The Age of Atonement: The Influence of Evangelicalism on Social and Economic Thought 1785–1865* (Oxford: Clarendon, 1988).

Hodgson, Dorothy L., *The Church of Women: Gendered Encounters Between Massai and Missionaries* (Bloomington, IN: Indiana University Press, 2005).

Janssen, Flore and Lisa C. Robertson (eds), *Margaret Harkness: Writing Social Engagement 1880–1921* (Manchester: Manchester University Press, 2018).

Jansson, Siv, '*The Tenant of Wildfell Hall*: Rejecting the Angel's Influence', in *Women of Faith in Victorian Culture: Reassessing the Angel in the House*, ed. by Anne Hogan and Andrew Bradstock (Basingstoke: Macmillan, 1998), pp. 31–47.

Jarrett, Susan C., 'Classics and Counter-Publics in Nineteenth-Century Historically Black Colleges', *College English*, 72 (2009), 134–59.

Jay, Elisabeth, *Faith and Doubt in Victorian Britain* (London: Macmillan, 1986).

——, 'Introduction', in *Dreams: Three Works by Olive Schreiner*, ed. by Elisabeth Jay (Birmingham: Birmingham University Press, 2003), pp. ix–xxviii.

——, 'Introduction', in *Life of Charlotte Brontë*, ed. by Elisabeth Jay (London: Penguin, 1997), pp. ix–xxxii.

——, *The Evangelical and Oxford Movements* (Cambridge: Cambridge University Press, 1983).

——, *The Religion of the Heart: Anglican Evangelicalism and the Nineteenth-Century Novel* (Oxford: Clarendon, 1979).

—— 'Women Writers and Religion: "A Self Worth Saving, a Duty Worth Doing and a Voice Worth Raising"', in *Women and Literature in Britain 1800–1900*, ed. by Joanne Shattock (Cambridge: Cambridge University Press, 2001), pp. 251–74.

Johnston, Anna, *Missionary Writing and Empire, 1800–1860* (Cambridge: Cambridge University Press, 2003).

Jones, Peter d'Arcy, *The Christian Socialist Revival 1877–1914: Religion, Class, and Social Conscience* (Princeton, NJ: Princeton University Press, 1968).

Kaplan, Cora, 'Introduction', in *Olive and the Half-Caste*, ed. by Cora Kaplan (Oxford: Kaplan Oxford University Press, 1999), pp. vii–xxvi.

Kern, Kathi, '"Free Woman Is a Divine Being, the Savior of Mankind": Stanton's Exploration of Religion and Gender', in *Elizabeth Cady Stanton, Feminist as Thinker: A Reader in Documents and Essays*, ed. by Ellen Carol DuBois and Richard Cándida Smith (New York: New York University Press, 2007), pp. 93–110.

Kirkwood, Deborah, 'Protestant Missionary Women: Wives and Spinsters', in *Women and Missions: Past and Present, Anthropological and Historical Perceptions*, ed. by Fiona Bowie, Deborah Kirkwood and Shirley Ardner (Oxford: Berg, 1993), pp. 23–41.

Kissack, Mike and Michael Titlestad, 'Olive Schreiner and the Secularization of the Moral Imagination', *English in Africa*, 33 (2006), 23–46.

Koven, Seth, 'Borderlands: Women, Voluntary Action and Child Welfare in Britain 1840–1914', in *Mothers of New World: Maternalist Politics and the Origins of Welfare States*, ed. by Seth Koven and Sonya Michel (London: Routledge, 1993), pp. 94–135.

——, *Slumming: Sexual and Social Politics in Victorian London* (Princeton, NJ: Princeton University Press, 2004).

Koven, Seth and Sonya Michel, 'Introduction', in *Mothers of New World: Maternalist Politics and the Origins of Welfare States*, ed. by Seth Koven and Sonya Michel (London: Routledge, 1993), pp. 1–42.

Krueger, Christine, *The Reader's Repentance: Women Preachers, Women Writers and Nineteenth-Century Social Discourse* (London: University of Chicago Press, 1992).

Labode, Modupe, 'From Heathen Kraal to Christian Home: Anglican Mission Education and African Christian Girls, 1850–1900', in *Women and Missions, Past and Present, Anthropological and Historical Perceptions*, ed. by Fiona Bowie, Deborah Kirkwood and Shirley Ardner (Oxford: Berg, 1993), pp. 126–44.

Langland, Elizabeth, *Telling Tales: Gender and Narrative Form in Victorian Literature and Culture* (Columbus, OH: Ohio State University Press, 2002).

Lauer, Laura, 'Soul-Saving Partnerships and Pacifist Soldiers: The Ideal of Masculinity in the Salvation Army', in *Masculinity and Spirituality in Victorian Culture*, ed. by Andrew Bradstock, Sean Gill, Anne Hogan and Sue Morgan (Basingstoke: Macmillan, 2000), pp. 194–208.

Lecaros, Cecilia Wadso, *The Victorian Governess Novel* (Lund: Lund University Press, 2001).

Ledger, Sally, *The New Woman: Fiction and Feminism at the Fin De Siècle* (Manchester: Manchester University Press, 1997).

Lerner, Laurence, 'Olive Schreiner and the Feminists', in *Olive Schreiner and After: Essays on Southern African Literature*, ed. by Malvern Van Wyk Smith and Don Maclennan (London: David Philip, 1983), pp. 67–79.

Levine, Philippa, *Feminist Lives in Victorian England: Private Roles and Public Commitment* (Oxford: Blackwell, 1990).

———, *Victorian Feminism 1850–1900* (London: Hutchinson, 1987).

Livesey, Ruth, *Socialism, Sex, and the Culture of Aestheticism in Britain 1880–1914* (Oxford: Oxford University Press, 2007).

———, 'Reading for Character: Women Social Reformers and Narratives of the Urban Poor in Late Victorian and Edwardian London', *Journal of Victorian Culture*, 9 (2010), 43–67.

Lloyd, Naomi, 'Evangelicalism and the Making of Same-Sex Desire: The Life and Writings of Constance Maynard 1849–1935' (unpublished doctoral thesis, University of British Columbia, 2011).

———, 'Religion, Same-Sex Desire, and the Imagined Geographies of Empire: The Case of Constance Maynard (1849–1935)', *Women's History Review*, 25 (2016), 53–73.

Longmuir, Anne, 'Reader Perhaps You Were Never in Belgium', *Nineteenth-Century Literature*, 64 (2009), 163–88.

Mace Emily H., 'Feminist Forerunners and a Usable Past: A Historiography of Elizabeth Cady Stanton's *The Woman's Bible*', *Journal of Feminist Studies in Religion*, 25 (2009), 5–23.

Manktelow, Emily, *Missionary Families: Race, Gender and Generation on the Spiritual Frontier* (Manchester: Manchester University Press, 2013).

Marcus, Sharon, *Between Women: Friendship, Desire, and Marriage in Victorian England* (Oxford: Princeton University Press, 2007).

Mason, Emma, *Women Poets of the Nineteenth Century* (Tavistock: Northcote, 2006).

Matus, Jill L., 'Introduction', in *Cambridge Companion to Elizabeth Gaskell*, ed. by Jill L. Matus (Cambridge: Cambridge University Press, 2007), pp. 1–9.

Mazzanti, Robert, 'Lyndall's Sphinx: Images of Female Sexuality and Roles in *Story of an African Farm*', in *Flawed Diamond: Essays on Olive Schreiner*, ed. by Itala Vivan (Coventry: Dangaroo, 1991), pp. 121–34.

McClintock, Anne, *Imperial Leather* (London: Routledge, 1999).

McClisky, Claire, '(En)gendering Faith?: Love, Marriage and the Evangelical Mission on the Settler Colonial Frontier', in *Studies in Settler Colonialism: Politics, Identity and Culture*, ed. by Fiona Bateman and Lionel Pilkington (Basingstoke: Palgrave Macmillan, 2011), pp. 106–21.

McClisky, Claire, Daniel Midena and Karen Valgårda (eds), *Emotions and Christian Missions: Historical Perspectives* (Basingstoke: Palgrave Macmillan, 2015).

McGavran, James Holt, Jr., 'Introduction', in *Romanticism and Children's Literature in Nineteenth-Century England*, ed. by James Holt McGavran Jr (London: University of Georgia Press, 1991), pp. 1–13.

McKean, Matthew, 'Rethinking Late-Victorian Slum Fiction: The Crowd and Imperialism at Home', *English Literature in Transition, 1880–1920*, 54 (2011), 28–55.

McWilliams-Tullberg, Rita, 'Women and Degrees at Cambridge University', in *A Widening Sphere: Changing Roles of Victorian Women*, ed. by Martha Vicinus (London: Methuen, 1980), pp. 117–45.

Melnyk, Julie, 'Introduction', *Women's Theology in Nineteenth-Century Britain: Transfiguring the Faith of their Fathers*, ed. by Julie Melnyk (London: Garland, 1998), pp xii–xviii.

Midgley, Clare, 'Can Women be Missionaries? Envisioning Female Agency in the Early Nineteenth-Century British Empire', *Journal of British Studies*, 45 (2006), 335–58.

———, 'From Supporting Missions to Petitioning Parliament: British Women and the Evangelical Campaign against *Sati* in India, 1813–30', in *Women in British Politics, 1760–1860: The Power of the Petticoat*, ed. by Kathryn Gleadle and Sarah Richardson (Basingstoke: Macmillan, 2000), pp. 74–92.

———, *Women Against Slavery: The British Campaigns 1780–1870* (London: Routledge, 1992).

Miller, Lucasta, *The Brontë Myth* (London: Jonathan Cape, 2001).

Mitchell, Sally, *Dinah Mullock Craik* (Boston, MA: Twayne, 1983).

Morgan, Sue, 'Introduction: Women, Religion and Feminism: Past, Present and Future Perspectives', in *Women, Religion and Feminism in Britain, 1750–1900*, ed. by Sue Morgan (Basingstoke: Palgrave Macmillan, 2002), pp. 1–19.

Morgan, Sue and Jacqueline deVries, 'Introduction', in *Women, Gender and Religious Cultures in Britain, 1800–1940*, ed. by Sue Morgan and Jacqueline deVries (Abingdon: Routledge, 2010), pp. 1–10.

Mumm, Susan, 'Women and Philanthropic Cultures', in *Women, Gender and Religious Cultures*, ed. by Sue Morgan and Jacqueline deVries (Abingdon: Routledge, 2010), pp. 54–71.

Nelson, Claudia, *Boys Will be Girls: The Feminine Ethic and British Children's Fiction 1857–1917* (New Brunswick, NJ: Rutgers University Press, 1991).

Nixon, Jude, *Victorian Religious Discourse: New Directions in Criticism*, ed. by Jude Nixon (Basingstoke: Palgrave Macmillan, 2004), pp. 1–26.

Nord, Deborah Epstein, '"Neither Pairs Nor Odd": Female Community in Late Nineteenth-Century London', *Signs*, 15 (1990), 733–54.

Oliver, Evelyn Dorothy and James R. Lewis, *Angels A to Z*, 2nd edn (Canton, MI: Visible Ink Press, 2008), p. 202, books.google.co.uk/books?isbn=1578592127 (accessed 28 July 2013).

Parker, Pamela Corpron, 'Elizabeth Gaskell and Literary Tourism', in *Literary Tourism and Nineteenth Century Culture*, ed. by Nicola J. Watson (London: Palgrave Macmillan, 2009), pp. 128–38.

Peterson, Linda, 'Women Writers and Self Writing', in *Women and Literature in Britain 1800–1900*, ed. by Joanne Shattock (Cambridge: Cambridge University Press, 2001), pp. 209–30.

Phipps, Pauline, 'Constance Maynard's Languages of Love', *Women's History Review*, 25 (2016), 17–34.

——, *Constance Maynard's Passions: Religion, Sexuality and an English Educational Pioneer, 1849–1935* (Toronto: University of Toronto Press, 2015).

——, 'Faith, Desire, and Sexual Identity: Constance Maynard's Atonement for Passion', *Journal of the History of Sexuality*, 18 (2009), 265–86.

Poovey, Mary, *Uneven Developments: The Ideological Work of Gender in Mid-Victorian England* (Chicago IL: Chicago University Press, 1988).

Prevost, Elizabeth E., *The Communion of Women: Missions and Gender in Colonial Africa and the British Metropole* (Oxford: Oxford University Press, 2010).

Richardson, Angelique, 'Introduction', in *Women Who Did: Stories by Men and Women 1890–1914*, ed. by Angelique Richardson (London: Penguin, 2002), pp. xxxi–lxxxi.

——, *Love and Eugenics in the Late Nineteenth Century: Rational Reproduction and the New Woman* (Oxford: Oxford University Press, 2003).

Richardson, LeeAnne, M., *New Women and Colonial Adventure Fiction in Victorian Britain: Gender, Genre and Empire* (Gainesville, FL: University Press of Florida, 2006).

Rickard, Suzanne, 'Victorian Women with Causes: Writing, Religion and Action', in *Women, Religion and Feminism in Britain, 1750–1900*, ed. by Sue Morgan (Basingstoke: Palgrave Macmillan, 2002), pp. 139–57.

Robertson, Lisa C. '"We Must Advance, We Must Expand": Architectural and Social Challenges to the Domestic Model at the College for Ladies at Westfield', *Women's History Review*, 25 (2016), 105–23.

Rosman, Doreen, *Evangelicals and Culture* (London: Croom Helm, 1984).

Ross, Cathy, *Women with a Mission: Rediscovering Missionary Wives in Early New Zealand* (London: Penguin, 2006).

Ross, Ellen, 'Introduction', in *Slum Travellers: Ladies and London Poverty 1860–1920*, ed. by Ellen Ross (Berkeley, CA: University of California Press, 2007), p. 1–39.

——, 'Margaret Harkness', in *Slum Travellers: Ladies and London Poverty 1860–1920*, ed. by Ellen Ross (Berkeley: University of California Press, 2007), pp. 89–90.

Samson, Jane, 'Ethnology and Theology: Nineteenth-Century Mission Dilemmas in the South Pacific', in *Christian Missions and the Enlightenment*, ed. by Brian Stanley (Richmond: Curzon, 2001), pp. 99–122.

Sanders, Valerie, *Eve's Renegades: Victorian Anti-Feminist Women Novelists* (Basingstoke: Macmillan, 1996).

Schaffer, Talia, *Romance's Rival: Familiar Marriage in Victorian Fiction* (Oxford: Oxford University Press, 2016).

Schlossberg, Herbert, *Conflict and Crisis in the Religious Life of Late Victorian England* (London: Transaction Publishers, 2009).

Schueller, Malini Johar, 'Nation, Missionary Women, and the Race of True Womanhood', in *Messy Beginnings: Postcoloniality and Early American Studies*, ed. by Malini Johar Schueller and Edward Watts (New Brunswick, NJ: Rutgers University Press, 2003), pp. 155–74.

Schwartz, Laura, *A Serious Endeavour: Gender, Education and Community at St Hugh's 1886–2011* (London: Profile Books, 2011).

Scotland, Nigel, *Squires in the Slums: Settlements and Missions in Late Victorian London* (London: Tauris, 2007).

Semple, Rhonda, 'Missionary Manhood: Professionalism, Belief and Masculinity in the Nineteenth-Century British Imperial Field', *Journal of Imperial and Commonwealth History*, 36 (2008), 397–415.

——, *Missionary Women: Gender, Professionalism, and the Victorian Idea of Christian Mission* (Woodbridge: Boydell, 2003).

Setran, David, *The College Y: Student Religion in the Era of Secularisation* (New York: Palgrave Macmillan, 2007).

Shattock, Joanne, 'Introduction', in *The Works of Elizabeth Gaskell*, ed. by Joanne Shattock, Vol. 1, *Journalism, Early Fiction and Personal Writings* (London: Pickering and Chatto, 2005), pp. xxi–xxxiv.

Shelston, Alan, 'Introduction', in Elizabeth Gaskell, *Ruth*, ed. by Alan Shelston (Oxford: Oxford University Press, 1998), pp. vii–xx.

Shields, Juliet, 'The Races of Woman: Gender, Hybridity, and National Identity in *Olive*', *Studies in the Novel*, 39 (2007), 284–300.

Showalter, Elaine, *A Literature of Their Own: British Women Novelists from Brontë to Lessing*, exp. edn (Princeton, NJ: Princeton University Press, 1999).

——, 'Introduction', in *Daughters of Decadence: Women Writers of the Fin De Siècle*, ed. by Elaine Showalter (London: Virago, 1993), pp. vii–xx.

——, *Sexual Anarchy: Gender and Culture at the Fin De Siècle* (London: Bloomsbury, 1991).

Showalter, Nathan, *The End of a Crusade: The Student Volunteer Movement for Foreign Missions and the Great War* (London: Scarecrow, 1998).

Sill, Ulrike, *Encounters in Quest of Christian Womanhood: The Basel Mission in Pre- and Early Colonial Ghana*, Studies in Christian Mission (Leiden: Brill, 2010).

Smith, Margaret, 'Introduction', *The Letters of Charlotte Brontë*, ed. by Margaret Smith, 3 Vols (Oxford: Clarendon, 1995), Vols I–III, I, pp. 1–26, II, pp. xvii–xxxi, III, pp. xv–xxvi.

Smith, Susan E., *Women in Mission: From the New Testament to Today* (New York: Orbis, 2007).

Sondheimer, Janet, *Castle Adamant in Hampstead: A History of Westfield College* (London: Westfield College, 1983).

Spivak, Gayatri Chakravorty, 'Can the Subaltern Speak', in *Marxism and the Interpretation of Culture*, ed. Cary Nelson and Lawrence Grossberg (Urbana, IL: University of Illinois Press, 1988), pp. 271–313.

——, 'Three Women's Texts and a Critique of Imperialism' (1985) repr. in *Feminisms: An Anthology of Literary Theory and Criticism*, ed. by Robyn R. Warhol and Diane Price Herndl (New Brunswick, NJ: Rutgers University Press, 1991) pp. 798–814.

Stanley, Brian, 'Christianity and Civilization in Evangelical Mission Thought, 1792–1857', in *Christian Missions and the Enlightenment*, ed. by Brian Stanley (Richmond, VA: Curzon, 2001), pp. 169–97.

Stephens, Barbara, *Emily Davies and Girton College* (London: Constable, 1927).

Stevens, Laura M., *The Poor Indians: British Missionaries, Native Americans, and Colonial Sensibility* (Philadelphia, PA: University of Pennsylvania Press, 2004).

Stokes, John (ed.), *Eleanor Marx (1855–1898): Life, Work, Contacts* (Aldershot: Ashgate, 2000).
Stoler, Ann Laura, 'Cultivating Bourgeois Bodies and Racial Selves', in *Cultures of Empire: A Reader, Colonizers in Britain and the Empire in the Nineteenth and Twentieth Centuries*, ed. by Catherine Hall (Manchester: Manchester University Press, 2000), pp. 87–119.
Stone, Lawrence, *The Family, Sex and Marriage in England 1500–1800* (London: Weidenfeld and Nicolson, 1977).
Sutton-Ramspeck, Beth, *Raising the Dust: The Literary Housekeeping of Mary Ward, Sarah Grand and Charlotte Perkins Gilman* (Athens, OH: Ohio University Press, 2004).
Swaisland, Cecilie, 'Wanted – Earnest, Self-Sacrificing Women for Service in South Africa: Nineteenth-Century Recruitment of Single Women to Protestant Missions', in *Women and Missions, Past and Present, Anthropological and Historical Perceptions*, ed. by Fiona Bowie, Deborah Kirkwood and Shirley Ardner (Oxford: Berg, 1993), pp. 70–84.
Sypher, Eileen, *Wisps of Violence: Producing Public and Private Politics in the Turn-of-the-Century British Novel* (London: Verso, 1993).
Talley, Lee, '*Jane Eyre's* Little-Known Debt to *The Methodist Magazine*', *Brontë Studies*, 33 (2008), 109–19.
Thormählen, Marianne, '"Horror and Disgust": Reading *The Tenant of Wildfell Hall*', *Brontë Studies*, 44 (2019), 5–19.
Thorne, Susan, 'Missionary-Imperial Feminism', in *Gendered Missions: Women and Men in Missionary Discourse and Practice*, ed. by Mary Taylor Huber and Nancy C. Lutkehaus (Ann Arbor, MI: University of Michigan Press, 1999), pp. 39–65.
Thwaite, Ann, 'What Is a Tract?', in *From the Dairyman's Daughter to Worrals of the WAAF: The Religious Tract Society, Lutterworth Press and Children's Literature*, ed. by Dennis Butts and Pat Garrett (Cambridge: Lutterworth Press, 2006), pp. 36–48.
Tigges, Wim 'A Feminist Mirage of the New Life: Utopian Elements in *The Story of an African Farm*', in *The Literary Utopias of Cultural Communities 1790–1910*, ed. by Maguérite Corporaal and Evert Jan Van Leeuwen (Amsterdam: Rodopi, 2010), pp. 189–208.
Tosh, John, *Manliness and Masculinities in Nineteenth Century Britain* (Harlow: Pearson, 2005).
Twells, Alison, 'Missionary Domesticity, Global Reform and "Woman's Sphere" in Early Nineteenth-Century England', *Gender and History*, 18 (2006), 266–84.
———, *The Civilizing Mission and the English Middle Class, 1792–1850: The Heathen at Home and Overseas* (London: Palgrave Macmillan, 2009).
Twycross Martin, Henrietta, 'The Drunkard, the Brute and the Paterfamilias: The Temperance Fiction of the Early Victorian Writer Sarah Stickney Ellis', in *Women of Faith in Victorian Culture*, ed. by Anne Hogan and Andrew Bradstock (Basingstoke: Macmillan, 1998), pp. 6–30.
Vallone, Lynne, 'Women Writing for Children', in *Women and Literature in Britain 1800–1900*, ed. by Joanne Shattock (Cambridge: Cambridge University Press, 2001), pp. 275–300.
Valman, Nadia. *The Jewess in Nineteenth-century British Literary Culture* (Cambridge: Cambridge University Press, 2007).

Vance, Norman, *The Sinews of the Spirit: The Ideal of Christian Manliness in Victorian Literature and Religious Thought* (Cambridge: Cambridge University Press, 1985).

Vicinus, Martha, *Independent Women: Work and Community for Single Women 1850–1920* (London: Virago, 1985).

———, 'Introduction', in *A Widening Sphere: Changing Roles of Victorian Women*, ed. by Martha Vicinus (London: Methuen, 1980), pp. ix–xix.

———, 'Introduction', in *Suffer and be Still: Women in the Victorian Age*, ed. by Martha Vicinus (London: Indiana University Press, 1972), pp. vii–xv.

———, '"One Life To Stand Beside Me": Emotional Conflicts in First-Generation College Women in England', *Feminist Studies*, 8 (1982), 603–28.

Vickery, Amanda (ed.), 'Golden Age to Separate Spheres? A Review of the Categories and Chronology of English Women's History', *The Historical Journal*, 36 (1993), 383–414.

———, *Women, Privilege and Power: British Politics 1750 to the Present* (Cambridge: Cambridge University Press, 2001).

Walkowitz, Judith, *City of Dreadful Delight: Narratives of Sexual Danger in Late-Victorian London* (Chicago, IL: University of Chicago Press, 1992).

Watson, J. R., 'Soldiers and Saints: The Fighting Man and the Christian Life', in *Masculinity and Spirituality in Victorian Culture*, ed. by Andrew Bradstock, Sean Gill, Anne Hogan and Sue Morgan (Basingstoke: Macmillan, 2000), pp. 10–26.

Watson, Nicola, *The Literary Tourist: Readers and Places in Romantic and Victorian Britain* (Basingtoke: Palgrave Macmillan, 2006).

Watts, Ruth, 'Rational Religion and Feminism: The Challenge of Unitarianism in the Nineteenth Century', in *Women, Religion and Feminism in Britain, 1750–1900*, ed. by Sue Morgan (Basingstoke: Palgrave Macmillan, 2002), pp. 39–52.

Werner, Winter Jade, *Missionary Cosmopolitanism in Nineteenth-Century British Literature* (Columbus, OH: Ohio State University Press, 2020).

Wheeler, Michael, *Death and the Future Life in Victorian Literature and Theology* (Cambridge: Cambridge University Press, 1990).

Williams, C. Peter, *The Ideal of the Self-Governing Church: A Study in Victorian Missionary Strategy* (Leiden: Brill, 1990).

Williams, Perry, 'Pioneer Women Students at Cambridge, 1869–81', in *Lessons for Life: The Schooling of Girls and Women 1850–1950*, ed. by Felicity Hunt (Oxford: Blackwell, 1987), pp. 171–191.

Williams, Peter, '"The Missing Link": The Recruitment of Women Missionaries in Some English Evangelical Missionary Societies in the Nineteenth Century', in *Women and Missions: Past and Present, Anthropological and Historical Perceptions*, ed. by Fiona Bowie, Deborah Kirkwood and Shirley Ardner (Oxford: Berg, 1993), pp. 43–69.

Willis, Chris and Angelique Richardson, 'Introduction', *The New Woman in Fiction and In Fact: Fin de Siecle Feminisms*, ed. by Chris Willis and Angelique Richardson (Basingstoke: Palgrave, 2000), pp. 1–38.

Wilson, Linda, *Constrained by Zeal: Female Spirituality Amongst Nonconformists, 1825–75* (Carlisle: Paternoster, 2000).

Winnifreth, Tom, *A New Life of Charlotte Brontë* (London: Macmillan, 1988).

Woodman, Ross, 'The Idiot Boy as Healer', in *Romanticism and Children's Literature in Nineteenth-Century England*, ed. by James Holt McGavran Jr (London: University of Georgia Press, 1991), pp. 72–95.

Yeo, Stephen, 'A New Life: The Religion of Socialism in Britain, 1883–1896', *History Workshop*, 4 (1977), 5–56.

Zlotnick, Susan, 'Jane Eyre, Anna Leonowens, and the White Woman's Burden: Governesses, Missionaries and Maternal Imperialists in Mid-Victorian Britain', *Victorians Institute Journal*, 24 (1996), 27–56.

Index

adaptation 10, 12, 21, 32, 48–61, 116–18
Africa 172, 193–4, 215, 217–19; *see also* South Africa
agency 34–8, 58–63, 68–75, 91–4, 96–9, 113–15, 149–50, 191–4, 216
agnosticism 15, 145–6, 161–2, 167, 171–6; *see also* doubt
androgyny 8–9, 42n47, 175–6, 178, 182n64, 184n99
angels 1, 23, 31, 56–7, 64, 112–13, 119, 135, 159–60, 167, 195
'Angel of the House' 9, 48, 61, 63, 75, 105n25, 197
Anglicanism 3–4, 16n12, 95, 135, 146, 186–7, 192–3, 197, 209–10, 215
Apocalypse 9, 120, 152, 160–3, 176–7; *see also* millenarianism
Apostles 8, 28, 177
archives 4, 9–11, 64, 104n12, 187–9, 190, 204, 215–17
art 12, 132, 152, 162, 178
Atonement 109, 135–6, 174–6, 188, 209, 224n118
authority 12–15, 34–9, 47, 61, 66–7, 75, 96, 149–52, 156–7, 168, 174, 186–8, 196–7, 201, 216–19, 229
autobiography 11, 22, 29–36, 78n34, 110–11, 149–51, 190–200; *see also* life writing

Balfour, Clara 50–6, 64, 67, 69, 99
Baptists 21, 24, 34, 79n56
Bedford College 186, 207, 219n3
Belstead School 188–9, 189–90, 194
Bible 8, 28–30, 54, 73, 86–96, 102, 114–15, 124, 133–6, 153–60, 162, 166–7, 172–7, 195, 200, 203, 205
Bishop, Matilda 192–3

biography *see* autobiography; collective biography; life writing; missionary biography; spiritual biography
Brainerd, David 22–3, 28, 37, 59, 195
Brontë, Anne 109, 128–31; *The Tenant of Wildfell Hall* 128–9
Brontë, Charlotte 1–2, 12, 14, 97, 103, 108–11, 121–31, 136, 148, 227; *Jane Eyre* 103, 108–21, 130–1; *Shirley* 110; 'The Missionary' 113–14; *Villette* 110–11, 117–18
Brontë, Patrick 109, 122, 129
Brontë myth 108, 122–31, 139n50, 140n67
Brooke, Graham Wilmott 217–19
Brooke, Margaret 199–200, 215, 217–19
Burma mission 21, 35–6, 54, 63
Butler, Josephine 146, 151, 153–4, 194
Butterworth, Joseph 21, 36

'Calling' 1–2, 26, 64–6, 93, 95–7, 112–14, 119–20, 134, 150–60, 173–6, 190–4, 203, 210
Calvinism 22, 106n32, 135, 146, 164; *see also* dissent; Methodism
catechism 82, 104n5, 105n17, 117, 162, 180n22
celibacy 66–71, 79n65, 154, 158
child obituary literature 27, 31–2, 60, 82, 87–92, 104n3, 117; *see also* 'holy child' characters; obituary literature
children's literature 12, 51, 53, 82–95, 103n1, 104n12, 105n29, 109, 112, 117, 227
chivalry 9, 37
Christ 9, 22–3, 88–90, 109, 114–17, 135–6, 151–9, 161–75, 182n64, 184n99, 209, 213

Christian Socialism 133–6, 141n99, 146–7, 171–8, 184n110, 187, 224n118
Church Missionary Society (CMS) 3–4, 11, 211, 214–19
class 84–5, 89–90, 97, 101, 111, 115–16, 129, 134, 147–8, 171, 177–8, 197, 210–11; *see also* indigenous cultures
collective biography 20n74, 21, 47–8, 56–65, 75
college newsletters 11, 187–8, 204–15
colonialism 5, 217–19, 224n127; *see also* empire; imperialism
conversion narratives 22–5, 34, 58, 62, 109, 123–5, 139n58, 198–200
converts 4, 68–9, 72–5, 86–90, 105n28, 116, 130, 173, 211–17, 224n127, 228
correspondence 4–5, 11, 22–3, 35, 42n42, 65–75, 122–33, 187–91, 200–4, 206–12, 215–18, 223n80
Cowper, William 51, 126
Craik, Dinah Mullock 14, 83–4, 95–103, 111–18, 136, 198, 219n3, 227; *Bread upon the Waters* 96–103, 136; *Olive* 97–8; *The Half-Caste* 96–103

Davies, Emily 186, 189, 192, 194
deathbed accounts 23–38, 57–65, 72–5, 86–95, 117–20, 130–6, 160–70
depression *see* melancholy
diaries 9–11, 22–5, 30–5, 62, 100–2, 187, 190–4, 198–200
didacticism 8–12, 24–5, 48, 56–63, 83–8, 101–3, 126, 181n34, 227
disability 102–3, 118, 171, 176–7
dissent 8, 47, 95, 132, 193
domesticity 2, 7–8, 22–4, 47–8, 50, 58–9, 61, 92, 123, 126–9, 131–2, 148–50, 187, 196–200; and the female missionary figure 8, 47–8, 52–4, 57, 60, 66–8, 96; and fiction 14, 82–4, 86; and missions 3, 24, 26–8, 32, 50, 54–5, 63–4; *see also* marriage
domestic mission movement 2, 82–5, 103n1, 111–15, 128–32, 172–8, 204–13
doubt 13, 27, 33, 96, 100–3, 109, 123–6, 146, 161–73, 190, 203; *see also* agnosticism

Eddy, Daniel C. 51, 55, 57
editing 11, 13–14, 23–30, 38, 41n13, 48–51, 55–7, 61–3, 65–6, 70–3, 100–2, 172, 190, 207–18
Elijah 152, 155, 167; *see also* Mendelssohn's *Elijah*
E.M.I. 51, 53
emotion: in conversion 23–5, 34–5, 41n16, 93–9, 115–17, 123–6, 152–3, 159, 196–201; history of 10–11; missionary 11–12, 33, 56–8, 66, 72–3, 83–4, 93–103, 111–20, 131, 163–5, 187, 200, 216, 227; religious 6, 8, 11–12, 30, 33, 68, 80n87, 91, 106n41, 188; *see also* melancholy; sentiment
empire 5, 54, 84–5, 145; *see also* colonialism; imperialism
eugenics 146, 160
evangelicalism: culture 7–13, 21, 32, 36–8, 48–52, 82–5, 110–12, 161; doctrines 22–9, 36, 56–63, 72, 78n30, 88, 92, 95–8, 101, 113–17, 125, 130–3, 151, 176; enthusiasm 25, 32, 41n16, 67–70, 94, 109, 119, 132, 138n41; feeling 8, 55, 91, 126; revivals 4, 22, 40n3, 82, 217; simplicity 8, 31, 41n28, 89–90, 95–6, 105n28, 106n47, 117, 119, 121, 139n47, 218; *see also* Atonement; emotion; Incarnationism; piety

family *see* domesticity
Fellowship of the New Life 147, 162
Female Missionary Intelligencer 4, 11, 66
femininity 21–2, 24–8, 32–4, 39, 47–8, 51–60, 68–9, 75, 83–4, 110–11, 126–35, 148–50, 158–9, 175–8, 187, 196–7, 204–5; *see also* domesticity; marriage
feminism: anti-feminism 6, 186; first-wave 6, 15, 137, 145–8, 151, 157, 161–3, 167, 170–3, 177–9, 179n4, 186–92, 213, 224n99, 229; proto-feminism 1, 12, 118; second-wave 6, 15, 108, 146, 168, 187, 229
foreign mission movement 24–6, 82, 111, 119, 132, 172, 188; *see also* mission field
Freethought 161–2, 172, 190, 203; *see also* agnosticism
friendship 13, 34, 52, 122–3, 177–8, 188, 196, 205, 210, 216

248 Index

fundraising 2, 60, 69, 99, 110, 122, 215–16

Gardner, James (Revd) 51, 55, 59–60
Gaskell, Elizabeth 14, 83, 103, 108–9, 131–3, 148, 227; *Life of Charlotte Brontë* 121–31; *Mary Barton* 132; *North and South* 136; *Ruth* 131–7
girls' schools 13, 204, 220n9, 228–9
Girton College 186, 190, 192, 200–1, 205–8
'Girton girl' 187, 205
Governesses' Benevolent Institution 99, 101–2, 107n56
governess fiction 1, 14, 83–4, 92–103, 104n9, 106n39, 108–20, 197
Grand, Sarah 15, 145–53, 167–8, 172, 174; *The Heavenly Twins* 147–51, 153–61
Grierson, Margaret 51–3, 56, 60, 82

hagiography 37, 57, 78n34, 151, 190
Harkness, Margaret 15, 145–7, 161, 170–9; *In Darkest London* (or *Captain Lobe*) 147, 171–8
'heathenism' 24, 39, 49, 54–5, 63–4, 85–90, 97–8, 111, 114, 151, 216; *see also* indigenous cultures
heroism 12, 14, 24, 36–9, 49, 56–60, 68–71, 75, 95–101, 108, 113, 116, 122, 126–7, 133–6, 148–53, 157–66, 175, 202, 218, 227
High Church *see* Anglicanism
'holy child' characters 14, 83–95, 106n39, 116–7, 120, 134, 168
hymns 23, 206, 220n11

imperialism 5, 17n24, 25n41, 38, 54, 80n91, 104n10, 139n43, 225n127; *see also* colonialism; empire
Incarnationism 147, 171–6, 189, 209
India 3, 24–6, 37, 47, 63–5, 70, 73–4, 85–6, 119, 215
indigenous cultures 2, 4–5, 8–9, 69, 71–5, 80 ns 75 and 91, 105n28, 111, 216–17, 225n127; *see also* 'heathenism'
intimacy 13, 52, 55, 140n61, 158, 196–9; *see also* friendship

Japan missions 212, 215–17, 219
journals *see* diaries
Judson, Adoniram 33, 38–9, 53–5, 64
Judson, Ann 14, 21–5, 28, 29, 30–40, 47–50, 54–8, 60, 70, 73, 96, 99, 101, 109, 112–14, 151, 191–2, 195, 204, 227; *Address to Females in America Relative the Situation of Females in the East* 39, 63; *Memoir of Ann Judson* 21–4, 28–40, 47–53, 75, 99, 101, 109, 111, 113–14, 191–2, 204
Judson, Sarah (née Boardman) 31, 51

Kilham, Hannah 49, 51, 65
Kingsley, Charles 42n49, 122, 141n99, 186
Knowles, James Davis 14, 24–5, 28–31, 33–9, 49–53, 62–3, 75, 82, 87, 100, 192; *see also* Judson, Ann

Lady Margaret Hall (LMH) 186–8, 192–3, 199, 205, 207–15
letters *see* correspondence; diaries
life writing 1, 9–15, 19n60, 22–8, 32, 34–6, 40 ns 1 and 3, 47–50, 62, 66, 72, 75, 111–12, 173; *see also* biography
London Missionary Society (LMS) 3, 11, 17n24, 20n72 and 73, 62, 129
Lumsden, Louisa 189, 192, 200
Lyon, Mary 193

marriage: arranged 13, 32–3, 118–19; missionary 13, 32–4, 54–5, 63–8, 102, 114, 118–19, 177, 200; plot 12–13, 97, 101–3, 227–8; reform 146, 154, 158, 169–70, 177–8, 179; romantic 12–13, 32, 55, 65, 79n62, 99, 101–2, 114, 118–19, 158, 176
Martyn, Henry 36–7, 84, 109, 116
martyrdom 25–8, 56–8, 65, 71–3, 96, 118, 121, 128–33, 135–6, 151, 157, 163, 170, 176, 202–4, 212–13, 218–19, 228
Marx, Eleanor 146, 171
masculinity 8–9, 36–8, 42n47 and 49, 55, 121, 158, 170, 175, 198, 202
Maurice, F. D. 141n99, 186
Maynard, Constance 187–90, *189*; education 187–93, 196–8, 205–6; life writing 190–5, 200–4, 206–7, 211–12; missionary work 188, 190, 193–200, 202–12; relationships 192, 197–200
Meade, L. T. 187, 205; *A Sweet Girl Graduate* 187, 205
melancholy 30, 123–7, 157, 191
memoir *see* biography
Mendelssohn's *Elijah* 154, 155
Methodism 22, 28, 41n24, 77n15, 85, 109, 119, 135, 139n47; *see also* dissent; Wesley

middle class 3, 7, 25, 76n5, 84, 90–2, 132, 145–6, 151, 196
militancy 8–9, 39, 69, 96, 99, 118, 149, 151, 155–6, 169–70, 173–4, 187, 193–6, 202–7, 210–11, 213, 218
millenarianism 5, 147, 163; *see also* Apocalypse
mission: field 1–6, 10, 13, 24–9, 34, 37–9, 47, 52–4, 61–9, 71–2, 77n25, 83–6, 98, 109–12, 117, 158, 173, 196, 215–19, 228; history 2–5, 9, 217; schools 13, 66–71, 113, 208, 215, 225n147; supporters 3, 16n4, 36, 38, 48, 50, 52, 58, 61–2, 73, 75, 208–9
missionary: biography 1–2, 9, 11–14, 20n74, 21–2, 24–5, 28–30, 47–51, 56–63, 72–5, 82–3, 86–7, 90–2, 100, 103, 108–11, 115–26, 156–7; candidates 4, 63, 68–71; newsletters 4–5, 11, 13, 65–75, 201, 217–18, 228; wives 2–3, 24, 35–9, 48, 50, 64–75, 84, 92, 103, 118–19, 151, 173, 194, 217
Moberly, Annie 192, 205
More, Hannah 32, 50, 55
motherhood 50, 53–4, 59, 68, 101, 197–8, 212
Mount Holyoke College 193
'muscular Christianity' 187, 220n11

networks 13, 21, 206, 228
Newell, Harriet 21–8, 32–7, 39, 49, 51–2, 73, 76n8, 101, 118, 124; *Memoir of Harriet Newell* 14, 21–8, 32–7, 39, 49, 101, 109, 114, 124, 192
Newell, Samuel 33, 35
'New Man' 158–61, 170, 177–9
Newnham College 186, 208
New Woman 9–10, 12, 15, 137, 145–8, 151, 157, 161–3, 167, 170–3, 177–9, 181n41, 202, 228–9
nobility 34, 37, 70, 96, 98–102, 115–16, 127, 167, 169, 202, 205, 210
nursing 1, 6, 53–4, 63, 98, 131, 134–5, 170, 208, 216–17, 223n80
Nussey, Ellen 14, 108–10, 122–31, *123*, 136, 137n12
Nussey, Henry 110

obituaries 5, 10, 22–3, 26, 29, 39, 62, 66, 72–5, 78n30
obituary literature 22–3, 27, 31, 60, 92
orphans 69, 74, 86

passivity 12–14, 27–8, 31, 36–7, 50–1, 54–62, 66–72, 75, 83–4, 87, 90–3, 101, 112, 114, 117–18, 121, 130, 133–5, 150–2, 156–7, 165, 167, 176, 193
philanthropy 3, 6, 7, 19n50, 59, 61, 80n91, 89, 110, 128, 132, 141n96, 179n5, 184 n.114, 193, 209–10, 213–15; *see also* fundraising
piety 22–4, 26–7, 29–30, 35–9, 51–2, 59–63, 68–71, 112, 121, 126–7, 131, 151–2, 156, 158–9, 192, 227
positivism 161, 165
prayer 23, 38, 69, 87–8, 90–1, 94, 115, 124, 154, 160, 163, 198–201, 216
preachers 8, 23, 39, 93, 131, 147, 150, 210; *see also* woman preachers
professionalism 2–4, 6, 13, 48, 61–9, 74–5, 82, 98–9, 101, 103, 115, 146, 170, 191, 201, 204–6, 212, 215–19, 228
prophets 8, 152, 155, 174; *see also* Elijah
proselytising 22, 54, 57, 68, 87, 89, 93, 116, 128, 149, 156, 193, 200–1, 209, 214, 216–17
prosopography *see* collective biography
Providence 2, 13, 23, 26–7, 50, 92, 94, 98, 114, 148, 154, 160
psalms *see* Bible
publishing 4, 13, 21–3, 31, 39, 82–5, 104n12, 122, 125, 135, 140n70, 147–50, 172, 190, 215

race 5, 85, 97–8, 100, 107n53, 111, 120, 178, 187; *see also* indigenous cultures
Religious Tract Society (RTS) 21, 34, 51, 56–8, 104n12, 172
respectability 3, 7, 24, 27, 50, 83, 109, 112, 122, 128–32, 135–6
Revelations (Book of) 136, 178; *see also* Apocalypse; millenarianism
Royal Holloway 188, 192–3, 196, 204–5, 207, 211, 214

saints 24, 27–8, 30, 36, 39, 87–8, 93–4, 112, 124, 126, 133, 150–1, 161, 202
Salvation Army 145–7, 170–8
sati 74–5, 120, 160
Schreiner, Olive 15, 145–7, 161–72, 214, 229; *Dreams* 147, 161–6, 168, 172; *The Story of an African Farm* 147, 161, 164–70

Index

science 97–8, 145, 147, 161, 164–5, 171–2, 203, 209, 217, 223n92
Second Coming *see* Apocalypse; millenarianism
secular 4–7, 84, 104n10, 145–7, 154, 161, 179, 186–8, 190, 192–3, 203–5, 207–9, 227–8; *see also* agnosticism
sentiment 55, 60, 72, 83–95, 147, 150, 175, 197
separate spheres *see* domesticity
sermons 7, 25–7, 32, 50, 62, 64, 68–9, 89–90, 114
settlements 172–8, 188, 204, 208–13, 220n16, 223n77
Shaftesbury (Lord) 194
Sherwood, Martha 14, 82–9, 92–5, 98, 103, 106n39, 111–12, 198, 227; *Caroline Mordaunt* 92–5, 99–100; *The History of Little Henry and his Bearer* 84–93; sisterhoods 3, 159, 215
Slade Art School 190, 200
slums 85, 145, 173–9, 213
socialism 15, 145–7, 161–2, 171–3, 177–8, 179n4, 229; *see also* Christian Socialism
social purity movement 146, 148, 150, 156, 168–9, 179n4, 224n99
Society for the Promotion of Christian Knowledge (SPCK) 3
Society for the Promotion of Female Education in the East (SPFEE) 3–4, 11, 62, 65–6, 76n2, 79n63
Society for the Propagation of the Gospel in Foreign Parts (SPG) 3, 11, 214–15
South Africa 146, 162, 215
spiritual biography 22–8, 30–2, 34, 39, 48, 83, 102, 109, 125, 130, 147, 149; *see also* life writing
St Hugh's College 192, 214
St Leonard's School (St Andrews) 189, 192, 200
Stretton, Hesba (Sarah Smith) 14, 82, 84–5, 89–95, 103, 112, 227; *Jessica's First Prayer* 89–93, 95, 106n33, 119; *Jessica's Mother* 90
Sudan Mission 215, 217–19
suffrage movement 186, 213–14
suffragettes 164, 213–14, 229
Sunday schools 51, 59–60, 67, 82–5, 89, 95

Taylor, Hudson 4, 217
teachers 66–72, 94, 111–12, 114–17, 188–90, 192–9, 201, 203, 205–7, 211–12, 215–16, 219; *see also* governess fiction
Temperance 128–9, 214; *see also* domestic mission movement
theology 4, 7, 9, 13, 34, 42n39, 90–1, 111–13, 121, 135–6, 164, 182n64, 209
Thompson, Jemima 48–9, 58, 61–75, 92
tracts 12, 14, 53, 56–9, 82–96, 100, 103, 108–9, 112, 115–20, 147, 158, 168, 172, 227
transcendentalism 150, 161–2, 165
Tristram, Katherine 202–3, 211–12, 215–17, 219

Unitarianism 109, 125, 132–3, 135–6, 186; *see also* dissent
universal kinship 97–8, 209–10; *see also* race
University Women's Settlement (Southwark) 188, 209–10
utopianism 147, 162, 171

Venn, Henry 69, 80n75, 217
vocation *see* calling

Webb, Beatrice (née Potter) 146, 170
Wesley, John 22–4, 28, 36
Wesleyan Methodist Missionary Society (WMMS) 3, 48; Ladies' Committee 48, 61–2, 66–75
Westfield College 4, 187–93, 196, 200–8, 211–12, 215–19
Wilberforce, William 21, 37
women preachers 8, 22, 28, 95, 132; *see also* Methodism and dissent
women's colleges 11, 13, 179, 186–8, 192–3, 196–7, 204–5, 207–15, 228–9; *see also* college newsletters; Girton College; Lady Margaret Hall; Newnham College; Royal Holloway; Westfield College
Woods, Leonard 14, 24–8, 30–4, 36, 62, 192; *see also* Newell, Harriet
Wordsworth, Elizabeth 186, 192–3, 196–7, 199, 205, 219

zeal 25, 28, 49–50, 59, 70, 120, 132, 150, 206
zenana 3, 8, 47